MEN COPING WITH GRIEF

Dale A. Lund, Ph.D.
University of Utah Gerontology Center

Death, Value and Meaning Series
Series Editor: John D. Morgan

Baywood Publishing Company, Inc.
AMITYVILLE, NEW YORK

Library of Congress Catalog Number: 99-087525
ISBN: 0-89503-211-2 (cloth)
ISBN: 0-89503-212-0 (paper)

Library of Congress Cataloging-in-Publication Data

Lund, Dale A.
    Men coping with grief / Dale A. Lund.
    p. cm - - (Death, value, and meaning series)
    Includes bibliographical references and index.
    ISBN 0-89503-211-2 (cloth) - - ISBN 0-89503-212-0 (pbk.)
    1. Grief. 2. Bereavement- -Psychological aspects. 3. Death- -Psychological aspects. 4. Loss (Psychology) 5. Men- -Psychology I. Title. II. Series.

BF575.G7.L86 2000
155.9'37'081- -dc21   99-087525

Preface

In May of 1994, the 12th International King's College Conference on Death, Dying and Bereavement focused primarily on issues related to men. The conference theme was "Helping the Bereaved Male." Dr. John D. Morgan (Jack), the person most responsible for creating and organizing these annual conferences, had a great deal of foresight in selecting this particular focus for the conference. While the popular press had already started to address issues and topics specifically about men, there appeared to be a mood, usually not shared publicly, among members of many professional groups that it was not politically correct to examine concerns from an exclusively male perspective or to focus primarily on men. The assumption was that because men were not among the many powerless, neglected, or disadvantaged groups in our society, it would be inappropriate and selfish to focus on male concerns. Further, this logic continued, men did not deserve special attention because they already have had it throughout history.

I had a disturbing and shocking personal experience with this issue of political incorrectness in March 1993, when I had a meeting in my office with a young female teaching assistant. We were discussing my previous week's sociology lectures and discussions regarding gender inequality and sexism when she said I was a sexist. I have always taken great pride in how I present numerous examples of past and present gender inequality and discuss the very serious negative consequences to both men and women when we socialize them into overly narrow and rigid gender roles. I end these lectures with an attempt to personalize the material by suggesting that everyone has an obligation to do something to help eliminate gender inequality by saying, "You are part of the problem if you do not become part of the solution." I very much enjoy teaching this class with over 400 students because I believe it gives me a chance to make a difference in educating others about the pervasive, long-lasting and ill effects of social inequality and how each of us can contribute to making changes to improve the quality of people's lives.

Prior to my conversation with this teaching assistant, I had never been called a sexist, at least to my knowledge. I was personally relieved, however, when later in our conversation she said that I was a sexist, not because I had said something specifically sexist, but because I was a man. She said, "All men are sexists because men have power." In her opinion, my membership in a biological category did not allow for me to differ from anyone else who shared my gender membership. She was not interested or the least bit impressed by my argument that I was making a positive impact on students and trying to reduce problems of gender inequality. I tried to explain, discuss, debate, listen, and understand, but her views were carved in stone. She had no room for information or knowledge that did not fit her preconceived opinions and expectations. To this day I do not know what became of this young woman. Some day I hope to learn that she opened her mind to see and discover more than just what she expected or wanted.

This incident continues to have a powerful effect on me because someone defined me in a way that is the complete opposite of how I see myself, and her opinion was based exclusively on one single biological trait. My education, research, and personal life have taught me that while our group memberships, even those which are biologically based, are influential in shaping who we are, what we think, what we do, and how we feel, there is considerable diversity within each group or category. I do not believe, however, that our biological sex is such an all-powerful trait that it can dictate uniformly and rigidly how we will grieve. Our biology plays an interactive role along with many cultural and personal life experiences in creating our grief-related feelings and adjustments.

My experience with this female teaching assistant, combined with my views about the relative importance of gender in shaping our lives, gave me added incentives for accepting the invitation to be one of the keynote speakers at the 12th King's College Conference on Bereavement. I was delighted to present on the topic of older men coping with the deaths of their wives for three reasons. First, the invitation encouraged me to speak on male grief experiences at a time when some professionals thought it was politically incorrect to be interested in topics focused on men. Because men are not a disadvantaged group is no reason to neglect learning more about their lives and discovering ways to help them deal more effectively with grief. Surprising, bereavement and grief are stressful aspects of life that we know less about men than we do women. The conference at King's College was a timely and important event because it helped draw international attention to the neglected topic of male grief. Second, my presentation gave me an opportunity to present research findings which showed tremendous diversity among men in how they were experiencing grief. If biology were the only important influential agent then we would not see the wide range in coping abilities, strategies, and outcomes that characterize the way men grieve. Third, it is often forgotten that men and women share much in common. We exaggerate the differences between men and women when we only ask how they differ and not what they have in common.

I selected the title of this book, *Men Coping with Grief,* rather than other possible titles because it more accurately reflects a focus on the full range of variation that exists among men. Other possible titles that highlighted masculinity or male grief would convey an assumption that all men use traditionally masculine or male strategies. The title also conveys a practical focus on coping which I hope readers will find useful in developing specific ways to help those with the greatest need. In the "Introduction" to this book and most chapters, the reader will find many examples of men coping with grief in ways that would be considered feminine, or at the very least unexpected. The same can be said of the ways women grieve, because some women use traditionally viewed masculine strategies. We can best advance our understanding of grief and identify more effective ways to intervene to help people if we do not restrict our thinking to long-lasting stereotypes based solely on group categories and memberships.

The King's College Conference also was important to the development of this book because it provided the impetus and foundation for most of the chapters. Jack Morgan, also the consulting editor with Baywood Publishing Company, asked me to edit a book on the theme of the 12th Annual Conference and invite many of the conference speakers to submit chapters based on their presentations. Some of the invited presenters did not submit chapters and not all of those who submitted their work have chapters included in this book. Some additional authors were invited to contribute chapters because their expertise would help strengthen each of the three sections of the book: conceptual issues, research, and interventions. This book reflects an appropriate broad range of perspectives about the ways men cope and grieve. While there may not be an ideal flow from chapter to chapter, the primary value of this book lies in its broad coverage of topics and varied types of chapters. Some authors relied on quantitative approaches and others used more personal and qualitative styles. Some chapters will be of greater interest to professional clinicians and others will be of greater value to educators or researchers. Although my efforts took much longer than all of the contributors (including me) would have preferred, I am pleased with the final product and hope that each reader will find something of interest, importance, and practical use in *Men Coping with Grief.*

Acknowledgments

This book represents the culmination of the efforts of many people. First to be acknowledged should be Dr. Jack Morgan who served as the consulting editor for the book and also was the King's College Conference organizer. Near the conclusion of the 12th annual conference with a theme on "Helping the Bereaved Male," Jack invited me to edit this book. While I was a bit reluctant because I had an upcoming sabbatical leave scheduled, I was honored by his invitation and now I am both proud and relieved that the book is completed. I also am appreciative of Jack's patience and prodding during the long process of gathering and reviewing chapters and doing my own writing.

Next, I want to thank each of the chapter authors for their willingness to submit their work for inclusion in the book, timely completion of needed revisions, and patience far greater than I deserved. Many interruptions occurred during the process of preparing this book and the authors were most understanding and encouraging. I hope that each author will be pleased with the final product and feel that the wait was worthwhile.

Also, I would like to express appreciation to Dr. Michael Caserta who stepped in near the end to co-author a chapter with me and review the book and section introductions. Brandi Devey, our Center's executive secretary, was extremely helpful as my pace quickened in the last few weeks. She typed several chapters and other parts of the book and remained very patient when I needed to make more changes.

I am grateful for the loving support of my wife, Patty, my two rapidly growing children, Matt and Angie, and my mother, Pearl. My work in the area of grief and bereavement makes these relationships even more meaningful because observing others who are experiencing significant losses makes me more thoughtful and appreciative of the support that I have had.

I hope that those who read this book will gain understanding, empathy, and valuable knowledge that will benefit them personally and professionally. And finally, I hope that we begin asking more questions about what people have in common and not just how we differ from one another.

Contents

Introduction

The primary purpose of this book is to bring together, in a single publication, a very diverse group of authors who have considerable knowledge to share about the ways men grieve and how their bereavement experiences impact various aspects of their lives. Bereavement refers to both the situation and the long-term process of adjusting to the death of someone with whom a person feels close. The adjustment process is multidimensional in that the loss can affect nearly every aspect of a person's life including emotions, identity, social interactions and relationships, spirituality, intimacy and sexuality, work productivity, health, and even death. The term bereavement also has been used in reference to losses other than death, such as the loss of a home, personal belongings, career, and independence, due to such things as natural disasters, relocations, retirements, and health impairments. Although many people use the term grief to refer to the same process, it is more accurate to describe grief as the affective or emotional responses experienced during the early phases of the overall bereavement process. These feelings frequently include disbelief, confusion, shock, numbness, sadness, anger, and guilt. Feeling abandoned, lonely, depressed, and being preoccupied with thoughts of the deceased person and the events surrounding the death are often components of grief.

Given these definitions, it is obvious that multidisciplinary perspectives are needed to more fully understand the experiences of bereaved persons and identify effective ways to provide appropriate assistance when needed. The authors of the chapters have expertise in history, philosophy, journalism, poetry, sociology, psychology, anthropology, social work, nursing, health education, gerontology, religious studies, and business. They represent professions in academics, research, clinical service, business, the clergy, and many more. Each chapter author offers his or her insights, opinions, personal experiences, and supporting evidence to explain what we should know about the ways men grieve, why they grieve in a particular way, and how this knowledge might be applied to assist them. Many of the authors appear to agree with one another on some issues but, as you might expect from such a diverse group of professionals, their viewpoints represent challenges, opposition, and inconsistencies as well. Again, the purpose of this book is to bring together a wide range of knowledge about male grief and not to identify and advocate for just one single viewpoint.

DO MEN AND WOMEN GRIEVE DIFFERENTLY?

Although this question is not of central importance in this book, it is somewhat implicit that men must grieve differently or we would not be compiling a book specifically about men. The most accurate answer to this question, however, based on what knowledge we have available, is that we are only beginning to know and understand how men and women differ in their grief. For many years we have relied on cultural beliefs, practices, norms, values and oftentimes, stereotypes to answer questions about gender differences. Our popular culture now stresses the importance of group memberships and social categories and how they make each of us unique. Race, ethnicity, religion, gender, age, and geographical location are all important influential agents in shaping our lives and personalities.

As a sociologist, gerontologist, and researcher, however, I believe that while most of the intentions are good and purposeful, we are becoming so narrow in our "search for differences" that we are ignoring much of what we all have in common. We must not avoid asking equally important questions such as "What do we have in common? or "In what ways do men and women grieve similarly?" Men and women do have different life experiences and perceive their experiences according to their gender. But, let us not forget that men and women have much in common. Most men and women eat, sleep, attend school, get report cards, play with friends, drive cars, attend church, get married or find partners, become parents, raise children, buy homes, pay taxes, learn to use technology, watch television, listen to radios, read newspapers, try to stay well, avoid accidents, engage in recreation activities, develop hobbies, try to find meaning in life, seek happiness, and experience many kinds of losses throughout their lives. Nearly all of us readily acknowledge that these experiences can create individual differences but we seem to fail to recognize that these are also shared experiences and very likely create a great degree of similarity. It has simply become more fascinating and interesting to keep asking questions about how we differ.

How is this discussion relevant to grief and bereavement? Put most simply, I believe that we must be careful not to overstate or exaggerate the differences between men and women in the ways they grieve and avoid all that they have in common. We should not just search for differences but should pay equal attention to our similarities, even if we run the risk of asking boring questions. In one of our research studies (see Chapter 9) we concluded that the bereavement experiences and outcomes of older bereaved men and women were characterized more by their similarities than differences. In another research study, we found that bereaved men and women were again very similar in their adjustments and that they seemed to benefit equally from their participation in self-help groups. These men and women also reported that they enjoyed participating in gender mixed support groups because they learned they had much more in common than expected (also see Chapter 9).

I would like to conclude this introduction by presenting two quotes from different participants in a spousal bereavement study. One quote is from an eighty-year-old man at one year following the death of his wife. Another quote is from a seventy-two-year-old woman at six months after her husband's death. Please guess which quote is from which person.

> You know, I got tired of looking in the mirror and seeing how depressed I was. I felt like I deserved better. I started to look at it as a challenge. You can't expect others to change it for you . . . to take away the pain. People need to be responsible for themselves. It is something you have to do alone, so you just do it.

> This is the most horrible thing that has ever happened to me. Nothing could compare with it. It's been terrible. The only thing that has kept me going is to know that when I feel sad and need to cry and to talk to someone about how I feel I can turn to my daughter. Without my daughter I could not have made it this far. We have always been close. She's been there when I needed her. I love her and I'm so thankful that I have her.

Surprising, the first quote was from a woman and the second was from the man. Both were coping with the death of their spouse, but their comments are not consistent with the expected norms. The widower noted his dependency on his daughter and his close relationship with her to help him in his grief. However, one reviewer of this book noted that many men rely on women to help them organize their lives. This man was still quite unusual for admitting his dependency, need to cry, and openly expressing his feelings to his daughter.

Conversely, the widow did not want to rely on others and defined her bereavement situation as a challenge. Our culture encourages men to view life difficulties as challenges to overcome and assert power and control rather than passively accept losses and move on. If we relied on existing stereotypes or narrow expectations about how men and women grieve then we would inappropriately relate to these two different people. Knowing what is most common and expected can be useful information but it should not blind us in recognizing the wide range of grief responses.

ORGANIZATION OF THE BOOK

The book is divided into three parts. Part I consists of seven chapters which deal primarily with conceptual issues related to death, bereavement, grief, gender, and masculinity. Collectively these chapters provide a foundation for understanding the ways in which men grieve by examining a continuum of issues ranging from histori-cal, philosophical, and cultural to specific situations and personal experiences. These chapters provide an excellent review of the most relevant theoretical and research literature needed to understand the lingering traditional views of masculine grief and the diversity in the ways that men actually grieve.

Part II of the book includes five chapters, each presenting original research findings regarding men in various grief situations. Again, there is considerable diversity among these chapters in the types of studies conducted and the conceptual frameworks selected by the authors. Most of the focus is on grieving fathers and husbands but the findings presented are relevant to other bereavement situations.

Part III consists of seven chapters, all interrelated because of their focus on ways to help men in grief. Included in this section are chapters discussing a wide range of helping techniques from interventions and therapies designed for highly skilled professionals to self-help groups and generic helping strategies. The suggestions and recommendations included in these chapters are relevant to clinical and mental health professionals, educators, clergy, support group leaders, family mem-bers, friends, and those who are grieving. Many of the discussions also are applicable to those who are interested in changing cultural mes-sages related to gender, grief, and mental health to make our values, norms, and beliefs less rigid, more accurate, and less judgmental.

These three sections of the book are not mutually exclusive divisions. There is considerable overlap among many chapters because the authors were not requested to simply address one of the three issues: conceptual, research, or clinical. Many of the chapters present discussions of all three topics. Decisions about the book sections and sequence of chapters were made somewhat arbitrarily to achieve the best possible continuity for those who want to read the book from a logical beginning to an end. The division into three sections should also be helpful to those who have special interest in one of organizational topics, but these readers are advised to carefully review other chapters because they will likely find additional information related to their main interest. Please critically examine the chapters in this book, learn from them, apply the knowledge, help change and improve lives, and enjoy your reading.

PART I

Conceptualizing and Describing Death, Grief, and Masculinity

The seven chapters included in this section of the book provide a broad foundation or context for understanding how men grieve. Each of these chapters contributes to the way we conceptualize issues about death, bereavement, grief, gender, and masculinity. These chapters provide excellent reviews of existing literature, descriptive accounts of personal grief experiences, examples of various grief and loss situations, and overall, the "bigger picture" of men and grief.

Each chapter author has his or her own unique writing style and was not required to follow any particular organization for their chapter. While this flexible style may challenge the reader's desire for more continuity, it allowed each author the freedom to express their knowledge and expertise in their most preferred manner. This is important to note at the beginning of the book because the first chapter differs from all of the other chapters in that it is a printed version of a keynote address by an internationally recognized philosopher and writer, Sam Keen. His speech was the lead presentation at the 12th International King's College Conference on Death, Dying, and Bereavement in London, Ontario, Canada in 1994. The conference theme was "Helping the Bereaved Male." His presentation, "Building Your Ship of Death for the Longest Journey Over Endless Seas," appears as the first chapter in this book because his messages provide the broadest context for the remainder of the book. Sam presents a philosophical view of death and relates it to issues of human existence. He discusses death in different times and cultures so that we may gain a greater awareness of our past and where we may be headed regarding "death liberation." He addresses thought-provoking questions but appropriately does not answer them in simple ways for us. His chapter challenges the typical medical model application to grief and bereavement which other authors in this book continue to use. This chapter is stimulating, entertaining, and critical.

Chapter 2, "The Ontology of Masculinity: The Roots of Manhood" by Neil Thompson, continues with a philosophical and historical approach initiated by Sam Keen. His chapter provides an analysis of male-specific grieving, particularly the emotional inexpressiveness of boys and men by placing the discussion in the context of the social construction of masculinity and the ontology of insecurity. These macro- or cultural-level issues help us to better understand how boys, men, and professionals deal with grief.

Ken Doka and Terry Martin's chapter, "Take It Like a Man: Masculine Response to Loss," continues the discussions about masculinity presented in the first two chapters but adds several important points that must not be overlooked as we examine the ways men grieve. These authors note the importance of recognizing the diversity that exists within each gender role and the problems that result when we define one gender role always in relation to the other gender. They distinguish between masculine and male grief and argue that gender is only one factor that influences grief. Doka and Martin also provide excellent references and practical suggestions for clinical interventions.

Chapter 4, "The Vietnam War: An Ongoing National Grief Response," by Angeline and John Bushy, adds significantly to our understanding of how societal-level issues can impact individual lives. The Vietnam War is a highly relevant case in point, because an entire country or world was involved in the conflict. The Bushy's examine the post-war effects on those who served in the military at that time. They describe the confusion and pain and the continuing barriers to resolve these difficulties. Also, a reviewer of this book noted that it is important for us to acknowledge that survivor guilt and emotional numbing can interfer with a healthy grief process. This chapter provides information on grief theories and a valuable discussion about treatments, healing, and helping suggestions.

John Hart writes about "Gay Men: Grieving the Effects of Homophobia" in Chapter 5. He provides additional knowledge about the ways in which society or culture influence the lives of individuals by internalizing messages about homosexuality and homophobia. Hart does an excellent job of illustrating how these negative values, norms, and beliefs create losses for gay men which involve grief responses. He concludes by offering suggestions for positive coping responses and describes a workshop designed to help gay men begin a process of grief. Both Chapters 4 and 5 are important to this book because they provide good examples of the diversity in macro-level situations (e.g., war and homophobia) that can create grief and loss to individuals.

Chapter 6, "Emerging From the Anguish: A Father's Experience with Loss and Grief" by Kent Koppelman, is absolutely essential to this section of the book because it provides a description of the intense emotional responses which accompany grief. Mr. Koppelman presents a very powerful, empathic, and personal description of what it was like to experience his son's death. His willingness and ability to share such personal feelings is commendable and illustrative of the fact that not all men are inexpressive about their grief. He also mentions in the chapter how surprised he was that his expectations about specific grief reactions did not always happen and that, at times, his wife was strong and he was weak.

The final chapter in this section, "Research on Gender Differences in Bereavement Outcome: Presenting a Model of Experienced Competence" by Susan Allen and Bert Hayslip, provides a most appropriate conclusion to this section of the book. Their chapter offers a very well-organized and comprehensive review of literature, particularly regarding research studies and those focused on men and women experiencing spousal bereavement. Another valuable contribution that Allen and Hayslip make is the presentation of a model appropriate to understanding and predicting adjustments to bereavement and grief. Their model of "experienced competence" is solidly based on the research literature and highlights the importance of each person's locus of control, coping self-efficacy, history of coping competence, and self-esteem. These characteristics can be used to guide clinical interventions and other helping strategies. Part II of this book focuses primarily on research-based knowledge and begins with another chapter by Hayslip and Allen accompanied by Laura McCoy because they provide a research test of their theory.

CHAPTER 1

Building Your Ship of Death for the Longest Journey Over Endless Seas

Sam Keen

I take the title for my chapter, the mood, and the wisdom from an unlikely source, D. H. Lawrence. It is my belief that D. H. Lawrence has a wisdom about how we deal with death that is superior to almost anybody who has ever written. He remembers things that Elisabeth Kübler-Ross has not even forgotten yet, or doesn't know.

I'd like to start off with a little reading:

> Now it is autumn, and the falling fruit and the long journey toward oblivion. The apples falling like great drops of dew to bruise themselves and exit from themselves. And it is time to go. To bid farewell to one's own self and find an exit from the fallen self. Have you built your ship of death? Oh, have you? Oh, build your ship of death for you will need it. We are dying! So, all we can do is now to be willing to die and to build the ship of death to carry the soul on the longest journey. A little ship with oars and food and little dishes and all accoutrements fitting and ready for the departing soul. Now, launch the small ship. Now, as the body dies and life departs launch out the fragile soul in the fragile ship of courage. The ark of faith with its store of food and little cooking pans and change of clothes upon the flood's black waves, upon the waters of the end, upon the sea of death where still we sail darkly, where we cannot steer and have no port.

The reflections that I want to do on death today are done for the point of view of an amateur. There is an enormous difference whether we deal with death as *their* death and *their* grief or *my* death and *my* grief. It is the difference between dealing with death objectively and dealing with it as an existential fact, as the PRIMAL existential fact.

As a philosopher, I am dedicated to trying to understand human existence through the mirror of the life of Sam Keen. I can best understand what's going on in my culture by reading my own psyche and my own soul.

As a philosopher, it is my hope, in some way, to be a physician of the spirit and a physician of the soul. And first of all, of course, a physician to my own spirit and my own soul. Philosophy is about the healing—or if you want—the saving, the salvation of the soul. Not particularly or necessarily in a religious sense of the soul. Therefore, philosophy, whatever else it is, is not about the ego. It is not about what is culturally accepted as wisdom. Philosophy is very often exactly the opposite.

Somebody once said, "philosophers are perverts!" And it's true! You remember Socrates? That was the charge made against him. Everybody pretty well understood the cultural norms until Socrates came on the scene. Euthyphro comes along and he's going to turn his father in for impiety. Socrates said, "Oh, good! You can tell me what piety is." And he starts asking Euthyphro questions. At the end of the dialogue Euthyphro has no idea, whatsoever, what piety is. And, for this, Socrates was charged with perverting the youth of Athens, twisting them around. His reward was a hemlock milk shake.

Philosophy is always doing that, always turning things over. Philosophy is about appearance and reality.

Philosophers, being perverse creatures, usually assume what most people think is reality is only an appearance; and vice-versa.

So, what I'm going to be doing today is looking at the cultural ways we think about death and deal with death—and trying to turn that over to suggest that maybe we're dealing with it all the wrong way.

Another way of saying this is: a philosopher is always trying to read symptoms and trying to find out what is underneath the symptom. In back of this is the understanding that one way to further disease people is to confuse the symptom with the disease. And I suspect that's what we're doing in dealing with death these days.

The structure of my remarks is going to follow a scheme that I learned a long time ago from Paul Tillich. Paul Tillich always said that there were three kinds of questions that any religion, philosophy, or therapy has to ask. First, "What's wrong with us? What's the disease? What's the pathology?" Second, "What would we look like if we were whole? Healed?" We don't even have a word for this, you notice—a state of positive health, or "the ideal," or however we're going to talk about it.

Third, "How do you get from one to two? What are the means of healing?"

My remarks are going to follow these three questions. First, I will look at the pathology of death. Then, at a good way of dying, an ideal way of dying. And, third I will ask, "is there any way to achieve a better death?"

The pathology of death in the post-modern world. Books like this on death and grief look like symptoms of hope; and indeed they are. Because, this wouldn't have happened thirty years ago. Death has come out of the closet. We're living in a time of death liberation where we talk about death in ways that we did not before. The question of death is on our minds. We see documentaries on television about death. There is certainly a death revolution, a death liberation.

So, it's tempting to believe that we are beginning to deal with death in a way which is more creative. But, there's a danger here. Let me make an analogy. There are other kinds of liberation that we've had. We've had a sexual liberation movement, a women's liberation movement, and now, a man's liberation movement. One of the things you always have to ask about a liberation movement is, "What is being liberated? And at what cost? Are there any new forms of bondage that go along with liberation movements?" Let's jump backwards a little bit to get some leverage on the question.

I think the sexual liberation movement in some ways increased our bondage. It liberated us to talk about sexuality. But, it also identified a whole lot of conduct and sexual feelings as repressive. Remember the height of the sexual revolution. I don't know if any of you are veterans of this. Today, veterans of the sexual revolution are sort of like veterans of the Second World War. With AIDS and everything, some of you have only heard about this period. There was a time, not so long ago, when we were taught that to liberate ourselves sexually, to achieve sexual freedom, meant to connect any two or more pairs of genitals of consenting adults. That was about the only requirement. Getting together in any constellation was not only okay, but was apt to produce liberation.

This indiscriminate sexuality was promoted by Playboy magazine and Cosmopolitan. Erica Jong talked about women finally getting sexually liberated and having the right to the "zipless fuck." We had the impossible idea that sex was anything any two consenting adults did without too much emotional involvement, without the burden of connecting it with love, *and* it was supposed to free us.

We had the Richian orgasm. Probably many of you didn't have one. It's colder up here in Canada. Salvation by orgasm proved inadequate when they discovered that women could have more orgasms than men.

There was a discounting procedure, four of hers for one of yours. After that the vibrator replaced that part of the male anatomy of which we are so fond, when it turned out that there were only clitoral orgasms which made the penis, essentially, an obsolete piece of equipment. There was even a question as to whether women should bother with men.

And this went on and on to all kinds of silliness and, finally, we discovered the "O" spot. Oh, excuse me . . . it's the "G" spot. I was never any good at these things. I kind of thought the "O" spot was when somebody finally says, "OH! OH! OH!" Anyway, it turned out that after a lot of monkey business what we discovered was that sexual liberation ended up in trivializing sex because it stripped sexuality of it's numinous quality, its sacredness. It overlooked the fact that genitals are connected with human beings; and human beings are connected with people who have histories, and dreams, and hopes, and continuity, and make children. It turned out that sexual liberation really focused on the wrong things, in some ways. We've had to re-own the notion that when we touch another person we're not just touching flesh, we're touching their spirit. All really vital and whole-hearted sexuality is the touching of incarnate spirits. Sexuality that does not honor the other's spirit, their history, their story, the totality of who they are, is less than what it might be. So, sexual liberation turned out to produce a very strange kind of new repression.

We are in the middle of death liberation. I'm afraid if we aren't very careful we are going to liberate people to have more and more trivial and alienated deaths. Why?

First of all, death is not a natural phenomenon. We do not understand anything about how people die, when they die, or the meaning of death until we understand that. Another way of saying this is, human beings are the only bio-mythic animals. We are the only animals for whom our biology and our mythology are inextricably connected. We are those animals who cannot separate biology from the stories that we tell about ourselves. We are that animal that has a neo-cortex. We are that animal that is conscious. We are, therefore, that animal that is self-conscious, that reflects upon ourselves. We are the animals that must necessarily tell stories about ourselves. And one of the primary stories we have to tell about ourselves to know how we get along with our lives is, "What is the meaning of death?"

Every culture has a mythology, a repertoire of stories about what it means to be human. The name of the game of being human is inevitably, "What is the name of this game?" We are that animal that must tell a story about ourselves. And when we're talking about stories that large we're talking about "myth."

There are certain things that are biologically hard wired. Nature gives us a certain amount of hardware, but all of those protocols by which we are going to deal with death are not built into the hardware that we get at birth. The moment we come into life somebody starts shoving software disks into us, programs. The culture shoves them in, the family shoves them in. And these stories—these myths—form us, they inform us.

So, in every culture you are going to have stories about what the meaning of death is, why people die. In some, people are thought to die because they've offended the gods. Many primitive mythologies assume that death comes as a result of breaking a taboo. It is not natural, doesn't just happen. You've offended a god, or you have done something you ought not to have done. In every culture we have to ask, "What are the stories that govern death?" and "What kind of death do they focus on?"

In any culture, the operative myth of that culture is invisible to it. In Eskimo culture, in the old days they took the old people out and left them on an ice flow and thought the god Sedna would comfort them as they were dying. I can look at that and say, "Oh, that's very mythological isn't it?" But when I look my own culture where we take people to the hospital and have weird people, always dressed in white (never in rainbow colors, or like a clown), I don't see that as mythological. That's science. That's modern medicine. In order to decipher death, and what we are doing, and, more importantly, what we are NOT doing, we have to look at our own culture in terms of its mythology.

One of the best ways that we can get a handle on this is to look at the heros of a given culture, to look at where the myth is incarnate, to look at the death upon which a given culture focuses. Every culture has a focal death. Every culture has somebody who, in their dying, becomes a model for what that culture takes to be the meaning of life and the meaning of death.

Let me do a bit of retrospective history here, because I think that's going to help us get a handle on our culture. In an agricultural culture the model for death is the seed. The seed goes into the ground, and there's darkness, and the seed dies, and the seed disintegrates, and then it comes to fruition again. You'll find that in every agricultural culture the seed is likened unto the soul. So, death is taken merely as a passage, as a transition, as a transformation. And that mythology is always about going down into the darkness and rituals of going down into darkness and disintegration create the assurance that where there is death there will be rebirth.

Mythology is not just something in the head, it's in the bodies of people; it's in the way that they experience nature. In the degree that the natural order, is a maternal order, the soul is also something that is regenerated. You have the idea of rebirth or transmigration of soul or of reincarnation. The soul cannot die. It is a continual cycle. So, death is just a part of the cyclical existence of the human soul.

This is an assurance that we don't have any more, because we don't look at nature that way. We don't experience ourselves that way.

Let's take another death, the death of Socrates. In the pre-modern world there were two deaths that gave people the meaning of life, the death of Socrates and the death of Jesus. They were the focal points of the Greek and Christian mythologies.

Remember Socrates' last words? Socrates is dying, the poison has reached his waist and he leans over and says, "Crito I owe a cock to Asculepius." That's very interesting. Because Asculepius is the god of healing. Socrates, in the middle of dying says, "I am being healed. I owe a cock to Asculepius." Almost all of ethics after the time of Socrates, in Aristotle, in the Stoic ethics—is a reflection on the life and death of Socrates.

First of all, Socrates was given a chance to escape and he didn't escape. Why didn't he escape? Because, in his view, the highest good was found only in community. So, you don't have individualism. As an individual he could have escaped. But, no. In essence, Socrates said, "Human beings are human only when they are social; only when they're in a community. And a community can only exist when there is law. And Athens has the law. And even if the law is wrong I cease to be human if I do not honor that law. It has condemned me and I will take the poison."

Socrates also said that his reason told him that the soul was not born and would not die. Therefore, he should go to his death voluntarily without fear. He says, "All of my life I have been practicing dying. And now, when it comes to the act of actual doing it should I be afraid? Should I run away? That would show that my entire life was a fraud."

Socrates taught that philosophy is the practice of dying. By that he meant that the well lived life is a life where we move away from sense knowledge and get in touch with that which was central to the human being, namely the soul. To die was merely to finish the process of getting to the essence of the soul, to be liberated from the bondage of the body and time. In that, for the Greek mind, there was an enormous kind of comfort. Socrates was a comforter.

I'll switch cultures. Jesus goes to his death, also, voluntarily. Again, just to begin the comparison, look at the signal deaths of two cultures. We're dealing with a death that is chosen, voluntary, but could have been avoided in either the case of Socrates or Jesus. Jesus comes along, lives his life, and for whatever reasons he is condemned, and he does not try to escape that. He does pray that "this cup" could be taken from him. For him, death is obedience to what he conceives of as the will of God. Not reason, but a direct obedience to God, which is the meaning of life. Life is obedience. Life is obedience to a covenant with a personal God. To refuse to follow that path of obedience would have been to deny the meaning of life. So, in the death that is accepted, in the suffering that is accepted, is the re-affirmation of the meaning of life.

Now I'll take a third one. One of the few deaths, in the modern world, that has become focal has been the death of Che Chevera. For the communist world, before the fall of the Berlin Wall and the collapse of the Soviet Union, the only hero who was looked up to was Che Chevera. After the Cuban revolution he voluntarily went to South America and was killed and became a martyr. Some say that one of the reasons the Soviet Union supported Cuba for so long was because they had the only martyr of the revolution who really moved the young.

Three focal deaths, three stories, three incarnate mythologies, each of which tells us how to die, what to die for, and what the ideal death is. Now, I want to switch to the modern world.

Forget what you know, forget your expertise for a minute and let's just read the newspaper together, let's watch television together and ask ourselves the question, "What is the death that is focal, or exemplary in modern culture?" What do we see? How do we see death portrayed? What is the face of death that we see?

First, the one that doesn't concern us. Right now the death we see most is in Ruwanda and Bosnia, third world death, the death that comes out of anarchy, disintegration, and poverty. We see the death where tribal consciousness and tribal hatred are re-emerging.

As we see those bodies floating down the river in Ruwanda, and read the stories of incredible savagery of the Tutsies and the Hutu, we say, "Isn't it awful?" And then we say under our breath, "Thank God we are not as they. Thank God we are not primitive. Thank God we are really civilized. Thank God we don't have deaths like that. Thank God."

So, the horror of death in the third world is strangely a comfort to us—because it is not our death. It is not the death to which we are called. It is not the one we think about. We can, perhaps, give some minor charities. But there is also in us, and we don't like to admit this, great relief. "Thank God it is not our death."

Let's focus on what our death is. Our death is, first of all, death in the hospital. How many of you work in hospital settings or work largely with terminal people? How many of you work with cancer? The signal death in our culture is medicalized. Probably the death that becomes a signal for us more than anything else is death by cancer or AIDS. AIDS is ideologically tinged in the popular imagination because it is associated with sexuality. In the degree that we don't deal with sexuality well we also don't like to deal with AIDS. It's a feared death.

Now what does this tell us? The debate in our culture is largely about what we do, not with death, but with death in *terminal situations*. The medical crisis in North America is largely the crisis of both (A) focusing on death in terms of the terminal deaths—that is death at the end of life and (B) focusing on medicalized death—people who are terminally ill.

I want to call your attention to something about our focus on death that is very different than any other deaths that we've ever looked at in terms of mythology. If I asked the question, "What did Socrates die from?" A medical pathologist might possibly say, "Well, hemlock does this . . ." and give me a clinical description of the death. But that wouldn't be to the point, would it? Or what did Jesus die from? Blood loss? That isn't the issue; that isn't the question. The question in both cases is, "What did Socrates die *for* ?", "What did Jesus die *for* ?"

Now I want to try an experiment. I hope you're not too sophisticated for it to work. I would like for you to put aside your professionalism for a minute and just do a sentence completion for me with the first thing that comes to mind. All you do is complete these two sentences. He died for _____. She died for _____. Usually, "his country" is the answer. "He died for his country." Or, "He died for honor," "He died for work." "She died for love," or "She died for family." But, in fact, it's true isn't it, that we don't have very clear ideas of anything that's worth dying for and, therefore, worth living for. So, the question in our culture—now this is very pivotal—all focuses on two words: *for* and *from* and the difference between dying *for* something and dying *from* something. Speaking in terms of how we live and how we die, the most important question we can ask ourselves is "Do you die *for* something or do you die *from* something?" We die *from* something. The deaths that we choose to focus on are largely deaths in which we feel ourselves to be victims of something.

Increasingly, we are a society where there is a rush to victimization; where illness, and especially catastrophic terminal illness, is usually thought of as something that happens to a person, a victim. Disease and illness is something that happens to us. Not a choice.

Thus, we medicalize the problem of dealing with illness and disease. We turn it over to a physician. It's as if we take our bodies to doctors and say, "Here, I'm dropping this off. Fix it." There are alternative movements where we're beginning to understand our responsibility. But, by and large, the central fact in terms of the way that we think and deal with disease and death is as victims.

In our imagination, death is, therefore, an enemy. Physicians are taught that death is an enemy that they must try to defeat at all costs. But death is an enemy that eventually defeats us.

Death comes to be the wastebasket in which we put everything that we are ashamed of.

In North America stress is a problem and a virtue, and leisure is taboo. In the degree that we are governed by the modern myth of progress, ideally we are in control of things. We're independent; we're striving for individuation; we are not rational; we are not co-dependent. We stand on our own two feet. "I can take care of myself."

The horror of death comes because it is exactly the opposite. We're not used to being out of control; we're not used to having to be taken care of, certainly not in any graceful way. We're not accustomed to surrendering; we're not accustomed to limitations; we're not accustomed to not being able to triumph. So, all of the things that are negative in our psyche are put in the wastebasket of death.

What that means is that people are forced to learn to deal with these things when they're terminal. In the degree that we start dealing with death when people are terminal, we are bound to fail. Most of you are being asked to do the impossible, the absolute impossible. To try to teach somebody to die well when they're dying is usually about seventy-seven years too late to begin the process of education. There is no way of teaching somebody to die well—you may teach them to die better than they would die otherwise, but the process of death education is a process that should begin at birth. It should be a self-conscious part of education or it's not going to be done well.

So, here we are trying to deal with it in medicalized situations. Education for death should not belong to the medical profession. I repeat, it should not belong to the medical profession. I don't think it should belong to the psychiatric profession either, incidentally. Dealing with death is, and should be, an amateur enterprise. The word amateur comes from love. Another way to say it is that death is a subject for dilettantes; which comes from the same word, a delight. Those who most delight in life should be the ones who teach about death. To be taught right it has to be taught in the context of love, where you are enfolded within a context of love and of life and growth and vitality. It is in that context that the lesson of death is best taught. That is to say, it is taught all of life.

I've looked at some of the mythologies of death in modern culture— let me look at some alternatives. What would be a wholehearted way of death? How would it look differently? First of all, let me go to what is maybe the most extreme example, the tradition of yogi death. A person, who, for a lifetime, has practiced meditation, and learned wisdom and compassion, will come to the end of life and will die voluntarily.

This is very interesting. I know many cases where this actually happens. Somebody says, "I am at the end of my life and I am ready to die. I yield." Such a person does not die *from* a disease, they die in a time of readiness and ripeness. They die because to surrender at the time of ripeness is the final act of wisdom, and of courage, and of hope in a human life.

If you live constantly learning to let go and to surrender to what is deepest, you are all the time learning to die. The most erotic of all practices, that is the practice which increases love and compassion most, is the practice of learning to die.

For the last two years I've lead groups into Bhutan, high in the Himalayas, the last of the great Buddhist kingdoms. There the essence of life is to learn to be compassionate and wise. Death is something that you practice all along. Part of that culture is a book called the *Tibetan Book of the Dead,* which is a practice. It's not morbid, it's about letting go.

In a minute we're going to see that there are other places where letting go may have some very positive, powerful, and quite desirable effects. I won't mention them yet for fear that I'll blow the story.

In our culture, the only one I know who practiced it was Scott Nearing. Scott Nearing was a philosopher, an organic farmer who believed deeply in the connection with the earth. When he got to be 100 years old he said, "I've lived long enough." He stopped eating and died. Almost an inconceivable thing in the United States for somebody to do that! Inconceivable. Was it suicide?

I go down tomorrow to visit a friend of mine who has ALS, Lou Gehrig disease. It's one of the most punishing diseases in the world, because you lose everything except your mind. A marvelous man I've known for thirty years, powerful—now is lying in bed. The only way he can communicate at all is slightly moving his arms to punch a computer, which is translated into a voice box. Now he's so debilitated it's only "yes" or "no" or small answers like that. His wife is with him, a woman he married about three years ago when they knew quite well what they were dealing with. As his body has withered away, his face has become more and more beautiful. He has achieved some kind of acceptance of death that is almost beyond my power of imagination to conceive.

I remember a couple of years ago when he could still walk a bit, I was there and my wife said to him something like, "Well Dick, you're certainly dealing with this beautifully." He typed back. He said, "What else could I do?" My wife said, "Well, you could piss and moan a little it." He got this seraphic look on his face and typed out. "I never thought of that." So whole-hearted.

Traditionally, philosophy said practice dying every day. Let's see what it would mean to believe that. I think I'll do a little segue here. I'm going to go from treating your death and other people's death to my death. Which I don't like to think about any more than you like to think about your death.

I was raised in a way that death wasn't a problem, because Jesus was going to take care of it. He died for my sins. He died for my sins even when I didn't particularly have any. I mean, I had to invent sins to ask to be forgiven. For, how could I be forgiven, and therefore be saved, and therefore have immortal life unless I allowed Him to be the savior of my sins? Since I didn't think I had sins, that was proof that I did. You got it? Believe in the Lord Jesus Christ and thou shalt be saved! It was a question of eternal life. I believed it as much as I could believe it, and I tried. I was earnest.

I was brought up in a very loving home. I didn't come from a dysfunctional family. I believed that if I believed the right things God was going to solve the problem of death for me. When you think that, you try very hard to believe it. Doubt isn't a mental problem, doubt erodes your immortality, doubt opens you up to death. That's the reason not to doubt. That's the reason to keep a religious framework that assures you that there is eternal life. The authorities tell you that, the Pope tells you that, the Bible tells you that. Somebody assures you that there's eternal life. My faith eroded simultaneously with the death of my father in 1964. When death hits someone you love it's more powerful than all theories, more powerful than all explanations. The death of somebody you love deeply wipes explanation away from the universe.

Death is the rock upon which all systems shipwreck. It is the unknowable. It is the question for which there is no answer, and the one we've been looking for most of all. It is the great, primal mythic question, the great terror.

Usually, those of us who are good have been good so we won't die. We're going to shine in the eyes of Mother and Daddy and God and do the right thing. In the depth of the psyche there is the infantile notion that if we are perfect we will not die.

How do I deal with it? How do I deal with my death? What I've learned gradually over the years is a certain kind of ritual. Every day death visits me. Every day I experience some utter horror. It's not the horror of being terminally ill, as far as I know.

It's interesting, as soon as you start talking about death people assume that you're terminally ill. You can't talk about death in this society without somebody saying . . . somebody told me you had cancer. Not that I know of. I'm trying to learn about dying. I'm sixty-two, it's time to think about it.

Every day death, comes. It usually comes to me when I'm going to sleep—that is, when I'm yielding control. Or, I wake up in the middle of the night and I have to go pee at 2 A.M. and I look in the mirror and say, "Oh my God! How did a seventeen-year-old kid like you get a face like that?" You know, being male you look in the toilet to see if there's blood in your piss, or something like that. "How's that mole doing, there? Is it changing shape, or not?"

For me the terror is not about the process of dying, I could handle it. A friend of mine who had leukemia said, "Dying would be a great way to live if it weren't for the final act."

I think the process of letting go could be very like a total body orgasm. Lay that burden down. Can you feel it? I mean, it's got to be similar. In orgasm there is a place, if you notice, that you're very careful so you will come back. Death must be sort of like, "I'm going all the way, thank you. I'm lettin' go of everything and it ain't gonna be pretty."

For me the ultimate terror is about being dead. D-E-A-D. The fear that death means "end of report," end of Sam Keen, end of everything that I love, end of consciousness.

I can't even think that thought without imagining myself not being there. Then something in me deep, deep, deep, primal—and it isn't neurotic—rises up and says, "No. God damn it. No! No!! It is not acceptable! And if you don't know it, you haven't confronted your own death. It is not acceptable!" I don't believe it and you don't believe it in your gut of guts, all the rationalizations aside. This is what I don't like about Elisabeth Kübler-Ross. All of those things aside, it is not acceptable! And, we don't like it.

Now, what do I do with that? Can I be angry? I didn't sign the contract. When I was born the small print wasn't even there, because my eyes were better and I could have seen it. I wasn't asked if I wanted to die. I wasn't given life and this was the condition. Thus, the terror and the horror. . . . That's what terror is. At the bottom, terror isn't about suffering. At the bottom of terror is annihilation. That's a good reason to keep death out there.

When I feel the threat of annihilation, I feel the center of my stomach being scooped out; and I feel my balls going limp; and I feel any power going out of me. I want to run away. I want to deny. For many years I did.

Then I began to learn something else. The primary rule I have learned about dealing with the life of a spirit is: when you meet a demon don't run. When they open up their mouth to swallow you, go right in. Go toward them. Go toward the unacceptable thing. Don't dilute it down.

I don't know if it's true or not—it's true enough, whether it happened or not. Supposedly, there's a culture in New Guinea where the right of passage for men involves drinking poison. It's a strange kind of poison; it could be absorbed in the esophagus, but it's neutralized in the stomach. So, if you take the poison and you go "gulp," "Ah"—you're safe. But, if you gag you're dead.

It's like the time when my son was a little boy and he had to take medicine, so we mixed it with a spoonful of honey. He wouldn't take it. We mixed it with orange juice. He wouldn't take it. So, we have this drink we used to make out of "tiger milk," we called it. It was brewer's yeast and all this stuff that was supposed to keep you living forever. We mixed up that. He loved it. We had a pint. He wouldn't take it. Now we have the problem, "how do you get the pint of medicine down when before it was only half a spoonful?" You can swallow a spoonful of terror and it won't contaminate your days. As a matter of fact, far to the contrary.

Some strange things happen when we begin to deal with death in terms of taking that terror raw and taking it into ourselves. I began to notice, for instance, that when I didn't run away from terror, and I would hold the terror right there and look at that terror, I could immediately go back, retrospectively, into my new life and see all of the armoring I had done in order to protect myself from that terrible knowledge. I could see what a good boy I was. Oh, I was good for the early part of my life. I could see how hard I'd worked. I could see what being famous was like. I could see what performing was like. I could see that some tincture of death had colored most of my activities. I had my immortality projects, as Ernest Becker had said. I saw my armoring, and my power, and my effort to control other people and control myself was all an armoring against death.

And, as I would take the fear of death straight, that armoring would begin to loosen. I didn't have to be so perfect. I didn't have to be trustworthy, loyal, helpful, friendly, courteous, kind, obedient, cheerful, thrifty, brave, clean, and reverent.

I discovered, also, that in the degree that I would accept the terror of death, and the terror of life, that something began to happen which was very interesting. The wonder began to return. They are siamese twins!

When ever we encounter the holy we encounter a mystery which is at the same time a mysterium tremendum, et fascinane. It's awesome; it's overpowering; it's terrifying. It is a terrible thing to fall into the hands of a living god . . . or goddess. Kali, the goddess of Creation, wears skulls around her neck. To take life raw means that which gives us life also kills us.

Terrifying thing. It's also a wonderful thing. A wonder, the mystery of it all, the privilege of being here. It remains, with a terrible face and with the wonder of it all, a mystery which is ultimately indecipherable. To live in that mystery is to live with the consciousness of being an explorer, the taster of that mystery, a questioner.

So, gradually, what happened was I did this. I realized that my whole sense of the life of the spirit changed. I didn't have the answers anymore. I didn't have a series of religious answers. What I had was that I'd finally learned to fall in love with the questions. As Rilke said, "To learn to love the questions themselves."

The great mythic questions: "Where did I come from?", "What is my ultimate destiny?", "What ought I do?", "How close can I be to other people?", "What is the meaning of death?", "How do I heal myself?", "How do I forgive?", "How do I be forgiven?" All those great questions become daily bread. Not frustrating because I don't have the answers. Those questions face me into the wind.

The experience of realizing that the world is ultimately mysterious, beyond explanation. Therefore, the end of my existence, my death, is ultimately mysterious. It returns to me the sense of the mystery of life. Also, it returns me to my body.

In my own experience, a great deal of my early religious life was a life of disincarnating, or discarnation. Christianity, although it said the "word became flesh," it didn't believe it—or it believed it only from the neck up. It was very suspicious of the life of the flesh, the life of sensuality and of sexuality.

It wasn't easy for me to own the connection between the sensual and the sacred and the sexual. The wonder of life is that daily, moment by moment, instant by instant, I am given gifts. Gifts of simple beauty— the gift of color, touch, and taste. My life is a receiving of an overflow-ingness from the world; hopefully, also, a returning of that overflowing-ness. If you want to put it in crude terms, the payoff for living daily with death is that we live daily, also, with wonder.

Then you might ask the question, "Well, what about when I come to the end of my life?", "What about if I were terminal?", "How do I deal with those that are terminal?" My friend Dick, with whom I've shared many dreams and many, many years, and now he can't talk. I ask myself, "Well, how do I deal with Dick?" My life, at this point, is very rich. So, there's a part of me that's ashamed when I go there to tell him about riding horses and all the things that I do. Another part of me knows what is best in me and what is best in him and I have to give that. He loved that when he could share it then he loves that now. He doesn't have answers. He doesn't have to have answers. The people who have the answers are the ones that get cut off from him, because they can't live with his tragedy; and the only way that helps him with his tragedy is when people really connect with him. Of course, really connecting with another person is our connecting with them at the point where life is mysterious to us, where the questions are still real with us. We do not connect with the dying as professionals. We connect to the dying as amateurs who are also dying. So, those are some of the ideals. I see I'm at the end of the hour.

I would like to close as I began, with some words of D. H. Lawrence about the mystery of life and then of death. This is called "Terra Incognita" (Unknown Country):

> There are vast realms of consciousness still undreamed of, vast ranges of experience like the humming of unseen harps we know nothing of within us. Oh, when man escaped from the barbed wire entanglement of his own ideas and his own mechanical devices there is a marvelously rich world of contact and sheer fluid beauty. And, fearless, face to face awareness of our now naked life. And me, and you, and other men, and women, and grapes, and ghouls, and ghosts, and green moonlight, and ruddy orange limbs stirring the limbo of the unknown air. And eyes, so soft, softer than the space between the stars. And all things, and nothing, and being, and non-being alternately palpitate. When at last we escape the barbed wire enclosure of "know thyself" knowing we can never know. But, we can touch, and wonder, and ponder, and make our effort, and dangle in a last fastidious, fine delight as the fuchsia does— dangling her reckless drop of purple after so much putting forth and slow mounting marvel of a little tree.

And then finally:

> Sing the song of death. Oh, sing it. For without the song of death the song of life becomes pointless and silly. Sing, then, the song of death, and the longest journey, and what the soul carries with him, and what he leaves behind, and how he finds the darkness that enfolds him into utter peace at last, at last beyond innumerable seas.

CHAPTER 2

The Ontology of Masculinity–
The Roots of Manhood

Neil Thompson

Gender is not only a basic dimension of society at a broad level, but also a significant aspect of personal identity. Masculinity and femininity are fundamental to the individual's sense of self. This chapter explores the significance of gender, particularly masculinity, in coping with the existential demands of human existence. It considers the costs and benefits of gender differentiation insofar as it affects dealing with grief and other life challenges. The analysis presented is premised on the existentialist philosophy of writers such as Sartre and de Beauvoir, and the development of their ideas in relation to social work [1, 2]. A key aspect of this theoretical framework is that of *ontology*—the study of being. Ontology raises fundamental questions about meaning, value, and purpose. It is therefore of major significance in relation to issues of life, death, grief, and loss.

Feminist analysis has shown us that male and female patterns of thinking and feeling are differentiated at an early age through the gender-specific process of socialization: "blue for a boy, pink for a girl" [3]. A particularly significant aspect of this process is the establishment of differential sets of norms with regard to the expression of emotion. In broad terms, men are discouraged from expressing "feminine" emotions of loss, sadness, and tenderness, and this can produce a significant psychological block at times of male grief when powerful feelings enter into conflict with the individual's sense of self and conception of the social world (or, *Weltanschauung* as philosophers refer to it). This is not simply a conflict of the *psychological* (grief) and the *social* (socialization); it is, more fundamentally, the site of an ontological crisis. It challenges our sense of self or personal identity and, as such, has profound consequences for the way in which we experience our existence.

A key concept is that of "ontological security," as used by Laing [4] and further developed by Giddens [5]. This refers to a sense of personal wholeness and the integration of personality. The absence of such security on a longer-term basis is associated (for example, by Laing) with schizophrenia. On a short-term basis, ontological security can also be undermined at times of crisis, reflecting the breakdown of homeostasis associated with the crisis situation. This chapter explores one particular aspect of ontological security, that of masculine identity, and the threat posed by the experience of grief and loss.

MASCULINITY AND SELFHOOD–
THE ONTOLOGICAL BASIS

As we grow and develop, we establish a sense of self, a personal identity that acts as a source and symbol of security and stability. Each of us develops a sense of uniqueness and individuality which becomes a very important part of our emotional and psychological well-being. However, identity is not simply about uniqueness—there are also significant social or group aspects integrated into each person's identity. For example, cultural or religious affiliation, national or regional identity, are all significant dimensions of a person's sense of self [6]. Similarly, gender definitions and expectations are part of culture yet they are shaped by individual experience. Our perceptions of who we are, and the perceptions of others, are heavily influenced by gender. Indeed, gender is a primary social indicator of identity. The following quotation from a noted psychologist highlights the central role in our self-concept and our interactions with others.

> It would probably be true to say that one of the first things we notice about somebody, if not *the* first thing, is whether they are male or female; it almost seems as if we have to have this information about a person if we are able to interact with them properly. We also expect people to be able to identify us correctly as male or female and if they cannot, or do not, we would probably be most offended. Our name, age and sex are standard pieces of information on all official forms and our sex, of course, is one of the facts which appears on everyone's birth certificate. Our sex, therefore, is a fundamental part of our self-concept and of our interactions with others [7, p. 674].

Recognizing the centrality of gender to our identity helps to illustrate that identity is both personal *and* social—it straddles both dimensions of existence, that which is unique to each of us and that which we share with others. It is the interplay between the personal and the social aspects that gives identity its particular ontological character—its role as a bridge between the subjective world of personal experience and the broader context of the objective social world. For men, then, masculinity is part of one's relationship with the world; it is a filter through which the world is experienced. Masculinity is not simply an objective social category, it is a fundamental part of a man's existence (as indeed is femininity for women).

Appreciating the significance of the interrelatedness of the personal and the social point is hindered by the traditional academic division of labor, with psychology demonstrating an interest in the individual and sociology in social collectivities. The different academic traditions within these disciplines have tended to produce a divide between the two subjects, with relatively little analysis of the overlap between them. Consequently, human action tends to be conceptualized in either psychological terms *or* sociological terms, bearing little or no testimony to the intricate complexities of "lived experience" (le vécu) that can be understood in terms of a dialectic of subjective and objective factors. An existentialist approach, by contrast, draws on ontology, the study of being, that conceives of human existence as both psychological and sociological—simultaneously experienced at both a personal and social level. This approach also values the unique contribution of each discipline.

Masculinity can be seen to be an important ontological concept, as it operates at both an individual and social level. As Segal comments:

> "masculinity" gains its meanings, its force and appeal, not just from internalised psychological components or roles, but from all the wider social relations in which men and women participate which simply take for granted men's authority and privileges in relation to women [8, p. 284].

The "authority and privileges" that patriarchal societies bestow upon men are encapsulated in "messages" from society about how men should think, feel, and act, messages that become internalized; they become part of the basic ontological structure of the individual's personality. There are two key issues that flow from this:

1. Socialization is commonly seen as the process whereby an individual is "inducted" into his or her society by learning the appropriate social values, norms, and expectations. However, what also needs to be appreciated is that this is a reciprocal process—

as the individual becomes part of society, that society becomes part of the individual.

2. Masculinity, as a set of social expectations, not only shapes how men should behave, but also how they should think and feel. Gender-related social expectations have a significant bearing on the experience and expression of emotion. This point will receive greater attention later in the chapter.

A person's gender can be seen, then, as a dimension of his or her being. For men, masculinity becomes a filter through which our everyday experience passes, a framework for making sense of the world. This is reflected in the use of language which shows clear gender differences. For example, Tannen argues that men's speech patterns demonstrate a focus on status, while women's speech patterns show a focus on intimacy and sharing [9]. The language we use provides a framework for interpreting the world and our everyday experience [10]. It acts as a "window on the world," and so we can see that the gendered nature of language ensures that the pane of glass is, for men, masculine-tinted.

The significance of this may be difficult to appreciate at first, as a masculine perspective is commonly seen as a social norm. This is illustrated by de Beauvoir's concept of "alterity" (or "otherness"). That is, women are defined *in relation to* men. Women are seen as "the other," the "spare rib":

A man never begins by presenting himself as an individual of a certain sex; it goes without saying that he is a man. The terms *masculine* and *feminine* are used symmetrically only as a matter of form, as on legal papers. In reality, the relation of the two sexes is not quite like that of two electrical poles, for man represents both the positive and the neutral, as is indicated by the common use of *man* to designate human beings in general; whereas woman represents only the negative, defined by limiting criteria, without reciprocity [11, p. 15].

While this argument has major implications for understanding the patriarchal nature of social organization on a macro level, it is also significant at a micro level in terms of individual thoughts, feelings, and actions. In particular, two important points arise:

1. Men are less likely to appreciate the extent to which they are influenced by social expectations of masculinity as such expectations are so strongly grounded in everyday experience.

2. When masculinity is challenged, men are likely to feel that their very being is under threat, as the preponderance of masculine norms makes it very difficult to disentangle what is specifically masculine from what is more broadly human.

An understanding of what happens when masculinity is threatened is very much related to emotional expressiveness, particularly during times of loss and bereavement.

GENDER DIFFERENTIATION: COSTS AND BENEFITS

Sex-role stereotyping is a significant aspect of social organization and raises a wide number of issues. One particular set of issues relates to the costs and benefits of gender differentiation. This is often over-simplified to a position in which the power and privileges of patriarchy that most cultures bestow upon men are recognized, but the costs of sexism for men are usually ignored. Clatterbaugh draws attention to the price men have to pay for the benefits of masculinity when he states:

> One of the striking commonalities throughout much of the litera-ture on men and masculinity is agreement about the cost of being masculine. Even if men themselves are not oppressed, those who assume a traditional masculine role tend to pay a price . . . Mas-culinity, too, is a form of alienation largely produced by the relations of production in which men control and are controlled [12, p. 117].

Similarly, Bowl argues that: "There is much to be gained from loosen-ing up the prevailing concept of masculinity. . . . Our existing conception operates as a straightjacket limiting communication between men, and between men and women, and limiting fulfilling experiences" [13, p. 30].

One of the recognized costs of masculinity is the phenomenon com-monly known as "emotional inexpressiveness," as captured in the phrase "big boys don't cry." However, it is important to note that this is somewhat misleading. It is not simply that men are discouraged through the socialization process from expressing emotion—it is only certain emotions which are seen as "unmanly" [14]. For example, the expression of anger or aggression is seen as suitably masculine, as is the expression of joy in certain circumstances, such as success at a sporting event. It is, therefore, not simply that women may express emotion while men may not. The range of emotions are structured according to gender—emotions reflect and reinforce differential gender expectations in society. Unfortunately, grief is an emotion that tends not to be associated with masculinity, and this can therefore present a dilemma for men when strong feelings of grief clash with deeply ingrained social expectations against their expression, thereby creating the potential for an ontological crisis. This is a cost of masculinity that is especially significant, particularly in relation to how well-equipped—or otherwise—men may be to deal with the emotional challenges of human existence. The following comment from Phillips illustrates just how costly such a rigid gender-specific emotional response can be:

> If power is in the interests of men, why are so many men emotionally disconnected? Why do nearly one in every two divorced men sever the emotional connection with their own children as soon as the connection with the children's mother is dissolved? [15, p. 19].

It is therefore an issue which merits closer attention.

MASCULINITY AND LOSS

The experience of loss is one example of the range of existential demands that characterize human existence. The dominant conception of masculinity, with its emphasis on holding back the expression of sadness and grief, presents challenges for the effective management of loss. It creates artificial barriers that add to the difficulties of handling bereavement and loss. For example, studies of the responses of parents to the loss of a child have shown significant gender differences, with fathers being less willing to express their grief openly. As Littlewood comments:

> Kennel, Slyter and Klaus (1970) found that the fathers in their study tended to deny the fact that they were grieving, despite grieving in fact for as long or longer than their partners. Wilson et al. (1982) have found that fathers were more unwilling than mothers to agree to discuss their dead child. Obviously, a disinclination to report aspects of grief could account for some of the apparent differences between maternal and paternal grief [16, p. 144].

The reluctance to acknowledge, and work with, one's grief can turn the existential demand of loss into an existential crisis, a breakdown of ontological security. Loss can disturb or even shatter our everyday sense of reality. Where this occurs, one's sense of reality is, temporarily at least, thrown into disarray, and this feeling of confusion and uncertainty can add to the distress of the grief. For men, this can present a major dilemma in which masculine notions of coping do not sit easily with the demands of the situation, creating additional tensions and pressures. A man's sense of personal security can be seriously challenged and undermined by such an event—ontological insecurity is experienced.

Ontological insecurity is the absence of a sense of "rootedness," of being anchored in social reality. It is a term that describes a breakdown in the individual's taken-for-granted relationship with the social world. It contrasts with the everyday experience of ontological security which Giddens defines as: "Confidence or trust that the natural and social worlds are as they appear to be, including the basic parameters of self, and social identity" [17]. This is closely related to the concept of "homeostasis," as used in crisis theory. Giddens illustrates this in a later work when he comments on the relationship between crises and ontological security.

> The maintenance of a framework of "ontological security" is, like all other aspects of social life, an ongoing accomplishment of lay actors. Within the production of modes of interaction in which the mutual knowledge required to sustain that interaction is "unproblematic," and hence can be largely "taken for granted," ontological security is routinely grounded. "Critical situations" exist where such routine grounding is radically dislocated, and where consequently the accustomed constituting skills of actors no longer mesh in with the motivational components of their action [18, p. 124].

Giddens's notion of "radical dislocation," as used here, is an apt term for the experience of loss in general, but applies particularly well to the male experience of grief in which culturally codified expectations of thoughts, feelings, and actions can leave men inadequately equipped to cope when the floodgates of pain and distress are opened by bereavement.

Consequently, a crisis situation such as a bereavement can be seen to challenge and undermine ontological security and lead to a recon-sideration of meaning and values:

> As a rule, questions about the purpose and meaning of life are rarely addressed. Within the complacency of homeostasis we take such matters for granted and, if they do arise, they are usually dismissed by jokes about "the meaning of life" etc. However, at a time of crisis, such issues tend to loom large. Feelings of loneliness, emptiness and meaninglessness are characteristic of crisis as it is, in effect, an existential experience insofar as it replaces the

security of homeostasis with doubt and existential uncertainty [19, p. 17].

The crisis of loss reintroduces the ontological dimension which, in everyday life, remains submerged and unquestioned. Loss presents an existential challenge—a challenge for which traditional masculinity can be seen to have few answers.

Feminist analysis has brought our attention to the privileges and benefits for men in societies characterized by patriarchal social relations [11]. Against these, however, must be balanced the risk of ontological crisis brought about by the inadequacy of traditional masculine patterns of emotional response in dealing with the intensity of a bereavement. Such a crisis may have disastrous consequences. For example, Ridley points out that a high proportion of people who take their own lives have experienced a major upheaval in the previous year. In addition, she notes the significance of gender insofar as the suicide rate for males is twice that for females, and male deaths are more likely to be characterized by violence [20]. In sum, masculinity can be seen to be detrimental at two levels—first, it leaves men vulnerable to ontological insecurity and crisis at times of loss and upheaval; and, second, if ontological insecurity is experienced, the emotional inexpressiveness of masculinity leaves men ill-equipped to deal with it.

CONCLUSION

Traditional constructions of masculinity have been shown to be problematic, especially in relation to the existential challenges of loss and bereavement. An uncritical acceptance of stereotypical norms of masculinity carries with it many costs, not least of which are the emotional barriers associated with the expectation that "big boys don't cry." Such barriers can lead to a crisis of ontological insecurity, a process whereby the grieving trajectory can be distorted and rendered far more problematic than it needs to be. There is therefore a high price to pay for traditional conceptions of masculinity. Segal captures this point when she argues that:

> The influence of feminism may of course make men less certain of the desirability of what they see as their masculinity. What the pro-feminist men's movement literature and practice make clear is that, once aware of it, at least some men are very unhappy with the idea that they are caught up with a system which is exploitative of and oppressive to women, gays, and certain other men [8, p. 290].

The critique of masculinity is therefore one to be promoted and pursued in the interests of a more constructive response to grief in particular, and a more enlightened approach to existence in general. It highlights the need to develop an approach to gender socialization more in keeping with the existential reality we face, that is, a more *authentic* approach.

> Masculinity reflects a set of expectations concerning gender-specific characteristic behaviours, attitudes and outlook on life. As such, it is a *Weltanschauung,* a "window on the world." However, as this "window" tends to be fairly rigid and stereotypical as a result of the process of socialisation into patriarchal roles and norms, it is a window of distortion. This relates closely to the existentialist notion of "bad faith" or "inauthenticity." . . . This is an important concept which helps us to understand the destructive potential of rigid sex-role stereotyping [14].

The relationship between ontology and masculinity is one that has received relatively little attention in research or practice but clearly has a significant bearing on the male experience of grief, and the success or otherwise of professional attempts to ease suffering and aid the process of "healing." Much can be gained by increasing our understanding of the ontology of masculinity, a great deal of progress to be made by developing further the critique of conventional conceptions of masculinity.

REFERENCES

1. N. Thompson, *Existentialism and Social Work,* Avebury, Aldershot, Vermont, 1992.
2. N. Thompson, *Child Abuse: The Existential Dimension,* University of East Anglia Social Work Monographs, Norwich, 1992.
3. T. Lovell (ed.), *British Feminist Thought,* Blackwell, Oxford, 1990.
4. R. D. Laing, *The Politics of Experience and the Bird of Paradise,* Penguin, Harmondsworth, 1967.
5. A. Giddens, *New Rules of Sociological Method* (2nd Edition), Polity, Cambridge, 1993.
6. R. G. Pugh, Language Policy and Social Work, *Social Work, 39*:4, pp. 432-437, 1994.
7. R. D. Gross, *Psychology: The Science of Mind and Behaviour* (2nd Edition), Hodder and Stoughton, London, 1992.
8. L. Segal, *Slow Motion: Changing Masculinities, Changing Men,* Virago, London, 1990.
9. D. Tannen, *You Just Don't Understand: Women and Men in Conversation,* Virago, London, 1992.

10. R. G. Pugh, *Effective Language for Health and Social Work*, Chapman and Hall, London, 1996.
11. S. de Beauvoir, *The Second Sex*, Penguin, Harmondsworth, 1972.
12. K. Clatterbaugh, *Contemporary Perspectives on Masculinity: Men, Women and Politics in Modern Society*, Westview Press, Oxford, 1990.
13. R. Bowl, *Changing the Nature of Masculinity—A Task for Social Work?* University of East Anglia Social Work Monographs, Norwich, 1985.
14. N. Thompson, Men and Anti-Sexism, *British Journal of Social Work*, 25:4, pp. 459-475, 1995.
15. A. Phillips, *The Trouble with Boys*, Pandora, London, 1993.
16. J. Littlewood, *Aspects of Grief: Bereavement in Adult Life*, Routledge, London, 1992.
17. A. Giddens, *The Constitution of Society*, Polity, Cambridge, 1984.
18. A. Giddens, *New Rules of Sociological Method* (2nd Edition), Polity, Cambridge, 1993.
19. N. Thompson, *Crisis Intervention Revisited*, Pepar, Birmingham, 1991.
20. S. Ridley, Sudden Death from Suicide, in *Death, Dying and Bereavement*, D. Dickenson and M. Johnson (eds.), Sage, London, pp. 64-67, 1993.

CHAPTER 3

Take It Like a Man: Masculine Response to Loss

Kenneth A. Doka and Terry Martin

In recent years, there has been increasing interest in gender differences in grief. Specifically, attention has focused on ways that males respond to loss. Traditionally, many clinicians have seen aspects of the male role placing men at a disadvantage in grieving when compared to women. Women are seen as more ready to accept help and express emotion, both of which are viewed as essential to the process of grieving. Since men are perceived as less likely to show emotion or accept help, they are seen as having more difficulty in responding to loss. LeGrand, for example, states, "This does not mean men are not grieving; it does indicate that they may not accomplish the task as successfully as women" [1, p. 3].

The underlying assumption is that there are limited ways that one can effectively cope with loss. Staudacher expresses this succinctly: "Simply put, there is only one way to grieve. That way is to go through the core of grief. Only when experiencing the necessary emotional effects of your loved one's death is it possible for you to eventually resolve the loss" [2, p. 31]. Yet, this assumption is questionable. Were men and women to grieve in identical ways, one also would expect analogous expressions of emotion, duplicate behavior patterns, and feelings that would be indistinguishable from one gender to the other. In fact, there are many ways to cope with loss. To assert that only one pattern is acceptable is both empirically ungrounded and clinically unhelpful. Rando states this well:

> Many care givers strive to have male mourners respond to loss as do their female counterparts. This is an unwise, to say nothing of an almost fruitless goal [3, p. 358].

It may be that, in grief, we do with males what we do with females in many other areas—evaluate them against norms based upon the other gender. In this case, we evaluate male grief against norms of grief that are primarily based upon female samples and judge that they do not grieve as women do. Perhaps there are different patterns of grief and correspondingly specific strategies for coping and intervention that works best with males.

This chapter explores the phenomenon of masculine grief. Masculine, rather than male, was chosen to describe this pattern of grieving. Perhaps additional research will reveal that masculine grief is not wholly gender-specific, just as traditional (or feminine) grief is not a uniquely female experience. The chapter reviews gender differences between males and females that might affect the grieving process. This has been a traditional way to study different patterns. Next, patterns of grief, drawn from this research, are delineated. And, finally, the clinical implications of masculine grieving are explored, emphasizing the coping strategies and clinical interventions that may be useful to masculine grievers.

First and foremost, however, it is necessary to offer two critical caveats. First, any discussion of gender differences must take into account the wide variations within male and female roles. If anything, gender differences must be perceived as two overlapping, bell-shaped curves. Means and medians may differ on these curves, but should not obfuscate the overlap that exists between genders. Secondly, we need to reaffirm that gender roles are constantly reshaped by historical events, culture, class, religion, and other significant social variables and understand that whatever is true today for specific populations will likely differ in the future.

THE MALE MYSTIQUE

While culture and history frame gender experiences and expectations, it is clear that in contemporary U.S. society, the experiences of men and women are very different. Beginning with the games chosen in childhood, boys and girls develop different (though complimentary) social skills. While girls are learning to interact one-on-one or in small groups, to work cooperatively, and to have empathy for others, boys are learning to compete with one another. They practice leading and following and working with others on a "team" toward some common goal, usually defeating another "team" [4]. As adults, men are attracted to sports which emphasize a competitive role. Their friendships usually center around shared activities. Men, as well as boys, view their relationships with others—particularly other males—in terms of a hierarchy [5]. Often, there is a tendency to de-emphasize emotionality, especially the more tender emotions. Socialization into the male role means learning to control one's emotions. As a result, men tend to learn active and problem-focused solutions for coping with stress. In addition, men tend to value self-reliance. Solving one's problems and facing one's difficulties alone have long been defined as hallmarks of manhood [6].

Women's experiences are somewhat different from men. From an early age, girls at play tend to be more cooperative and to have consideration and empathy for others [4]. They are also taught to share confidences and draw support from one another. Emotional expressiveness is not repressed; in fact, females tend to learn more emotion-focused ways of coping [7]. Nothing in the female role denies the support or nurturance of others. To the contrary, the ability to offer and to accept such nurturance is defined as a critical mark of the women's role.

In response to the women's movement, the problem of defining contemporary models of male identity has merited increased attention. Rotundo historically reviews American definitions of the male role and notes both continuities and changes in male identity over the past 200 years [8]. In studying the twentieth-century male culture, Rotundo describes how mastery of one's emotions and enthusiasms was seen as a key developmental issue that separated boys from men: boys could not control their enthusiasm; men had to teach and model self-restraint. Among both men and boys, emotional mastery and stiff-lipped courage were seen as virtues [8].

However, early in the nineteenth century, men often shared intimate, caring relationships with other men. Since men were expected to invest much time in public and social affairs, relationships between men were perceived as natural and productive. This began to change later in that century for three reasons. With industrialization, the work role became more fundamental to one's identity. There were limited opportunities to bond with other men outside of work, inhibiting bonding. Second, the concurrent rise of individualism also isolated men from their peers. As men became older, established in their work and marriage, there was little time for sharing feelings and thoughts with other men. Congregating with other males began to be considered a mark of the boy—not the man. Finally, homophobia reared its unlovely head. Since homosexuals had been labeled as "unmanly," it was difficult to acknowledge feelings for other men that would allow one to build supportive connections with one another. By the twentieth century, contemporary visions of the male role had taken root, emphasizing the male as a rugged individual.

Some theorize that the roots of gender differences are biological. Because of testosterone, males are larger and more muscular. Bolstered by data that consistently link aggression to males, sociobiologists might argue that our male forebearers were naturally selected to defend hearth and family. For these ancestors, emotionality may have inhibited survival. For example, when the community was under attack, men who could ignore their dismay at the deaths of comrades could focus on repelling the invaders. Afterwards, the task of rebuilding could begin only if shock and grief could be laid aside. Likewise, the case could be made that conforming to society's rules, especially those involving conflicts and disputes, could be accomplished only if males curtailed their aggressiveness, perhaps through controlling, even suppressing emotions.

Recently, these conceptions of maleness have been challenged. Robert Bly, for example, offers a poetic vision of what the male role can be [9]. Drawing from ancient myths, he envisions a male role that encompasses a vigorous sense of masculinity with an ability to be emotionally rooted. Ironically, Bly sees the male first having to acknowledge significant griefs that have impaired his development— the griefs caused by lost fathers, dreams, and morality. Similarly, Sam Keen also sees men forging an identity out of a struggle with grief and guilt, burdened by the demand of work and performance [10]. To Keen, the essence of men is that they are spiritual warriors attempting to create meaning in their lives. Their quest is to fashion a new sense of male identity that allows for both emotionality and commonality in some yet undefined, but distinctly male way. Should the fledgling male movement succeed in redefining masculinity, it may very well change masculine patterns of grieving.

PATTERNS OF GRIEVING

Presently, though, the limited research linking gender with grieving suggests that men and women deal with grief somewhat differently, in ways that are highly reflective of traditional gender roles. This is not surprising, as each culture has norms that not only govern behavior, but emotions. Hochschild notes that these "feelings rules" tell someone what feelings ought to be suppressed [11]. Naturally, these feelings rules can differ by gender. Because a subset of these "feelings rules" relates to patterns of grieving, it is understandable that research has found some differences in patterns of grief. For example, a number of studies have found that outside of anger, men had a difficult time expressing emotions [12-15].

Research, though, on depression has been mixed. Osterweis, Solomen, and Green [16] found higher rates of depression in males, particularly boys who lost a father, while Goldbach, Dunn, Toedler, and Lasker [13] reported that women were more depressed after pregnancy loss than their husbands. This may suggest that the type and meaning of loss has more effect on depression than does gender. Yet, even if the type of loss is fixed, there is still confusion about gender and depression following bereavement. Jacobs and Kasl reported that the widows in their sample experienced significantly more numbness/disbelief and depression than females following the death of a spouse [17]. Still other studies report no gender differences in depression following the deaths of spouses [18-20]. Finally, Stroebe and Stroebe offered a different view of this data [21]. Since a sex main effect in the occurrence of depression has been well established, findings of no gender differences in the incidence of depression is evidence that widowers are relatively more affected than widows. As for findings of lower rates of depression among bereaved males, Stroebe and Stroebe suggested that this may be an artifact of higher rates of alcoholism, which often masks depression [21].

Studies have also shown that men and women tend to cope with grief differently. Glick, Weiss, and Parkes found that widowers spoke more about loss as a "dismemberment," while women looked at loss in terms of "abandonment" [12]. Men also availed themselves less of self-help groups [16]. Rando suggests that men, after the loss of a child, saw themselves as needing to be providers, protectors, and problem-solvers, making it difficult to accept and to receive help [22]. Similarly, Hogan and Balk found men to be more private, intellectual, introspective in their grief [23]. Glick, Weiss, and Parkes reported that the widowers in their research expressed a concern with being "realistic," i.e., focusing on solving the immediate problems of loss [12]. They also reported that men were more likely to experience social recovery earlier, often quickly returning to work. However, returning to work may itself be a coping mechanism, since it allows persons to become distracted from their grief. Studies of gay men responding to the loss of lovers and friends in the AIDS epidemic reaffirm the observations of some clinicians [2] that males may be more inclined to use substances such as drugs or alcohol to mitigate the grieving process. Studies did show that common coping patterns included both the use of sedatives and recreational drugs [24, 25].

In reviewing the limited literature on gender differences, it is critical to note three points. First, the experiences of bereavement are both highly individual and different. Carey, for example, documented that widowers and widows face different types of problems and discontinuities while widowers experienced disruptions in their home life and kin network [20].

Second, it is important to recognize that these differences may be mitigated by the type of loss or other variables such as social class. Further, there is most likely an interaction between gender differences in bereavement and age: differences seem less apparent in older cohorts. For example, Feinson found that any gender difference in her study seemed to disappear when social and demographic variables were factored [26]. Another study, exploring the reactions of older persons to spousal loss, found gender was unrelated to measures of adjustment and depression [27]. In fact, the majority of studies reporting differences involved younger samples. This is not surprising given the general agreement that both sexes, as they age, move toward androgyny [28].

Third, if there are differences, they may be more apparent earlier in the grieving process. Goldbach, Dunn, Toedler, and Lasker found in their testing that women early in grieving have higher scores on overall grief, difficulty in coping, and despair than men [13]. At a later time, though, this difference disappeared. Similarly, Lund, Caserta and Dimond found no significant differences between males and females on social and psychological bereavement outcomes [29]. Perhaps this simply reaffirms Lang and Gottlieb's own conclusions to their research: "Men grieve just as intensely as their wives, but their expression of grief may take different forms" [14, p. 250].

What are these forms or patterns of masculine grief? First, it seems that outside of anger, men seem to have a difficult time responding emotionally to the loss. As stated earlier, males have been taught to suppress emotions throughout their socialization. One thanatologist, Dennis Ryan, responding to the loss of his stillborn son, expressed this conflict well:

> I knew I could hide my feelings very well. I had learned that and counted it as a strength. People who thought similarly would never try to draw someone's feelings out unless they wanted to humiliate him or her. I was thankful to these, for there were times when I was very close to that fearful state of being out of control of my emotions. But I was spared that indignity [30, p. 128].

While anger is a natural and easy emotion for men to express, anger does not seem to have the therapeutic benefits of other forms of emotional release. For example, anger does not seem to buffer cardiovascular stress [7]. Men also tend to be reluctant to share their grief. This, too emerges from the protective role that men often assume. Again, Ryan's reaction is often typical: "I had cast myself in the role of the strong one and was trying to live up to that role" [30 p. 129].

This role of protector often serves to tone down emotional response in general; in this case, repression is the price of vigilance. Ironically, this characterization may also lead to a sense of failure and feelings of guilt, especially if the deceased was one of the "protected."

Rather than externalizing their grief, many men choose to confront their losses internally. Men are more comfortable in dealing with grief cognitively. Perhaps men respond initially to cognitions explaining the circumstance of their losses, rather than emotional cues. For example, a psychologist and his wife each lost both their parents within an eight-month period. His wife described her grief as a series of emotional waves, with the intensity of feelings, and concomitant responses, ebbing and flowing. The husband sought an internal explanation for his losses, stating that "I was always being over-whelmed by thoughts, not feelings." In another case, a young couple shared their disappointment with each other several months after the sudden death of their seventeen-year-old son. Responding to his wife's accusations that he failed to validate her grief, the husband stated: "I couldn't allow myself to miss (him) until I figured out what this meant to our family." This suggests that at least some men might attempt to evaluate their experiences cognitively, rather than experience them emotionally.

When some men do respond behaviorally to a loss, it usually involves immersion in some form of activity. Sometimes, this is work. It also may be intimately related to the loss. Men may wish to take legal or physical action in response to the loss. For example, one male client, whose son was lost and assumed dead after the crash of his training airplane, found solace by being actively involved in the search. Other men may take active roles in the funeral. Ryan, while noting concerns at his wife's emotional response to the loss, expressed his own grief by carving his son's memorial stone [30]. Men, too, may focus on the problems caused by the loss, actively trying to find appropriate solutions. After a twenty-year-old daughter was killed when she lost control of her car, her father spent several weeks rebuilding a neighbor's fence that was damaged in the accident. He later described this activity as crucial to "getting me through those first two months." When these coping mechanisms are not helpful, there may be a tendency to seek escape in alcohol and drugs.

CLINICAL APPLICATIONS

These coping patterns have at least three major implications for clinicians. First, male efforts to problem-solve and protect may provide incentives to begin counseling or some other therapeutic activity. Participating in a therapeutic process may be reframed as a problem-solving and protective action—a way to assist others in the family. For example, the counselor may be able to effectively utilize typically masculine approaches, such as competition and mastery. Or, the counseling process may be framed as a way for men to master the process of grieving. With counseling, it may be affirmed, they may cope with loss better than others. Counseling can also be offered as a tool for growth.

Since some males may perceive cognitions as more important (and perhaps less threatening) than feelings, counselors should focus on thoughts about the loss as well as emotional responses. Mastering thinking and its consequences, emotional management and behavioral control have long been hallmarks of cognitive and cognitive-behavioral therapy. In particular, cognitive reframing and mood monitoring, increasing pleasant events, and identifying and challenging dysfunctional thoughts are techniques that should be included in the counselor's arsenal of therapeutic methods in treating male grief. Similarly, current task models of loss are highly compatible with masculine models of loss and can be presented for consideration during the counseling process [31].

Second, when dealing with emotions, counselors should find ways to allow emotional expression in ways compatible with the client's perception of the male role. Sometimes, for example, some clients may find it more comfortable to discuss "reactions" rather than "feelings." In fact, traditional methods for enabling emotional catharsis (e.g., probing for feelings, recreating highly emotionally-charged events) should be used with circumspection. In some cases, coping responses such as humor or sarcasm may represent forms of emotional release. These modes of expression should be respected by the clinician, and, in some cases, encouraged.

The men's movement has also developed a series of active interventions that allow emotional expression. Men are empowered to wail, shout, dance, or act out in other ways, all in the supportive presence of other males. While this movement still seems limited to a small segment of the male population, it may suggest and validate options that can be presented to male clients.

Third, active interventions may be very effective with male clients. Clinicians should encourage, when possible, any tendencies or desires to take an active and problem-solving focus. This may be done in a number of ways. For example, some men may wish to do things for a person who is dying. Ashley recounts how helpful it was for a father to assist his dying son in completing certain business [32]. Some men may take active roles in planning and personalizing the funeral. Even after the funeral, therapeutic rituals may offer powerful opportunities to express loss and to enfranchise grief.

Bibliotherapeutic techniques or reading self-help literature may also be highly effective with masculine grievers. Bibliotherapy, in general, has been found to be a useful resource for the bereaved [33]. The fact that it is active, cognitive, self-regulated, and solitary in nature may make it especially well-suited to some of the masculine grieving style.

Physical activity can be an effective form of coping. Exercise, for example, is often used as an outlet for anger and aggression. While running is a solitary activity suited for some men, others choose weight lifting or some form of organized sports activity. The playing field, ball diamond, bowling alley, or gym may provide opportunities for companionship as well as support.

It is critical for counselors to respect differences among the ways that some males respond. Gender role is only one factor that influences grief. As with other grieving clients, a key role of counselors is to normalize and validate, and support their attempts to cope. In some cases, it may mean validating a client's desire to cope in a way that he perceives as not being in accord with gender expectations. For example, one client needed reassurance that his expressions of emotion and his strong need for his wife's support at the death of his father were both appropriate and manly. Another man sought validation of his desire to sleep with an article of his late-wife's clothing. In other cases, some men may need to see that their ways of coping are, in fact, manifestations of grief. For example, a man who becomes intensely involved in work on his child's memorial fund may need to recognize that this, too, is a way of coping.

The patterns of male grieving, as well as the evaluation of different interventions, are areas begging for considerable research. Such research should differentiate between both male responses to different types of losses, as well as significant variables such as age, socialization experiences, culture, and class that might affect some men's grief. Extensive research with large samples of men may reveal very different ways that people cope with loss.

Perhaps, as previously suggested, it is more accurate to speak of "masculine" patterns of grief than male grief. This implies that this pattern of grief is gender-related but not necessarily gender-specific. There may exist, too, a pattern of coping with grief that emphasizes more relatedness and emotionality. This "feminine" pattern of grief may be formed in some females, as well as males.

As research continues, both clinicians and educators need to be sensitive to the many ways that gender roles may influence the grieving process. As with other significant variables such as culture, we must acknowledge that each gender's ways of coping have both strengths and limitations. There are advantages and strengths in expressing emotionality and seeking support. But there are also complementary strengths in stoically continuing in the face of loss and in seeking melioration in cognitive and active approaches. We can learn from both types of responses. Different modes of coping are just that—different, not deficiencies.

REFERENCES

1. L. LaGrand, *Coping with Separation and Loss as a Young Adult,* Charles C. Thomas, Springfield, Illinois, 1986.
2. C. Staudacher, *Men and Grief,* New Harbinger Publishers, Oakland, California, 1991.
3. T. Rando, *Treatment of Complicated Mourning,* Research Press, Champaign, Illinois, 1993.
4. J. Lever, Sex Differences in the Games Children Play, *Social Problems, 23,* pp. 478-487, 1976.
5. C. Gilligan, *In a Different Voice: Psychological Theory and Women's Development,* Harvard University Press, Cambridge, Massachusetts, 1982.
6. J. Gray, *Men are from Mars, Women are from Venus: A Practical Guide for Improving Communication and Getting What You Want in Your Relationship,* HarperCollins, New York, 1992.
7. R. Barnett, L. Beiner, and G. Baruch (eds.), *Gender and Stress,* Free Press, New York, 1987.
8. E. Rotundo, *American Manhood: Transformations in Masculinity from the Revolution to the Modern Era,* Basic Books, New York, 1993.
9. R. Bly, *Iron John: A Book about Men,* Vintage, New York, 1990.
10. S. Keen, *Fire in the Belly: On Being a Man,* Bantam, New York, 1991.
11. A. R. Hochschild, Emotion Work, Feeling, Rules and Social Support, *American Journal of Sociology, 85,* pp. 551-573, 1979.
12. I. Glick, R. Weiss, and C. M. Parkes, *The First Year of Bereavement,* Wiley, New York, 1974.
13. D. Goldbach, D. Dunn, L. Toedler, and J. Lasker, The Effects of Gestational Age and Gender on Grief, *Orthopsychiatry, 61,* pp. 461-467, 1991.
14. A. Lang and L. Gottlieb, Marital Intimacy after Infant Death, *Death Studies, 17,* pp. 233-256, 1993.
15. R. Schwab, Paternal and Maternal Coping with the Death of a Child, *Death Studies, 14,* pp. 407-422, 1990.

16. M. Osterweis, F. Solomon, and M. Green (eds.), *Bereavement: Reactions, Consequences and Care,* National Academy Press, Washington, D.C., 1984.
17. S. C. Jacobs and S. V. Kasl, The Measurement of Grief: Age and Sex Variation, *British Journal of Medical Psychology, 59,* pp. 305-310, 1986.
18. L. Radloff, Sex Differences in Depression: The Effects of Occupation and Marital Status, *Sex Roles, 1,* pp. 249-265, 1975.
19. P. E. Bornstein, P. J. Clayton, J. A. Halikas, W. L. Maurice, and E. Robbins, The Depression of Widowhood after Thirteen Months, *British Journal of Psychiatry, 122,* pp. 561-566, 1973.
20. R. Carey, Weathering Widowhood: Problems and Adjustments of the Widowed during the First Year, *Omega, 10,* pp. 163-172, 1979.
21. M. S. Stroebe and W. Stroebe, Who Suffers More? Sex Differences in Health of the Widowed, *Psychological Bulletin, 93,* pp. 279-301, 1993.
22. T. Rando, The Unique Issues and Impact of the Death of a Child, in *The Parental Loss of a Child,* T. Rando (ed.), Research Press, Champaign, Illinois, 1986.
23. N. Hogan and D. Balk, Adolescent Reactions to Sibling Death: Perception of Mothers, Fathers, and Teenagers, *Nursing Research, 39,* pp. 103-106, 1990.
24. C. Hughes and D. Fleming, Grief Casualties on Skid Row, *Omega, 23,* pp. 109-118, 1991.
25. J. Martin, Psychological Consequences of AIDS Related Bereavement among Gay Men, *Journal of Consulting and Clinical Psychology, 56,* pp. 856-862, 1988.
26. M. C. Feinson, Aging Widows and Widowers: Are There Mental Health Differences? *International Journal of Aging and Human Development, 23,* pp. 241-255, 1986.
27. A. Futterman, D. Gallagher, L. Thompson, S. Lovette, and M. Gilewski, Retrospective Assessment of Marital Adjustment and Depression during the First Two Years of Spousal Adjustment, *Psychology and Aging, 5,* pp. 277-283, 1990.
28. D. Gutmann, *Reclaimed Powers,* Basic Books, New York, 1987.
29. D. Lund, M. Caserta, and M. Dimond, Gender Differences through Two Years of Bereavement among the Elderly, *Gerontology, 26,* pp. 314-320, 1986.
30. D. Ryan, Raymond: Understanding Grief, in *Disenfranchised Grief: Handling Hidden Sorrow,* K. Doka (ed.), Lexington Books, Lexington, Massachusetts, 1986.
31. W. Worden, *Grief Counseling and Grief Therapy: A Handbook for the Mental Health Practitioner* (2nd Edition), Springer, New York, 1991.
32. M. Ashley, Being There with a Dying Son, *Public Welfare, 44,* pp. 38-43, 1986.
33. K. Doka, The Therapeutic Bookshelf, *Omega, 21,* pp. 321-326, 1990.

CHAPTER 4

The Vietnam War: An Ongoing National Grief Response

Angeline Bushy and John R. Bushy

BACKGROUND

The United States' involvement in the Vietnam War ended in April 1975. The battles stopped almost a quarter of a century ago, but if the end of a war means peace, many of our citizens are still waiting for it to happen. The Vietnam War was a conflict that forever altered America's psyche—it split families, alienated friends, and put an end to America's innocence. The personal and national grief continues to this day over a conflicting series of events during that period of history. The personal pain is intensified by political and military facts about the war that only recently have been made public. This chapter examines the ongoing grief response to the Vietnam War among veterans, their significant others, and the nation as a whole. Various dimensions of the lingering response to those experiences are examined using theoretical frameworks of grieving. The information herein is from the literature on the responses to the Vietnam War, as well as our professional and personal experiences with veterans who served during that time.

It is important to reiterate that, given the opportunity, most people exposed to the extreme rigors of war and battle will cope fairly effectively with subsequent events in their lives. Nevertheless, war can take a terrible toll on humans, as noted by Homer in the *Iliad* and Shakespeare in *Henry the IV* [1, 2]. Observers of veterans note that similar reactions to battles have occurred throughout history. Moreover, the majority of war-survivors experience post-war sequela without manifesting acute disabling symptoms upon being exposed to subsequent life-traumas. Even if the response is not overtly manifested for some who served in that war, the silent pain persists [3, 4].

Conversely, the low number of reported stress casualties during the Vietnam War does not reflect the high incidence of Post Traumatic Stress Disorder (PTSD) that veterans still exhibit two decades after the battles [1, 2]. This is exemplified by the following statement by one distraught veteran: "If there is a lesson to this, which there is not, it is very simple. You don't have to be Nam to be in Nam." The number of individuals directly involved in the Vietnam War was substantial. Of the total number of men and women who served (3.14 million) in Southeast Asia during the War, 36 percent were exposed to high war zone activity and 20 percent report having witnessed atrocities. Approximately 58,000 died, 300,000 were wounded, and 75,000 were seriously wounded.

Often forgotten but certainly impacted are the thousands of bereaved relatives, friends, and support personnel who survived major losses during those confusing years. War takes a toll on both sides, as well as among those caught in the middle of the conflict. In the Vietnam War it is estimated that more than 900,000 Vietnamese were wounded, 250,000 were killed, 300,000 were missing in action, 100,000 were incarcerated, and anywhere from six to ten million have been resettled. Placed in context with other wars, these statistics can yield insights on the magnitude of the Vietnam War.

For instance, comparing civilian casualty rates, World War I had an estimated 5 percent, World War II had an estimated 50 percent, and the Vietnam War had an estimated 80 percent rate. Interestingly, statistics about the enemy in Southeast Asia are not widely discussed. Nonetheless, those casualties directly and indirectly impact a significant number of Asian-American citizens. The deliberate silence on the Vietnam experience regarding this phenomenon is described as a collusion and sanitization which also has hindered national healing [5-8]. While all wars are horrible from a psychiatric point of view, the one in Southeast Asia was particularly egregious, especially when compared to the more recent ones in the Persian Gulf and in the Falkland Islands.

The more recent military conflicts were comparatively brief, involved mostly professional soldiers, had a clearly defined enemy, used tactics that were primarily offensive in nature, and generally did not pose direct threats to home and family. Comparatively, the Vietnam War involved more than 40 percent draftees who were assigned to the area, had an ambiguously defined enemy, coupled with the lack of public support for the war. Non-support, in many instances, took a hostile nature and was directed at military personnel who served. Conversely, experts speculate that idealistic soldiers who volunteered to go to Vietnam may have had more mental health problems than counterparts who were drafted to serve. Perhaps this observation also is a factor in delayed resolution to the Vietnam experience.

THE MALE EXPERIENCE

Even though women served in the military, and were indirectly affected by the war, most of the information on the Vietnam experience is from the male perspective. There is a range of perceptions and misunderstandings about the experience. For instance, extremely strong and differing emotions exist between those who were drafted and those who were conscientious objectors. Conflicting views also exist between soldiers sent to Vietnam and those assigned to military installations in other parts of the world during that time. Surprisingly, there are divergent perspectives between combat and non-combat soldiers who served in the Southeast Asian theater of war.

Recently, this phenomenon was reinforced among a group of six men who meet on a regular basis during the twentieth anniversary of the war's end. The goal was to discuss personal experiences with the hope of resolving misperceptions regarding their Vietnam experience [1-3]. Of the six, three served in the military, one had been a conscientious objector, one got lucky (had a high lottery number) and was not drafted, and the other was too old to serve in Vietnam but was active in the anti-war movement in the United States. Interestingly, since the end of the war, two of the Veterans had become pacifists and actively promoted those beliefs. Although everyone's circumstances were quite different from the others, conflicting in some cases, each participant had the best intentions of not criticizing other members' perspectives. Soon after the discussions started, however, it became obvious that chasms existed which probably could not be bridged despite initial good intentions by the group as a whole.

More specifically, one of the veterans in the group, a former marine captain, described his war experience as being in "continuous combat in Nam." Routinely, soldiers under his command were killed in the action. The man said he could not keep track of his men and described one emotional situation where an eighteen-year-old had joined the unit only a few hours prior to being killed. The veteran asked, "What was I supposed to tell his parents? I never even met the kid"; then mocked, "Tag'em and bag'em." Even though the group perceived this man to be of utmost gentleness and decency, the final comment caused non-veterans in the group to bristle. No one commented but all realized that individual histories reinforced existing walls among them. Instantly the veterans assumed a more comfortable military manner when recalling their war experiences. The conscientious objector cynically noted, "You're doing it again!" Veterans in the group understood the inference, but the old covenant was too strong and too comforting to relinquish.

History proved to be the least complex factor that divided the group. Certainly not the only one. For example, among the Vietnam veterans, military assignments were different. Unlike the marine, another veteran reported not experiencing similar memories of extreme desolation during his tour of duty. Neither could the man who described himself as being a "lottery winner" (hence, not drafted) comprehend the conscientious objector's frame of reference. The more the participants talked, the further apart their perspectives seemed to be. After eight meetings (and with unexpressed relief) the men decided to "hang it up" and discontinue meeting. One individual remarked, "I think we quit with a sense of relief and humility. Initially, we hoped to understand each other a little better. We did not expect to settle any issues or cast out demons. What surprised me was to hear how many demons exist and how much power they still had over all of us" [2, p. 5D].

THE NATIONAL EXPERIENCE

The dynamics of this men's group parallels national divisions regarding the Vietnam experience. On the one hand, for individuals who refused to go or protested the war, he or she worried about the confusion and pain this caused those who served and their families at home. How did a person make peace with the fact, however unintentional, as a conscientious objector one indirectly encouraged "the murdering enemy" to kill boys that one grew up with or one's best friend. Those who served in the war, on the other hand, noticed the United States was trying to save another government that was not worth saving. The confusion was greater when the soldier noticed the people in that strange country were not even interested in our kind of help. Conflicting ideals had soldiers reflecting as to, Why did I go? Why am I here? "Conviction or fear of being viewed as a coward? Regardless of the role one assumed during Vietnam, only individuals having the most self-satisfied and self-serving ideologies are able to avoid questioning the appropriateness of their war experience" [5, 9, 10].

Even though this chapter focuses on men and their grief response to the Vietnam experience, a few words are in order for female soldiers as well. A significant number of female Vietnam veterans served during the war, many of whom were nurses assigned to military hospitals in

Southeast Asia. Coupled with the usual war-related stressors, it was not unusual for female veterans to also experience sexual harassment and even assault by male peers and superiors. Yet, until recent years, females' issues seldom have been addressed. One can speculate since the war was for the most part a masculine experience, perhaps women, too, experience a masculine grief response. Could this be reflected in their post-war PTSD symptomology as well?

Why the unresolved personal and national conflict—two decades later? Could the confusion be associated with not having closure on the various losses that were experienced? In the remainder of this chapter these losses will be examined using theories of grief as the frame of reference. The discussion will be interspersed with comments from veterans to better illustrate the relationship between the theory and their war experiences.

OVERVIEW OF GRIEF THEORIES

Grief is an intense emotional response often described as a deep and violent sorrow. Yet, it is a natural and necessary process that is part of adjusting to a loss. Loss may be the death or separation from a loved one, intense disappointment at not receiving an anticipated reward, failure to experience a normal life-developmental event, or the loss of comrades as in the case of war. During war, soldiers experience many other losses. Be it real or imagined, there is the "overnight" loss of one's youth, innocence, and the longed-for associated life experiences. Soldiers continuously are surrounded by death—friends, comrades, even that imposed on the enemy. Those who live often experience guilt for surviving as they struggle to give the war-experience a meaning.

Social theorists put forth a range of grief and bereavement theories and each has its own set of terms to describe the progressive process. All view grief to be an individual process that is not necessarily sequential in nature. They describe progression and regression in the healing process. Everyone grieves in his or her own way, and the process is influenced by major life events as well as the day-to-day activities. If a loss remains unresolved, the grief process becomes prolonged to the point of dysfunction [10-14].

Some theorists list specific phases for grieving. However, succinct stages can be difficult to differentiate and the process generally is not experienced in textbook fashion by the bereaved. A few never adequately adjust to a loss, consequently can remain emotionally fixed in one particular dimension of the process. The activities related to the twentieth anniversary of the Vietnam War reinforced that our nation has not brought closure to that experience. With the admonition that it is not linear and each person experiences grief differently the ensuing discussion elaborates on the bereavement process.

The first response (phase) to a loss or crises is *shock and numbness*. Initially, the person denies the loss, expresses shock, and may withdraw from routine social situations. Other behaviors often exhibited are short attention span, difficulty concentrating, disorientation to time and the actual sequence of events, impaired decision-making ability, resistance to new experiences, stunned disbelief, and failure to accept reality. This preliminary phase may last only a few hours to several weeks or months. In some cases, the preliminary phase can last for years. More specifically, even today it is not unusual to hear a Vietnam veteran say, "It didn't mean nothing," after describing an atrocity or intense battle in which the person was involved.

This preliminary response to loss is followed by a *searching and yearning* phase. During this time the person experiences rage at those who inflicted the pain, at society for allowing the events to occur, and even at oneself for being part of the event, even if given no choice about one's role. Other behaviors often seen during this part of the process are resentment, guilt, restlessness, impatience, depression, giving double meanings to recent life-events, dreaming about the event, bitterness, testing reality, emotional instability, difficulting sleeping, preoccupation with the loss, and complaints of physical discomforts, e.g., headaches, gastro-intestinal distress, back pain, heart palpitations, frequent sighing, and lethargy. Each person uses different coping strategies to reduce the discomfort, some of which may be more healthful than others.

Commonly used coping strategies include immersing oneself in work, meditating, exercising, talking about the experience, isolating oneself, and using chemical substances. This phase also varies in length of time from individual to individual and from situation to situation. Based on the responses that were elicited during the twentieth anniversary of the war's end, one might speculate that our nation as a whole seems to be stuck in this dimension of the grief process.

Finally, there is the *reorganization and resolution* phase of the grief process when the anger, sadness, and mourning decrease in frequency and intensity. The individual accepts the reality of the loss and incorporates the event into his or her belief system. In the case of veterans, they experience a sense of relief and renewed energy. The person resumes routine eating and sleeping habits, makes better decisions with greater ease, has increased self-self-esteem, finds reason to smile, and plans for the future. As a nation, we have not yet come to that point regarding the Vietnam experience [5, 15, 16].

DYSFUNCTIONAL GRIEF RESPONSE

A person must be allowed and encouraged to grieve for healthy adjustment to occur. It can become very stressful for the person, and others in the immediate environment, when grieving continues for an extended time. Behaviors associated with prolonged grief are chronic sorrow, anger, loneliness, sadness, shame, anxiety, and guilt. The appropriate time frame for grieving to be completed is not delineated and cultural factors play a significant role in the process. Some propose the longer one grieves for a particular loss, the more likely this behavior is to continue. Others propose that denying the loss, or failing to completely work through the grief process, can be detrimental to the long-term health of the body and mind. Prolonged grief often is associated with certain diseases, especially cancer and other chronic health problems. Dysfunctional grieving can be an outcome of the following situations:

- Actual or perceived loss of an object or self, as seen before the traumatic incident occurred. The sensation can be exacerbated by other losses which occur during or after the event.
- Loss of physical, psychological, or social well-being.
- Thwarted grief response or lack of resolution of previous loss(es).
- Absence of anticipatory grieving. That is to say, a lack of personal awareness of something going wrong or an impending loss.
- Guilt feelings for surviving when others, particularly peers, did not (survivor's guilt).

These factors are evident among most Vietnam veterans in varying degrees. To this day, many describe a number of problems in their lives that have origins in a previous role of soldier, that is one who is trained for war and killing. Moreover, reorganization and resolution must be the national goal regarding the Vietnam experience, as well as for individual solidiers.

POST-TRAUMATIC STRESS DISORDER (PTSD): A SYMPTOM OF UNRESOLVED GRIEF

An examination of the epidemiologic data on Vietnam veterans has implications for the assessment and treatment of their lingering grief [11, 17, 18]. For example, differences have been found in severity of post trauma symptoms among veterans and civilian populations.

On the one hand, full-blown PTSD is common among many Vietnam veterans, especially those exposed to pre-combat, combat, and post-combat experiences. Comparatively, the general population that has been exposed to violence demonstrates fewer of those kinds of symptoms. This finding is surprising when considering that soldiers are "trained" to anticipate combat, function as a unit during military maneuvers, remain stoic, and not "fall apart" during combat operations. Consequently, when a soldier survives while a comrade is injured or dies, the survivor questions what could have been done to prevent the incident from occurring or resulting in more favorable outcomes. To this day, a number of veterans question what a different set of circumstances might have had for certain comrades, and even on the ultimate outcome of the war [1, 2, 4, 11, 19].

When comparing civilian populations who have been exposed to a mass killing, bombing of public facilities, and random violence, that activity generally is perceived to be a random event. Consequently, those kinds of actions are more likely to shatter the public's perception of personal safety. In the past decade there has been an increasing number of random terrorist acts in our country that have harmed greater numbers, such as the bombing of the Oklahoma City Federal Building and the World Trade Center, as well as the Uni-bomber's prolonged history of activities. The long-term impact of those terrorist-like activities on the general population are yet to be measured. Comparing veterans with civilian populations, one finds that PTSD symptomology also differs. Specifically, civilian populations exposed to a mass violence seem to have more intrusive recollections with less emotional numbing. In contrast, among veterans who were in combat zones, survivor guilt and emotional numbing are more pronounced [3, 18].

The National Vietnam Veterans Readjustment Study [3, 5, 10] focused on those differences and reported that of all male veterans who served in Vietnam, nearly one-third suffer from PTSD. Of all female veterans who served, more than one-fourth suffer from the disorder. Besides gender, there seem to be cultural and racial variations in the incidence and symptoms of PTSD. For instance, the incidence of PTSD among African-American veterans is 21 percent, compared with Hispanics having about a 28 percent rate. The increased prevalence among African Americans, compared to white counterparts, is attributed to increased combat exposure. The differences between Hispanics and whites is explained only in part by increased combat exposure. Questions remain about the variations in prevalence of PTSD in veterans comparing on demographic factors such as gender, ethnicity, and race.

This national study also found a strong relationship between PTSD symptomology and post-war readjustment problems in virtually every domain of the afflicted veteran's life. For example, among veterans having significant problems in readjusting to civilian life, there was a higher rate for those who were in combat situations. Readjustment problems in veterans are evidenced by occupational instability (e.g., going from job-to-job, frequent and/or ongoing unemployment), chronic health problems, as well as extended service-connected disabilities. Of Vietnam veterans, 53 percent report work-related symptomology with an unemployment rate of 15 percent. As for mortality rates, Vietnam veterans are more likely than non-veterans (general population) to die from suicide and automobile accidents. For African-American veterans, the rate is twice that of Caucasian counterparts [1-3, 8, 11].

Even though a significant number of veterans have sought treatment for their PTSD, some remain unnoticed. Of all Vietnam veterans, at least 11 percent of males and about 8 percent of females suffer in silence without having had any professional intervention for their symptoms. These individuals have significant stress reactions, but their symptoms probably are not of sufficient intensity to be classified as "clinically significant"; or, one can speculate that these individuals might be using coping skills that keep their symptoms less conspicuous.

Experts project that nearly 1.7 million Vietnam veterans will exhibit clinically significant stress reactions at some time during their lives. The prevalence rate for PTSD among Vietnam veterans is comparable to counterparts of World War II. Veterans of the more recent war, however, are twice as likely to have enduring psychological problems compared to those of other wars. Nearly three decades after the war, Vietnam veterans complained of heightened arousal, jumpiness, irritability, insomnia, and experiencing recent events as if "reliving" past traumas. Significant negative psychological outcomes are most likely to be present in soldiers who were exposed to gruesome experiences, grotesque death, macabre stimulation, and human suffering.

Flashbacks and nightmares can be extremely debilitating for a person. Of those exhibiting PTSD symptoms, nearly 20 percent experience flashbacks of their war experiences which can occur during the day and night. Irrespective of combat exposure, soldiers who report more intrusive thoughts are more likely to experience chronic stress symptoms coupled with persistent feelings of isolation, detachment, and estrangement. Participation in war-time atrocities was found to be predicative of an increased incidence of flashbacks while participation in combat was found to be more predictive of avoidance behaviors in Vietnam veterans. They report having three major categories of disturbing war dreams. More than half of their nightmares are exact replications of actual traumatic events, another quarter are images of actual trauma-producing situations which are embellished with seemingly credible "might-have-been-events," and the others are hallucinatory-type thoughts and nightmares. Nightmares and the accompanying sleep disturbances can be very disrupting to the person, his or her significant other, as well as individuals in the immediate environment [3, 4, 6].

The prevalence of post-war psychological problems is significantly greater among veterans who experienced high levels of combat exposure and war-zone trauma. Many experience feelings of guilt for surviving. Guilt may be manifested by believing one "could have" or "should have" done something different, "done more," or "known better," which may lead to a more favorable outcome. Some experience feelings of extreme shame as they recall or recount the fateful event(s). The following descriptions are three men's post war experiences. These classic cases are based on formal and informal conversations with veterans, their families, and from the literature.

George was an army communication specialist. He started intense therapy sessions at a Vietnam Veterans Center four years ago in an effort to work through his war experiences. This decision was precipitated by his wife of twenty-three years threatening to leave because of his inability to communicate, his increasing use of alcohol, and "scary behavior" stemming from his flashbacks. He is a successful lawyer and a county commissioner. His struggles center on guilt, reporting: "I feel guilty for not experiencing the same outcome as my buddy Cliff, a helicopter pilot who was shot down at. . . ."

Carl was in a field artillery unit and has significant hearing impairment from exploding weapons. He, too, reports having survivors guilt, hyper vigilance, frightening nightmares, and years of insomnia. He says, "Why the person next to me and not me? Those thoughts never leave me, I struggle to control them, day in and day out, night after night."

Nick was a medic in the Navy who served two tours of duty. He brags "I didn't have any personal problems after Nam. After the war I bought a Harley and traveled across the United States and parts of Canada at least three or fours times in as many years . . . drinking off and on . . . married a few times." About ten years ago he enrolled in a nursing program "to get the official degree for what I already knew." A faculty member noted that he always sat in the very last row of the classroom and interacted very little with other students. Upon being asked about this behavior he reported, "I always sit with my back to the wall or the door . . . can't stomach the feeling that someone might be behind me . . . guess that war did that to me." Following graduation he established a fairly consistent work record in a VA Hospital, preferring to work night shifts in the coronary care, psychiatric, or emergency department where there was "more action." He started having flashbacks and nightmares when the Army Reserve Hospital Unit, of which he is a member, was mobilized to Germany for Desert Shield/Desert Storm. Even now these continue, precipitated by the sound of a helicopter and certain trauma cases in the emergency room. Flashbacks interfered with his ability to function in the hospital setting forcing him to seek professional counseling at least once a week.

These three cases illustrate the similarities of delayed war responses in veterans to those of prolonged and unresolved grief. In both instances the social rejection and alienation of friends and family can hinder a person's readjustment to the loss.

FAMILY DYNAMICS OF DELAYED GRIEF RESPONSES

Veterans with PTSD have more marital maladjustments in terms of self-disclosure, expressiveness, hostility, and aggression toward their partner. Compared with non-veteran counterparts, Vietnam veterans' wives, too, seem to be less communicative, and feel more angry and fearful of their partner. Children of veterans also are affected. Sixteen year old Lisa notes, "My neighbor cried every time he mowed the lawn. One day, I asked him why he was crying. He told me the sounds of the lawn mower always remind him of the helicopters during the war" [1, 2, 8, 10].

Shawn elaborates on his relationship with his father, "Whenever we tried to talk about the war, he became defensive and angry . . . sulked for a day or two . . . started to drink again . . . so I tried not to ever talk about that subject." Shawn's father responded in this way. "He asked so many questions, but I put him off by telling him that I didn't remember. I thought that talking about it would not serve any real purpose. I knew it wasn't being fair to him if he was interested. Talking is more difficult for those of us who went home just before the United States pulled out of Nam. We didn't have anything to feel proud about. Those of us who got back home in one piece thought we would have a hero's welcome, like our dads and uncles after World War II and Korea. Surprise! When we got off the military buses we were met by war-protestors throwing things and spitting at us [1-3].

Many Vietnam veterans describe a persistent feeling of restlessness, as illustrated by Nick in the previous section. Interestingly, of all homeless men, about 40 percent are estimated to be veterans and more than half of these served during Vietnam. A complex pattern of factors contribute to the high incidence of homelessness in Vietnam veterans including pre-military experiences (e.g., childhood trauma, placement in foster care during childhood, conduct disorders), military experiences (e.g., assignments in a combat zone, witnessing atrocities), and post-military experiences (e.g., social isolation, poor work histories, mental illness, substance abuse). Additional research is needed on the phenomenon of homelessness among veterans. Subsequently, interventions must be tailored to address this national public health concern [6, 10, 18, 19].

DISCUSSION

Obviously, adjusting to losses is a painful process. Are there ways to make the grieving process easier for a person, in this case Vietnam veterans, their loved ones, and our nation? The literature indicates that the experience of grieving can be eased somewhat by assuming an active and participatory role in the grieving process. Active participation infers allowing sufficient time to feel the loss, leaning on family and friends for support and encouragement, and taking "care" of oneself through healthful behaviors. In some cases, there may be a need for professional intervention for the individual and family systems, and participating in a bereavement support group. Professional support services are offered by the community-based Veterans Administration Vietnam Veteran's Centers across the fifty states [12-14].

The literature reflects diverse approaches in dealing with the lingering grief that is associated with PTSD, including acute in-patient treatment, short-term and long-term outpatient programs dealing with the co-morbidity of PTSD and substance abuse, self-help veterans' "rap" groups, as well as individual, family, and group therapies. Vietnam group participants consistently discuss issues related to anger, impulse control, unresolved feelings about the country of Vietnam and its culture, guilt, depression, and problems in their primary relationships. The most effective therapies consist of multiple interventions including verbal expression, identification of the problem, interpretation of its meaning, and peer support. Treatment programs should be designed to include the following goals.

1. Create a place of safety and trust where veterans can find and integrate acceptance of their sense of self as well as their behaviors during the Vietnam War.

2. Provide a safe and accepting arena for a veteran to tell his or her story, confront the war-related trauma, and accept it's personal impact. In other words, allowing the person to integrate the personal

dimension of the war experience in order to give those events a personal and/or spiritual meaning. This may include telling about the positive qualities of an individual's war stories and experiences, even when these occurred in severe combat situations. Often, intermingled with stories of death, atrocities, fear, and disaster are reports of good times with buddies, camaraderie, feelings of prowess, and moments of spiritual enlightenment.

3. Encourage a veteran to examine what he or she did to survive. Emphasize that the story did not end with one's return from combat. Identify what was gleaned from the experience(s). Obtain and integrate stories related to the veteran's post-combat and pre-combat with the combat experiences.

4. Educate veterans and their significant others about PTSD. Reframe current symptoms in a more positive frame of reference. Discuss the chronic nature of PTSD and identify strategies to effectively self-monitor stimuli that predispose the onset of a "bad-spell." Learn to identify specific noises, odors, social situations, certain seasons of the year, or particular holidays that precipitate war-related memories and flashbacks.

5. Provide an opportunity for veterans to mourn the loss of comrades, as well as one's youth and other important life experiences, in a meaningful, acceptable, and safe environment.

6. Help individuals to express emotions in an appropriate manner (e.g., anger and depression) and learn to modify avoidance behaviors (e.g., substance abuse and social isolation).

7. Address issues of guilt and shame with others who experience similar feelings on a long-term basis.

8. Facilitate resolution and foster integration of painful memories so the person can begin to see him- or herself as progressing from a passive "victim" role to that of an active survivor. Subsequently, the person must learn to integrate the two selves, specifically that of a war soldier with that of a peace-loving veteran.

9. Learn to care about day-to-day events, "let-go" of adrenalin-rush-producing behaviors, and appreciate a calmer existence.

10. Address issues of treatment non-compliance behaviors.

11. Redirect energies toward learning effective problem-solving skills on the part of the veteran and his or her significant others.

HEALING A NATION

Other creative approaches have been initiated across the nation to address the lingering pain and grief associated with the Vietnam experience among the public and among veterans. One notable effort has been the creation of the National and State Vietnam Memorials to recognize those veterans. Others are organizing tours for veterans to re-visit Vietnam and Southeast Asian countries where they had tours of duty. Additionally, the public is being educated about the causes and symptoms of PTSD, coupled with acknowledgment on the twentieth anniversary of the United States' withdrawal from a war that probably could never have been won.

Some communities are offering a course on the Vietnam War in local high schools. Often the course is taught by veterans of that war. These courses have had a favorable response from instructors and students alike [1-3]. One faculty member has these observations about the experience:

> Becoming a teacher resulted from my Vietnam experience. What is there to understand about the war? It was terribly cruel and stupidly violent. War isn't the enemy, though, ignorance is. The best way to overcome ignorance is to teach the subject matter. Some vets took refuge in using drugs and alcohol. But, over the years, I found that many people were interested in what I had to say. Talking about it helped me to work through many things that I had blocked out of my mind for years.

Raymond, a student whose father also was a Vietnam veteran, had this to say about the elective course:

> Vietnam was an incredible atrocity. My dad fought communism and his country shunned him . . . saw him as a killer. This course helped me learn more about my dad and why he is the way he is. When I tell him about the course he starts to talk about his war experiences. The course has brought us closer; he seems relieved to talk about it, too.

In sum, this chapter examined the lingering and unresolved grief of Americans to the Vietnam War, which ended more than two decades ago. Grief theory was used to examine the responses and behaviors of soldiers who served there, their families, and our country as we continue to be haunted by the ghosts of that unresolved military conflict. This phenomenon needs further research to avoid similar outcomes in the future and to develop appropriate interventions for individuals who experience the lingering consequences of war.

REFERENCES

1. D. Meichenbaum, Examples of Illustrative Special PTSD Populations: Vietnam Veterans and Other Combat Experiences, in *A Clinical Handbook and Practice Therapist Manual: Assessing and Treating Adults with Post Traumatic Stress Disorder*, Institute Press, Waterloo, Ontario, pp. 56-69, 1994.
2. F. Ochberg (ed.), *Post-Traumatic Therapy and Victims of Violence*, Brunner Mazel, New York, pp. 3-25, 1988.
3. H. Halloway and R. Ursano, The Vietnam War Veteran: Memory, Social Context and Metaphor, *Psychiatry, 47*, pp. 103-109, 1993.
4. B. Van Der Kolk, The Biological Response to Psychic Trauma, in *Post-Traumatic Therapy and Victims of Violence*, F. Ochberg (ed.), Brunner Mazel, New York, pp. 26-38, 1988.
5. E. Hauff and P. Vaglum, Vietnamese Boat Refugees, *Actu-Psychiatrica Scandinavia, 88*, pp. 162-168, 1983.
6. C. Figley, Coping with Stress on the Home Front, *Journal of Social Issues, 49*, pp. 51-72, 1993.
7. C. Engel and A. Engel, Post Traumatic Stress Disorders in Precombat Sexual and Physical Abuse in Desert Storm Veterans, *Journal of Nervous and Mental Illness, 181*, pp. 683-688, 1993.
8. L. O'Brien, What Will Be the Consequences of the War in Bosnia? *British Journal of Psychiatry, 164*, pp. 443-447, 1994.
9. R. Scurfield, Interventions with Medical and Psychiatric Evacuees and Their Families: From Vietnam through the Gulf War, *Military Medicine, 157*, pp. 88-97, 1992.
10. D. Lund, M. Caserta, and M. Dimond, The Course of Spousal Bereavement in Later Life, in *Handbook of Bereavement*, M. Stroebe and W. Stroebe, and L. Hansson (eds.), Cambridge University Press, Cambridge, Massachusetts, 1993.
11. D. Lund, M. Caserta, and M. Dimond, Gender Differences through Two Years of Bereavement among the Elderly, *The Gerontologist, 26*:3, pp. 314-320, 1986.
12. E. Constantino, Bereavement Crisis Intervention for Widows, *Nursing Research, 30*, pp. 351-353, 1981.
13. M. Diamond, Bereavement and the Elderly: A Critical Review with Implications for Nursing Practice and Research, *Journal of Advance Nursing, 6*, pp. 461-470, 1981.
14. J. Bowlby, *Attachment and Loss Vol. III: Loss, Sadness and Depression*, Basic Books, New York, 1980.
15. A. Shalev, Debriefing following Traumatic Response, in *Individual and Community Response to Trauma and Disaster*, R. J. Ursano, B. McCaughey, and C. Fullerton (eds.), Cambridge University Press, Cambridge, Massachusetts, 1984.
16. R. Kleber, C. Figley, and B. Gersons, *Beyond Trauma: Cultural and Societal Dynamics*, Plenum Press, New York, 1995.

17. F. Weathers, T. Keanse, and B. Litz, Military Trauma, in *Traumatic Stress: From Theory to Practice,* J. Freddy and S. Hobfoll (eds.), Plenum Press, New York, 1994.
18. N. Wilson and C. Kneisl (eds.), *Psychiatric Disorders,* Addison Wesley-Nursing, Menlo Park, California, pp. 669-732, 1995.
19. M. Clark, Care of Men (Ch. 22), in *Nursing in the Community,* Appleton & Lange, Stamford, Connecticut, pp. 523-551, 1999.

CHAPTER 5

Gay Men: Grieving the Effects of Homophobia

John E. Hart

This chapter begins with the assumption that most people who are raised in North American culture, whether gay or straight, are taught to be homophobic. Since homophobia is learned, it can also be unlearned. The process of undoing the damage caused by both internalized and externalized homophobia is long and frequently difficult. It involves not only getting in touch with the painful wounds which many gay men have borne for decades, but also being willing to experience the pain of loss which has lain dormant for many years. It is critical for gay men who wish to strive toward authentic wholeness to be willing to journey within and grieve the losses associated with their experience of homophobia.

HOMOPHOBIA: WHAT IT IS AND HOW IT OPERATES

Homophobia is the term coined in 1972 by George Weinberg in his book *Society and the Healthy Homosexual* [1] to describe prejudice against gay men. In one sense, the word is a misnomer because even though some people may actually fear men who both love and are sexually attracted to other men, the feeling which most aptly describes how they react to these men is more akin to hatred than to fear.

Everyone, including every gay man who is raised in North American culture is taught to some extent to despise gays. It is part of the way in which we are socialized. Religion uses both dogma and scripture to label homosexuality as sinful, perverse, unnatural, and against the laws of God. Psychiatrists identified homosexuality as a psychiatric disorder until 1973, when the American Psychiatric Association removed homosexuality from its *DSM-III: Diagnostic and Statistical Manual of Mental Disorders.* It took until December of 1994 for the American Medical Association to urge its members to seek a greater understanding of their homosexual patients and to acknowledge that the care which gay male patients receive is greatly improved when the physician recognizes and acknowledges sexual orientation in an open and non-judgmental way. The legal system in the United States does not afford the same protections to gay men that it provides to non-gay men. It is still a criminal offense in many states for consenting adults of the same sex to express their love sexually. Finally, the media aggravates the situation even further by portraying gays in either grossly stereotypical ways or in ignoring their existence altogether.

In general, most people have little knowledge about and even less understanding of homosexuality. Yet, they both fear and loathe it. These attitudes are conveyed to others in ways that are both blatant and subtle. Men in this culture are raised to be strong, independent, and self-sufficient creatures. Women on the other hand are taught from a young age to form relationships with others. Women are encouraged to work together with their sisters and to support each other in making sure that a task gets done. Men are encouraged to do the job themselves without asking for help from anyone lest they be perceived as weak or "soft like a woman."

People tend to have a very narrow definition of what it means to be a gay man. They tend to think only in terms of the sexual when it comes to gay men. Many seem to believe that gay men spend their entire lives in hot pursuit of sex. People completely forget that in addition to being people who are not only in touch with our sexuality, but who are also able to celebrate it, we live lives much like their own. We have jobs; we take care of our homes and our families; we pay bills; we walk the dog and feed the cat; and we complain about having to pay taxes. We are all around you in every trade and profession. We police your streets; we attend to you medically; we entertain you on stage and screen; we till the soil and grow the crops; we cook your food and then serve your meals; we service your cars; we transport you across vast oceans; we mend your clothes; and tend your souls. We truly are everywhere.

It is amazing how quickly young boys who may in actuality be gay, pick up on and internalize the negative message, whether blatant or subtle, which their parents or others put out about homosexuals and homosexuality. I can still hear the scorn and derision voiced by the mother of a boyhood friend who had been to see a stage show starring a popular, yet rather effeminate entertainer, on the previous night. Years later, I found out that the man actually was gay. However, he was stereotyped by my friend's mother and described as "being that way," which made it clear to my friend and me that men were not to behave in ways which she considered unmanly. It seems sad to me that people are so readily willing to compartmentalize others because they may look or act a particular way. As long as the entertainer was busily entertaining, then he was acceptable as a person. However, once he allowed himself to be himself by being "that way," then he became unacceptable. We are so used to fitting people into categories or boxes, that it is often difficult to deal with those who do not meet our pictures of how a particular category of people should be. For example, many people either knew or assumed that celebrities like Liberace, Paul Lynde, and Jim Nabors were gay because they frequently presented themselves to the world in a stereotypical way. On the other hand, a Hollywood idol like Rock Hudson, or a football star like David Kopay, is much more difficult to accept as gay by the general public because they do not meet society's expectations of how a gay man should be or act.

Even though I was only ten or eleven when I heard her description of the entertainer, her words struck me like a bolt of lightning. I had been experiencing strong physical and emotional attractions to male neighbors and to other males whom I watched on television since I was six or seven years old. At this point in time I had a crush on Spin or Marty, or possibly both of them, from the Mickey Mouse Club show. In addition, I was also attracted to Dick West, the Range Rider's sidekick.

I was never told directly that the feelings I was experiencing were "bad or wrong," but on some level I knew it intuitively. I also knew enough not to talk about them and to hide a part of who I was. I knew that I needed to become invisible. In order to survive in my milieu it was necessary to shut down, to conform, and to hide a vitally precious part of my personality, an aspect of myself that is integral to who I am as both a gay man and a human being. Today, as an adult who has worked long and hard on learning to love and accept himself as he is, I realize that my shutting off and neglecting an important piece of my personhood was a loss and it needed to be grieved. This loss of self, this subjugation of my gayness, that part of me that is both beautiful and life-enriching, was for too many years a deep, dark, shame-filled secret. This enigmatic aspect of me called "gayness" has been transformed from a soot-covered lump of coal into a sparkling diamond, once my internalized homophobia had been unearthed and healed through a lengthy and fiery process of grieving.

The term "homophobia" pertains to a form of oppression and system of beliefs that considers gay men to be sick, perverted, immoral, threatening, disgusting, inferior to heterosexuals, and deserving to be hated. Homophobia parallels sexism because it is intended to ensure that people conform to traditional gender roles ascribed to biological sex. In North American culture, most people, homosexual as well as heterosexual, are taught to be homophobic and to hate homosexuality. The level of hatred ranges from accusations of "Faggot!" screamed at any young boy who appears to be or who "acts different," to bumper stickers which urge the faithful to "Kill a fag for Christ!" Even though North Americans picture themselves as the champions of freedom, it is oftentimes difficult to express that freedom on a personal level. People are encouraged to conform to societal standards and any type of difference is looked upon with suspicion, derision, and scorn.

I remember an incident from the time I was twelve or thirteen. My friend Wayne's teenage sister asked me to look at my fingernails. I dutifully bent my fingers back toward my wrist and looked down at my nails. She congratulated me for not being a "queer." She then enlightened me by informing me that one could always tell whether or not a man was "queer" by the way in which he examined his fingernails. If he bent his fingers backwards to look at them, then that was all right. However, if he extended his hand and held it at a distance, "like a girl," to examine his fingers, then you knew for sure that he was a "queer." Luckily for me at the time, I unwittingly passed her test.

Since homophobia is a kind of prejudice that is learned, it can also be unlearned. This entails recognizing and confronting the prejudice within ourselves as well as within those around us who help to keep it alive. Patience and constant vigilance will be required if one truly wishes to root out his/her prejudices. Remember too, one needs to be gentle with oneself, for no one is perfect. It took time for one's homophobic attitudes to become ingrained, and it will also take time to loosen their grip.

Homophobia tends to operate on several levels and can be described in personal, interpersonal, institutional, and cultural terms. *Personal Homophobia* or prejudice encompasses negative feelings, like disgust, pity, and repulsion; beliefs, such as all gay men are sick or immoral; and stereotypes which a person may hold about gay people, for example, that all gay men are effeminate or that you can tell a gay man by how he looks. When this form of homophobia is experienced by gay men themselves, it can be defined as internalized homophobia.

Interpersonal Homophobia occurs when one's personal beliefs and feelings about homosexuality are acted out against another. Harassment and oppression of all kinds, ranging from name-calling to gay bashing, fall into this category. I live in a gay neighborhood in the inner-city and in the past it was not uncommon to see carloads of young toughs driving through the neighborhood on weekend nights screaming the words "queer," "faggot," or "gay boy" at any male who "looks" gay and who happens to be walking down the street. If one responds to their taunts, he is leaving himself open to the threat of being beaten, robbed, scarred both externally and internally, and possibly murdered.

Institutional Homophobia or *Heterosexism,* describes the ways in which society's institutions, such as schools, churches, businesses, and the military, discriminate against others on the basis of their sexual orientation or identity, whether perceived or real. It serves to reinforce the notion that being heterosexual is in some way superior to being gay or lesbian. In many situations, laws, codes, and policies enforce this institutional form of discrimination. For example, the Senior Prom is usually the social event of the year for many in the graduating class of a high school. Anyone who attends is expected to bring a date. It seems quite logical for a young gay man to invite another gay man to be his date and escort him to the prom. However, it would take a huge amount of courage and the strength of a lion for a young gay man to buck the system by inviting another male as his date, unless he has the support of his parents, teachers, and friends. Even then, it may not be legal in his city, state, or province for him to be escorted by another male.

Cultural Homophobia occurs when oppression is legitimized by sets of unwritten rules or norms. For example, a gay man working for most large North American corporations would rarely consider displaying his male lover's photo openly on his desk at the office, unless he felt very secure about both his identity and his job status. On the other hand, it is both common and accepted, perhaps even expected, for a heterosexual man to openly display photos of his wife and children on his desk. This form of discrimination is reinforced on a daily basis by the media on television and radio shows, in the press, and in movies which depict everyone as heterosexual and male-female relationships as the only acceptable norm in our culture.

For many people who were raised in North American culture, homosexuality is seen primarily in terms of sexual behavior. This perception can create problems in a culture that is obsessed with sexuality, while simultaneously in denial about it. North American society emphasizes one "right" way of being, that is, acting out traditionally masculine and feminine roles within the structure of the nuclear family. The existence of same-sex relationships challenges this traditional concept and is frequently perceived as a threat by many and leads them into oppressing anyone who is perceived as different.

North American culture tends to be patriarchal, that is, it is characterized by an enforced belief in male dominance, power, and control.
Maleness is highly prized, while femaleness is devalued and demeaned.
Homosexual males are often perceived by the dominant culture as
"being like or acting like women." Gay men are thought of in terms
of allowing themselves to be "used like women." This view of
homosexuality and homosexual males is both a reflection of the
dominant society's disdain and scorn for gay men as well as its devalu-
ing of women.

LOSSES ASSOCIATED WITH
HOMOPHOBIA

Coming to terms with living in a homophobic world can be incred-
ibly painful and difficult. It can also be an occasion for having to deal
with an enormous amount of loss. The fear of losing a job or an earned
promotion if he is "found out" is common for many gay men. The loss of
approval and acceptance from both family and friends is also a possibility for many. The loss of public acknowledgment and acceptance,
especially from potential allies who feel that they need to continue to
protect themselves by remaining in their closets, is likely to occur as
well.

Lack of safety is a major stressor for those living in a homophobic
society. Gay men (lesbian women and bisexual people as well) are
frequently threatened, harassed, and/or bashed, both verbally and
physically. In many cities, provinces, and states, the affirmation and
protection provided to heterosexual people is simply non-existent for
gay men. Living in an openly homophobic world where people are given
carte blanche to demean, oppress, and inflict cruelty on those who
are different, does little to enhance the self-worth and self-esteem of
gay men.

Most gay men know from very early childhood that they are different. They may not be able to label the difference or explain why they
feel the way they do, yet they know deep within themselves that they
are not like their heterosexual brothers or male friends. In reality, this
difference is a gift, but it frequently takes years for many gay men not
only to accept but also to celebrate their unique selves.

Because young gay men sense that they are different; because they
do not understand that this difference is both a gift and the core of who
they are; because there is usually no one in whom they can confide,
many young gay men isolate themselves rather than risk the wrath
and scorn of their family and school friends, should they be found out.
The result is painful isolation and loneliness. Some gay men are

fortunate enough to have groups like Boston's BAGLY (Boston Alliance of Gay, Lesbian, Bisexual and Transgendered Youth)[1] to provide support, role models, and a place to be gay in a safe environment.

Many gay men live out their lives in a state of hypervigilance, always at the ready to respond to very real outside threats. It doesn't matter whether one lives in a large city or a small town. Each setting has its own particular form of harassment and potential for violence. Beating, muggings, and gay bashing are not unique to large cities, since they frequently occur in small towns as well. Oftentimes these crimes go unreported because the victims fear reprisals from the perpetrators as well as the disbelief and mockery of the police. Sometimes, the comments and verbal harassment of small-minded people can wound just as deeply and cause possibly more pain than a physical beating.

Many families are well aware that their sons and brothers are gay, yet they are very often unwilling or unable to talk about it. Families, too, suffer from internalized homophobia. Even though they may indeed love their sons, parents may not be able to deal with conflicts frequently posed by their religious beliefs. Rather than face the issues squarely, everyone in the family constellation winds up living under the suffocating pall of denial, allowing his feelings to be squelched. Nothing is talked out and nothing gets resolved until eventually there is a painful emotional explosion that either brings the family together or drives it farther apart.

Frequently feeling scared and alone, believing that they are unique and different, many young gay men entertain suicidal thoughts and oftentimes act them out, thinking that they have nowhere to turn and that no one would understand or accept them. They know that their churches consider them to be sinful perverts teetering on the brink of eternal damnation; that some in the medical and mental health professions think that they are sick; and that their acts of love are considered criminal in many parts of the land. They frequently suffer in silence from depression and despair and believe that there is no way out but to end it all. Many do.

Since there is little or no support for young gay men in any but the most progressive of cities; since many gay adults fear any association of any sort with young gay men lest they be accused of pederasty and risk arrest; and since it is impossible for many gay teachers to be role

---

[1] BAGLY (Boston Alliance of Gay, Lesbian, Bisexual and Transgendered Youth), 617-227-4313 Monday-Friday, 9:00 AM to 5:00 PM. Also, Fenway Community Health Center's Peer Listening Line: 800-399-PEER, Monday-Friday, 4:00 PM to 10:00 PM.

models publicly lest they put their jobs on the line and livelihoods at risk, gay invisibility frequently is the rule and results in a self-fulfilling prophecy of even more invisibility.

MYTHS AND LACK OF INFORMATION

Society teaches all children that both the accepted and the expected way to be in North American culture is heterosexual. The message they are given is that they are supposed to grow up, get married, and raise a family. There are few role models for gay young people in this culture. The images they see on television, the people they see in advertisements, and the sports heroes whom they admire, are all represented as being heterosexual. Since most potential gay role models remain invisible, little is known about them. Fear and ignorance join forces with misogyny and sexism to create myths about gay men. There are countless myths about gay men, and the perception of these myths cause feelings of loss. They include statements like the following:

- Homosexuality is unnatural.
- Gay men act like women.
- He just hasn't met the right woman.
- Most gay men would change if they could.
- Gay men really want to be women.
- Gay men recruit young boys.
- Gay men hate all women.
- There seem to be very few happy homosexuals.

These and other myths present a distorted image of who gay men are, what gay men do, and how gay men interact and behave.

In addition to these myths, lack of information about the lives and cultures of gay men has combined with the lack of equality for gay men in areas of heterosexual privilege such as:

- Living openly with a partner and being accepted by family, neighbors, friends, and colleagues;
- Benefits derived from property laws, income tax regulations, and probate laws;
- Access to home, life, health, and motor vehicle insurance at couples' rates;
- Unrestricted access to one's partner or significant other in the event of an accident or other medical emergency;

- Paid bereavement leave following the death of a partner;
- Being acknowledged, supported, and validated by one's religious community.

These myths make sure that gay men and the realities of their lives continue to remain hidden.

Although things are slowly improving, there is still an information gap about gay men. We have made a lot of progress from the days when I was in junior high school and used to try to sneak a peak at the "homo . . ." card in the local library's card catalog, without getting caught doing it. Yet even though there is considerably more material in print today which deals with the lives of gay men, not everyone has easy access to that material.

There are very few gay characters on television shows to provide positive images of gay men dealing with their daily lives. Gay characters are not frequently seen on the movie screens either, unless they are portrayed as either tragic victims or mincing queens. These images need to change but they won't change until television producers and movie makers realize that they are not going to lose contracts and that their profits are not going to diminish simply because they present an honest and realistic picture of what it means to be a gay man.

As I have noted earlier in this chapter, the experience of loss connected with one's homosexuality begins early in life for many gay men. In February of 1993, the Massachusetts Governor's Commission on Gay and Lesbian Youth published a report[2] on making schools safe for gay and lesbian youth and, in August of 1994, they published a second report[3] dealing with making health and human services accessible and effective for gay and lesbian youth. I have used some of the challenges and stresses on gay and lesbian youth referenced in both of these reports published by the Governor's Commission as a basis for the losses that I reviewed in the previous section.

Each one of these challenges and stresses represents a potential loss for gay male youth and, at some point in his life, must be dealt with if the gay man is to integrate his being gay into his self-definition. Through the process of internalization, people come to own and accept

---

[2] Making schools safe for gay and lesbian youth: Breaking the silence in schools and in families, *Education Report of the Governor's Commission on Gay and Lesbian Youth,* 1993.

[3] Prevention of health problems among gay and lesbian youth: Making health and human services accessible and effective for gay and lesbian youth. *Education Report of the Governor's Commission on Gay and Lesbian Youth,* 1994.

at gut level the feelings and beliefs which the dominant society holds about them. The problem is that in a homophobic culture many negative messages are conveyed and then internalized by gay men. This subsequent negative perception of one's self-worth and value results in internalized homophobia.

During the early 1980s, HIV/AIDS was viewed as a gay disease in the United States and, in some quarters, it continues to be. In our sex-phobic culture, HIV/AIDS was, and sometimes still is, seen as something shameful and even sinful. Overlaying internalized homophobia with the shame associated with HIV/AIDS can be thoroughly overwhelming for many HIV+ gay men.

Living within the constraints of a culture which is both oppressive and repressive can be a daily challenge for many gay men. Dealing with homophobia is an ongoing daily process. It is frequently not safe to express terms of endearment to one's partner in public, let alone touch or hug in public. We take it for granted and find it quite acceptable when a man and a woman greet each other or bid one another farewell with a hug and a kiss. Yet when two men engage in the same behavior, eyebrows are raised, people look askance, and derogatory comments are made. These seemingly little incidents are sources of stress and the basis for loss in the lives of gay men and they need to be acknowledged.

Living in the "Age of AIDS" has brought incredible losses to the gay male community. The grief brought about by having to endure the death of one friend after another is enormous. Sometimes I have the image of men lined up at a turnstile. One man dies, and another passes through the turnstile into the mysterious realm of HIV-disease as he is told that he is HIV+. It is almost impossible to fathom being able to process this gigantic mound of cumulative grief. Yet, if one is to remain healthy and sane, this monstrous task must be undertaken as one is able to do so.

Gay men are also in need of grieving an entire way of interacting with each other since the advent of "safer sex." It was once thought that gay men were expected to use the prescribed precautions only for a limited amount of time. It was supposed that a cure for AIDS would be found and then many men felt that they would be able to go back to their former ways without risk. The reality that gay men have been challenged to change behaviors for the remainder of their lives is finally beginning to sink in for many men. This is both an enormous change and an enormous loss for men who were used to the sexual freedom that was the hallmark of the seventies, and this change *must* be acknowledged, discussed, and grieved.

PROPOSED WORKSHOP ON GRIEVING
THE EFFECTS OF HOMOPHOBIA

This workshop can be done using either a full- or half-day format. It focuses on the issues of shame and guilt, and is an attempt to provide gay men with a way to begin looking at their internalized homophobia. Several of the exercises are variations of exercises in a curriculum I developed for the Massachusetts Department of Public Health's Bureau of Substance Abuse Services, called *The Gay/Lesbian/ Bisexual Client in Substance Abuse Treatment: Creating a Welcoming Environment*. Ways to begin working with the painful losses which result from homophobia are explored, resulting in a diminishment of its negative effects.

Dealing with the impact of internalized homophobia is similar to recovering from internalized shame in that it tends to work best in a group setting. When one member of a group has the courage to take a risk by sharing openly a long held shameful secret from his past, he opens the door for others in the group to share their own secrets. People usually identify with what is being said. Very often they will feel compassion for both the person sharing and themselves, realizing that their own secret isn't really as bad as they had feared. It is critical that a safe space be created for the participants to explore the roots of their current negative feelings about their gay selves and not feel that they are going to be judged or shamed yet once again.

After a period for participant introductions and expectations, the ground rules around the issue of safety need to be established. The facilitator asks the participants "What 'gound rules' work for you?" and, together with them, develops a list and records it on a sheet of newsprint. The following points need to be included on the list.

Confidentiality

This means not revealing information about particular individuals to people who did not participate in the workshop. It would be acceptable, however, to talk in general terms about what you as an individual did in the workshop.

Respecting Differences

This means having a willingness to listen respectfully to the opinions of others, a willingness to share one's own opinions and experiences, and a willingness to disagree if they are different from the experiences and opinions of others.

Taking Care of One's Own Needs

This means a commitment to do what is best for oneself. It might include taking a break to stretch, temporarily "spacing out," or possibly saying exactly what is on one's mind. Each participant is invited to examine the ways he uses to take care of himself. It is important to discern for oneself whether or not one is using them to avoid difficult issues or unintentionally, to interrupt the participation of other members of the group.

Speaking from One's Own Experience

This means using "I" statements to talk about one's perceptions and one's life, as opposed to making judgments about others' lives or speaking for other participants. The bottom line is that people need to feel comfortable enough to express their true feelings without judgmental comments from either the facilitator or other participants. All participants need to agree to abide by the ground rules as they are listed, and the list needs to be posted on the wall of the training room for the remainder of the workshop. The group is broken into dyads next and safety/support issues are handled.

The first workshop exercise is called an "Essence Game." This relatively simple technique, originally developed by my colleague and mentor David Smith, Ph.D., helps people to get at their core feelings and beliefs about a particular topic, and then verbalize what it is that they truly believe. It also allows the facilitator to identify whatever baggage or emotional bias each participant is bringing with him. The technique works to focus the group, helps each participant feel that he has an important role to play in the discussion, and, finally, provides a way to enhance safety by making room in the discussion for diverse opinions.

The "Essence Game" is an exercise which involves asking a series of open-ended questions to get at the attitudes, beliefs, and feelings of the participants. In order to use this tool successfully, the trainer must be able to create a safe space for participants to not only have their own attitudes, beliefs, and feelings, but also to be able to express them openly and not feel judged by others in the room.

The exercise can either be done aloud by quickly going around the group and asking for a response from each participant, or it can be done using a written format. It is important to instruct the participants to give the first answer that comes to mind. Once everyone has given a response, go back and review and discuss the responses. Once again, it is important that answers not be judged.

Some sample statements and participant responses follow:

Being a man means . . .
> Sample Responses
>> Being strong
>> Being responsible
>> Being "butch"
>> Being fearless
>> Being the breadwinner

Being gay means . . .
> Sample Responses
>> Being tender
>> Feeling like a social outcast
>> Having vision
>> "Selective closetedness"
>> Being emotionally, physically, and sexually attracted to
>> members of the same sex

The most difficult thing about being gay is . . .
> Sample Responses
>> Feeling different
>> Watching all your friends die
>> Loneliness
>> Not feeling accepted, understood, or included by my family
>> Having to guess whether someone else is

The thing I like best about being gay is . . .
> Sample Responses
>> Being able to be affectionate with whomever I want
>> The perspective on the world which it gives me
>> Being clear about my sexuality
>> Being with Wayne
>> Men!!!

This exercise is intended to get the discussion process moving. It also helps to facilitate the process of identification among participants. Men who have been labeled by other people's homophobic cruelty sometimes think that their particular situation is unique and that they personally are the only ones experiencing the pain associated with homophobia. When participants share their responses to the open-ended questions, they frequently open doors for other participants who might have been reluctant to admit having similar feelings. If one participant has the courage to share his feelings with the others, he creates space for them to have and perhaps share their feelings also. Participants begin to realize that their experiences and feelings are not so unique, and that others in the room have had similar feelings and are dealing with them. Therefore, they too gain hope about dealing with their particular issues, and mutual support frequently is the result.

A brief didactic session on homophobia is conducted next and the following terms are discussed and clarified:

Biological Gender

The biological basis for being who one is, i.e., male or female. It is determined at the chromosomal and hormonal level. It is fixed and cannot be changed.

Gender Identity

The sense which a person has of him/herself as a male or female. It also refers to the way a person expresses him/herself as a male or female. Gender identity is influenced by social norms.

Gender Role

Societal expectations about how males and females should behave. It refers to those characteristics or behaviors which society says are proper to an individual of a particular sex. Gender role is flexible and may be changeable.

Homophobia

A persistent, irrational fear and dread of homosexuality and homosexual people.

Heterosexism

The unconscious assumption and value statement that everyone is heterosexual, and, if they are not, they should be.

Sexual Identity

The combination of one's biological gender, gender identity, gender role, and sexual orientation.

Sexual Orientation

This term refers to a person's attractions and behaviors. The sexual orientation of a homosexual involves emotional and sexual attraction or behavior directed toward a person or persons of the same sex; while that of a heterosexual is directed toward a person or persons of the opposite sex. The bisexual is one whose emotional and sexual desire or behavior is directed toward persons of both sexes, though not necessarily at the same time.

This term not only refers to what people do in bed, but also to who they are as complete human beings. Since people are complex and are not static, they do not always fit neatly into distinct categories of sexual/affectional orientation. Human sexuality is also a dynamic condition and many people change positions on the continuum of sexual/affectional orientation.

The *Homophobic Message Exercise* comes next, following a brief break. This exercise focuses on examining the impact of the homophobic messages which participants received from any number of people, frequently authority figures such as parents, teachers, and clergy, when they were young, on their perceptions and experiences of being gay. Workshop participants are asked to recall any homophobic messages that they had directed at them when they were either young or during the recent past. The sources of the messages are identified next.

It is important that the participant now try to recall and identify someone, even a grandparent, from whom he received support and love at the time he was also experiencing the homophobic messages. Even though it may be difficult for them to recall, most people, unless they were abused, have had an experience of acceptance and unconditional love, even from a pet such as a cat or a dog, no matter how briefly, at some point in their lives. It is important to reconnect the participants with these feelings in order to instill the hope that if they were able to experience unconditional love and acceptance even once in their lives, they now know that they are at least capable of having this experience, and if they have had it once, they may have it again.

Finally, participants are asked, if they wish, to try to translate some of the negative self-talk into a more positive affirmation of themselves. The point of this exercise is to both expose the homophobic lies from the past and to try to rewrite the inner dialogue that frequently replays in our minds, turning it into something more positively reinforcing.

A sample of the responses from participants in past workshops follows. Each participant is given a grid which is divided into four segments. Each segment is labeled as follows: Homophobic Messages; Who Labeled You?; Who Supported You?; and New Message. Participants are then asked to recall experiences of homophobia from their past and to fill in each labeled box.

Homophobic Messages	Who Labeled You?
Called a "fruit" when I was in high school.	My father and my classmates
What are you, a boy or a girl?	Neighborhood children
All gay people are going to Hell!	Parish priest
You throw like a girl!	Baseball coach
You are sick and disgusting	Mother

Who Supported You?	New Message
Grandmother	I am a gay man, and I am proud of it.
My dog	I accept myself just as I am.
A friend	I am a good and worthwhile person.
Teammate	I can throw a baseball well enough.
My sister	I know that my mother was wrong.

A discussion of these responses follows. Each participant is asked to recall a loss associated with each message and to then think about whether or not he has ever grieved these losses.

The group breaks for a few minutes and then moves into the next exercise which examines the issue of support. Participants divide into pairs and each person in the dyad has ten minutes to think about and then share his answers to the following questions with his partner.

1. Is there someone in the workshop setting whom you feel you could use as a support person?
2. Who in your personal network is a source of support for you?
3. Where is it safe for you to share/express your feelings?
4. Name someone with whom you can share your feelings honestly. This may/may not be the same person whom you identified as a support.
5. Are some feelings more acceptable to you than others? If so, identify them.

After ten minutes of sharing, the person who was listening switches roles and takes his turn at answering the questions.

Recalling An Early Loss, an exercise which focuses on examining one's earliest memory of loss, follows next. Participants are led through a gentle guided meditation in which they recall an early loss. During the process portion of this exercise, participants will examine the various lessons they learned and internalized about how one experiences and deals with/does not deal with loss just by having observed significant others who were around them at the time of their earliest loss. Discussion will focus on how what people learned from their earliest loss carries over into their current lives and how they experience loss in the present time.

One participant who grew up in a broken home described an incident involving the death of a cat. The cat, a Blue Persian named Smokey, was the young man's "best friend" when he was a boy. The boy was shy and withdrawn, and, even at a very young age, had a sense of "being different." Smokey was always there as a companion to whom the boy could confide his secrets and dreams. Smokey was the only source of unconditional love and acceptance in the boy's life. One day after school, the boy, who was seven or eight years old at the time, found Smokey dead in the back yard. He had been poisoned. The boy gently picked up the body of his lifeless cat and ran into the house crying to his mother. The mother asked what was wrong and the boy extended his arms showing her the lifeless cat. She quickly assessed the situation, and told the boy to "just throw him in the trash and we'll get you another cat later." Needless to say, the boy was devastated! It took the boy a long time during his adult years and with the help of a therapist to learn how to get in touch with his feelings and to be able to grieve effectively.

This exercise is followed by a break for lunch and then a brief didactic session on grief and loss, with attention given to the "little losses" which occur in our lives daily and which we frequently fail to recognize or acknowledge. The "little losses" range from something so seemingly mundane as moving from one location to another, to fairly major events like retiring from a job or getting a divorce. These "little losses" which we shrug off so quickly sometimes have an impact on us on a very deep level, yet we rarely take the time to process them. These losses slip through the cracks because we usually do not realize their significance and believe that they do not warrant the time it would take to deal with them. In addition, many men have been taught not to feel at all. From early boyhood they are told "not to cry," "to be brave little soldiers," and that "real men keep their feelings to themselves." Kenneth Doka suggested during his plenary session at the 1994 King's College Conference that many men cannot even respond to the word "feeling," so he works with them using the word "reaction" instead. Grief is differentiated from mourning and Worden's tasks of mourning and manifestations of normal grief which he outlines in his book *Grief Counseling & Grief Therapy* are discussed [2]. The Rando's process of mourning is examined [3]. Finally, specific strategies for dealing with grief are suggested.

The final exercise provides participants with an opportunity to continue their healing process by creating something, a drawing, a poem, perhaps a paragraph or two of prose, which depicts a loss directly related to homophobia. Participants are given the opportunity to process their creations by sharing something about the loss in a small group setting and later in the larger group.

Participants are asked to comment on the following questions:

1. What feelings or reactions does your creation represent?
2. What are the meanings of the various colors and shapes?
3. What gifts came into your life as a result of the loss?
4. What would you have missed out on if the person or thing which you lost had not been a part of your life?

Before concluding the workshop, participants are asked to recall the people in their lives whom they identified as supports. They are reminded that they can call on these people for support if difficult feelings surface for them in the days following the workshop.

Although this workshop is new, the technique has worked well with clients in the past who have used it to deal with shame and guilt. It is important for everyone, but more especially for gay men, to identify and examine closely the beliefs and attitudes they hold about themselves, if they intend to change those beliefs and attitudes. Changing the way a person thinks can have a profound effect on how he feels. In the words of Stephen Levine, poet and teacher of meditation, "To heal is to touch with love that which we previously touched with fear" [4].

Finally, a few words of caution regarding the workshop. I cannot emphasize enough the importance of the safety issue for the participants in the workshop setting. The workshop must be facilitated by someone who is both qualified and skilled. The facilitator needs to have done his/her homework regarding his/her own issues related to both grief and homophobia. In addition, prior to the day of the workshop, the facilitator should have obtained written permission to take part in the workshop from the therapist of any participant who is currently in therapy.

The workshop is intended to assist participants in either beginning or continuing their process of dealing with both grief and homophobia. It is not meant to be seen as some kind of "shortcut to growth and healing." Dealing with grief and homophobia can be both a painful and lengthy process. It is important to remind participants of this reality several times throughout the day. It is also important to keep reminding them about the issue of safety, and their responsibility to do whatever is necessary to take care of themselves.

CONCLUSION

All gay men have suffered losses due to their experience of homophobia, both externalized homophobia and internalized homophobia. This chapter suggests creative methods using both didactic and experiential exercises for gay men to get in touch with these losses, to grieve the pain associated with their losses, and to continue their journey toward authentic wholeness. As a result of participating in this workshop, gay men are able to access the losses caused by homophobia in their lives both in the present and in the past. Participants are assisted in finding ways to process these losses in a safe and supportive setting. Gay men taking part in the workshop are encouraged to be aware of and to respect their own and others' levels of comfort throughout the process. Participants leave with the awareness that they are not alone in their experiences of grief and homophobia, that there is no "right" or "proper" way to grieve these losses, and that their personal process of grieving is absolutely perfect for them.

Gay men are disenfranchised grievers. Their losses, whether related to homophobia or to the countless catastrophic losses associated with HIV/AIDS that they have endured for the past fifteen years, have been largely discounted by the larger society. If gay men are going to recover from the devastation of their experience of loss, they must begin the process of healing by declaring and dealing with these losses to the extent that they are able.

AUTHOR'S NOTE

This chapter was written six years ago in 1994. Since then, I have made modifications to the workshop and have updated the definitions used in the workshop's didactic section.

REFERENCES

1. G. Weinberg, *Society and the Healthy Homosexual,* St. Martin's Press, New York, 1972.
2. J. W. Worden, Attachment, Loss, and the Tasks of Mourning; Normal Grief Reactions, in *Grief Counseling & Grief Therapy* (2nd Edition), Springer Publishing Company, New York, pp. 10-18, 20-30, 1991.
3. T. A. Rando, What is Grief? in *Grieving: How to Go On Living When Someone You Love Dies,* Lexington Books, New York, 1988.
4. G. J. Stern, Internalized Homophobia, *A Few Tricks Along the Way,* The Crossing Press, Freedom, California, 1994.

REFERENCES NOT CITED IN TEXT

Blumenfeld, W. J., *Homophobia: How We All Pay the Price*, Beacon Press, Boston, Massachusetts, 1992.

Bozarth, A. R., *Life is Hello, Life is Good-Bye*, CompCare Publishers, Minneapolis, Minnesota, 1982.

Clark, D., *The New Loving Someone Gay*, Celestial Arts, Berkeley, California, 1987.

Eichberg, R. *Coming Out: An Act of Love*, Plume/Penguin Books, New York, 1991.

Gonsiorek, J. C., Mental Health Issues of Gay and Lesbian Adolescents, *Journal of Adolescent Health Care, 9*, pp. 114-122, 1988.

Hart, J. E., *Substance Abuse Treatment: Considerations for Lesbians and Gay Men*, Mobile AIDS Resource Team (MART), Boston, Massachusetts, 1991.

Isensee, R., *Growing Up Gay in a Dysfunctional Family*, Prentice Hall, New York, 1991.

Isensee, R., *Love Between Men*, Prentice Hall, New York, 1990.

James, J. W. and Cherry, F., *The Grief Recovery Handbook*, Harper & Row, New York, 1988.

Jennings, K. J. (ed.), *Becoming Visible*, Alyson Publications, Boston, Massachusetts, 1994.

Miller, J., *Healing Our Losses*, Resource Publications, San Jose, California, 1993.

Pharr, S., *Homophobia: A Weapon of Sexism*, Chardon Press, Inverness, California, 1988.

Staudacher, C., *Men and Grief*, New Harbinger Publications, Oakland, California, 1991.

Woodman, N. J. (ed.), *Lesbian and Gay Lifestyles*, Irvington Publications, New York, 1992.

CHAPTER 6

Emerging from the Anguish:
A Father's Experience with
Loss and Grief

Kent Koppelman

When the call came on the evening of September 13, 1989, it was after 11:00. My wife answered the phone. It was the Houston County Sheriff. Jason, our nineteen-year-old son, had been in a car accident and was being taken to Lutheran Hospital. The sheriff was calling from his car phone and the tone of his voice suggested that this was serious. The ambulance was turning into the hospital parking lot as we arrived. When Jan got out of the car she started running to the ambulance which had backed up to the emergency room doors. I did not run. I walked quickly behind Jan trying to be calm, trying not to let my worst fears take over. Perhaps it was Jan's brief glimpse of Jason that caused her to believe he was dead. While I sat in a private waiting room, hoping, Jan was in the bathroom trying to overcome her nausea. I was desperately repeating words like "sustained (an injury)" or even "seriously injured" or even "maimed." No matter how ugly those words sound, they sounded better to me at that moment than "dead." But it was not to be.

When the doctor finally came back into the room, she spoke simply, directly. She said Jason was in an accident, and he "didn't make it." Jan took the news more calmly than I because she had prepared herself for such a statement. I had not, and I was overwhelmed with agony. Large tears splashed down my cheeks as I groaned and bent over and groaned again. I could barely hear Jan and the doctor talking. It took several minutes before I could regain some control.

The doctor asked if we wanted to see Jason's body. We did. A few minutes later we were escorted to the room where Jason's body lay. They had cleaned him up as best they could, some dried blood remained around the fingernails and someone had placed a blue shower cap on his head, presumably to hide the badly damaged skull. The doctor had explained that Jason died instantly from a severe head injury which occurred when the car flipped over onto its top.

Jan immediately went to his right side, I to his left. My stubborn optimism refused to yield to the announcement of his death, and all the way down the hall I kept thinking of the miracle of Lazarus. At Jason's side I clutched his hand as hard as I could, as if I could infuse some of my warmth, some of my life into him. As I felt the coolness of his palm and stared at that familiar face with no breath blowing softly between parted lips, I was forced to accept the fact that my son was dead.

The pain was so intense I don't know how I could have tolerated it had it not been for the numbness. My entire body felt numb. In my brain the numbness was like a soft buzz of radio static (the volume turned low). Jan and I touched Jason's body, despite how cool and lifeless it felt. We touched and kissed him and told him how much we loved him. It made no sense, but neither did his death. We had to express our love even though his ears could not hear nor could his body feel the caresses. This was the beginning of a lengthy grieving process, which I would come to recognize as an effort to say goodbye.

No one is prepared to confront the death of their child, but I was especially overwhelmed by the myriad of decisions to be made. Jan and I met with the funeral director to discuss the funeral. What Bible verses . . . what music selections . . . who would give the eulogy? What clothes would Jason want to be buried in? Would he care? I didn't know but I did know that he didn't want to die, not now, not at nineteen. We had to select a coffin, wandering aimlessly amid the wood and metal cylinders. We had to pick out lots at the cemetery. Should we buy three lots or two? Would Tess understand why we would only want to buy three? We couldn't take the chance so we bought four. We were told we could resell the lot if we didn't need it. We hoped we would not need it, but hope was a hollow word on this day. We were about to bury our son.

For several days the buzzing in my brain continued and the numbness bore down on my body like a load of cement. In some ways this was good. The numbness helped me to get through the public visitation and the funeral, but it was draining me of energy. I had the constant sensation of moving slowly, as though I was walking deep down under the water. Every step, every thought seemed to require enormous effort. Although I wasn't sleeping well, that was not the reason for this feeling. I have gone without sleep before, and I know how that feels. This was different. Everyday at mid-afternoon I would feel exhausted, hardly able to function.

I was still struggling with this burden when I returned to work a week later. Because I was a college professor, I had a "staggered" work schedule. And so I staggered through it. I taught classes on Monday evenings and late afternoon on Tuesday, Wednesday, and Thursday. This schedule gave me time to go home and rest before each class, and after class I always felt exhausted. Teaching has always required considerable energy because I help students examine sensitive social issues such as sexism, racism, and homophobia. I bring my enthusiasm and commitment to the classroom, and students have appreciated that, but now I was having to blot out a piece of reality during that classroom time. This was also true when I was in my office, at committee meetings, or engaged in any of the various duties of a teacher-education professor, from advising students to observing a student teacher to meeting with area teachers.

Sometimes people offered consolation by talking to me about the accident or telling me of similar tragedies experienced by other family members. Although they meant well, such conversations made being at work even more difficult. On campus I needed to focus on my work. I did not need to be reminded of my pain or anyone else's pain. The people who helped me the most were those who simply said how sorry they were, and some would give me a hug. That helped. When you are struggling with despair, you need people to say they care about you, and you need to know that they mean it. After one full week back at work, I was still teaching and fulfilling my other responsibilities with this sense of gravity that had increased two or threefold.

On Wednesday morning, one week after returning to work, I awoke at 5:00. I had been waking up at this time every morning. This was part of the reason I lacked energy, and I knew if I could just sleep a little longer each morning I could function more effectively. In desperation I folded my hands and prayed. It was a prayer whispered in the dark by a man of little faith who freely confessed his doubts. I prayed to have the burden lifted, not for myself, but because I still had a family and they needed me. Afterwards, I thought I would lie in bed for a few more minutes and then get up. Unlike the previous mornings, I fell asleep, and I dreamed.

In the dream I saw Jason and his two closest friends. Their conversation was mundane, trivial, normal, so normal that I was briefly convinced that this was reality and that Jason's death was simply a horrible nightmare. A powerful wave of emotion—joy, relief, perhaps even a kind of ecstasy—swept over my body. I distinctly felt it while I dreamed. It did not take long before I realized that there was too much in what I was seeing that was inconsistent with reality. I reluctantly accepted the conclusion that I was dreaming, but I tried to take advantage of this opportunity to give Jason a hug and tell him how much I loved him. When I moved toward him to do that, I woke up. It was disappointing to be denied such a simple pleasure in my own dream. After I awoke I described the dream to Jan, and then I wept.

The effect of this dream was dramatic. I graded papers all morning and realized by the end of the morning that I was not feeling so tired. I went for my usual noon swim and came home still feeling energetic. Since the accident I had usually been too tired to continue working by this point in the day, so I would lay on the couch before going to teach. Instead I worked until the time came to go to class. Even without a break, I had no trouble mustering the energy and enthusiasm required to teach, and the time passed quickly. After class I came home for supper. I should have felt absolutely exhausted. Even before the accident I would usually come home from a class feeling tired. But now I felt fine. I worked at the computer for two hours and then decided to stop and relax for a couple of hours before going to bed. The next day I functioned more like I used to before the accident. From this point on I had bad days and good days, but nothing like the energy I experienced on the day following the dream.

A few weeks later I was at the clinic for my annual physical examination. I asked the doctor if he could explain my lack of energy and then the burst of energy following my dream. He began by saying that the medical profession still has a great deal to learn about the brain and brain functioning, but what I experienced sounded like the symptoms of clinical depression which are chemically induced in the brain. He said it was possible that a dream could provoke a chemical reaction in the brain which could counteract the effects of the chemicals causing the depression. I don't know if this is what happened to me, but I know that after the dream I was able to return to a semblance of normality in my daily life.

Other men have had dreams similar to mine, but the effect has not been as dramatic for them. I have talked to several men who lost an adolescent child and every one of them had a dream where they saw their child again, perhaps weeks later, even months later, but they all agreed it was an important part of their grieving process. By contrast, I have also talked to women who lost a child and none of them had such a dream. Is this a difference between men and women? Perhaps because women traditionally spend more time with their children they have enough memories to satisfy the need to remember and cherish the child. Perhaps for men such dreams are an anguished effort to expand an inadequate memory base. I don't know, but I know my dream gave me an opportunity to say goodbye to Jason and I cannot believe that women have any less need to do this. It is essential if one is to become reconciled with a death that you do not expect, a death that comes suddenly, especially the death of a child.

My wife's experience with saying goodbye came at the funeral. We shared our feelings of grief with each other from the first, and we continued to talk. In one of those conversations, Jan told me about the emotional dilemma she experienced at the funeral. She kept thinking about Jason, that this was her son in the coffin, and even though he was not alive it was all she had left of him. She did not know how she would be able to leave the cemetery, to leave him behind.

During the funeral the family sat in a reserved section. Jan sat on one side of Tess, our thirteen-year-old daughter, and I sat on the other. Several family members sat behind us. To our right was a door which lead out to the parking lot where the hearse was parked with cars behind it to drive to the cemetery. The funeral began with dreadful recorded organ music which Jason would have hated. At that moment a scraping sound seemed to come from the door leading to the parking lot. I wondered if the wind was gusting outside and if I should get up and make certain the door was closed. Suddenly the door flew open banging against the outside wall as if a child had burst through, anxious to get outside and enjoy the day on such a warm September afternoon. For Jan, the door incident assured her that Jason was no longer there, no longer in the coffin. He had probably stayed as long as he could, but he would never have tolerated that music. So he had left, abruptly, forgetting to close the door, and her belief that this had happened made it possible for her to say goodbye to his body at the cemetery and leave the coffin behind.

When the door incident occurred, I had the same sense as Jan, that it had to be Jason's spirit leaving, but my rational mind interrupted such speculations, rejecting the possibility of supernatural signs. I began to speculate on more practical explanations such as a strong gust of wind, but later, at the cemetery, I noticed little or no air movement. I can remember watching mosquitoes float lazily up and land on the front of my shirt as we all stood with our heads bowed in prayer. I still cannot explain what occurred; I can only believe what I choose to believe.

Although I had not read death and dying literature thoroughly, I had read enough to know of some potential consequences. What surprised me was how many I did *not* experience. I was prepared to feel anger at Jason for dying, for being careless while he was driving. This didn't happen. I worried that my marriage might suffer, that my family might fall apart under the burden of this tragedy. That did not happen. I was prepared for the possibility of a significant decline in my productivity at work. That did not happen. In each case, I think I know why.

Jan and Tess and I had spent six weeks in Europe during the summer of 1989. Jason had decided to stay home and work, so I asked him to take care of the lawn while we were gone. We came home in mid-August and I was pleased to see that Jason had just mowed the lawn, but in the stacks of mail I discovered a letter from the "Weed Commissioner" demanding that I mow my lawn or the city would do it for me and send me a bill. The letter stated that they had received complaints of weeds "four to five feet high." When I confronted Jason with the letter he simply shrugged and said, "I don't do weeds." I had too much to do to discuss this with him, but as the day went on I thought about what I wanted to say to him and I tried to feel a sense of "righteous wrath." It surprised me to discover that I was unable to generate any wrath, righteous or "un." Something deep inside me had apparently decided to accept Jason as he was.

I mentioned this revelation to a friend who said it was a sign of my maturation as a parent. I'm not so sure, but I do believe it was this acceptance which resulted in my inability to be angry with Jason for the accident. And there was reason to be angry with him. The accident occurred on a cloudless night, no weather problems or road problems. Jason was apparently not paying attention as he approached a curve in the road and the car went off on the shoulder. He was not able to control the car and it went into a ditch, flipping onto its top and killing him. The accident was clearly his fault, but I could not feel anger toward him. Jason had many good qualities, and deserved to be loved for them. He also had flaws, one of which was a tendency to be careless, an unwillingness to focus on the task at hand, especially if the task was uninteresting or mundane. In one moment it became a fatal flaw.

Each of us has flaws that cause us to make mistakes. As one friend said, "If everyone died each time he did something stupid there would be no one left on the planet." Because I had accepted Jason, flaws included, I could not be angry with him over the weeds nor could I be angry with him over the accident. It was just a case of Jason being Jason, probably driving a bit too fast, certainly being a bit careless, not paying attention. He should not have had to pay such a high price for such a minor flaw in his character, but he did.

The times I can recall feeling angry have usually been when I have encountered people mouthing pious nonsense about God calling Jason home. It is as if these people have some notion of a kindly, anthropomorphic god with a flowing white beard who sits on a throne in heaven and says, "I really like (that person), bring (him or her) to me." Among the many absurdities of such a vision is that in this instance God would have had to say, "Bring Jason to me and don't botch the job. Kill him good and proper. I don't want him lingering on a respirator. I suggest you flip his car over and smash his brains all over the place. That should do it." I am appalled that people could actually believe in such a ridiculous and ultimately brutal concept of God.

There was a time when I felt angry with God. It never became intense as I was not (and am not) certain that God exists; but, if God does exist, I thought that He should have to bear some responsibility for the death of my son. God is supposed to be omnipotent. What good is power if you don't use it to stop something tragic and evil from happening? My feelings became more obvious during my search for the biblical passage I wanted to use in the manuscript I had begun to write. I began with the version that said, "not one sparrow falls to the ground without your father's *consent*," because I wanted to blame God for what happened to Jason. But the more I thought the more I became reconciled to the King James Version, which says, "one of them shall not fall on the ground *without* your father." If I am to believe in God, it must be a God who suffers with us, who shares our pain. A God who inflicts suffering is not worthy of belief.

My relationship with Jan and Tess has been affected by Jason's death, but it has not torn us apart. Perhaps the factor that helped us the most was the way Jason died. It would probably have been much different if Jan or Tess or I had been in the car (or if Jan or Tess had been driving the car) and survived. Although I would like to think I could be understanding and forgiving in such circumstances, I can imagine the bitter feelings and the accusations I might have harbored, and I cannot be certain I would have overcome them. I can also imagine the guilt I would have felt if I had been in the car and survived the accident, even if Jason had been the driver. Jan and I discussed this, and we both agreed. No matter how rational one tries to be, rationality does not always take precedence over the powerful and often irrational feelings of guilt, which can arise under such tragic circumstances. Jason spared us that. He died alone.

Instead of blaming each other, we focused on trying to help each other. It was strange how consistently Jan was able to be strong when I felt weak, and how I was able to be strong when she felt weak. From the very beginning we seemed to take over for each other as if we were working "shifts." This was a reflection of our relationship with each other, and it suggests that if some marriages are destroyed by a tragedy, they may have already been flawed. The part Tess played was to get on with life and her wide range of activities. She has done as much as anyone to rebuild our life together as a family. She has been a constant reminder that we need to move forward, that we still have a life to live, that Jason would want us to enjoy whatever gifts life offer. I know she has been affected by Jason's death, but she has used it to approach life with an appreciation far deeper than can be found in most adolescents.

I believe I was able to remain productive in my professional life in part because I firmly believe in the importance of the work I do, but another factor was the value of my deliberate attempt to create and engage in a grieving process. Our culture only has a few brief rituals to represent the grieving process—public and private visitations, the funeral, the burial. All of them occur immediately after the death and shortly thereafter we are expected to resume our lives. Our culture does not have an adequate grieving process to help us to heal compared to some other cultures. Instead, each individual has to "invent" such a process. My process was to pursue activities which responded to a feeling or addressed need.

Jan and I knew that writing could help us, so we each began to write regularly about our emotions, our state of mind. We both began by writing about the scene at the hospital, but as we continued to write we moved in different directions. I went forward to record the events as they happened—the details of the funeral preparations, the private and public visitations, the funeral itself—but Jan wanted to write about the past. She wrote about the last time she saw Jason, and later she wrote an anecdote, which a college counselor had told her, about Jason behaving like a role model during a Freshman orientation meeting. She continued moving back in time to other memories of Jason. I was trying to describe and understand the experience of loss forced upon us, but she was trying to recapture the life of the son she had lost. Later, when I began to think about reworking my writing into a manuscript I remembered her stories and decided to include such stories in my writing.

I needed to do more than write. I needed to do something for Jason, for his memory. I needed to create the illusion of his presence. I needed to do things that helped me to think of him and to love him as I did when he was alive. Jan did not feel this need as much as I did. She needed time—time to feel, to remember. At work she daydreamed frequently, reviving old memories. At home she went through our pictures, memorabilia from past vacations, old report cards, anything to help her remember and reconstruct the times she shared with Jason. For me, feeling was dangerous. When I would think about my memories with Jason, the feelings aroused were those of pain and loss and I could only weep. This made me feel helpless. I needed to do things to give me a sense of purpose and meaning in this meaningless death. Writing helped, but I needed to do more.

I decided to organize Jason's writing. I went through all of his papers and took every kind of poetry and prose I could find. I was proud of his poems, especially the ones he wrote during his freshman year at college. My favorite is the one where he is lying in bed at night in his dorm room recalling how his father used to read to him every night. It is written in words of love. After I had gathered and arranged all his writing, I wanted to do more than just duplicate the pages, I wanted to make a booklet. Jan created a cover, which was printed on a heavier stock of paper, and Jan also suggested including Jason's high school graduation picture. We made fifty copies to distribute to family and friends.

Another project was to create a scholarship fund with the $3000 sent to us by family and friends. Jan and I met with a representative from a local foundation to discuss what it would take to set up an independent scholarship fund. We were told it would require a minimum of $15000. This project was only partially satisfying. It gave me a long-term goal, but I needed to have something to do immediately to help me deal with my pain.

To satisfy that need, I decided to write letters to some of Jason's "heroes." I thought about all of the people he admired in the film industry from writers to reviewers to directors. There were seven people I could identify who were especially significant to him. I wanted them to know how much they had meant to him and to thank them for enriching his life. I thought about it carefully, and I was certain that this would help the healing process *only* if I took my satisfaction from writing the letters. If I allowed myself to look for a response from any of these celebrities, I would probably be disappointed and hurt. I didn't need any more pain.

I eventually wrote letters to seven people to share the brief story of my son's life and to thank them for the part they played in it. In each letter I assured the recipient that he did not need to respond to me. Even so, three of the seven responded. George Lucas sent a signed poster, as did Steven Spielberg. Garrison Keillor did even more. He telephoned and talked to Jan and offered to do a benefit for Jason's scholarship fund. It was like a burst of light for two people struggling through a fog of pain.

I had also tried to find books to read. I found a few and friends sent a few, but most of these books concerned terminal illness so they offered little consolation. When people know they are dying, they have a chance to resolve things—heal old wounds, pay old debts, say goodbye to old friends and the family. With an unexpected death, you are left with questions, aching for reasons, seeking sense in senseless events, trying to say goodbye to someone who is not there. This frustration with my reading compelled me to reread my own writing. What I had written seemed like a good start for a manuscript. I continued writing regularly, but now I began to think of writing for a wider audience. I began to consider how my writing could be shaped into a book, and eventually I settled on a structure, which intersperses stories of a boy's life in a narrative describing the grief and healing which followed his death. This became my most important healing activity, and it helped me to manage my grief. I believe this is why I continued to be productive in my professional life.

Eventually I completed the first draft of the book, and after several more years and numerous revisions it was published in 1994 by Baywood Publishing Company under the title *The Fall of a Sparrow: Of Death and Dreams and Healing*. With this project concluded, I had a sense that the "doing" phase of my grieving process was over. Through this book I have given Jason a place in the world, a place he should have occupied as a living presence, but that dream died with him so what life there was is preserved in this book. It is not as good as his living would be, but it will have to do.

I'm not sure what the next phase will be, but I know healing takes a long time, perhaps a lifetime, and I will have to attend to it. Many things have helped. Certainly the most important event was Garrison Keillor's benefit for Jason's scholarship fund. Keillor also had a son whose name, coincidentally, was Jason and who was about the same age as our Jason. This benefit was a significant event for my family, for Jason's friends, for everyone who attended. It represented an affirmation of life and love and family. It reminded us not to let our pain overwhelm our sense of the joy of life. It reminded me of Jason. Since the accident I have often wondered if I could ever recapture my enthusiasm for life and work. Keillor's performance said I could, and that I should. I needed to hear that.

I wonder if the next phase of the grieving process is to confront the reality that a part of me died with Jason. I am not the person I was. That person had a son and a daughter whom he loved deeply, and he shared their hopes and fears, dreams and frustrations. The father I am now has only one child, a daughter, and while he can love her and share her life it is not the same as it was before. There is an absence which makes a difference, because the person I am now cannot (and will not) forget the son who was. And that makes me a different person, not better or worse, just different.

If this is true then it means that I not only have to accept the death of my son, but also the death of the person I used to be. It is a hard thing to do. It is especially hard if you liked the person you were. I did like that person, and I hope I can keep the best parts of him for this new person I am to be. Writing about my process of grieving and healing was an important step in becoming reconciled to Jason's death. My book represents his life and the relationship we had. It represents an end to one journey, and perhaps it has made possible the beginning of another.

There is a Buddhist saying that, "Life is joyful participation in the sorrows of the world." This belief could be the basis for creating the person I must become, the father who has lost a son and cherishes his daughter. It could also be the basis for creating a new perception of the family I now belong to—father, mother, daughter. I am aware that this process of creation has already begun, but I have not participated in it fully. My wife and daughter have done most of the work. My awareness of their efforts was expressed when I wrote the dedication for the book, which came to me almost effortlessly. It is the proper ending for this essay:

To

Jan and Tess

Who have loved
Amid the charred ruins of a family

And created in the ashes
Like the phoenix

A new family:

Smaller than before
But just as beautiful

CHAPTER 7

Research on Gender Differences in Bereavement Outcome: Presenting A Model of Experienced Competence

Susan E. Allen and Bert Hayslip, Jr.

Of the life events humans experience, the loss of one's spouse is among the most stressful. Research suggests that conjugal bereavement is accompanied by a host of negative personal and social-psychological consequences (e.g., higher suicide rates, deteriorating health, more complaints of depression, greater alcohol consumption) [1-5]. Why bereaved individuals are at increased risk is, however, not well understood, in part reflecting the fact that bereavement is a complex process whose outcomes depend on the presence or absence of predisposing premorbid characteristics (e.g., concomitant non-bereavement related stress, illness) [6].

This bereavement puzzle has also been difficult to solve due to the cross-sectional nature of most bereavement studies wherein bereaved persons are compared to non-bereaved controls, who may differ from conjugally bereaved persons along a number of dimensions that may also correlate with bereavement outcome, i.e., health status, income, sex, age, access to resources, support from others [4, 6-8].

GENDER AND BEREAVEMENT OUTCOME

Among the factors known to mediate the effects of bereavement on the individual, gender has received perhaps the most attention. Carey concluded that widowers were significantly better adjusted than were widows during the first year of bereavement [9]. While being forewarned, thus allowing one to grieve in an anticipatory way, seems important for widows, it is not for widowers, according to Carey's research. Widows who were more highly educated, who had higher incomes, and who lived alone made better adjustments after their spouses' death; this was not the case for widowers. Interestingly, those with stable, happy marriages and those with constant, pervasive marital problems appeared to be better adjusted. Not facing the death and/or deterioration prior to death and uncertainty about what life would be like after the death were the major problems to be overcome by the widows and widowers in this study. Others have also found women to have more difficulty in coping with conjugal loss than men [10-12].

Balkwell [13] and Stevenson [14], in contrast, have found that widowers are more likely to be socially isolated and less apt to express their feelings, perhaps indicating that men may have a more difficult bereavement than do women, though there are wide individual differences in grieving among widows [15, 16]. Gass found that among widowers, the sudden death of their spouses related to greater self blame and greater use of coping strategies versus those whose spouse died of a chronic illness [17]. Moreover, widowers whose spouses died of a chronic illness reported receiving more social support, suggesting that the personal impact of spousal death as well as available resources may jointly influence bereavement for men.

DeFrain, Jakub, and Mendosa found that among grandparents whose grandchild had died of SIDS, women tended to talk through their grief to a greater extent than did men, who kept their feelings bottled up to a greater extent [18]. Over time, the authors observed, gender differences in coping with loss tended to dissipate, however.

Rubin who studies gender difficulties in reaction to the loss of an adult child, found women to experience more difficulty than did men who resembled those in a nonbereaved control group [19]. These gender differences were greatest when persons were asked about the previous year, but were reduced when asked about the present.

At thirteen-months post bereavement, Shuchter and Zisook found men to drink more and express themselves less while women felt more helpless and were more likely to define the loss of their husbands in terms of his protective function [12].

Carroll and Shaefer found that men and women responded somewhat differently to the death of their child due to SIDS, wherein women sought support within the family to a greater extent than did men [20]. For men, a current pregnancy related to less adaptive coping, while for women the presence of other living children was related to less support seeking.

Stroebe and Stroebe, who studied thirty men and thirty women over two years who were conjugally bereaved, found that societal expectations about gender appropriate role behaviors were a more powerful determinant of the success of grief work for men than for women [21]. While focusing on one's loss in an active emotional manner was especially beneficial for men who were presumably more able to ignore the male stereotype of controlling one's emotions, such was not the case for women.

Perhaps the most widely cited gender difference in bereavement outcome, with men being a greater risk for mortality and illness, are those studies by the Stroebe's [22, 23]. Stroebe and Stroebe found that while over eighteen months, spousal death resulted in a greater loss of social support for widowers than for widows, but there were no gender differences in bereavement outcome [21]. While selection bias may be important here, the joint effects of gender and extent of perceived support were not reported, however.

Gallagher-Thompson, Futterman, Farberow, Thompson, and Peterson report that women tend to be more depressed than men regardless of bereavement. Thus, the greater risk of mortality and illness for men takes on a special urgency, underscoring the need for available, helpful support networks, and greater attention to coping styles and impact of loss as important for widowers [24]. In their study, men were also more likely than women to drop out of the study due to death [25].

Sanders emphasizes the crucial role of social support for widowers, who may have previously relied on their wives for emotional sustenance [25]. In contrast, when a child dies women grieve more deeply than do men and unfortunately, are also more likely to be isolated from others [26]. Arbuckle and DeVries found that child bereavement was more stressful for women, and that widowed women were more hopeless about completing future plans than were widowed men [27].

Wortman, Silver, and Kessler explored more carefully the dimensions along which gender differences in bereavement outcome can be understood [28]. While financial strain was most salient for women, interpersonal difficulties (particularly with children) were most troublesome for men. In each case, such tasks had been previously handled by the deceased spouse, underscoring the complementary nature of marital bonds broken through death. Though not reported to date, the weight of such factors for each gender may vary over time, resulting in greater vulnerability for men versus women over the course of their adjustment.

Thompson, Gallagher, Cover, Gilewski, and Peterson, in a thirty-month longitudinal study, found that with the exception of anxiety, where widowed women had higher levels, bereaved men and women scored similarly on the Brief Symptom Inventory [29]. Over a year, women declined to a greater extent in somatization than did men, but after thirty months this difference disappeared. A similar lack of gender differences in bereavement outcome has been found by Gallagher, Breckenridge, Thompson, and Peterson [11], by Lund, and his colleagues [30, 31], Faletti, Gibbs, Clark, Pruchno, and Berman [32], and by Van Zandt, Mou, and Abbott [33]. Worden and Silverman [34] did not find men and women to respond differently to the loss of spouse four months after the death in terms of CES-D scores, confirming the findings of Robinson and Fleming [35].

Gass found that widowed men and women each appraised their bereavement as equally manageable, yet women used mixed coping strategies (help seeking/avoidance) to a greater extent than did men [36]. Interestingly, while greater individual resources predicted less dysfunction for widows, such was not the case for widowers, wherein resources and dysfunction were independent. Perhaps widowers were less skilled at asking for support from others. Gallagher, Lovett, Hanley-Dunn, and Thompson found minimal differences across gender in the use of specific coping strategies across a 2-1/2-year post-bereavement period [37]. Women, however, used self-talk more than did men, while men were more likely to report keeping busy as a coping strategy.

Meuser, Davies, and Marwit, who studied older widows and widowers, did not find gender to predict Texas Revised Inventory of Grief (TRIG) scores [38]. Similarly, Caserta and Lund [39] did not report gender differences in bereavement adjustment over a two-year period among the widows and widowers, and Ponzetti did not find differences between men and women among both parents and grandparents in response to the death of a child [40]. Levy, Martinkowski, and Derby did not find gender to differentiate four patterns of bereavement adjustment defined in terms of both the extent of depression and stability of pattern over an eighteen-month time frame.

Solie and Fielder used the Bem Sex Role Inventory to categorize forty-five widows into sex role groups, and found that androgenous widows experience a more positive adjustment to bereavement than do feminine, masculine, or undifferentiated widows [42]. Results of the study suggest a relationship between the breadth of a widow's behavioral repertoire and her ability to cope with loss. Rather than viewing males as biologically predisposed to suffer more than females from the stress of bereavement, some researchers emphasize the importance of gender-typical behaviors within society [37, 38].

SAMPLING EFFECTS, OUTCOME SPECIFICITY, AND BEREAVEMENT

Participants in bereavement research are generally volunteers recruited from various sources, who agree to help the researcher(s) by answering interview questions or being tested on a variety of measures. Since the potential sample is made up of volunteers who agree or don't agree to participate for various reasons, it is possible that the actual sample will be biased by the self-selection of those who agree to help. As Stroebe and Stroebe have pointed out, "whether a bereaved person agrees to participate (in research) or not is undoubtedly influenced by his or her mental and/or physical health state, which are precisely the variables that such studies are attempting to measure" [43, p. 2]. Stroebe and Stroebe found that overall acceptance rates were relatively low, although rates varied widely among studies [43]. Studies having the highest acceptance rates tended to be associated with highly credible sampling sources, such as hospitals and religious institutions. No studies reviewed reported differences between participants and nonparticipants in sociodemographic characteristics. For example, Lund, Caserta, and Dimond, found no differences between acceptors and refusers in socioeconomic status, sex, age, or rate of remarriage [30]. Similarly, Valanis and Yeaworth found no differences in race or sex of participants versus non-participants [44].

Psychological characteristics may also influence willingness to participate in bereavement research. For example, expected death, such as death resulting from a terminal illness, may be associated with higher rates of participation, perhaps because an expected death is less disrupting for a surviving spouse than an unexpected, sudden death. Furthermore, Lund, Caserta, and Dimond found that reported reasons for nonparticipation included ". . . too busy, too upset, in poor health, or because of advice received from adult children," implying that at least some refusals were due to poor physical and/or mental health [30].

Levy, Darby, and Martinkowski found little evidence for a selective participation bias among widowed spouses [45]. Refusers and participants' Bereavement Risk Index scores were nearly identical, except for the fact that refusers had exercised less control over their emotions at the time of the loss, and that they were less likely to be working outside their homes.

Despite the finding of Levy et al., it is nevertheless possible that only women who are experiencing more severe difficulties or men who are experiencing less severe adjustment problems volunteer for bereavement research [45]. Alternatively, as men may prefer not to discuss their feelings as a coping mechanism, only those who are open to self disclose are likely to participate, thus representing those men who have more insight into the impact of loss upon them, for whom support from others may be more available, facilitating their adjustment to loss. Stroebe and Stroebe found that among refusers, men were more depressed and less isolated, whereas for women refusers were less depressed and more self sufficient [43]. This suggests that the absence of gender difficulties in bereavement outcome may reflect a convergence among genders regarding levels of adjustment in terms of its impact on available samples.

While we know a great deal more about the impact on conjugal bereavement on women, this may simply reflect the greater number of older women surviving into later life. Such women may have more support available to them or be more receptive to help from others. In this light, most of those participating in a self-help research project were female [46].

The apparent inconsistencies in some studies can also be traced, at least in part, to the wide variety of outcome measures used to determine adjustment. For example, while some studies look at mortality rates and physical illness, others examine self-reports of depression, grief, life satisfaction, and even remarriage. With such a lack of standardized definitions of adjustment, there is little wonder that results are inconsistent. Furthermore, as women are more likely than men to participate in research, this suggests, as mentioned before, the strong likelihood of a selection bias among those men who do participate. Feinson concluded from the results of both a literature review and her own work that while mortality studies provide support for the notion that widowers in some age groups are at higher risk than widows, the studies of psychological distress do not provide support for the perception that widowers suffer more than do widows [47].

As Lund has observed, there is great diversity in how bereaved spouses cope with their loss [48]. The personal impact of the death, i.e., suddenness or centrality of the loss [49], the availability of helpful social support, and the extent of effective coping skills, all emerge as likely mediating variables that interact with gender in determining bereavement outcomes. Given the substantial lack of gender differences in many, but not all bereavement research studies to date, it may be that gender interacts with other variables in relating to bereavement outcome. Women, for example, may be more skilled in seeking support from others, while men may be more personally and unexpectedly impacted by their loss, because women usually outlive their husbands.

COPING WITH BEREAVEMENT

Recent evidence suggests that bereaved individuals confront their grief in ways that fit most closely with their own personal styles. As Caserta, Van Pelt, and Lund have found, "Because people differ in what is particularly problematic for them, their strategies to manage grief also vary" [50, p. 123]. Some bereaved persons rely on the support of family and friends [15, 51, 52], others make use of their own "intrapersonal coping resources" [17], while still others use a mixture of various coping strategies [49]. As Allen and Hayslip have pointed out, if a behavior "leads to increased realization of and adaptation to the loss," it can be considered a successful coping strategy [53, p. 18]. However, research has shown that some coping strategies may be associated with poor bereavement outcomes [51]. For instance, the use of alcohol, self-blame, refusing to express feelings or acknowledge the loss to others, and avoiding reminders of the lost loved one, have all been found to be associated with poorer adjustment to bereavement [16, 17, 54].

Some researchers have suggested that bereaved individuals tend to select coping strategies that best fit their situations and personal styles. For example, Folkman, Lazarus, Pinley, and Novacek compared the coping strategies of 141 older adults and seventy-five younger married couples in response to stressful life events [55]. They found that the older adults rated the stressors in their life as being relatively unchangeable, and therefore they made more frequent use of coping strategies that were "emotion focused," such as accepting responsibility for the problem, reappraising the problem in a positive light, and distancing oneself from the stressor. These older individuals also tended to use escape-avoidance strategies, such as wishing the problem away, to a greater extent than did the younger subjects. The younger adults, on the other hand, were more likely to rate more of their life stressors as changeable, and to more frequently use problem-focused strategies which served to directly eliminate or control the stressors in their life. Although Folkman et al. did not study bereavement coping directly, their study sheds some light on the preference of individuals in different situations or with different perceptions for a variety of coping strategies [55].

In a study directly examining bereavement coping, Gass studied the use of coping strategies among older widowers [36]. She found that men whose spouse had died suddenly and unexpectedly were more likely to use problem-focused, self-blame, emotion focused, and wishful thinking strategies than were those whose spouse's death had been anticipated.

Thus, bereaved individuals facing different bereavement tasks may select different coping strategies. Caserta, Van Pelt, and Lund asked for coping advice from seventy-one older bereaved adults [50]. They found that the strategies of remaining occupied, developing new skills, reestablishing social linkages, increasing social participation, and engaging in meaningful, ongoing projects and activities were all effective for different bereaved individuals. However, the authors concluded that "provided a person has a full range of resources available, the strategies which the person finds most comfortable seem to work best for that person" [50, p. 132]. Other researchers have found that, at least among older bereaved individuals, those who report using a variety of coping strategies tend to show fewer symptoms of psychological distress [11, 30]. Furthermore, the coping strategies selected may differ according to the phase of bereavement. Gallagher, Lovett, Hanley-Dunn, and Thompson found that certain strategies, such as expressing sadness, decreased over time, while others were used more often later in bereavement [37]. Very few researchers, however, have studied changes in coping strategies over time.

Close examination of the literature on the course of typical bereavement suggests an alternate explanation to the "stages" theory of bereavement espoused by many [53, 56]. Recovery may indeed occur continuously over time. According to this view, the "stages" typically reported in the literature may simply represent different levels of mobilization of coping strategies. Certain behaviors may be associated with different points in a continuous process. For example, the "shock and numbness" phase may represent a point in time when the bereaved's construct system has been largely invalidated, but coping strategies have not yet been mobilized. Early in the process of reconstruction, the task may seem overwhelming, leading to the most intense period of negative affect. As headway is made and progress is seen, grief diminishes and mobilization of further strategies is encouraged. Only persons who fail to mobilize strategies or whose strategies fail will remain in conflicted or chronic states of grief.

Successfully accomplishing the task of reconstruction involves coping with and eventually overcoming the major problems brought about by bereavement. The bereaved may be viewed as faced with two major sets of problems. First, the "assumptive world" described by Parkes [2] has been violated; cognitions usually relied upon are now invalid and a new reality must be apprehended. Kelly has shown how using invalid constructs can lead to anxiety, despair, psychological maladjustment, and organic illness [57]. Secondly, a major source of reward or reinforcement has been removed from the person's life. Reinforcement may be positive (affection, attention) or negative (lessening of anxiety or loneliness). The point is that a source of reward has been removed and must be replaced to at least some degree if "reconstruction" is to take place.

Although Pearlin and Schooler's call for a differentiation of resources and responses has been fulfilled somewhat by researchers of coping strategies, it has gone almost entirely unheeded by bereavement researchers [7]. The factors used as predictor variables in most research studies are not organized in any logically consistent way, and interrelationships among variables are not adequately considered. Further problems stem from a failure to operationalize terms. Bereavement is generally thought of as loss of a close relationship, but how close? Studies may erroneously assume that all forms of bereavement are comparable. Finally, predictor variables are often confounded with outcome variables. For example, poor outcome might be defined as a preponderance of negative affect, while "guilt" is used as a predictor variable. Obviously, guilt cannot logically be used as both a predictor and an outcome variable unless quite sophisticated statistical techniques are employed.

ANTICIPATION OF LOSS AND COPING

Despite these problems, several factors have emerged as probably contributing to bereavement outcome. In addition to gender, a most well-documented factor is whether or not the death was anticipated [49]. While it is true that those who have ample warning of the death of a love object appear to fare better in bereavement than those who experience sudden loss [53, 57, 58], it appears that the causative agent may be the use of anticipatory cognitive coping strategies rather than preliminary emotional expression. Clayton, Halikas, Maurise, and Robbins [59] conducted a study of widows and found that contrary to Lindemann's [60] original hypothesis, anticipatory emotional responses such as grief, sadness, and depression did not lessen the sadness experienced after the loss. However, Parkes studied the course of bereavement in widows and widowers over a period of four years and compared the responses of those who had at least two weeks notice that death was imminent to those who experienced a sudden loss [58]. Those in the "short preparation" group were far more likely to experience prolonged periods of shock and anxiety and to mobilize defenses such as denial and avoidance. Members of the short preparation group also exhibited social and vocational functioning inferior to that of members of the longer preparation group as long as four years after the death. Parkes interprets these results as reflecting the overwhelming anxiety which may result from a sudden discrepancy between the assumptive world and reality. The results are not reflected in increased sadness and sorrow, but rather in increased disorganization and the mobilization of less effective coping strategies.

QUALITY OF THE LOST RELATIONSHIP AS A FACTOR IN BEREAVEMENT

The nature of the lost relationship is often cited as an important factor in predicting bereavement outcome. From Raphael's extensive work in the field, she concludes that the more ambivalent and/or dependent the lost relationship, the more problematic the bereavement process is likely to be, and the greater the probability of poor outcome [56]. Kitson found that widows with high levels of ambivalence suffered the poorest adjustment to loss [61].

Unfortunately, however, studies of the impact of the nature of the lost relationship on bereavement outcome are typically plagued with theoretical and methodological shortcomings. First, the nature of the relationship is almost invariably measured after loss has occurred. At this point, ambivalence may reflect the conflict associated with poor coping. Second, persons with a high degree of ambivalence may also have a longstanding character disorder, and may react poorly to the stress of bereavement as a result of the disorder.

SOCIAL SUPPORT AND BEREAVEMENT

Numerous studies have shown that a lack of such support can be detrimental to bereavement outcome. Vachon et al. found that among widows, isolation and the lack of support were highly predictive of continued distress two years after a loss [62]. Others have found a lack of social support to be related to more intense distress early in bereavement [12], an increased strain in adjusting to life as a widow(er) [15], and poorer long-range adjustment to bereavement [12, 63].

Originally, researchers measured social support by the frequency of contacts with network members. More recently, however, it has become generally recognized that the impact of social support may be more complex and multidimensional than first assumed. In his extensive work in the area, Lund has noted that the qualitative dimensions of the social network, such as the degree of perceived closeness, shared confidences, opportunities for self-expression, mutual helping, and frequency of contacts, were more important predictors of bereavement outcome than were structural characteristics, such as size, strength of ties, and network density [50].

The type and timing of support have also recently been given attention in the bereavement literature. Schuster and Butler studied a sample of older widows and widowers and found that social support received shortly after the death of a spouse was more influential in predicting bereavement outcome than was support received later in the bereavement process [64]. Walker, MacBride, and Vachon also studied the timing of support, and concluded that shortly after the death, support from a small dense network is most helpful, but, as time goes by, such a dense network may hinder the bereaved individual's need to take on new social roles [65]. Furthermore, Schuster and Butler have found that instrumental support, such as assisting with the daily tasks of life, was just as important to the mental health of the bereaved as affective support [64].

Hirsch studied twenty young widows and found that lower density of social network (characterized by more relationships that are functionally independent of one another) is correlated with better adaptation to widowhood, using several measures of adaptation [66]. Bankoff studied the effects of various types of support systems on outcome in widowhood [15]. He emphasized that simply measuring the frequency of interpersonal contact is not a sufficient predictor of adjustment. According to the author, social networks include the dimensions of size, composition, frequency of contact, and degree of intimacy.

A number of other studies have related various aspects of the social support system to adjustment to bereavement. These include intimacy [67], interaction with family members [60], and stability of the social network [68]. Dimond, Lund, and Caserta found that structural aspects of the social support network (such as size and interrelatedness of members) were less important in predicting bereavement outcome than were qualitative aspects of the social network (such as a sense of closeness to network members) [51]. Raphael, on the other hand, emphasizes the importance of independent relationships (a structural variable) in recovering from bereavement [56]. Similarly, Lopata notes in her work with widows that those who had not built a social life outside their husbands had poorer outcomes, because they were left directionless in the task of identity reconstruction [68].

With regard to social support systems and their importance in bereavement, Maddison and Walker point out that perceived resources are more important to outcome than resources as measured objectively [69]. This makes intuitive sense; a widowed person would not be likely to utilize any source of support that is not perceived as available and helpful.

PERSONALITY AND BEREAVEMENT

It is not well known what personality variables might contribute both to failure to establish supportive relationships and to poor bereavement outcome. In fact, only a few studies have addressed the relationship between personality variables and recovery from bereavement. Parkes reported a high incidence of previous depressive illness in patients with complicated grief reactions [1]. This suggests a possible link between personality variables associated with depressive tendencies and those connected with poor bereavement outcome, but this is by no means the only viable interpretation of these findings. Parkes and Weiss found that highly dependent persons were at risk of poor bereavement outcome, as were anxious or hostile persons, or persons who had difficulty expressing feelings [70]. Similarly, Raphael infers from the general literature and her own interviews that persons whose personalities lead them to form dependent, clinging, or ambivalent relationships, or who are unable to express and accept strong feelings, are likely to suffer poor bereavement outcomes [56].

More recently, self-esteem has been studied as a mediating personality variable in coping with loss and bereavement. Lund, Dimond, Caserta, Johnson, Poulton, and Connelly found that low self-esteem, even prior to bereavement, is likely to be predictive of coping difficulties two years following the death of a spouse [71]. Johnson, Lund, and Dimond found an interdependent relationship between self-esteem and coping with bereavement [72]. Whereas higher self-esteem appears to some degree to mitigate coping difficulties, failure to cope can also lower self-esteem.

PREVENTABILITY OF LOSS AND BEREAVEMENT

Another factor theorized to be related to bereavement outcome is the perceived preventability of loss [50]. Bugen argues that the impact of the death of a central love object is likely to be intensified if the mourner views the death as preventable [49]. According to this model, preventability refers to the general belief that factors contributing to the death were not well controlled, or that survivors in some way contributed to the death. Perceptions of preventability are more likely to occur when the cause of death is unknown or when the bereaved was present at the time of death. Prolonged grief is the expected result of loss that is viewed as preventable.

A MODEL OF BEREAVEMENT ADJUSTMENT

Based on the literature on coping strategies and bereavement, we developed the concept of "experienced competence," which takes into consideration the locus of control, coping self-efficacy, history of coping competence, and self-esteem. In our study of 193 bereaved individuals, we found that subjects high in experienced competence reported less loneliness and depression, greater life satisfaction, and the use of more high-level coping strategies in response to bereavement over a six-month time interval than did those scoring low on measures of experienced competence. The Allen and Hayslip (1990) model emphasizes the role of the individual as an active agent in bereavement adjustment. Their focus upon experienced competence adds a cognitive component which may lend insight into variations in adjustment among individuals. Our model is based upon several assumptions:

1. Bereavement presents the widowed person with two major sets of problems: Much of the "assumptive world" has been invalidated, and a major source or reinforcement has been removed. The greater the life change resulting from the loss and the less the loss is anticipated, the greater is the violation of the assumptive world. Reinforcement is removed and basic assumptions are invalidated to the extent to which the lost relationship was a central one. Further, (self) punishment may be added to the removal of reinforcement in the case of loss perceived as preventable. Together, life change, anticipation of loss, centrality of relationship, and perceived preventability combine to yield the impact of loss.

2. The problems described above are aversive to the widowed person, such that the individual may be motivated to reconstruct the assumptive world and obtain new sources of reinforcement. However, in order to do so, there must be adequate resources and utilization of these resources in the mobilization of active coping strategies. Rotter's [73] construct of locus of control, Bandura's [74] construct of self-efficacy, and Seligman's [75] notion of learned helplessness would all predict that only if individuals perceive a causal connection between their behaviors and outcomes will these resources be utilized and coping strategies mobilized. The initiation of the "grief work" will depend upon a personal sense of control over outcome and confidence in one's ability to solve the problems associated with bereavement.

3. This sense of control and confidence in one's ability to cope with bereavement problems comprises a person's experienced competence in the bereavement situation. A sense of control depends upon a general belief in contingency between behavior and outcome, while confidence in coping ability depends upon coping self-efficacy deriving from a

perceived connection between past attempts to cope and good outcome. High self-esteem will both lead to and result from successful coping efforts. Thus, the following make up the variable experienced competence: locus of control, coping self-efficacy, prior history of coping competence, and self-esteem.

4. If "impact" is considered to be the bereavement problem and the solution to this problem depends upon active coping deriving from a sense of experienced competence, then resources help to determine the success of those strategies mobilized in the present situation. This is congruent with Lieberman's finding that low-level resources predict poor outcome, but high-level resources are insufficient to predict good outcome in coping with life stressors [76]. For resources to contribute to good outcome, they must 1) be of sufficiently high level and 2) be utilized. Even high-level resources are not useful unless active coping strategies which utilize these resources are mobilized.

5. Resources must include only what is perceived to be available. Feelings regarding these resources and utilization of resources are outcome variables which depend upon coping success. For example, the number of persons reported to be available and perceived as open to intimate relationships is a better measure of resources than is the presence of intimate relationships. This is because the formation of intimate relationships is a behavior and not a resource, and it is a behavior that depends upon the availability of persons open to intimacy *and* the mobilization of strategies which utilize this social resource. In addition to social resources, there are health/behavioral capacity, cognitive, economic, emotional, and community resources.

Allen and Hayslip found that persons high in experienced competence fared better on broad measures of adjustment following bereavement than did those low in experienced competence [53]. They also found that individuals for whom the loss was more impactful showed more bereavement adjustment difficulties, more negative moods, more depression, more loneliness, more symptoms of distress, and lower life satisfaction than did those for whom the impact of loss was not as great, and that persons with high levels of perceived resources fared better on both broad and specific measures of bereavement adjustment than did those with low levels of perceived resources.

While a test of our model provided support for the roles of experienced competence, impactfulness of loss and extent of resources in understanding bereavement outcomes, it was limited to the exploration of such outcomes over a short-term (6 month) time frame. Moreover, it failed to explore the role that gender differences in bereavement adjustment might play in mediating the effects of these influences on the long-term functioning of bereaved individuals. The next chapter presents a study which incorporates gender in concert with experienced competence, perceived resources, and impact of loss in exploring bereavement outcomes over a long-term (3 year) time frame.

REFERENCES

1. C. Parkes, Bereavement and Mental Illness, *British Journal of Medical Psychology, 38*, pp. 1-26, 1965.
2. C. Parkes, *Bereavement: Studies in Grief in Adult Life*, Basic Books, New York, 1972.
3. C. Parkes and K. Brown, Health after Bereavement, *Psychosomatic Medicine, 34*, pp. 449-461, 1972.
4. K. Rowland, Environmental Events Predicting Death for the Elderly, *Psychological Bulletin, 84*, pp. 349-372, 1977.
5. S. Schleifer, S. Keller, M. Camerino, J. Thornton, and M. Stein, Suppression of Lymphocyte Stimulation following Bereavement, *Journal of the American Medical Association, 250*, pp. 374-377, 1983.
6. F. Norris and S. Murrell, Older Adult Family Stress and Adaptation Before and After Bereavement, *Journal of Gerontology, 42*, pp. 606-612, 1987.
7. L. Pearlin and C. Schooler, The Structure of Coping, *Journal of Health and Social Behavior, 19*, pp. 2-21, 1978.
8. J. Schultz, Death and Dying and Effectiveness of Counseling, *Vocational Guidance, 26*, pp. 365-370, 1978.
9. R. B. Carey, Weathering Widowhood: Problems and Adjustments of the Widowed during the First Year, *Omega, 10*, pp. 163-174, 1979-80.
10. A. Futterman, M. Gilewski, and J. Peterson, The Effects of Late Life Spousal Bereavement Over a 30-Month Interval, *Psychology and Aging, 6*, pp. 434-441, 1991.
11. D. Gallagher, J. Breckenridge, L. Thompson, and J. Peterson, Effects of Bereavement on Indicators of Mental Health in Elderly Widows and Widowers, *Journal of Gerontology, 38*, pp. 565-573, 1983.
12. S. Shuchter and S. Zisook, The Course of Normal Grief, in *Handbook of Bereavement* (pp. 23-43). M. S. Stroebe, W. Stroebe, and R. O. Hansson (eds.), Cambridge, Cambridge, England, 1993.
13. C. Balkwell, Transition to Widowhood: A Review of the Literature, in *Marriage and Family: Coping with Change*, L. Cargan (ed.), Wadsworth, Belmont, California, pp. 312-322, 1985.
14. J. Stevenson, *Death, Grief, and Mourning*, Free Press, New York, 1985.
15. E. A. Bankoff, Social Support and Adaptation to Widowhood, *Journal of Marriage and the Family, 45*, pp. 827-839, 1983.
16. P. R. Silverman, *Widow to Widow*, Springer, New York, 1986.
17. K. Gass, Appraisal, Coping, and Resources: Markers Associated with the Health of Aged Widows and Widowers, in *Older Bereaved Spouses*, D. Lund (ed.), Hemisphere, New York, pp. 79-94, 1989.

18. J. D. DeFrain, D. K. Jakub, and B. L. Mendosa, The Psychological Effects of Sudden Infant Death on Grandmothers and Grandfathers, *Omega, 24*, pp. 165-182, 1991-92.
19. S. S. Rubin, Adult Child Loss and the Two-Track Model of Bereavement, *Omega, 24*, pp. 183-202, 1991-92.
20. R. Carroll and S. Shaefer, Similarities and Differences in Spouses Coping with SIDS, *Omega, 28*, pp. 273-284, 1993-94.
21. M. S. Stroebe and W. Stroebe, Determinants of Adjustment in Older Widows and Widowers, in *Handbook of Bereavement*, M. S. Stroebe, W. Stroebe, and R. O. Hansson (eds.), Cambridge, Cambridge, England, pp. 208-226, 1993.
22. W. Stroebe and M. S. Stroebe, *Bereavement and Health: The Psychological and Physical Consequences of Partner Loss*, Cambridge University Press, Cambridge, 1987.
23. M. S. Stroebe and W. Stroebe, The Mortality of Bereavement: A Review, in *Handbook of Bereavement*, M. S. Stroebe, W. Stroebe, and R. O. Hansson (eds.), Cambridge, Cambridge, England, pp. 175-195, 1993.
24. D. Gallagher-Thompson, A. Futterman, N. Faberow, L. Thompson, and J. Peterson, The Impact of Spousal Bereavement on Older Widows and Widowers, in *Handbook of Bereavement*, M. S. Stroebe, W. Stroebe, and R. O. Hansson (eds.), Cambridge, Cambridge, England, pp. 227-239, 1993.
25. C. Sanders, Risk Factors in Bereavement Outcome, in *Handbook of Bereavement*, M. S. Stroebe, W. Stroebe, and R. O. Hansson (eds.), Cambridge, Cambridge, England, pp. 255-270, 1993.
26. S. Rubin, The Death of a Child is Forever: The Life Course Impact of Child Loss, in *Handbook of Bereavement*, M. S. Stroebe, W. Stroebe, and R. O. Hansson (eds.), Cambridge, Cambridge, England, pp. 285-298, 1993.
27. N. W. Arbuckle and B. DeVries, *The Long Term Effects of Later Life Spousal and Parental Bereavement on Personal Functioning*, paper presented at the Annual Scientific Meeting of the Gerontological Society, New Orleans, Louisiana, November 1993.
28. C. B. Wortman, R. C. Silver, and R. C. Kessler, The Meaning of Loss and Adjustment to Bereavement, in *Handbook of Bereavement*, M. S. Stroebe, W. Stroebe, and R. O. Hansson (eds.), Cambridge, Cambridge, England, pp. 349-366, 1993.
29. L. Thompson, D. Gallagher, H. Cover, M. Gilewski, and J. Peterson, Effects of Bereavement on Symptoms of Psychopathology in Older Men and Women, in *Older Bereaved Spouses*, D. Lund (ed.), Hemisphere, New York, pp. 3-15, 1989.
30. D. Lund, M. Caserta, and M. Dimond, Testing for Gender Differences through Two Years of Bereavement among the Elderly, *The Gerontologist, 26*, pp. 314-320, 1986.
31. D. Lund, M. Caserta, M. Dimond, and K. Shaffer, Competencies, Tasks of Daily Living, and Adjustments to Spousal Bereavement in Later Life, in *Older Bereaved Spouses*, D. Lund (ed.), Hemisphere, New York, pp. 135-152, 1989.

32. M. Faletti, J. Gibbs, M. Clark, R. Pruchno, and E. Berman, Longitudinal Course of Bereavement in Older Adults, in *Older Bereaved Spouses,* D. Lund (ed.), Hemisphere, New York, pp. 37-51, 1989.

33. S. Van Zandt, R. Mou, and D. Abbott, Mental and Physical Health of Rural Nonbereaved Elders: A Longitudinal Study, in *Older Bereaved Spouses,* D. Lund (ed.), Hemisphere, New York, pp. 25-35, 1989.

34. J. W. Worden and P. S. Silverman, Grief and Depression in Newly Widowed Parents with School-Age Children, *Omega, 27,* pp. 251-261, 1993.

35. P. J. Robinson and S. Fleming, Differentiating Grief and Depression, *Hospital Journal, 5,* pp. 77-88, 1989.

36. K. Gass, Health of Older Widowers: Role of Appraisal, Coping, Resources, and Type of Spouses Death, in *Older Bereaved Spouses,* D. Lund (ed.), Hemisphere, New York, pp. 95-110, 1989.

37. D. Gallagher, S. Lovett, P. Hanley-Dunn, and L. Thompson, Use of Select Coping Strategies during Late-Life Spousal Bereavement, in *Older Bereaved Spouses,* D. Lund (ed.), Hemisphere, New York, pp. 111-121, 1989.

38. T. M. Meuser, R. M. Davis, and S. J. Marwit, Personality and Conjugal Bereavement in Older Widow(er)s, *Omega, 30,* pp. 223-235, 1994-95.

39. M. Caserta and D. Lund, Bereavement Stress and Coping among Older Adults: Expectations versus the Actual Experience, *Omega, 25,* pp. 33-46, 1992.

40. J. J. Ponzetti, Bereaved Families: A Comparison of Parents' and Grandparents' Reactions to the Death of a Child, *Omega, 25,* pp. 63-72, 1992.

41. L. H. Levy, K. S. Martinkowski, and J. F. Derby, Differences in Patterns of Adaptation in Conjugal Bereavement: Their Sources and Potential Significance, *Omega, 29,* pp. 71-81, 1994.

42. L. J. Solie and L. J. Fielder, The Relationship between Sex Role Identity and a Widow's Adjustment to the Loss of a Spouse, *Omega, 18,* pp. 33-40, 1987-88.

43. M. Stroebe and W. Stroebe, Who Participates in Bereavement Research? A Review of Empirical Study, *Omega, 20,* pp. 1-29, 1989.

44. B. Valanis and R. Yeaworth, Ratings of Physical and Mental Health in the Older Bereaved, *Research in Nursing and Health, 5,* pp. 137-146, 1982.

45. L. H. Levy, J. F. Darby, and K. S. Martinkowski, The Question of Who Participates in Bereavement Research and the Bereavement Risk Index, *Omega, 25,* pp. 225-238, 1992.

46. D. Lund and M. Caserta, Older Bereaved Spouses Participation in Self-Help Groups, *Omega, 25,* pp. 47-62, 1992.

47. M. C. Feinson, Aging Widows and Widowers: Are There Mental Health Differences? *International Journal of Aging and Human Development, 23,* pp. 241-253, 1986.

48. D. A. Lund, Conclusions about Bereavement in Later Life and Implications for Interventions and Future Research, in *Older Bereaved Spouses,* D. Lund (ed.), Hemisphere, New York, pp. 217-231, 1989.

49. L. Bugen, Human Grief: A Model for Prediction and Intervention, *American Journal of Orthopsychiatray, 47,* pp. 196-206, 1977.
50. M. Caserta, J. Van Pelt, and D. Lund, Advice on the Adjustment to Loss from Bereaved Older Adults: An Examination of Resources and Outcomes, in *Older Bereaved Spouses,* D. Lund (ed.), Hemisphere, New York, pp. 123-134, 1989.
51. M. Dimond, D. Lund, and M. Caserta, The Role of Social Support in the First Two Years of Bereavement in an Elderly Sample, *The Gerontologist, 27,* pp. 599-604, 1987.
52. I. Glick, R. Weiss, and C. Parkes, *The First Year of Bereavement,* Wiley, New York, 1974.
53. S. Allen and B. Hayslip, *A Model for Predicting Bereavement Outcome in Adulthood,* paper presented at the Annual Scientific Meeting of the Gerontological Society, Boston, Massachusetts, November 1990.
54. J. Bowlby, *Attachment and Loss: Loss, Sadness, and Depression* (Vol. 3), Basic Books, New York, 1980.
55. S. Folkman, R. Lazarus, S. Pinley, and J. Novacek, Age Differences in Stress and Coping Processes, *Psychology and Aging, 2,* pp. 171-184, 1987.
56. B. Raphael, *The Anatomy of Bereavement,* Basic, New York, 1983.
57. G. Kelly, *The Psychology of Personal Constructs,* Norton, New York, 1955.
58. C. Parkes, Determinants of Outcome Following Bereavement, *Omega, 6,* pp. 303-323, 1975.
59. P. J. Clayton, J. A. Halikas, W. L. Maurise, and E. Robbins, Anticipatory Grief and Widowhood, *British Journal of Psychiatry, 122,* pp. 47-51, 1973.
60. E. Lindemann, Symptomatology and Management of Acute Grief, *American Journal of Psychiatry, 101,* pp. 144-148, 1944.
61. G. G. Kitson, H. Z. Lopata, W. M. Holmes, and S. M. Meyering, Divorcees and Widows: Similarities and Differences, *American Journal of Orthopsychiatry, 59,* pp. 291-301, 1980.
62. M. L. S. Vachon, J. Rogers, A. W. Lyall, W. J. Lancee, A. R. Sheldon, and S. J. J. Freeman, Predictors and Correlates of Adaptation to Conjugal Bereavement, *American Journal of Psychiatry, 139,* pp. 998-1002, 1982.
63. A. Duran, C. Turner, and D. Lund, Social Support, Perceived Stress, and Depression Following the Death of a Spouse in Later Life, in *Older Bereaved Spouses,* D. Lund (ed.), Hemisphere, New York, pp. 68-78, 1989.
64. T. Schuster and E. Butler, Bereavement, Social Networks, Social Support, and Mental Health, in *Older Bereaved Spouses,* D. Lund (ed.), Hemisphere, New York, pp. 55-68, 1989.
65. K. Walker, A. MacBride, and M. Vachon, Social Support Networks and Crisis of Bereavement, *Social Science & Medicine, 11,* pp. 35-41, 1977.
66. B. J. Hirsch, Natural Support Systems and Coping with Major Life Changes, *American Journal of Community Psychology, 8:2,* pp. 159-171, 1980.
67. M. Lowenthal and C. Haven, Interaction and Adaptation: Intimacy as a Critical Variable, *American Sociological Review, 33,* pp. 20-30, 1968.

68. H. Lopata, On Widowhood: Grief Work and Identity Reconstruction, *Journal of Geriatric Psychiatry, 8,* pp. 41-55, 1975.
69. D. Maddison and W. Walker, Factors Affecting the Outcome of Conjugal Bereavement, *British Journal of Psychiatry, 113,* pp. 1057-1067, 1967.
70. M. Parkes and R. S. Weiss, *Recovery from Bereavement,* Basic, New York, 1983.
71. D. Lund, M. Dimond, M. Caserta, R. Johnson, J. Poulton, and J. Connelly, Identifying Elderly with Coping Difficulties after Two Years of Bereavement, *Omega, 16,* pp. 213-224, 1985-86.
72. R. J. Johnson, D. A. Lund, and M. F. Dimond, Stress, Self-Esteem, and Coping during Bereavement among the Elderly, *Social Psychology Quarterly, 49,* pp. 273-279, 1986.
73. J. Rotter, Generalized Expectancies for Internal versus External Control of Reinforcement, *Psychological Monographs, 80,* p. 609, 1966.
74. A. Bandura, Regulation of Cognitive Processes through Self Efficiency, *Developmental Psychology, 25,* pp. 729-735, 1989.
75. M. Seligman, *Helplessness: On Depression, Development and Death,* Freeman, San Francisco, 1975.
76. M. Lieberman, Adaptive Processes in Later Life, in *Life Span Developmental Psychology: Normative Life Crises,* N. Daton and L. Ginzberg (eds.), Academic, New York, 1975.

PART II

Research on Grief

The five chapters which comprise this part of the book all make contributions to our understanding about the ways men grieve by adding research findings to our knowledge base. Other chapters in this book also present findings from research, but these five chapters have research type questions, data collection, and data analyses as focal points. These five studies do not represent much of the diversity that exists among completed research about men and grief because four of the five deal with widowers and one makes use of funeral directors as respondents. These projects, however, do provide evidence regarding some of the messages conveyed in the introduction to this book. Most important is the recognition that while the typical man may differ from the typical woman in their responses to grief, they also have much in common. Also, there is a wide range of coping responses and outcomes among men, just as there is among women. As Doka and Martin reported in Chapter 3, gender is only one factor that influences how we grieve.

The first chapter in this section (Chapter 8), "The Role of Gender in a Three-Year Longitudinal Study of Bereavement: A Test of the Experienced Competence Model" by Bert Hayslip, Jr., Susan Allen, and Laura McCoy-Roberts, provides a research test of the bereavement coping model they described in Chapter 7. Again, the key factors in this model are locus of control, coping self-efficacy, history of coping competence, and self-esteem with availability of resources and impact of loss as mediating variables. The authors concluded that only minimal differences were found between men and women, with widowers experiencing slightly less difficulty coping with bereavement. Although much of this chapter is quite technical and statistical in nature, their model of experienced competence is a valuable and helpful conceptual tool to predict bereavement outcomes and guide the development of interventions for both men and women.

Chapter 9, "When the Unexpected Happens: Husbands Coping With the Deaths of Their Wives" by Dale Lund and Michael Caserta, presents the results of two more studies of spousal bereavement. This chapter focuses primarily on comparing widowers of different ages to determine the extent to which age and life circumstances impact how men grieve the loss of their wives. Their findings revealed that men in their seventies appeared to have the greatest difficulty with grief, depression, and coping, but they also showed considerable benefits from participating in gender-mixed support groups. Some of the high degree of difficulty for these men might be attributed to their life circumstances of experiencing additional loss of status due to retirement and the loss of a companion with whom they were expecting to spend greater amounts of time over the coming years. Conversely, men in their fifties appeared to be the most effective in coping with their grief. The authors discuss these issues further, along with highlighting the diversity among men in how they grieve and cope with loss.

Douglas O'Neill and Robert Mendelsohn, authors of Chapter 10, "American Widowers With School-Age Children: An Exploratory Study of Role Change and Role Conflict," report on the results of their unique study of widowers adjusting to being a single parent. Their chapter identifies the importance of sociodemographic factors which influence the way men adjust to the role changes and role conflicts created by their loss. They make use of an interactionist perspective and show how this conceptual framework not only helps to understand the way men grieve but can be helpful in guiding practical interventions. This chapter could have been included in Part I of this book because of the comprehensive description of their perspective, but it was more appropriate to include it here because they provide unique research findings.

Chapter 11, "Gender Differences Related to Sexuality in Widowhood: Is it a Problem for the Male Bereaved?" by Kathryn Hustins, is a relatively brief chapter but it examines an important and often ignored topic. Hustins found that men were much more likely than women to develop a sexual relationship with another person by the end of the first year of widowhood. Many men, however, experienced value conflict between their religious beliefs and sexual interests and practices. The author appropriately recommends more education regarding sexuality in widowhood and the value in seeking professional help when needed.

Paul Sakalauskas takes the reader to a small but unique research sample of funeral directors and reports, in Chapter 12, what he learned from their opinions about the ways men and women differ in their coping styles. In his chapter, "Male Attitudes on Funeral Rites and Rituals," Sakalauskas focuses primarily on the gender differences that funeral directors observe when they interact at various times with bereaved family members. As expected, men were reported to be most concerned with the costs associated with the funeral and women were most concerned about the appearance of the body and with social relationships related to family and friends. While some gender differences were identified, the author argues that men should not be forced into expressing their grief in ways that might be inconsistent with their upbringing. Similar to Sakalauskas, most of the chapter authors in this section of the book conclude with some recommendations regarding ways to help, intervene, or prevent serious long-term coping difficulties. The next part of the book presents chapters which focus primarily on practical, clinical, and helping strategies.

CHAPTER 8

The Role of Gender in a Three-Year Longitudinal Study of Bereavement: A Test of the Experienced Competence Model

Bert Hayslip, Jr., Susan E. Allen,
and Laura McCoy-Roberts

The role of gender in concert with experienced competence, perceived resources, and impact of loss was explored in the context of a three-year longitudinal study of bereavement outcome. Results suggested that while the effects of experienced competence, perceived resources, and impact of loss were substantial, gender differences in bereavement outcome were minimal as were the interactions among gender and these influences on bereavement adjustment. The few gender effects that did emerge suggested that men have a less difficult time than women in coping with bereavement. In light of the expectation that gender would play an important role in adjusting to loss, factors influencing the lack of gender effects found in this study are discussed.

The previous chapter reviewed research on gender differences regarding the impact of bereavement and presented a model of bereavement adjustment that supports the roles that experienced competence, perceived resources, and impact of loss play in influencing bereavement outcomes over a six-month period of time. The study presented in this chapter longitudinally explores the extent to which gender differences in bereavement outcome are mediated by the effects of coping competence, personal impact of the loss, and the extent of resources utilized by bereaved persons, building on the short-term longitudinal research of Allen and Hayslip [1]. While main effects for gender would not be surprising, the real foci here are the interactions between gender, time of measurement, and the proposed mediators of bereavement adjustment reviewed in the preceding chapter.

SUBJECTS

Volunteers consisted of 147 conjugally bereaved persons and forty-six persons bereaved of a close relative other than spouse. All persons volunteered for participation by responding to announcements made at bereavement groups and widowhood association meetings or placed in newspapers and senior citizens' newsletters. The median length of time bereaved for the widowed group was from one to two years, while the median for the nonwidowed bereaved group was from two to three years. All persons had been bereaved for ten years or less. Although all widowed individuals responded to the questionnaire with regard to loss of a spouse, 48 percent had suffered an additional loss of a close friend or relative in the past two years. For most persons (56% of the sample), the loss was of a relative other than mother, father, child, or sibling. Of the nonwidowed bereaved group, 11 percent had lost a child, 35 percent their mother, 30 percent their father, 9 percent a sibling, and 15 percent another close relative. In both groups, the most common cause of death of the loved one was prolonged illness (48% for widowed, 39% for nonwidowed bereaved), followed by sudden or brief illness (37% for widowed, 25% for nonwidowed), accident (9% for widowed, 19% for nonwidowed), and finally "other" (4% for widowed, 17% for non-widowed). Although no formal data were gathered on whether death resulted from suicide, informally gathered data (letters, telephone conversations) suggested that a high percentage of persons in the "other" category had lost their spouse or relative to suicide. Five percent of the widowed group had been widowed twice.

Widowed persons ranged in age from twenty-six to eighty-two with a mean age of fifty-eight, and were mostly female (129 females and 18 males). Nonwidowed bereaved subjects ranged in age from twenty to seventy with a mean age of 40.6, and were also predominantly female (35 women and 11 men). A high percentage of subjects in both groups were caucasian (99% of widowed and 96% of nonwidowed sample). The remainder were primarily Latin American in the widowed group and Black in the nonwidowed bereaved group. With regard to religion, both groups were primarily Protestant (62% for widowed persons and 74% for nonwidowed bereaved) or Catholic (29% for widowed and 17% for nonwidowed persons). Of the remainder, the largest number were Jewish. For both groups, the median education level was "some college." More variability existed in the education level of the widowed than the nonwidowed group. For example, in the widowed group, 13 percent had not finished high school and 10 percent had earned advanced degrees. Those figures for the nonwidowed bereaved group were 2 percent and 4 percent, respectively. Widowed persons had been married to their deceased spouse from one to fifty-five years, with a mean of 29.4 years. Nonwidowed bereaved subjects had been married from zero to forty-nine years, with an average of 20.6 years. Twenty-five percent of the widowed subjects had been married more than once, while only 7 percent of the nonwidowed bereaved subjects had been married more than once. Volunteers had from zero to ten living children, with a mean of 2.5 for the widowed subjects and 2.1 for the nonwidowed bereaved subjects.

With regard to current living situation, the majority of widowed persons lived alone in their own home (65%) followed by living with a child (10%). The remainder lived alone with a pet (6%), alone in an apartment or boarding house (5%), with current spouse (3%) or other relative (3%), with friend or roommate (2%), or "other" (6%). The majority of the nonwidowed bereaved lived with a spouse (65%). The remainder lived with a friend or roommate (16%), alone in an apartment or boarding house (7%), with another relative (5%), alone with a pet (2%), or "other" (5%).

With regard to occupation, the largest group of widowed persons was retired (36%) followed by those who worked part time (13%), were temporarily unemployed (3%), or "other" (2%). The largest number of nonwidowed bereaved subjects worked full-time (36%) followed by those who worked part-time (29%), were temporarily unemployed (10%), were homemakers (9%), were retired (2%), or "other" (1%). Income (combined with spouses if married) ranged from less than $5,000 per year to $50,000 per year for widowed and from less than $5,000 to more than $50,000 for nonwidowed bereaved persons. The median income range was from $16,000 to $25,000 per year for the former group and from $26,000 to $35,000 per year for the latter.

In addition to the current bereavement situation, the majority of persons had suffered other major losses through death at some point in their lives. Of the widowed group, 15 percent had lost a child, 82 percent their father, 73 percent their mother, 88 percent another close relative, 79 percent a close friend, and 46 percent a sibling. For the nonwidowed bereaved group, 18 percent had lost a child through death, 70 percent their father, 49 percent their mother, 88 percent another close relative, 42 percent a close friend, and 33 percent a sibling. Whereas 72 percent of the widowed persons had attended to were attending a bereavement group. Only 12 percent of the nonwidowed bereaved persons had attended or were attending a bereavement group.

With respect to health, 7 percent of the widowed and 15 percent of the nonwidowed bereaved claimed that their health was poorer than that of their age peers, on the average. Nineteen percent of the former group and 13 percent of the latter said that they currently had a major medical or psychiatric illness. Many individuals in both groups had sought psychiatric or psychological help in dealing with bereavement (23% of widowed and 30% of nonwidowed bereaved subjects).

The previous chapter provides a broader theoretical background within which the principal independent variables explored in this study can be understood, based on the model developed by Allen and Hayslip [1].

VARIABLE 1: EXPERIENCED COMPETENCE

Experienced competence was measured in four ways. The first experienced competence component was termed *prior strategies,* derived from a scale designed for the present study called the *Coping Competence Scale* (described below). The second measure of experienced competence was termed *coping self-efficacy,* derived from the Coping Self-Efficacy Scale (CSES), also designed for this study (described below). The third measure of experienced competence consisted of Levenson's revised Locus of Control Scales [2]. The fourth and final measure of experienced competence was Rosenberg's revised version of the Guttman Scale of Self-Esteem [3].

The Coping Competence Scale

This scale includes items from seven coping categories found in the bereavement literature to be used by widowed persons. The categories are 1) cognitive coping strategies, 2) social coping strategies, 3) behavioral coping strategies, 4) affective coping strategies, 5) seeking support and guidance, 6) focus on spouse (including items related to illusion and sanctification), and 7) denial/avoidance.

For each item, the bereaved person was asked to indicate: 1) whether or not the strategy has been used previous to bereavement (to cope with a major loss or change), 2) how helpful the strategy was viewed as being at that time, 3) whether or not the strategy has been used in coping with conjugal bereavement, and 4) how helpful the strategy has been viewed as being in dealing with conjugal bereavement.

The *prior strategies* score was calculated as the total number of coping strategies mobilized prior to bereavement to cope with a major loss or change. The number and type of strategies mobilized in coping with conjugal bereavement is *not* included in this score but is instead considered a dependent measure (see below).

The Coping Self-Efficacy Scale (CSES)

Bandura states that, in order to measure self-efficacy, individuals should be presented with self-efficacy scales representing tasks varying in difficulty, complexity, or some similar dimension [4]. The scale should be fitted to the domain being measured.

The CSES designed for this study consisted of items related to bereavement tasks, such as learning to feel comfortable alone in social situations or overcoming feelings of extreme remorse and sadness. Notice that these are *coping tasks* rather than *coping strategies*. A panel of ten Ph.D. psychologists rated sixty intuitively-derived items as representing various levels of difficulty for most people. Twenty intuitively derived items thought to represent each of three levels of difficulty were presented to the above panel of psychologists. The three possible levels were: 1) not difficult for most persons, 2) moderately difficult for most persons, and 3) highly difficult for most persons. Eighty percent agreement among the ten psychologists was required in order for the item to be retained. The ten items with the highest agreement for each level (yielding a total of 30 items) comprised the original scale. However, based upon alpha coefficients, two items from level one were dropped, yielding a total of twenty-eight items. With these items omitted, the alpha coefficients were .89 for the scale as a whole, .71 for the group of level 1 items, .81 for level 2 items, and .81 for level 3 items.

When the scale was administered, persons were asked to judge for each item whether or not they believed they could successfully complete the task (responding "yes" or "no"). The number of points received for endorsing each item corresponded to the number indicating the level of difficulty, such that higher scores reflect higher levels of coping self-efficacy.

Locus of Control

Levenson's [2] revision of Rotter's [5] Locus of Control Scale (I-E Scale) was the third indicator of experienced competence. Levenson's instrument contains three scales measuring internal locus of control (I scale), control by powerful others (the P scale), and control by chance or fate (the C scale). Twenty-four items in a Likert format comprise the instrument. Levenson found that the P and C scales are positively correlated with one another, and both correlate negatively with the

I scale ($p < .01$). For purposes of this study, scores on the combined P and C scales were subtracted from scores on the I scale.

Rosenberg's Revised Guttman Self-Esteem Scale

Rosenberg's ten-item revision of the Guttman Self-Esteem Scale represented the final measure of experienced competence, and has a test-retest reliability of .92 [3]. High scores on the self-esteem scale indicate a high degree of self-satisfaction and acceptance. The prior strategies, coping self-efficacy, locus of control, and self-esteem scores were summed to create an Experienced Competence score, and a median split on time 1 scores was used to differentiate persons for this independent variable.

VARIABLE 2:
AVAILABLE RESOURCES QUESTIONNAIRE

A series of questions were developed to assess perceived resources of the following types: cognitive/educational, social/interpersonal, health/behavioral capacity, economic, emotional, and community. Some items were taken from indices reported by Arling to have been used by Project PLEA (Piedmont Life Enrichment for the Aged) [6]. Other items were intuitively derived, based on the existing literature. In tests of reliability, coefficient alphas were .79 for the scale as a whole, .79 for the cognitive/educational subscale, .74 for the social/ interpersonal subscale, .81 for the health/behavioral capacity subscale, .88 for the economic subscale, .77 for the emotional subscale, and .69 for the community subscale. It should be emphasized that only resources perceived to be available were measured; the degree to which they were mobilized and feelings about the value of mobilizing these resources were considered dependent measures, and were tapped by instruments measuring outcome.

On the basis of scores on this questionnaire, persons were divided into high and low resource groups in the following manor. Those scoring in the bottom half of the Coping Resources Questionnaire (CRQ) at time 1 as a whole or scoring in the bottom third on any CRQ subscale at time 1 were placed in the low perceived resource group. All other persons were placed in the high perceived resource group.

An *Impact of Loss Questionnaire* developed for this study contained items related to the following four areas: 1) centrality of the lost relationship prior to bereavement, 2) degree to which the death of spouse or loved one was perceived as preventable, 3) degree of life change associated with the loss (and other simultaneous life crises), and 4) degree to which death of spouse was anticipated or expected.

As discussed above, each of these appears related to bereavement outcome. They are assumed to measure the degree to which reinforcement has been removed (or punishment initiated, in the case of perceived preventability) and the extent to which the construct system has been invalidated. Where relevant, items were taken from the Horowitz and Wilner *Impact of Events Scale,* omitting items that appeared to be confounded with the use of ineffective coping strategies [7].

Items measuring centrality of the lost relationship focus upon the emotional intensity of the relationship before bereavement and the degree to which the marital relationship was a central focus in the life of the bereaved spouse. Those items measuring the degree to which loss was anticipated or expected include questions about the suddenness of death as well as the general expectation before bereavement that one's spouse might die. Life-change items focus upon the pre- and post-bereavement differences in everyday life. Finally, questions designed to measure perceived preventability of death focus upon the degree to which the person believed that external factors contributing to the death were well-controlled and the degree to which the individual perceived himself or herself to have done everything possible to prevent the death.

Reliability statistics yielded coefficient alphas of .77 for the scale as a whole, .86 for the centrality subscale, .81 for the preventability subscale, .56 for the life change subscale, and .81 for the anticipation subscale.

Items measuring life change, perceived preventability, and centrality of the lost relationship were assigned positive values, while items measuring anticipation of loss were assigned negative values. Overall positive scores indicated a high impact of loss. A median split of scores at time 1 was utilized in order to derive high and low impact groups.

DEPENDENT VARIABLES

Variable 1: Coping Strategies Mobilized

It will be recalled that the total number of coping strategies mobilized in response to loss or change prior to bereavement was listed as an independent variable above. Two related dependent measures were derived from the *Coping Competence Scale* (described above). The first was the absolute number of coping strategies reported mobilized in the current bereavement situation.

Variable 2: Cognitive, Social, Affective, and Behavioral Strategies

The second dependent measure derived from the *Coping Competence Scale* was the total number of coping strategies reported mobilized in the current bereavement situation that fit into the categories of cognitive, social, affective, and behavioral strategies, based upon existing literature.

Variable 3: Revised UCLA Loneliness Scale

This instrument is described by Russell, Peplau, and Cutrona as eliminating the positive response bias that presented a problem with the earlier version of the scale [8]. Statistical analysis shows that the measure is more related to other ratings of loneliness than to mood states or personality variables, but is related to feeling abandoned, depressed, empty, isolated, and self-enclosed and with not feeling satisfied or sociable. A coefficient alpha of .94 was obtained by the authors.

Variable 4: Profile of Mood States (POMS)

A revised version of an earlier instrument (Psychiatric Outpatient Mood States) was described by McNair and Lorr [9]. Five factors were clearly delineated through factor analysis: tension/anxiety, anger/hostility, depression/dejection, fatigue/inertia, and vigor/activity. Items from all but the last factor listed above (vigor/activity) were used in the present study. Kuder-Richardson reliability coefficients for three of the four factors used in this study are above .90. The scale differentiates psychiatric patients from normals and is sensitive to improvement with treatment [9].

Variable 5: Life Satisfaction Index-Z

The LSI-Z is a shortened, revised version of Neugarten, Havighurst, and Tobin's Life Satisfaction Index-A, designed to measure the evaluations of life satisfaction and to be relatively independent of measures of activity level and social participation, wherein this instrument measures zest versus apathy, resolution, and fortitude, congruence between desired and achieved goals, self-concept, and mood tone [10]. The revised LSI-Z was shortened to contain thirteen items and has a coefficient alpha of .79 [11].

Variable 6: Hopkins Symptom Checklist (HSCL)

The HSCL is a self-report symptom inventory comprised of items representative of symptoms frequently seen in outpatients. Persons are instructed to rate themselves on each symptom using a 4-point scale of distress with reference to their experience in the past seven days. A series of factor analytic studies by Derogatis and his colleagues revealed five primary symptom dimensions labeled somatization, obsessive-compulsive, interpersonal sensitivity, depression, and anxiety [12]. Subsequent studies utilizing large samples have supported this factor structure. Coefficient alphas reported in the literature for the fifty-eight-item version of the scale are as follows: .87 for the somatization subscale, .87 for the obsessive-compulsive subscale, .85 for the interpersonal sensitivity subscale, .86 for the depression subscale, and .84 for the anxiety subscale. For purposes of this study, a short version (44 items) of the HSCL was employed, utilizing only those items reported by Derogatis, Lipman, Rickels, Wenhuth, and Covi to principally load on each of the five factors [13].

Variable 7: The Beck Depression Inventory (BDI)

The BDI is a self-report inventory designed to measure the behavioral manifestations of depression. The Pearson split-half reliability is reported as .86; the Pearson biserial r between BDI scores and clinical judgments of depth of depression is in the range of .65 to .67 [14].

Variable 8: The Bereavement Experience Questionnaire

The Bereavement Experience Questionnaire (BEQ) is a self-report, Likert-type scale containing sixty-seven items measuring distress related to conjugal bereavement [15]. The BEQ is composed of eight subscales: guilt, anger, yearning, depersonalization, stigma, morbid fears, meaninglessness, and isolation. Persons are asked to respond to experiences in the last month. Scoring for each item is coded on a 4-point scale. Higher scores indicate higher levels of bereavement-related distress. The BEQ was utilized in a study of perceptions of bereavement of widowed persons and helping professionals by Conway, Hayslip, and Tandy [16]. The authors indicated that the BEQ has acceptable validity and reliability [see 16]. Conway et al. found the BEQ scores of widows and helping professionals to differ significantly [16].

PROCEDURE

Within two weeks of volunteering, persons received a packet containing a letter of thanks for participating and a sheet of instructions, an informed consent form, an explanation of the study, and all of the instruments described above. Widowed and non-widowed persons received slightly different packets. For non-widowed persons, some wording of items on the Coping Competence Scale and Impact of Loss Scale was altered so that items did not refer to "spouse" or being "widowed." Also, widowed persons were asked to respond to the items on the Coping Competence Scale both with regard to widowhood and with regard to a previous loss, resulting in twice as many items on that scale for widowed as for non-widowed individuals. Aside from those differences, packets for widowed and non-widowed volunteers were identical. Persons were requested to return the packets in an enclosed, stamped, addressed envelope, within two weeks.

Upon volunteering, persons were told that the study would be conducted in two parts, and that they would be asked to fill out the same questionnaire again six months after the first time of measurement. As planned, packets identical to the first were sent six months from the date the first packet was sent. The procedure at six months was identical to that of the first time of measurement.

Three years after the original data had been collected, persons were again contacted by mail. In a letter from the original researcher, the findings of the earlier study were briefly outlined and persons were thanked for their participation. Enclosed with the letter was a packet, identical to the first two, with the exception of an additional item asking whether an additional death of a loved one had occurred within the interval between times of measurement. Individuals who had suffered an additional loss were asked to answer relevant items with the most recent loss in mind. Individuals were asked to complete the packet once again and to return it in the enclosed, stamped, addressed envelope. The procedure at this final time of measurement was identical to that of the first two.

By the second time of measurement, six months after initial testing, 18 percent of the original sample had dropped out. At the third time of measurement, three years later, another 34 percent had dropped out, leaving approximately 48 percent of the original sample.

RESULTS

Findings for individuals with complete data at all occasions were analyzed via a series of repeated measures MANOVA's (see Table 1),

Table 1. Adjusted Means for Measures of Bereavement Outcome

	Level of Impact				Extent of Resources				Experienced Competence			
	High		Low		High		Low		High		Low	
	M^a	F^b	M	F	M	F	M	F	M	F	M	F
BEQ^c	189.39	202.17	166.86	163.99	174.31	170.57	188.43	193.33	175.85	169.15	194.94	194.25
BDI^d	10.07	17.81	4.62	11.31	6.03	8.70	10.51	19.38	6.67	9.36	12.21	18.68
HSC^e	113.25	138.31	116.20	112.86	109.40	111.52	116.38	138.83	112.71	110.22	117.66	137.65
UCLA Loneliness	69.44	74.45	57.16	61.70	60.58	62.94	68.30	74.25	63.59	58.89	70.68	75.32
Life Satisfaction	15.11	20.92	9.96	15.61	12.57	12.31	14.77	22.98	12.17	11.99	16.75	23.26
POMS^f	38.46	53.68	34.64	30.39	28.48	35.47	39.05	53.14	36.26	26.22	40.28	54.41
Strategies Used^g	84.33	87.27	86.74	73.20	80.83	95.79	76.66	79.73	88.78	77.64	77.98	82.06
High Level Strategies Used^h	56.30	57.44	57.15	50.99	56.38	63.04	51.50	52.47	58.74	54.62	52.48	53.89
Overall Adjustment^i	434.75	507.35	389.46	395.87	390.32	402.60	437.46	501.94	407.28	385.85	452.55	503.59

[a]Males, *ns* = 5 to 10
[b]Females, *ns* = 35 to 60
[c]Bereavement Experience Questionnaire
[d]Beck Depression Inventory
[e]Hopkins Symptom Checklist
[f]Profile of Mood States
[g]Total Strategies Mobilized
[h]Total high level (cognitive, affective, social, behavioral) strategies mobilized
[i]Sum of BEQ, BDI, HSC, Life Satisfaction, POMS, UCLA Loneliness; lower scores indicate better adjustment

wherein gender was crossed with either the extent of impactfulness of the death, extent of resources, or level of experienced competence. In each case, the latter variables' distributions at the initial occasion of measurement were dichotomized to create two levels of the between-subjects factors of interest in the present study. Cell sizes were considerably smaller for males, ranging from 5 to 10 per cell, whereas those for females were much larger, varying between 35 and 50 per cell. As gender did not vary ($\chi^2_1 = .18$, $p > .05$) with the nature of the bereavement-related loss (spouse vs. other relative or close friend), data were collapsed across the specific nature of the loss. Moreover, equal proportions of males and females dropped out at the six-month ($\chi^2_1 = .03$, $p > .05$) and three-year ($\chi^2_1 = .26$, $p > .05$) occasions of measurement. Especially given the small number of males in the study, univariate effects were only explored if the multivariate effects were statistically significant, to avoid a capitalization on chance in the interpretation of findings.

A gender (male vs. female) by levels of experienced competence (high vs. low) by time (initial occasion of measurement, six-months, three-year follow-ups) repeated measures MANCOVA was initially carried out. Duration of time in months since bereavement was utilized as a covariate, as persons who had been bereaved for more than two years experienced fewer adjustment difficulties than did those who had been bereaved for two years or less (Multivariate $F_{8,87} = 7.25$, $p < .01$).

When experienced competence (EC) was crossed with gender, multivariate main effects for gender were not statistically significant, while those for EC approached significance ($F_{8,83} = 1.95$, $p < .06$). Post hoc univariate analyses suggested that persons who had higher EC scores also had lower BEQ scores, $F_{1,90} = 4.68$, $p < .05$, lower BDI scores, $F_{1,90} = 8.74$, $p < .01$, were less lonely, $F_{1,90} = 6.47$, $p < .01$, were more satisfied with their lives, $F_{1,90} = 12.30$, $p < .01$, and were less emotionally distressed (POMS), $F_{1,90} = 3.95$, $p < .05$. Neither the main effects for occasion, nor any of the remaining interactions were statistically significant at the multivariate level.

When gender was crossed with levels of perceived resources, analyses yielded a statistically significant multivariate main effect for resources, $F_{8,83} = 2.95$, $p < .01$, with persons reporting greater levels of perceived resources being less depressed, $F_{1,90} = 10.45$, $p < .01$, reporting fewer psychological symptoms of distress, $F_{1,90} = 4.32$, $p < .05$, being less lonely, $F_{1,90} = 4.12$, $p < .05$, being more life satisfied, $F_{1,90} = 7.92$, $p < .01$, and mobilizing more cognitive, behavioral, affective, and social coping strategies to cope with their loss, $F_{1,90} = 4.70$, $p < .05$. Multivariate main effects for gender were also substantial, $F_{8,83} = 2.27$,

$p < .05$, and were particular to depression, $F_{1,90} = 6.00$, $p < .01$, with males reporting less depression (BDI) than females. Men also tended, $F_{1,90} = 3.41$, $p < .06$, to report greater levels of life satisfaction than did women. The multivariate main effects for occasion of measurement as well as all of the interactions among occasion, gender, and level of resources were not statistically significant.

When gender was crossed with the degree of subjective impactfulness of loss, neither main effects for gender, occasion, or impact were found. However, a multivariate impact by occasion effect was obtained, $F_{16,352} = 1.87$, $p < .02$, particular to HSC scores, $F_{2,182} = 7.77$, $p < .01$, with those for whom the subjective impact of loss was greater reporting fewer psychological symptoms than those for whom the loss was more impactful at occasions 1 and 2. At occasion 3, however, each group's HSC scores were quite similar, suggesting a long-term reappearance of stressful symptoms for less impacted persons, versus those who reported more impact, for whom the level of symptoms declined. None of the remaining interactions were statistically significant.

A further similar set of exploratory analyses was carried out, controlling for the effect of occasion 1 scores on occasion 2 scores, and for the effect of occasion 2 scores on occasion 3 scores. In this set of ANCOVAs, the main effects of impact on HCS occasion 3 scores were found, $F_{1,96} = 4.13$, $p < .05$, favoring persons with less subjective impact (adj. $M = 63.2$ vs. adj. $M = 72.6$). A similar main effect of impact on occasion 3 total number of strategies mobilized was found, $F_{1,109} = 7.18$, $p < .02$, favoring those for whom the loss was more impactful (adj. $M = 37.8$ vs. adj. $M = 46.8$). Similar findings were found for occasion 3 cognitive, behavioral, social, and affective strategies, $F_{1,109} = 6.20$, $p < .01$ (adj. $M = 22.7$ vs. adj. $M = 30.8$) and occasion 2 BEQ scores, $F_{1,148} = 5.51$, $p < .02$ (adj. $M = 101.8$ vs. adj. $M = 108.6$).

These ANCOVAs also yielded a gender by resource interaction for occasion 3 HSC scores, $F_{1,96} = 4.28$, $p < .05$, with men who reported fewer resources surprisingly reporting lower levels of psychological symptoms (adj. $M = 65.7$ vs. adj. $M = 72.7$), while the opposite was true for women (adj. $M = 69.9$ vs. adj. $M = 59.4$). For total coping strategies mobilized at occasion 3, the gender by resource interaction approached statistical significance, $F_{1,93} = 3.47$, $p < .06$, with men who had less resources mobilizing fewer coping strategies than did those with more resources (adj. $M = 7.4$ vs. adj. $M = 9.7$), while the opposite was true for women (adj. $M = 10.1$ vs. adj. $M = 7.1$).

When the data was analyzed separately to examine differences across occasion from time 1 to time 2, and from time 2 to time 3, only the impact by time (time 2 vs. time 3) interaction was significant, $F_{8,84} = 2.76$, $p < .01$, wherein those who were less impacted had higher HSC scores over time (adj. M = 61.2 vs. adj. M = 70.5), relative to those who were more impacted, who returned to a relatively higher level of functioning over time (adj. M = 74.2 vs. adj. M = 67.2), $F_{1,91}$ = 12.22, $p < .01$. All other interactions with occasion were not statistically significant.

Occasion 1, occasion 2, and occasion 3 scores were then analyzed separately, thereby reflecting *different* proportions of the sample remaining at each occasion of measurement. When only occasion 1 scores were analyzed, main effects for gender were statistically significant, $F_{8,174}$ = 3.47, $p < .01$, wherein men had lower HSC scores (fewer symptoms) than did women (adj. M = 65.5 vs. adj. M = 73.6). Men also reported lower BDI scores (adj. M = 5.8) than did women (adj. M = 9.0) at occasion 1, $F_{1,181}$ = 6.30, $p < .01$. For all measures of adjustment except total strategies mobilized and CSAB strategies, scores for those with greater experienced competence suggested that such persons were functioning more adaptively, $F_{8,174}$ = 6.68, $p < .01$. A similar picture emerged for level of impact, $F_{8,174}$ = 2.17, $p < .05$, where persons who were less impacted functioning more adaptively. Such was also the case for persons reporting greater resources, $F_{8,174}$ = 3.64, $p < .01$.

At occasion 2, findings were similar ($p < .05$) for experienced competence, impact, and resources, but the above gender differences disappeared. At occasion 3, main effects for experienced and resource competence disappeared, while those for impact were substantially weakened ($p < .06$). Only in the case of HSC scores was a sex by resource interaction even somewhat substantial, $F_{8,96}$ = 1.75, $p < .09$, being particular to HSC scores, $F_{1,103}$ = 8.00, $p < .01$, and to life satisfaction, $F_{1,103}$ = 5.40, $p < .05$, wherein in each case males with fewer resources functioned more adaptively, while the opposite was true for women.

Overall adjustment scores were created by summing across the above measures of loneliness, life satisfaction, distress, symptomology, depression, and bereavement stress. A similar repeated measures ANCOVA yielded main effects for experienced competence ($p < .01$), impact ($p < .01$), and resources ($p < .01$) as described above. Persons' overall adjustment scores improved over time ($p < .01$). There were no gender effects or interactions between gender and either occasion of measurement, impact, resource, or experienced competence.

DISCUSSION

These findings in many respects break new ground regarding the process of bereavement, and in some ways they are quite surprising. Importantly, they clearly point up the importance of the perceived impactfulness of loss, the availability of resources, and the degree of coping competence as influences on bereavement adjustment.

Adjustment to Bereavement

The concept of experienced competence was derived from findings in the literature concerning locus of control, coping self-efficiency, learned helplessness, and self-esteem [1]. Indeed, the greater sense of control and confidence one has in one's ability to cope with difficult situations, the more successful will be one's attempts to adjust to traumatic life events, such as the death of a loved one [17]. In keeping with these findings, a highly significant main effect for experience competence was found. Persons high in experienced competence reported less depression, fewer bereavement adjustment difficulties, less loneliness, higher levels of life satisfaction, and fewer negative moods at all three times of measurement, than did persons low in experienced competence. Consequently, persons who presumably had a greater sense of control and confidence did appear to show higher levels of overall adjustment.

This finding is especially significant with regard to the relationship between locus of control and coping ability. It has been argued that there are two possible predictions that could be made with regard to locus of control and coping [18]. One is that persons with an internal locus of control will experience more distress when faced with uncontrollable events, because their basic beliefs in their own control over events will have been violated [19]. The second is that individuals with an external locus of control, those who already believe themselves to be helpless, will suffer more when confronted with uncontrollable events, because they will respond with resignation and depression, the results of learned helplessness, and will make only feeble attempts to recover [20, 21]. It is this latter prediction that is supported by the present finding that high levels of experienced competence are related to better overall adjustment in a bereaved sample. Persons with lower levels of experienced competence, i.e., those who perhaps believed they had little control or coping ability, responded to bereavement with higher levels of depression, and poorer overall coping.

The role of experienced competence in this study is in keeping with Bandura's claims about self-efficacy, defined as "people's judgements of their capabilities to organize and execute courses of action required to attain designated types of performance. It is concerned not with the skills one has, but with judgements of what one can do with whatever skills one possesses" [4, p. 391]. In other words, a widowed individual with low self-efficacy, when faced with the tasks of bereavement, will perceive himself or herself as unable to cope despite the skills and/or resources that are realistically available. According to Bandura, the stronger an individual's self-efficacy, the more vigorously and persistently will he or she make efforts to cope [4]. On the other hand, individuals low in self-efficacy will give up easily in the face of challenge. Since sustained effort is more likely to lead to success, it is not surprising that those with high self-efficacy in the present study fared better than did self-doubting individuals.

It is especially important to note that these findings held true over all three times of measurement. Experienced competence was important to adjustment both in the early phases of bereavement and the latter ones, and its importance did not diminish over time. Persons high in experienced competence at time 1 continued to show better adjustment six months and even three years later, compared to those low in experienced competence. Thus, it appears that the greater sense of control and confidence one has in one's ability to cope with bereavement, the more positive will be one's overall, long-term adjustment to loss.

According to Allen and Hayslip's model of bereavement, the true bereavement problem derives from the impact of the loss on the bereaved individual's life [1]. The loss of a loved one presents the bereaved with a radically altered assumptive world, as well as with the removal of a major source of reinforcement [22-24]. The impact of these changes will depend upon the combined influences of the degree of life change experienced, the centrality of the relationship, the perceived preventability of the death, and whether the loss had been anticipated. It was expected, then, that persons for whom the impact of loss was greater would face a greater bereavement task and would show poorer overall adjustment. Results tended to support this expectation. Persons high in impact of loss showed more symptoms of distress (HSC) at occasions 1 and 2, with a reversal at occasion 3. Thus, when a loss is less impactful, and the assumptive world is less radically changed, bereaved individuals are able to adjust more easily than are those for whom the impact is greater. Interestingly, however, it appears that high impactfulness may have positive benefits for persons at three years, with those who initially report less impact to perhaps have to re-work through the loss later on. High impactfulness may therefore sensitize people to the adjustments they must make later on it order to cope.

In this light, an additional post hoc finding which further supports the notion that greater impact presents a more challenging bereavement task is that subjects high in impact of loss reported mobilizing more coping strategies in response to bereavement and mobilizing more strategies which were of a higher level (i.e., cognitive, social, affective, and behavioral). It seems that, in response to the challenges that an impactful loss presents, bereaved individuals are likely to use a number of strategies in an attempt to cope with their altered assumptive world. The more difficult the task, the more strategies they mobilize. Despite their obvious attempts to cope, however, bereaved individuals facing an impactful loss still fared worse in overall adjustment than did those for whom the bereavement task is less challenging.

It is important to note that the impact of the loss is predictive of bereavement adjustment both in the short-term and in the long-term, but in complex ways. As would be expected, persons experiencing a highly impactful loss fared worse shortly following the death than did those experiencing a less impactful loss. Furthermore, those highly impacted individuals continued to show lower *overall* adjustment even many years after the loss, as compared to persons for whom the impact was not so great. Such was not the case when considering symptoms of distress (HSC), however.

Our model predicts that not only will the impact of the loss and the bereaved individual's sense of coping competence influence adjustment to bereavement, but that the resources perceived by the bereaved individual to be available to him or her will also play an important role [1]. It was therefore argued that individuals higher in perceived resources would show higher levels of overall adjustment than would those lower in perceived resources. Results strongly supported this expectation. Persons higher in perceived resources reported less depression, fewer symptoms of distress, less loneliness, higher levels of life satisfaction, and to mobilize their cognitive, behavioral, social, and affective strategies to cope with loss to a greater extent, presumably because the availability of resources make the use of such strategies more likely.

Importantly, perceived resources at the time of loss appears to be a powerful factor in both long- and short-term bereavement adjustment. Persons low in perceived resources showed poorer adjustment both early in the bereavement process and many years after the loss, as compared to those high in perceived resources. Thus, as with experienced competence and to a certain extent the impact of loss, perceived resources seem to play an important predictive role in the long-term adjustment to bereavement.

Thus, in accord with the Allen and Hayslip model of bereavement adjustment, experienced competence, impact of loss, and perceived resources, more so than gender, seem to be predictive of overall short-term and long-term adjustment to loss. This supports a view of bereavement as a complex process, which for some may not be resolved for many years, if ever.

Gender and Bereavement

Of particular interest here are the substantive lack of gender differences in our measures of bereavement adjustment as well as the absence of gender-specific paths of change over time and the lack of gender specific relationships with experienced competence, impactfulness of loss, and perceived resources. This suggests that, in contrast to previous research emphasizing gender differences in bereavement adjustment [e.g., 18, 25], the tasks of bereavement adjustment are universal, and consequently are not mediated by the effects of gender-specific role behaviors, coping skills, or accessibility of resources [see also 26]. Only in the case of the occasion specific analyses (reflecting different persons over time) do gender differences (favoring men) in adjustment emerge, and these disappeared at occasions 2 and 3, consistent with the findings of Lund et al. [17, 26] and Thompson et al. [27] who studied the same individuals over time.

The conspicuous lack of interactions with gender may, however, reflect a lack of statistical power in that for men, cell sizes were often quite small, ranging from 5 to 10. At face value, however, the lack of gender by resources interactions suggests that men are no less able to access available support in dealing with their loss than are women, as might have been expected on the basis of previous work.

In this light, the few gender differences in adjustment that did exist suggested that men responded to bereavement with less depression and experienced subsequent greater life satisfaction. On an occasion-specific basis, the gender by resource interaction at occasion 3 (controlling for occasion 2) suggested that men who reported fewer perceived resources to actually experience fewer distressing psychological symptoms and to report mobilizing fewer coping strategies to cope with an unanticipated loss [see 28] and/or the byproducts of being alone, i.e., more time alone, having to be more self-sufficient. Moreover, at occasion 1 men reported less depression than did women.

In spite of the fact that these findings reflect the self-reports of a relatively small number of men, they are nonetheless substantively consistent across independent (dissimilar) and dependent (similar) samples analyses. Namely, men in this sample seem to function more adaptively in spite of the relative paucity of resources. Either they are a select sample of highly functional men [see 29], such persons are unreporting the extent to which they are distressed, or, much less likely, they may reflect the differential attrition of those men who were experiencing greater bereavement difficulties. In that gender did not interact with attrition and persons who dropped out tended to have been widowed for a greater length of time and to have been better adjusted [30], the resulting sample of both men and women is somewhat negatively biased. In view of the findings for men, our feeling is that this particular subsample of men may be especially resilient. Rather than utilize others for support, the experience of loss may have sensitized them to their own inner strengths and resources, enabling them to carry on without either spouses, other close friends, or family. In contrast to previous findings that suggest men may not utilize other supports as effectively as might women and that men may be especially troubled by an inability to resolve interpersonal difficulties [see e.g., 31, 32], these findings suggest that bereaved men may indeed be more adaptive and self-sufficient than one might otherwise expect, consistent with the Carey [33] and Gallagher et al. [34] work. Thus, for some bereaved individuals, a more closed, encapsulated, self-initiated style of coping appears to be adaptive, in contrast to the prevailing wisdom suggesting that an other-directed, interpersonalized style of coping is better. Thus, this internalized coping style that this sample of men utilize indeed seems to be helpful in light of its impact on their psychological functioning. Similar, more positive views about the course of bereaved men's grief and adjustment have been put forth by Arbuckle and DeVries [35], Lund and Caserta [36], and Rubin [37].

Implications for Intervention

The findings of the present study have several implications for intervention and education with regard to bereavement. First, and perhaps most important, bereaved individuals and those closely involved with them need to be educated regarding the course and duration of bereavement. The present study provides encouraging information that a substantial majority of bereaved individuals do show significant improvement in adjustment over time, regardless of the initial devastating impact of the death. Time does appear to have a healing effect on the wounds inflicted by the loss of a loved one. However, it is important that the bereaved individual understand that the course of bereavement is not always smooth or linear. While improvements may occur fairly rapidly in some areas, in others adjustment may be slow or may even deteriorate. Similarly, adjustment to the life changes brought about by the death may take longer than the bereaved and his or her family expects. The present study found that even persons bereaved for seven years or more were continuing to show increases in adjustment in some areas. Thus, rather than suggesting that the bereaved individual "get over" the loss within a prescribed period of time, it should be expected that some aspects of his or her life will be forever altered and may never return to the pre-bereavement state. This is not to say that bereaved individuals must suffer without relief. In fact, most people adjust to loss quite well and are able to live their lives as fully as before. However, for those who have more difficulty, intervention might be in order.

Traditionally, intervention with bereaved individuals has focused on increasing the number and level of coping strategies utilized by the bereaved in response to the loss. It seems that the goal of intervention was to promote more active coping strategies and more intensive "grief work." For example, advice from various sources to helping professionals working with the bereaved includes encouraging the expression of emotion [38], teaching the bereaved to identify and express feelings [18], encouraging social support strategies, teaching new skills and new roles, encouraging the acceptance of help, the encouraging acceptance of the loss [39]. Rando suggests that helpers "design interventions that capitalize upon the griever's positive coping skills and compensate for deficient ones" [39, p. 125].

Results of the present study, however, indicate that simply using more active coping strategies is insufficient for improving adjustment. Persons in this study for whom the impact of the loss was high reported mobilizing more coping strategies than did those for whom the impact was low. However, the mobilization of these strategies for such persons did not always improve the adjustment of the bereaved, especially at occasion 3. In fact, low impacted persons showed poor adjustment (HSC scores) at the three-year follow-up. This suggests that traditional intervention techniques may not be the most effective in working with bereaved individuals who are experiencing adjustment difficulties. Instead, more effective intervention might focus on those areas shown to be most predictive of bereavement adjustment; namely, experienced competence, perceived resources, and the impact of the loss. These findings are further underscored by the fact that specific bereavement related measures were as significantly impacted by differences in competence, impact, and resources, as well as to a certain extent by gender, as were more broad-based measures of adjustment. Thus, it seems that the focus for intervention should be to also target specific issues as loneliness, grief, and difficulties in adjusting to the changes wrought by the death of a loved one.

Results of the present study indicate that levels of experienced competence early in the bereavement process are predictive of overall adjustment. These findings are consistent with results of another longitudinal study of elderly conjugally bereaved persons. Lund, Dimond, Caserta, Johnson, Poulton, and Connelly found that the best predictor of poor coping two years after the death of a spouse was low self-esteem at three weeks post-loss [40]. Thus, early intervention efforts aimed at bolstering self-esteem might be more effective than simply encouraging active coping techniques. This is not to say that coping techniques should not be taught. In fact, one means by which to bolster self-esteem might be to encourage techniques that will lead to successful experiences which may increase self-efficacy. Similarly, helping bereaved individuals begin to reconstruct a positive identity apart from the lost loved one may add to esteem and a sense of competence. Allen and Hayslip reported that persons in their study indicated informally that helping others helped them to overcome their sense of helplessness and depression [1].

Along with increasing experienced competence, intervention efforts might also focus on lessening the impact of the loss on the bereaved individual's life. The impact of the loss has been conceptualized in this study as being derived from the centrality of the lost relationship, the perceived preventability of the death, the degree to which the death was expected, and the degree of life change associated with the loss. Among these areas, the degree of life change seems to be most amenable to intervention. Many bereaved individuals when facing the loss of a loved one also face the loss of a major source of support, both emotional and practical. Widowed individuals may experience a sudden drop in income, a change in social support networks, and a major alteration in the roles that must be carried out, and even a geographical change if a decision is made to move to a new location. While many of these life changes must be accepted, others may be avoided or at least minimized. For example, Allen and Hayslip suggest that a widow who is forced to sell her home might be encouraged to locate an apartment close to her present neighborhood where she can attend the same church or make use of familiar community resources [1]. Other suggestions might include maintaining a familiar routine, keeping in touch with social contacts, and continuing with hobbies or pastimes that the individual enjoyed prior to bereavement. In this light, pre-post event disparity and degree of change have been shown to predict adjustment to nursing home placement [41].

Finally, intervention might focus on improving the bereaved individual's perception of the resources available to him or her. This might be done through such practical methods as educating individuals about community resources, encouraging them to seek social support, and helping them to view their emotional and cognitive resources in a more positive light [1].

LIMITATIONS OF THE STUDY

In spite of the salience of these findings for bereaved persons in general and bereaved men in particular, several limitations are to be noted. As the present study was exploratory in nature, several of the measures used were designed specifically for the purposes of this study. However, although validity estimate studies have not been established, alpha coefficients indicate adequate internal consistency for each instrument. Of the measures not designed for the present study, several were shortened or revised versions of well-established instruments. With the exception of one such measure (BEQ), reliability and validity of these versions have been well demonstrated in the literature. Moreover, for the Hopkins Symptom Checklist, coefficient alphas reported are based on a fifty-eight-item version as opposed to the forty-four-item version utilized in the present study.

A second limitation of the present study involves the lack of a non-bereaved control group. Since the focus of the study involved adjustment among bereaved individuals, a control group of non-bereaved subjects was deemed unnecessary. Nevertheless, certain statements regarding the impact of bereavement on adjustment must be made with caution. For example, it remains unknown whether bereaved individuals five years after the loss are different in terms of adjustment as compared to non-bereaved individuals.

The study is also limited in that the sample was made up of volunteers, most of whom were women. Recent research has indicated that persons who volunteer to participate in bereavement research may differ in important ways from individuals who choose not to participate [29]. Since the original sample here consisted primarily of women (164 females and 29 males), it is likely that a bias existed in favor of more depressed and less self-sufficient volunteers.

Furthermore, it is evident that attrition rates further biased the sample in favor of poor adjustment. By the final phase of the study, 52 percent of the initial sample had dropped out, though such attrition was unrelated to gender. An analysis of completers versus drop-outs indicated that the attrition was selective and had resulted in a less well-adjusted sample [30]. However, attrition can be viewed as only a partial limitation, in that it serves to answer questions regarding the extent of selective attrition which is integral to the longitudinal nature of the present study.

Another related limitation of the present study is the relative homogeneity of the sample. Volunteers were primarily female (85%), widowed (76%), caucasian (98%), and Protestant (65%), and most (72%)

had attended a bereavement support group. Generalizations to other samples must be made with care. Future research may do well to work with more heterogeneous samples.

Additional concerns exist regarding cohort-specific experiences with death, in that all persons in the present study had been bereaved within the last ten years. Bereavement-related concerns for this cohort are likely to be different than those for individuals bereaved in an earlier era. For example, as opposed to twenty years ago, society in general is more aware of the need for support during bereavement, and may be more sensitive to issues of death and dying. Cultural attitudes regarding appropriate bereavement behavior have likely changed in recent years. People are living longer, have access to hospice care, support groups, and other social programs, and may have more forewarning of death due to medical technologies which prolong the life of terminal patients. These issues, among others, may make it difficult to generalize the present findings to earlier bereavement-related cohorts. Similarly, since society and technology continue to change, it is difficult to say with any certainty how well these findings will generalize to future cohorts.

Other limitations relate specifically to the longitudinal nature of the present study. First, testing effects may be apparent. Answering questions about their experiences may have induced persons to further explore their thoughts and feelings, and in doing so they might have been changed in ways that would not have occurred had they not participated in the study. Furthermore, as persons became more familiar with the measures being used, they may have altered the manner in which they approached questions. For example, there is some evidence which suggests that repeated presentations of personality tests results in profiles of better adjustment as the individual becomes more familiar with the test [42]. Social desirability effects may also affect findings in that persons might have attempted to answer questions in a positive light in order to convince the researcher or even themselves that they were adjusting well to their loss.

Another limitation related to the longitudinal nature of the study relates to statistical regression toward the mean. As mentioned above, selective attrition resulted in a more extreme sample of volunteers over time [30]. Improvements in adjustment over time might, therefore, be in part attributable to regression that is related to attrition, as the most poorly adjusted individuals moved closer to the mean at a later time of measurement. Controls for this tendency, however, were instituted by taking data at more than two times of measurement and by using reliable measures. Thus, if regression plays a role in biasing these results, it is most likely only a small one.

A final limitation is the absence of pre-bereavement measures of adjustment. It is not possible, given the limits of the present study, to make statements about levels of adjustment prior to the death, and thus to determine with certainty that levels of adjustment are entirely related to bereavement. Moreover, individuals had been bereaved for varying amounts of time, a problem that was addressed via the utilization of length of time since one's loss as a covariate (see above).

Regardless of these limitations, our findings reveal important dimensions along which adjustment to loss might be understood, underscoring the diversity among persons in coping with loss as pointed out by Lund [43]. They also not only reinforce the universality of grief and bereavement among men and women, but also help to dispel the myth that men are necessarily more negatively impacted by loss, presumably because they have more difficulty in expressing their emotions or turning to others for support. Indeed, they suggest that many men might deal with the loss of a spouse, close friend, or other family member more adaptively than do women.

REFERENCES

1. S. Allen and B. Hayslip, *A Model for Predicting Bereavement Outcome in Adulthood,* paper presented at the Annual Scientific Meeting of the Gerontological Society, Boston, Massachusetts, November 1990.
2. H. Levenson, Distinctions Within the Concept of Internal-External Control: Development of a New Scale, *Proceedings of the 80th Annual APA Convention,* APA, Washington, D.C., 1972.
3. M. Rosenberg, *Society and the Adolescent Self-Image,* Princeton University Press, Princeton, New Jersey, 1965.
4. A. Bandura, Self-Efficacy Mechanism in Human Agency, *American Psychologist, 37,* pp. 122-147, 1982.
5. J. Rotter, Generalized Expectancies for Internal Versus External Control of Reinforcement, *Psychological Monographs, 80,* p. 609, 1966.
6. G. Arling, Resistance to Isolation Among Elderly Widows, *International Journal of Aging and Human Development, 7,* pp. 67-86, 1976.
7. M. J. Horowitz and N. Wilner, Life Events, Stress and Coping, in *Aging in the 1980's: Psychological Issues,* L. W. Poon (ed.), American Psychological Association, Washington, D.C., 1980.
8. D. Russell, L. Peplau, and C. Cutrona, The Revised UCLA Loneliness Scale: Concurrent and Discriminant Validity Evidence, *Journal of Personality and Social Psychology, 30,* pp. 472-480, 1980.
9. D. McNair and M. Lorr, An Analysis of Mood in Neurotics, *Journal of Abnormal and Social Psychology, 59,* pp. 620-627, 1964.
10. B. Neugarten, R. Havighurst, and S. Tobin, The Measurement of Life Satisfaction, *Journal of Gerontology, 36,* pp. 134-143, 1961.

11. V. Wood, M. L. Wylie, and B. Sheafor, An Analysis of a Short Self-Report Measure of Life Satisfaction: Correlation with Rater Judgements, *Journal of Gerontology, 24,* pp. 465-469, 1969.

12. L. Derogatis, R. Lipman, L. Covi, and K. Rickels, Neurotic Symptom Dimensions: As Perceived by Psychiatrists and Patients of Various Social Classes, *Archives of General Psychiatry, 24,* pp. 454-464, 1971.

13. L. Derogatis, R. Lipman, K. Rickels, E. Wenhuth, and L. Covi, The Hopkins Symptom Checklist (HSCL): A Self-Report Inventory, *Behavioral Science, 19,* pp. 1-15, 1974.

14. A. T. Beck, C. H. Ward, S. Mendelson, J. Mock, and J. Erbaugh, An Inventory for Measuring Depression, *Archives of General Psychiatry, 4,* pp. 561-571, 1961.

15. A. Demi, *Bereavement Experience Questionnaire,* personal communication, 1989.

16. S. Conway, B. Hayslip, and R. Tandy, Similarities of Perceptions of Bereavement Experiences Between Widows and Professionals, *Omega, 23,* pp. 37-51, 1991.

17. D. Lund, M. Caserta, M. Dimond, and K. Shaffer, Competencies, Tasks of Daily Living, and Adjustments to Spousal Bereavement in Later Life, in *Older Bereaved Spouses,* D. Lund (eds.), Hemisphere, New York, pp. 135-152, 1989.

18. W. Stroebe and M. S. Stroebe, *Bereavement and Health: The Psychological and Physical Consequences of Partner Loss,* Cambridge University Press, Cambridge, 1987.

19. N. Pittman and T. Pittman, Effects of Amount of Helplessness Training and Internal-External Locus of Control on Mood and Performance, *Journal of Personality and Social Psychology, 37,* pp. 39-47, 1979.

20. P. J. Ganellen and P. H. Blaney, Externality, and Depression, *Journal of Personality and Social Psychology, 52,* pp. 326-337, 1984.

21. J. H. Johnson and I. G. Saranson, Life Stress, Depression and Anxiety: Internal-External Control as a Moderator Variable, *Psychosomatic Research, 22,* pp. 205-208, 1978.

22. C. Parkes, Bereavement and Mental Illness, *British Journal of Medical Psychology, 38,* pp. 1-26, 1965.

23. C. Parkes, *Bereavement: Studies in Grief in Adult Life,* Basic Books, New York, 1972.

24. C. Parkes, Determinants of Outcome Following Bereavement, *Omega, 6,* pp. 303-323, 1975.

25. M. Stroebe and W. Stroebe, Who Suffers More? Sex Differences and Health Risks of the Widowed, *Psychological Bulletin, 93,* pp. 279-301, 1983.

26. D. Lund, M. Caserta, and M. Dimond, Testing for Gender Differences Through Two Years of Bereavement Among the Elderly, *The Gerontologist, 26,* pp. 314-320, 1986.

27. L. Thompson, D. Gallagher, H. Cover, M. Gilewski, and J. Peterson, Effects of Bereavement on Symptoms of Psychopathology in Older Men and

Women, in *Older Bereaved Spouses,* D. Lund (ed.), Hemisphere, New York, pp. 3-15, 1989.

28. K. Gass, Appraisal, Coping and Resources: Markers Associated with the Health of Aged Widows and Widowers, in *Older Bereaved Spouses,* D. A. Lund (ed.), Hemisphere, New York, pp. 79-94, 1989.

29. M. Stroebe and W. Stroebe, Who Participates in Bereavement Research? A Review and Empirical Study, *Omega, 20,* pp. 1-29, 1989.

30. B. Hayslip and L. McCoy-Roberts, *Selective Attrition Effects in Bereavement Research,* paper presented at the Annual Scientific Meeting of the Gerontological Society, New Orleans, Louisiana, November 1994.

31. J. D. DeFrain, D. K. Jakub, and B. L. Mendosa, The Psychological Effects of Sudden Infant Death on Grandmothers and Grandfathers, *Omega, 24,* pp. 165-182, 1991-92.

32. C. B. Wortman, R. C. Silver, and R. C. Kessler, The Meaning of Loss and Adjustment to Bereavement, in *Handbook of Bereavement,* M. S. Stroebe, W. Stroebe, and R. O. Hansson (eds.), Cambridge, Cambridge, England, pp. 349-366, 1993.

33. R. B. Carey, Weathering Widowhood: Problems and Adjustments of the Widowed During the First Year, *Omega, 10,* pp. 163-174, 1979-80.

34. D. Gallagher, S. Lovett, P. Hanley-Dunn, and L. Thompson, Use of Select Coping Strategies During Late-Life Spousal Bereavement, in *Older Bereaved Spouses,* D. Lund (ed.), Hemisphere, New York, pp. 111-121, 1989.

35. N. W. Arbuckle and B. DeVries, *The Long Term Effects of Later Life Spousal and Parental Bereavement on Personal Functioning,* paper presented at the Annual Scientific Meeting of the Gerontological Society, New Orleans, Louisiana, November 1993.

36. D. Lund and M. Caserta, Older Bereaved Spouses/Participation in Self-Help Groups, *Omega, 25,* pp. 47-62, 1992.

37. S. S. Rubin, Adult Child Loss and the Two-Track Model of Bereavement, *Omega, 24,* pp. 183-202, 1991-92.

38. B. Raphael, *The Anatomy of Bereavement,* Basic Books, New York, 1983.

39. R. Rando, *Loss and Anticipatory Grief,* Lexington Books, Lexington, Massachusetts, 1986.

40. D. Lund, M. Dimond, M. Caserta, R. Johnson, J. Poulton, and J. Connelly, Identifying Elderly with Coping Difficulties After Two Years of Bereavement, *Omega, 16,* pp. 213-224, 1985-86.

41. M. Lieberman, Adaptive Processes in Later Life, in *Life Span Developmental Psychology: Normative Life Crises,* N. Daton and L. Ginzberg (eds.), Academic Press, New York, 1975.

42. P. Baltes, H. Reese, and J. Nesselroade, *Life Span Developmental Psyhology: Introduction to Research Methods,* Lawrence Erlbaum, Hillsdale, New Jersey, 1988.

43. D. A. Lund, Conclusions about Bereavement in Later Life and Implications for Interventions and Future Research, in *Older Bereaved Spouses,* D. A. Lund (ed.), Hemisphere, New York, pp. 217-231, 1989.

CHAPTER 9

When the Unexpected Happens: Husbands Coping With the Deaths of Their Wives

Dale A. Lund and Michael S. Caserta

Most husbands do not outlive their wives. The 1990 Census of the United States reveals that while nearly 49 percent of women are widowed after age sixty-five only 14 percent of the men are widowed. After age eighty-five the rates of widowhood increase for both men and women. About 80 percent of these women are widows compared with 43 percent of the men [1]. Men may not know these exact statistics but their life experiences remind them that it would be unusual or unexpected if their wives were to die before them. Statistical odds do not operate like rules in our lives. No one can be guaranteed that death will occur at a particular time or in a specific way. A seventy-nine-year-old man in one of our research studies on spousal bereavement described the surprise he felt when his wife died unexpectedly. "I just can't believe this happened. My wife was healthy. She was strong. She took me to the emergency room three times in six months last year. I almost died twice. All of a sudden she has a heart attack and she's dead. I'm here and she's gone. This is crazy. Nobody thought I'd be the one to live the longest."

The focus of this chapter is on the ways in which men, particularly those in mid and later life, cope with the deaths of their spouses. We have learned a great deal from research on bereavement over the past twenty years but we know much less about older adults, especially men. Widows are more available and we have assumed that they are more willing to participate in research because we also believe that they are quite willing to discuss the personal and sensitive issues related to grief. Conversely, widowers are fewer in number and we expect men to be less interested in talking about their grief and even unable to express themselves. These factors contributed to the avoidance of including bereaved men in research studies.

During the 1980s our multidisciplinary research team at the University of Utah Gerontology Center conducted two studies which examined spousal bereavement among mid- and later-life adults. We were among some of the earliest researchers to study both men and women in the same projects. These studies will be mentioned later in more detail in this chapter but it is quite important to point out that the acceptance and full participation rates were similar for both men and women. The first study was a two-year longitudinal project with six interview/data collection periods involving significant amounts of time discussing or reviewing very sensitive and personal experiences. The second study, also two years in length, required participants to complete four detailed and sensitive questionnaires, and, for most subjects, to attend support group meetings for either two months or an entire year. The fact that widowers and widows had similar participation rates in these studies shows that some of our generally accepted beliefs about men not being willing to be expressive about their grief might be over-exaggerated.

Although some researchers have concluded that men and women differ in their grief responses in widowhood [2-4], the data from our two studies reveals far more similarities than differences. While men may be less likely to cry or cry less intensely than women, the widows in our studies shared similar difficulties with loneliness, depression, and nearly all psychosocial adjustments associated with bereavement [4]. We also found similarities between bereaved men and women with respect to their health and perceived stress levels and coping abilities overtime. One primary difference, however, was identified in our intervention study. Both men and women reported that loneliness was their single greatest difficulty during the first two years of bereavement and that completing the tasks of daily living was their second most difficult problem. The difference emerged in their specific tasks of daily life. As expected, these bereaved widowers age fifty and over were having great difficulty in shopping, preparing meals, and managing the household. The widows expressed having major problems doing home repairs, managing financial and legal matters, and taking care of their automobiles [5].

We also found that the bereaved men and women had similar predictors of what appeared to help them during their adjustments. Men and women who were highly competent in performing the diverse tasks of daily living, had relatively high self-esteem, and had opportunities to express themselves with others were coping much better than those who lacked these three factors [6]. Apparently, learning to be more competent in managing the new challenges of living in an "uncoupled" lifestyle helps to build more positive self-esteem and, in turn, helps in the bereavement adjustment process [5]. We concluded from these studies that while other people can be helpful to grieving widows and widowers, it is much more important to have a well developed set of internal coping resources to rely on. These internal resources include pride and confidence in oneself because they provide the motivation needed to cope with very stressful life experiences. When people feel that they are not deserving of a good life or that it simply does not matter if they feel miserable, they will not manage their grief very well. Conversely, when someone has always taken pride in his/her daily life and now finds themself in a terrible situation, they are more likely to engage in a course of action that will be helpful in managing their grief.

It is not the purpose of this chapter, however, to compare men and women in their grief experiences because we have already done so in several publications [4, 7-9] and authors of other chapters in this book also report on gender comparisons. It is interesting to note that although we published one of our first articles from these studies on a comparison of men and women, we followed much the same bias against examining men that was evident in early research by completing a detailed analysis of the widows bereavement adjustments [10] and not doing the same for men. This chapter helps fill that gap because we are now providing a much closer examination of the men who survived the deaths of their wives. More specifically, this chapter presents a descriptive analysis of the psychosocial adjustments and outcomes of bereaved husbands age fifty and over. Special attention is directed toward comparing men of different ages to determine whether or not their experiences are influenced by age.

Widowed men in their fifties may differ from men in their seventies and eighties because they are more likely to be employed full-time, have children at home, and be active participants in larger social networks. Married men in their seventies and eighties are more likely to be retired, spending increasing amounts of time with their wives, and have relatively smaller social networks. One situation is not necessarily better than another when widowhood strikes but we know very little about how these situations might impact the course of grief. Our research studies included men who ranged in age from fifty to ninety-three so these comparisons were possible.

METHODS

The data presented in this chapter are from the two federally-funded studies mentioned earlier that we conducted on spousal bereavement in later life. The first study was a longitudinal descriptive study in which recently bereaved older spouses were followed over a two-year period. The purpose of the second study was to examine the effectiveness of self-help groups for a similar sample of older widows and widowers. Two main common features of the design of the two studies were that each consisted of bereaved spouses aged fifty years and older who were identified through newspaper obituaries and both studies examined similar aspects of adaptation. Although the methodology for both studies are discussed in greater detail in numerous reports, a brief overview is presented below.

All potential bereaved participants in the first longidutional descriptive study were randomly assigned to either a home interview group (N = 104) or a mailed questionnaire group (N = 88) in order to test for an interviewer effect. No such effect was detected so the two groups were combined to form one bereaved sample (N = 192) [11]. Nonbereaved older adults who were currently married (N = 104) were identified through public voter registry records and were selected on the basis of age, gender, and socioeconomic status. In order to minimize the number of matches needed, a nonbereaved person was selected for each of the 104 bereaved respondents in the home interview group. Twenty-six percent of the bereaved respondents and 27 percent of the nonbereaved sample were men.

The 192 bereaved respondents either were interviewed or completed self-administered mailed questionnaires at three to four weeks, two months, six months, one year, eighteen months, and two years after their spouses' deaths. The 104 nonbereaved controls completed self-administered questionnaires according to the same schedule. The first two questionnaires for both the nonbereaved participants and the bereaved in the mail-questionnaire group were delivered by a research assistant but they completed them on their own and returned them by mail.

In addition to assessing the impact of self-help groups on a variety of bereavement outcomes, the intervention study also focused on the roles of group leadership and treatment duration by comparing those self-help groups led by widows versus professionals and short-term versus long-term formats. All groups met weekly for two months but the long-term groups continued to meet once a month for an additional ten months. Three hundred and thirty-nine recently bereaved spouses initially agreed to participate (241 were assigned to one of the intervention conditions and 98 were assigned to a control group). Men comprised 28 percent of the study sample.

All data were collected through self-administered questionnaires over four time points. The baseline measurement took place at two to three months after the death; the second measurement was obtained immediately after the completion of the eight weekly self-help meetings (roughly 4-8 months of bereavement); and the third followed the completion of the monthly long-term group meetings (approximately 14-17 months of bereavement). The fourth and final questionnaire was completed at two years following the death. The controls were assessed at the same four time periods but received no intervention.

A variety of bereavement adjustment measures as well as sociodemographic and other background information were obtained in both studies and are described elsewhere. Reported in this chapter, however, are measures of depression (first study), unresolved grief (second study), and perceived coping ability (both studies). In the first longitudinal descriptive study, depression was measured using the Zung Depression Scale [12] which consists of twenty Likert-type items that are summed for a total ranging from 20 to 80. A score above 48 for older populations is considered to be within the range for clinical depression, a higher score indicating a greater presence of depressive symptoms [13].

Unresolved grief, an indicator of adjustment we used in the self-help group study was measured using the Texas Revised Inventory of Grief (TRIG) [14]. This scale consists of thirteen Likert-type items that when summed, can range from 13 (low) to 65 (high). Also reported in this chapter is the measure of perceived coping ability used in both larger studies. This is a single-item indicator in which the bereaved were asked "How well do you feel you have coped with (the death of your spouse?)" on a scale of 1 (not well at all) to 7 (very well). The non-bereaved in the first study were similarly asked, "How well do you feel you would cope with (the death of your spouse?)" using the same 1-7 scale [15, 16].

RESULTS

Figures 1 and 2 present the changes in mean depression and perceived coping scores, respectively, for the men who participated in the first longidutional study we conducted. The trajectories presented in each of the figures represent a different age group: fifty to fifty-nine years, sixty to sixty-nine years, seventy to seventy-nine years, and those eighty years and older.

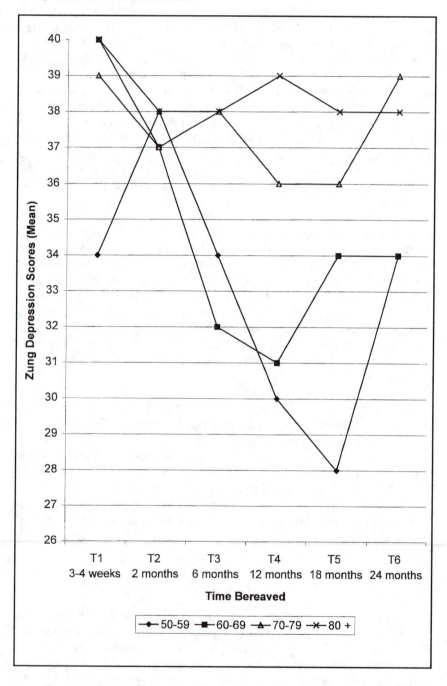

Figure 1. Depression levels of bereaved men over two years (*n* = 47).

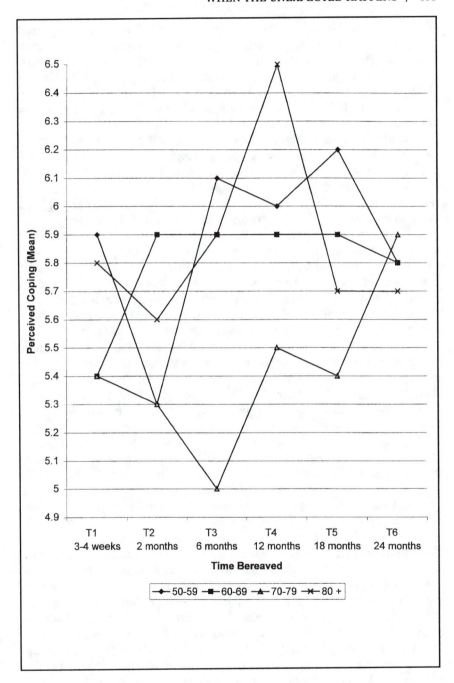

Figure 2. Perceived coping levels among bereaved men over two years (*n* = 49).

As seen in Figure 1, the youngest group of widowers reported an overall decline in depression levels from the second to eighteenth month of bereavement after an initial increase for the first two months. Although the mean scores for this group increased back to initial levels by the end of the study ($M = 34$), at no time point did they exceed the normal range [13]. The depression levels for men in their sixties showed a similar pattern of general overall decline although they had a higher mean initial depression level ($M = 40$). Whereas some fluctuation occurred, men in their seventies and eighties reported the highest overall depression levels over the two years but were not above the cut-off for clinical depression according to established criteria for older populations [13]. Those who were in their seventies had the highest depression scores at the beginning and at the end of the study.

According to the patterns diagramed in Figure 2, men in their seventies again reported the most difficulty coping with the loss throughout most of the study, never exceeding a mean score of 5.5 until finally improving to 5.9 at two years. Both the youngest and oldest cohorts (those in their 50s and those 80 and older) reported generally higher levels of coping ability. The only major exception to this pattern occurred at two months where the mean perceived coping ability of those in their fifties declined to 5.3 (from 5.9 at 3-4 weeks), but then returned to 6.1 four months later. The most stable pattern of perceived coping ability was observed among the men in their sixties who increased from 5.4 at three to four weeks to 5.9 at two months of bereavement, remaining virtually unchanged for the remainder of the two-year study period.

Figures 3 and 4 present the patterns of unresolved grief for the men in our self-help group intervention study. High scores on this scale indicate more difficulty with grief. Figure 3 consists of data from those who were in the control group (no intervention) while the data in Figure 4 represent the patterns of unresolved grief over time for those who participated in the self-help groups.

The mean level of unresolved grief among those who did not participate in the self-help groups (controls) was quite similar for each age group at two to three months of bereavement, ranging from approximately 44 to 46 (on a possible scale of 13 to 65). The men in the two youngest age groups (those <70 years old) showed greater declines in unresolved grief, the most dramatic changes over time being observed among those in their fifties. The mean grief level for men in this age group decreased by almost 18 points over the two-year period, indicating decreasing difficulties with grief. The level of unresolved grief for men eighty years and older eventually declined from 44 at baseline to 34 two years later, approximately the same mean score for men in their

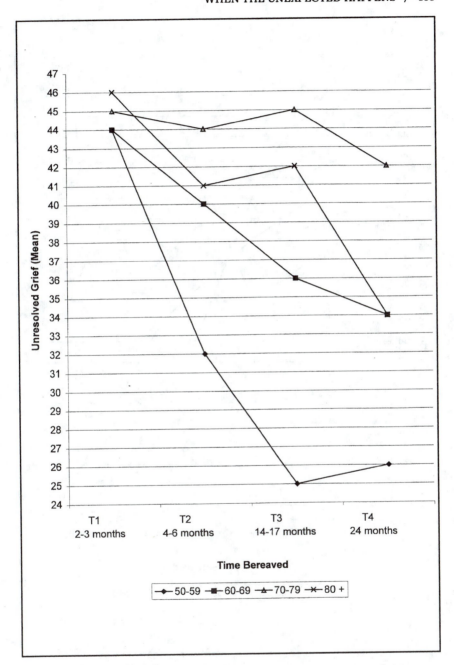

Figure 3. Levels of unresolved grief among bereaved men over two years (Non-Intervention Sample: *N* = 49).

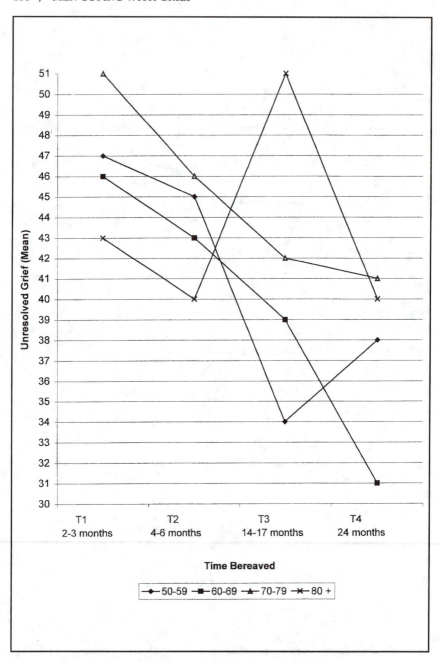

Figure 4. Levels of unresolved grief among bereaved men over two years (Participants in Support Groups: *N* = 34).

sixties at the two-year measurement. On the other hand, those in their seventies showed the least amount of change over the two years (mean scores ranged from 45 at baseline to 42 at two years), and their scores were clearly higher compared to the other age groups at the end of the study. Again, the widowers in their seventies consistently had the greatest difficulty with grief.

Similar to the bereaved controls of the same age, those less than seventy years old in the self-help groups showed an overall decline in unresolved grief over the course of two years (see Figure 4), which indicates improvement in their adjustments. Meanwhile, the oldest cohort showed a sharp increase (approximately 11 points) at fourteen to seventeen months of bereavement but then returned to a mean equal to 40 by two years. The increase in unresolved grief observed at the third data point coincided with the end of the monthly self-help group meetings. Unlike what was observed among controls, the level of unresolved grief for those in their seventies who received the intervention steadily diminished throughout the study. This age group had the highest mean TRIG score (51) at baseline which declined to 41 by the end of the study. Although this final score was not much lower than for those age seventy to seventy-nine in the control grouop, the controls showed virtually no change in unresolved grief from baseline whereas those in the self-help groups did. It appears that men in their sixties and seventies benefitted the most in terms of grief issues from participating in the self-help groups, whereas men in their eighties did not appear to benefit as much.

By comparison, when age is *not* considered and the level of unresolved grief is plotted over the course of the study for men in the self-help intervention versus those who were not, both groups show a similar decline over time (as depicted in Figure 5). Consequently, the self-help groups would appear to have no effect in unresolved grief. Only after controlling for the age group to which they belong does the treatment appear to have a differential impact on older widowers' grief levels, if not statistically, perhaps clinically. The oldest widowers (80+) did not show much improvement in their grief after being in the self-help groups and this distorts the overall benefit that the other age groups experienced.

Figure 6 compared the mean perceived coping ability of bereaved versus married nonbereaved men from our first study. This comparison with nonbereaved men is important because it focuses attention on how well men actually cope with bereavement compared to how similarly aged men expect their coping might be. The bereaved men reported greater coping ability (ranging from 5.4 at 3-4 weeks to 5.7 at 2 years) than what the nonbereaved men in the sample imagined their coping

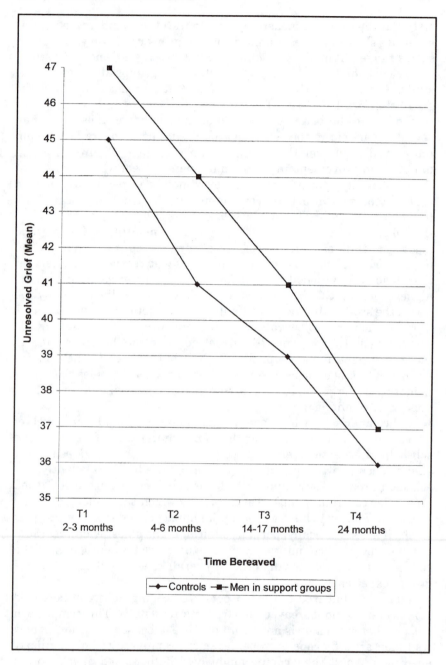

Figure 5. Changes in grief over two years: comparison of men in support groups and controls.

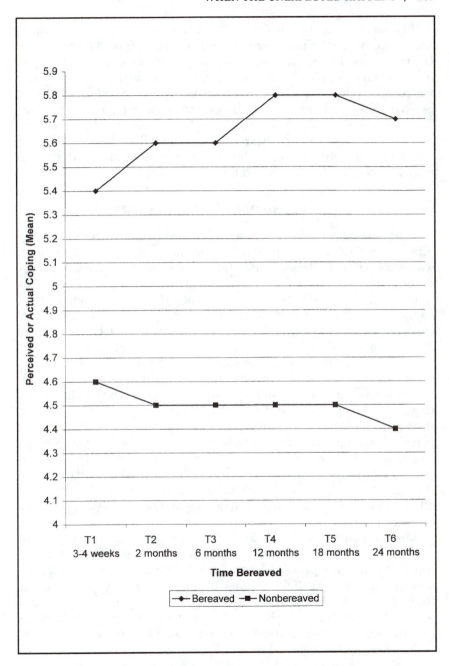

Figure 6. Perceived coping levels of nonbereaved and
bereaved men over two years.

ability would be if their wife were to die. The mean perceived coping ability scores for the latter group rarely deviated from 4.5 throughout the two years. These patterns closely approximate what was observed for the entire sample of men and women in the earlier study in which we reported that the difference in perceived coping ability between bereaved and nonbereaved groups was not moderated by gender [15]. These data show that it is quite possible that most of the bereaved men in this study were coping better than expected. Bereavement is a very stressful and difficult process but there is some evidence that these men are somewhat resilient and find ways to cope.

CONCLUSIONS AND DISCUSSION

The data analyzed and presented in this chapter reveal several interesting findings about grief experiences of mid- and later-life widowers. These findings deal with the potential influence of their age at the time of spousal bereavement, expectations of how well these men would likely cope with their grief, and the extent of variation in their adjustments. We have organized the findings into five major conclusions and provide some additional qualitative data to help explain or illustrate each point.

First, men in their seventies appear to have the greatest difficulty in adjusting to the deaths of their spouses. There were some minor exceptions to this conclusion but a pattern emerged in the data which showed that men in their seventies had the highest levels of depression at the beginning of the study and two years later. Although their perceived coping scores improved to the levels of the other men in the study, they had the slowest rate of recovery. Their scores on the unresolved grief scale remained the highest of all age groups throughout the study even though they started at similar levels to the others. This means that they were not managing grief issues very well even after two years.

Men in their seventies are likely to be near retirement or beginning the transition. This phase can potentially add further stress and frustration to the disruption of bereavement. The quote from a seventy-nine-year-old man at the beginning of this chapter conveyed his shock that he would outlive his wife, especially because he had been the one to battle health problems. He went on to say in his interview that he was also looking forward to spending more time with his wife and doing more traveling together. This was a common response for men who were planning more retirement activities with their wives. Another seventy-six-year-old man described himself in the following way after only three weeks following his wife's death. He was asked to write twenty statements about himself as a measure of his self-concept [17]. His answers give the impression that his self-image had been overwhelmed by his grief and saw himself only in terms of his loss situation. He made only four statements. "I am a very lonely man who misses his sweetheart. I know I will meet her again after I leave this life. I miss my sweetheart around the house. I miss her calling me to give a helping hand." These statements suggest that he had already grown familiar with spending a great deal of time in the house with his wife present and now he was lost without her. This is a typical grief response identified by Worden where the bereaved is required to adjust to an environment in which the deceased is absent [18].

Another seventy-five-year-old widower described his loneliness for his wife combined with lower self-esteem from being retired. At one year after his wife's death he said, "I've been a business executive all my life and I've had charge of lots of people. People look up to me, or did. Now they don't even look at me. I'm no longer the guy on the throne. I'm just another has-been. That's a discouraging thing, to be the head man for years and years. And then all of a sudden you're not even the foot. You're nothing, you know, you don't exist. That's a little bit of self-pity though, that shouldn't be." This is a rather extreme statement but it does reflect the double-douse of difficulty for men trying to cope with both the loss of status from work and loss of companionship and possibly status from being married.

Not all men in their seventies were equally devastated by the death of their wives. Another seventy-five-year-old man who recently remarried described himself this way. "I am a young man going on seventy-five. I am an artist, a music lover, a softy with my grandchildren, a loving and affectionate individual, a medium golfer, a traveler, a lover of art, a friendly person, love walking and like people." At the beginning of the study he was still employed as a business executive. About one year later he remarried and then retired within a few months. We did previously find that men who remarried were slightly better copers both before and after their remarriage [19].

Second, men in their fifties appear to have been the most effective in their coping and resolving grief issues. Although their depression scores fluctuated overtime they began the study with the lowest scores and also ended the project with less depression, especially compared with men in their seventies and eighties. Also, even though their coping scores varied overtime, men in their fifties had the most positive scores at three of the six time periods. With respect to their grief, men in their fifties showed by far the greatest improvement in resolving many of these issues.

Men in their fifties, especially compared with most men in their seventies, are likely to have employment relationships, larger social networks, and children at home. These characteristics can present additional challenges during times of grief but they also present opportunities for a sense of belonging, meaningful activities, and being needed by others. One fifty-nine-year-old man described his self-concept in terms that reveal a clear sense of belonging. He wrote these statements at two months after his wife's death. "I am still a father to eight children, owner of a business, still responsible to children and grandchildren, a member of a church, member of a community, a member of a club, a member of a religious study group, important to my business, and it seems like more people are watching me." It is clear that he still felt important and needed. It is also quite possible that men in their fifties expect to live many more years and they know that they will need to cope well if they want to continue to look forward to a future. One fifty-seven-year-old man said that, "I must pull myself together, for me and my kids. I have no choice but to do my best." Expecting to live another twenty to thirty years possibly served as a motivational factor to some of these younger men, even though having fewer years to live should not detract from coping well. We would never devalue the remaining years of any widower, regardless of their age. However, as we will report later, some of the oldest men in our studies apparently felt that they were too old to care much about their futures.

Third, men in their fifties, sixties, and seventies showed considerable improvement in resolving grief issues while participating in self-help groups, but men in their eighties showed only slight improvement two years later. The younger groups of men improved from nine to about fourteen points on the unresolved grief scale, but men in their eighties improved only three points over the course of two years.

Many of the men who participated in our self-help groups reported that one of the main reasons they agreed was to have an opportunity of meeting other people, especially to meet women. This was most common among men in their fifties, sixties, and seventies but less common among men in their eighties. One sixty-eight-year-old man said, "I refer to my support group as my harem, but I never say this when they are present." Many other positive comments were made about the support groups. Two men, both in their fifties, wrote, "The group helped us to talk about our problems and we were able to release some of our pent-up feelings." "Everyone could empathize each other's problems and everyone felt completely at ease to talk about anything. All group members tried to help anyone having particularly bad problems." Another sixty-seven-year-old widower said, "The groups helped us vent our feelings and learn more to cope better." A seventy-year-old man said, "We had a very fine rapport with members and our group leader. I felt like we were a family group, and we didn't want to say goodbye at the end." Another seventy-year-old stated, "They are a great group of people. I have a feeling of love for each one of them." These comments not only reveal the perceived helpfulness of the groups for most of the men but their statements also show that these men valued the companionship, sense of belonging, and the opportunities to be expressive of their personal and sensitive feelings in gender mixed groups. These comments run counter to many of the existing stereotypical assumptions about male grief.

It is not entirely clear why the men in their eighties did not appear to benefit as much from the support groups, but some possible explanations might be health problems that interfered with their attendance, feeling like they did not have as much in common with the others, or simply being less motivated to cope more effectively. One eighty-two-year-old widower said, "The groups were wonderful but I was not able to attend them all." Another eighty-year-old man reported, "I think they helped a lot of folks. I'm sorry I had to miss many of the meetings." Although the following quote came from a seventy-two-year-old woman who participated in the same self-help group as two older men, her comment may reflect what some of the eighty-year-old men felt but did not say. "The two old men talked too long and too much. They did not fit in with the three ladies." Similarly, a fifty-three-year-old woman said, "At first I did not care for the older men to be in the group, but later it did not seem to matter." It is quite possible that some of the oldest men felt what these women expressed. However, it is important to note that many women reported being grateful that men were included in their groups because they appreciated learning that "men were experiencing many of the same things." Obviously, special attention needs to be given to making all members of any support group feel valued, wanted, and important to the group, regardless of a person's age. We were quite pleased with the overall positive reports from the diverse participants in these support groups [20].

Fourth, spousally bereaved men age fifty and over consistently reported their actual coping abilities to be greater than similar aged men would expect their coping abilities would be if they were in the same situation. Because we were not able to ask the same bereaved men how well they thought they might cope with the death of their spouses and then compare their answers again after they became bereaved (i.e., asking the before and after question of the same men), we did the next best thing. We compared actual coping scores of bereaved men with hypothetical coping scores from non-bereaved currently married men. Even with the shortcomings of this kind of analysis, it is likely that bereaved men may end up coping more effectively than they would expect. When confronted with the realities of a very stressful situation, these men were resilient enough to report that they were coping quite well. In fact, many of the men felt proud of the new skills that they had been forced to learn because their wives were no longer present to do the tasks. Some men were learning how to cook, shop, and take care of the household [5]. As these men learned to become more competent in performing the tasks of daily living they also appeared to cope more effectively with their grief.

Fifth, even though some patterns of adjustment emerged in the data, it is obvious that men age fifty and over showed considerable variation or diversity in how well they were managing. Men in all of the age categories showed a great deal of variation on all adjustment measures throughout the two year study periods. Although the raw data for each male participant was not presented in this chapter it is apparent from Figures 1 through 6 that their bereavement adjustments were similar to "roller coaster" rides which we have discussed in other publications [4, 6, 7]. Their depression, coping, and unresolved grief scores illustrate the many ups and downs that characterize the bereavement process, unlike some of the stage theories of grief [21].

We reported earlier some quotes from men who were having great difficulty coping with their grief, but it is equally important to note that many men were managing their difficult situations very well. The following self-concept statements reflect very good coping at six months following the death of this sixty-eight-year-old man's wife. He wrote, "I am happy. I am loving, compassionate, proud of what I have accomplished in life, religious but not fanatical, enjoy yardwork, enjoy traveling, enjoy my work, enjoy sports—and watching sports, have a wonderful family, love to be outdoors, have many friends and enjoy being with them, but I get sad and miss my wife." Overall, his comments show continuing interest in lifelong activities, good relationships with others, but, still, an appropriate sense of sadness. In contrast to these positive feelings are the self-concept statements from an eighty-nine-year-old widower at three weeks after his wife died. "I am a little bit of nothing, I guess. I am a very small human being. I'd like to find a way out of the turmoil." Later in the study he continued to say that he was a nothing but he did report that he felt better when he kept busier.

We have, in many other publications, summarized some of the diversity that exists within each bereaved person and also among different persons [4-7, 9]. No description of the bereavement process would be complete without mentioning how important it is to know that the bereaved can feel quite good one moment but terrible the next moment. They can also be pleased with one aspect of their lives and adjustment but very dissatisfied with other parts of their adjustment. Similar diversity is also evident among different people. One person may manage very well from early grief through many years of widowhood. Yet, another person may manage poorly for a brief period of time and then find a way to make their life more meaningful and achieve a sense of peace with their loss. As we reported earlier in this chapter, those with good skills in managing tasks of daily living, high self-esteem, and opportunities to express their thoughts and feelings with others are most likely to manage their grief with greater satisfaction. Those who lack these three traits are at much greater risk for having long-term difficulty in coping with bereavement [22]. The men in our research studies have helped us to understand their diversity in coping and the factors that help create more positive outcomes.

One final, but very important point about the grief responses of men who experience the death of their wives has to do with the importance of being self-reliant and having a sense of purpose and direction in life. As gerontologists, we have learned to value the importance of these traits combined with an appreciation of continuity theory. Continuity theory suggests that most people try to maintain many of the same activities, interests, personality traits, and values as they age. Those who appear to be the most satisfied and content as they age are those who are able to maintain the greatest degree of continuity in their lives [23]. We suggest that men who have consistently, throughout their lives, been self-directed, maintained a sense of purpose, and had high self-esteem are much better prepared to deal with the death of a spouse in mid and later life. It is difficult to learn or acquire these traits in late life if they were not already in place earlier. Much of our attention directed toward helping people adjust with major life difficulties needs to be done in early development rather than waiting for the difficulties to occur. We can be more effective if we apply these principles in early socialization experiences of children so that they are in place when they are needed.

Sam Keen, in his book *Fire in the Belly,* makes a most salient point about men who grieve the death of their wives which also relates to our appreciation for continuity theory [24]. He passes along some advice that he received from a close personal friend when he was struggling with life losses. He reports that his friend told him that it was essential to ask yourself two very critical questions in your life and that is was important that they be asked in the correct order. The first question should be, "Where do you want to go on life's journey?" The second question should be, "Who do you want to accompany you on your journey?" If you ask these questions in the wrong order you end up placing more importance on following someone else's journey rather than the one you most want to have. It is quite possible, if you ask these questions in the wrong order and your spouse dies, you may experience greater difficulty because you will not know your own journey. It may be exceptionally difficult to develop a purposeful journey in widowhood if the direction was not already in place or the most central feature of the journey depended primarily on someone else. Again, this advice is most appropriate to apply as we influence the development of children and young adults. Having an identifiable, purposeful, and meaningful life journey can help each of us to cope more effectively with the many challenges and disruptions that are almost certain to come our way.

ACKNOWLEDGMENT

Funding for the two studies described in this chapter was provided by the National Institute on Aging (R01) AG 02193 and (R01) AG 06244.

REFERENCES

1. U.S. Bureau of the Census, Marital Status and Living Arrangements: March 1990, *Current Population Reports,* Series P-20, No. 450, Government Printing Office, Washington, D.C., 1991.
2. D. Umberson, C. B. Wortman, and R. C. Kessler, Widowhood and Depression: Explaining Long-Term Gender Differences in Vulnerability, *Journal of Health and Social Behavior, 33,* pp. 10-24, 1992.
3. W. Stroebe and M. S. Stroebe, *Bereavement and Health: The Psychological and Physical Consequences of Partner Loss,* Cambridge University Press, New York, 1987.
4. D. A. Lund, M. S. Caserta, and M. F. Dimond, Gender Differences Through Two Years of Bereavement Among the Elderly, *The Gerontologist, 26,* pp. 314-320, 1986.
5. D. A. Lund, M. S. Caserta, M. F. Dimond, and S. K. Shaffer, Competencies, Tasks of Daily Living, and Adjustments to Spousal Bereavement in Later Life, in *Older Bereaved Spouses: Research with Practical Applications,* D. A. Lund (ed.), Taylor & Francis/Hemisphere, New York, pp. 135-152, 1989.
6. D. A. Lund, Widowhood: The Coping Response, in *Encyclopedia of Adult Development,* R. Kastenbaum (ed.), Oryx Press, Phoenix, Arizona, pp. 537-541, 1993.
7. D. A. Lund, *Older Bereaved Spouses: Research with Practical Applications,* Taylor & Francis, Hemisphere, New York, 1989.

8. M. S. Caserta and D. A. Lund, Intrapersonal Resources and the Effectiveness of Self-Help Groups for Bereaved Older Adults, *The Gerontologist, 33,* pp. 619-629, 1993.
9. D. A. Lund, Bereavement, in *Clinical Geropsychiatry, Vol. 8 of Comprehensive Clinical Psychology,* B. Edelstein (ed.), Elsevier Science, Oxford, England, 1998.
10. M. S. Caserta, D. A. Lund, and M. F. Dimond, Older Widows' Early Bereavement Adjustments, *Journal of Women and Aging, 1*:4, pp. 5-27, 1989.
11. M. S. Caserta, D. A. Lund, and M. F. Dimond, Assessing Interviewer Effects in a Longitudinal Study of Bereaved Elderly Adults, *Journal of Gerontology, 40,* pp. 637-640, 1985.
12. W. W. K. Zung, A Self-Rating Depression Scale, *Archives of General Psychiatry, 12,* pp. 63-70, 1965.
13. M. A. Kitchell, R. F. Barnes, R. C. Veith, J. T. Okimoto, and M. A. Raskind, Screening for Depression in Hospitalized Geriatric Medical Patients, *Journal of the American Geriatrics Society, 30,* pp. 174-177, 1982.
14. T. R. Faschingbauer, *Texas Revised Inventory of Grief,* Honeycomb, Houston, Texas, 1981.
15. M. S. Caserta and D. A. Lund, Bereavement Stress and Coping Among Older Adults. Expectations Versus the Actual Experience, *Omega, 25,* pp. 33-45, 1992.
16. R. J. Johnson, D. A. Lund, and M. F. Dimond, Stress, Self-Esteem and Coping During Bereavement Among the Elderly, *Social Psychology Quarterly, 49,* pp. 273-279, 1986.
17. D. A. Lund, M. S. Caserta, and M. F. Dimond, Impact of Bereavement on the Self-Conceptions of Older Surviving Spouses, *Symbolic Interaction, 9,* pp. 235-244, 1987.
18. J. W. Worden, *Grief Counseling and Grief Therapy* (2nd Edition), Springer, New York, 1991.
19. V. K. Burks, D. A. Lund, C. H. Gregg, and H. P. Bluhm, Bereavement and Remarriage for Older Adults, *Death Studies, 12,* pp. 51-60, 1988.
20. D. A. Lund and M. S. Caserta, Older Bereaved Spouses' Participation in Self-Help Groups, *Omega, 25,* pp. 47-61, 1992.
21. D. V. Hardt, An Investigation of the Stages of Bereavement, *Omega, 9,* pp. 279-285, 1978.
22. D. A. Lund, M. F. Dimond, M. S. Caserta, R. J. Johnson, J. L. Poulton, and J. R. Connelly, Identifying Elderly With Coping Difficulties After Two Years of Bereavement, *Omega, 16,* pp. 213-224, 1985-86.
23. R. C. Atchley, A Continuity Theory of Normal Aging, *The Gerontologist, 29,* pp. 183-190, 1989.
24. S. Keen, *Fire in the Belly,* Bantam Books, New York, 1991.

CHAPTER 10

American Widowers with School-Age Children: An Exploratory Study of Role Change and Role Conflict

Douglas E. O'Neill and Robert Mendelsohn

The death of a spouse is considered the most traumatic of all life's experiences [1]. How the surviving spouse handles the loss and makes adjustments to this loss are areas of interest and concern for scholars as well as friends and relatives of the surviving spouse. More often than not studies of widowhood in the United States deal with the wife as the surviving spouse. These studies show how she, as the surviving spouse, must cope with the adjustments to loss and the challenges presented by this life cycle change.

The discipline of sociology also tends to address this life cycle event from the perspective of the widow rather than the widower. Helen Lopata's often quoted book *Widowhood in an American City* is an excellent example of research which has been done in the area of widowhood, but it also contains the underlying premise that the wife outlives the husband [2]. An abundant number of books, magazine articles, and scholarly journals articulate the problems, views, conflicts, and stresses that the widow rather than the widower encounters. These articles accentuate the needs and difficulties the wife has in adjusting to the loss of her husband. The different roles the husband performed in the marriage and the importance of these roles are addressed in these articles. However, for the widower there is a notable absence of studies or articles that deal with men as widowers and how they adjust to the death of their wives. This obvious difference in the amount of literature and research directed toward the widow versus the widower is largely due to the statistical data that show women live longer than their husbands [3].

The articles written for the widow address the issues of adjusting to conflicts, stress, and difficulties that accompany loss. The intent of the articles is to help the widow better understand the new roles with which she must now deal. On the other hand, very little research has been done on how the widower deals with similar difficulties, conflicts, and stresses that appear upon the death of his spouse. Narrowing the widower category to those with school-age children, even less literature and research are available. The importance of this single-parent family setting and the challenges it presents to the widower are topics that are seemingly overlooked.

The differences between men and women in adjusting to widowhood must be studied and analyzed to understand better how the loss of a spouse affects the traditional American family. By using traditional family roles and norms for husbands and wives, research can be done to better understand how strain and stress affect the widower. This chapter presents a review of relevant literature, proposes a conceptual framework to guide future research, and offers a research test of the conceptual framework.

Most research which deals with the widower views the topic from the perspective of the widower being an older man and home alone. The fundamental difference between the older widower and the younger widower is the age of the man and the children which were a part of the marriage with the deceased spouse. The marriage of the older widower and his deceased spouse spanned a length of time that fulfilled their parenting roles and their obligations to their children. The marriage of the younger widower and his deceased spouse, however, did not last long enough to realize their obligations to the children in their marriage. When literature is found which mentions the younger widower with school-age children at home, it is usually in passing with the topic of divorced fathers or single fathers as the main point of the research. Theoretical or practical aspects of widowhood (for younger men) are practically non-existent in research literature [4].

In the United States there are more than 35,000,000 families that have children under the age of eighteen at home. This investigation deals with the widower with school-age children who makes up only 0.3 percent of the total American families, or approximately 110,000 families. It is these families, where the widower is the principal parent, for which insufficient literature exists relative to social interaction and the social position of being a widower with school-age children. Significant interest currently exists in the American family and how parents are dealing with their children, especially those parents who are raising children alone because of divorce or choice of not to marry. This interest avoids the widower as a single-parent group completely or its significance as a single-parent family is too small to be sampled. This research will focus on the social interaction and position of this man and his family in American society.

REVIEW OF THE LITERATURE

Historical Overview of the Literature

It wasn't until the twentieth century that women were more likely than men to be a single parent raising the children apart from the father. Previous to this time, it was the man who was more likely to care and provide for the children as the lone parent [5]. Historically, the man became a single parent and assumed custody of the children by 1) the death of his spouse due to high maternal mortality, and 2) divorce or the absolution of the marriage because of desertion [5-7]. In the past when a family dissolution did occur, a legal framework was in place for the husband with social status and property to become a single parent. This framework was based on his ability to provide for the economic and social needs of the children and himself. Yet, if dissolution of the marriage was caused by the death of a spouse, there was more concern for the well-being of the children, who now had no mother. Society's primary consideration for this type of family was how would the widower be able to maintain and give appropriate care and nurturing for the surviving children. This apprehension about the man's ability to care for the children could be approached by different means. First, the children could be given up for adoption or given out to relatives. Second, a woman could be hired to fulfill the roles of nanny and housekeeper. However, a widowed man and a single woman in the same home could give the appearance of inappropriate behavior. In addition, hiring someone to care for the children was not always possible due to financial considerations. Third, the man could remarry as soon as possible so the children would have a mother [6, 7]. Fourth, the children could be brought up by the father, although it was not considered a practical idea or regarded as a real possibility by society or the widower. Because families were typically larger and because the father had to work full-time outside of the house, this option was unrealistic to most. According to Fox and Quitt, the option to remarry was an important advantage that widowers had over men who were divorced [8]. By remarrying, the widower was doing the socially acceptable thing and the marriage was recognized by society and most religions. This acknowledgment was very important in maintaining the social status and continuity of the family.

Overview of the Literature

The review of literature is divided into three segments: the traditional American family, crisis situations, and single men as parents. Segment one focuses on reviewing literature concerning essential areas of the family. In this segment, consideration will be given to what is considered the traditional American family and to the significance of roles in the family for the mother and father. Segment two contains overviews of literature reflecting on crisis situations in the family which lead to single parent status, specifically literature pertaining to men as single parents. This section looks at characteristics in crisis settings in the family. Divorce, desertion, and death are reviewed as events which can lead to a crisis in the family whereby the man can become a single parent. Last, the third segment provides a review of previous studies which discuss single men as parents and the findings of these studies.

The Traditional Family

The American nuclear family or what is commonly referred to as the "traditional family" is composed of two adults of opposite sex who live together in a socially recognized relationship with children who are biologically or socially related to either or both adults [9-11]. The function of the family is to fulfill the needs and desires which are attributed to specific tasks and obligations that the family maintains to operate in society. These diversified family tasks and obligations are acquired by the man and woman when they become married. Morgan reports Murdock stating that the fundamental functions of the family fall into spheres which are sexual, economic, reproductive, and educational in nature [9]. Families function to serve society at large and the individual needs of the members in the family, specifically the husband and wife. In traditional families, the husband and wife dyad provides economic support, the experience of bearing and rearing children, and a lifelong commitment to companionship, love, and affection to all members of the family unit [12]. As a system, the family confronts the same obstacles that are common to all social systems: task performance, goal gratification, integration and solidarity, and pattern maintenance. The nuclear family meets its functional requirements by the activities which are characterized by the family's differentiation, organization, boundary maintenance, and equilibrium tendency [13]. The family as a social system is organized in a manner that fulfills the needs of the unit and individuals alike in the areas of survival, continuation and growth. Martinson makes claim to the concept that the nuclear family's most important function in today's world is relief from the demanding, impersonal, and depersonalized bureaucratic world in which we live [11]. It becomes a harbor or safe haven for the individual who must confront the stresses and conflicts of today's world.

Roles for Husband and Wife

The structure of the nuclear family is commonly viewed as the assigned or culturally understood division of labor that exists between the husband and wife. Historically, the division of labor had more to do with the practical demands of running a household, and was not because of a gender specialization or function. Gender came into play by the roles in which it was most practical for the individual or couple to function and benefit the family unit. It was the inclination and skills of the husband and wife that helped to create gender specialization. The facts being what they are historically, it seems that early marriages functioned under the organization of the husband having the power in the family. Additionally, the division of labor was not gender-specific, as it appears to be in today's society [8]. Emile Durkheim looked at the division of labor as a complement of "differences that attract" rather than a factor of exclusion. Along with the concept of complementing opposites, Durkheim saw the division of labor as a producer of social solidarity [14].

Talcott Parson's socialization process uses sex-role differentiation to explore this paradigm in the family. His main contention is that the sex-role affiliation and differentiation plays an essential role in the functioning of the family unit. Parson's claim is that the mother role is the anchor between the mother-child and the family system, while the father role functions between the family system and the extra-familial social system. Parson's main interest is brought forward in his concept that the man's role is that of the occupational, i.e., he is the provider or "breadwinner." The husband's abilities at work help to determine the social status of the entire family. The man becomes specialized by his outside-of-family work, which deprives the husband/father of natural happiness within the family. For the married male, the family and his outside occupation must interrelate. The need to function in these two spheres at any given time or in the same time frame will cause role strain or conflict for the husband/father.

The woman's role is to be in control of the domestic unit, i.e, the home. In this role fall the tasks of caring for the children, providing emotional (therapeutic) support for all family members, and the physical tasks of housework and cooking. Stress of the mother/wife are the result of her expectation and/or desire to simultaneously fulfill her woman role(s) and the role of an individual person, which includes freeing of oneself from traditional restrictions. Additional stress, conflict, and adjustment factors enter the family when a specific role(s) must be and assumed by the surviving parent upon the death of a spouse, which in this study is the wife. When the man acquires the extra roles his wife once assumed, new demands will be placed on the husband's time and an understanding of these new roles will be necessary. This in turn puts more stress on the widower to function in his existing roles and to perform the tasks the additional roles will require. These additions then limit the time the man has for himself and for his children. When a women acquires a role that is usually associated with the husband, she is looked at as being honored. However a man, who picks up a role traditionally associated with woman, is not honored. Instead, his extra duties are looked upon as a burden or disgrace by many [15].

Although this postulate of specific roles for men and women may have been thought of as traditionally correct, it is becoming more evident that the family unit is evolving beyond this belief. Presently women are moving into roles that were thought of customary to men. They are working full-time jobs outside of the home in addition to their domestic duties. Traditionaly, men are more alienated when they, by choice or circumstance, acquire roles previously associated with women [12]. Although the husband usually recognizes the roles and responsibilities of his wife, he is isolated from their significance and worth until such time when he must assume them alone.

Crisis in Families

The origin of a crisis can have significant reverberations on how the family handles the crisis. If the crisis is caused from outside the family organization, the stress encountered by the family may actually help to solidify the family during its hardships. However, if the crisis is internal it may or may not reflect intra-family dysfunction and eventually cause its breakup.

When a crisis occurs in the family unit it may be as insignificant as how to get ready for the unannounced arrival of relatives for the weekend. On the other hand, complete role transition for one or more family members may result when spousal separation or the death of a spouse occurs [16]. When such a transformation of roles takes place, confusion, stress, major adjustment, and role overload may be experienced by those who now have new and old roles as their responsibility.

Martinson states that ". . . the family is the bottleneck through which all troubles pass, no other association so reflects the strains and stresses of life" [11, p. 350]. Hill notes that when a crisis occurs in a family, especially in a family living in an urban area, the family members will often present a collective front of solidarity to protect the family secrets and reputation during this time of crisis [17]. Hill found that this closed formation would only allow certain specified instruments from the outside to interact with the family. Those outside factions include immediate kin, family, friends, neighbors, the family physician, the family pastor, and the family lawyer.

A crisis-precipitating event is that which occurs without warning or with little previous understanding of such circumstances which becomes a major factor in how the family relates to and handles the stressor that has engulfed them [18]. The concept of a stressor ". . . is identified with a situation where there is little to no prior preparation and must therefore be viewed as problematic" [17]. Since no stressor is identical for each family, specific types of situations or circumstances cause the family and individuals to encounter obstacles that are unique or specific to their crisis. Hill refers to these obstacles as hardships, which follow in the footsteps of stressor. "Hardships may be defined as those complications in a crisis-precipitating event which demand competencies from the family which the event itself may have temporarily paralyzed or made unavailable" [17, p. 141]. It is pointed out by Hill that stresses that affect families are usually categorized by source of trouble (stressor), combinations of dismemberment-accession and demoralization, and types of impact of stressor events.

Hill discusses three categories of crisis in a modern family that lead to a family becoming dysfunctional or losing its continuity because of a major realignment of roles within the family [17]. First described by Hill is the concept of "dismemberment of family members." Dismemberment is used to explain an unwanted loss of a family member(s), either for a short period of time or permanently. Examples used by Hill for dismemberment are: 1) the death of a child, spouse, or parent, 2) hospitalization of a spouse or other family member, and 3) separation of family member by war.

Accession, the second concept, causes crisis in families because of lack of preparation for role changes by the member(s) of the family. This change may lead to the loss of family continuity or morale character. Some examples of accession are: 1) the unwanted pregnancy of a member of the family, 2) a member of the family who returns to the family after previously abandoning it, and 3) the addition of a step-father, step-mother, or step-children to an existing family.

The last concept Hill mentions is that of demoralization. Here the family unit is undermined by the loss of confidence and/or faith by a member who is counted on to play a role in the family that causes it to function smoothly. Family members who exhibit 1) nonsupport for other members or the family unit, 2) infidelity, or 3) problems of alcoholism, drugs, or gambling are examples of this concept.

The concept of demoralization can and does interact with dismemberment and accession, causing strain, conflict, and adjustment problems for all members of the family in crisis. The examples used in the preceding paragraphs illustrate some of the common crises that befall the modern family. It is the category of dismemberment within the family unit on which this study will focus. When dismemberment takes place, some type of demoralization will ensue, due to the disruption of family role patterns and the understood missing functions within the given family. "Dismemberment creates a situation in which the departed one's roles must be allocated, and a period of confusion-delay ensues while the members of the family cast learn their new lines" [17, p. 142].

Three Specific Crises in Which Men Become a Single-Parent

Desertion

According to Martinson, desertion is that state where a couple is not legally separated by divorce or annulment or where there is a separate maintenance agreement [11]. Fox and Quitt note that, historically, desertion occurs more frequently in lower class or low income families and is referred to in sociological literature as "the poor man's divorce" [8]. For those who are left as a single parent by desertion, difficulties abound because of not knowing the whereabouts of the deserter. This family posture causes stress for the lone parent as well as for other members of the family. For the remaining parent the problem of determining how the family will be supported and what action should be taken against the spouse that has abandoned the family are huge.

In countries where there is no option for divorce, desertion is the only alternative for a spouse who wants out of a marriage. In the United States, men whose spouse goes to the extreme of desertion have usually tried in vain to let the spouse know of their unhappiness in the marriage. This final extreme measure of desertion is usually pre-planned. The reasons why a wife leaves her husband include love affairs, her ability to achieve her own way in the world due to her own viable career, and her belief that her husband is unable to empathize and react to her needs [19]. Greif, in discussing the role of the husband and his wife before dismemberment, states that ". . . the father who is deserted by his wife is apt to have been more involved in the housework and child care during the marriage, to be earning less money, to have a marriage that ended because of infidelity, to have a wife who is less involved with the children after the breakup, and to have less satisfaction in a number of parenting areas" [5, p. 47].

Divorce

In today's American society, divorce is built on a Protestant framework that lawfully terminates the marriage. The premise of divorce as understood today is the legal dissolution of a valid marriage with the right of both parties to remarry. "Divorced men enter the single parent role with many of the same factors of demoralization as men who have been deserted by their wife [5, p. 8]. Greif notes that men who are divorcing for reasons other than desertion usually have not been actively involved with their children while they were married [5]. These same men, in most cases, did not want to end the marriage. This can cause stressful and difficult times for the father who must adjust to his new role as a parental figure and has no way to mourn his loss of marital status [9-11]. This sanction of divorce in American society has now made it the leading cause for marriage dissolution [3, p. 55], beating out the usual world-leading cause of marriage dissolution— death [20]. This legal change of marital status, the divorce decree [13], helps to set limits on the expectations, responsibilities, and roles that the man/father must now perform.

Death

Death is identified by Holmes and Rahe as the most stressful of all life events, as measured on the Social Readjustment Rating Scale [1]. This crisis disintegrates the nuclear family with a suddenness and intensity that is not associated with desertion and divorce. In this crisis there is no mending or repairing of the husband and wife team. There is no recourse for the surviving parent who must proceed alone with no counsel from lawyers or ex-spouse. Death as the cause for single parenthood and how it affects the husband/father of a nuclear family are topics that are rarely examined, especially when dealing with the men as single parents with school-age children under the age of eighteen [20]. Hanson and Bozett, in *Dimensions of Fatherhood* [6], have a chapter contributed by Jane K. Burgess in which she states:

> The problem with traveling on uncharted waters is that one has no "maps" with which to check one's course [7, p. 416].

So it is with writing a chapter on widowers as fathers.

Studies of Single Men as Parents

Arnold states that there is a considerable amount of literature on single-parent families headed by females who are either divorced or widowed [21]. However, there is a scarcity of literature and empirical research on the topic of single-parent families with school-age children under eighteen years of age [20] headed by the man due to the death of his wife. Arnold continues that one reason for this scarcity of research on widower's with school-age children is that there are so few families to sample and survey. With this population so numerically small, it logically follows that it is difficult to locate them. Other factors are the potential for a high financial cost in finding the widowers and then actually getting them to be part of the study.

Men as Single-Parents

Gasser and Taylor [22] and Mendes [23] have undertaken research that included the widowed man in their inquiries. However, grouping widowers with divorced men illustrates how some researchers deal with the dilemma of a small sample size. This lumping strategy is evidenced by the numbers of widowers found in various studies. In Gasser and Taylor's [22] study, a little more than 30 percent of the men are widowed; for Mendes [23], 30 percent. All of the studies mentioned above looked at variables such as role conflict, adjustment problems, attitudes, home-making, or problems the single parents were having.

The classification system previously mentioned in this chapter, which was outlined by Hill and discussed at length, makes an important point of delineating how studies such as those referenced above have noted the importance of differentiating between dismemberment and demoralization and have added dismemberment to demoralization [17]. It has been emphasized that the death of a spouse is a stand-alone crisis [17], but this crisis has not been researched by itself as a major event which brings about the changes, stress, and conflict of social position associated with being a widowed single parent.

Studies Specific to Widowed Men with School-Age Children

Very few investigations have addressed the issue of widowers with children from the social position of status and the role of the widower. Included is John Bedell's study *Role Reorganization in the One-Parent Family: Mother Absent Due To Death* [24]. In this study he examined widowed men with children from the city of Cleveland, Ohio. Bedell's study objective was an analysis of task function in the home setting. He wished to find out if the father and/or the children took up those functions of the wife/mother who was no longer a part of the family. He found, first, that widowers are a difficult group to sample and that generalizations about this group are made based on a very small sample. Secondly, he found that there is no universal replacement for any given task when it is to be performed.

A second study entitled *The Relationship between Adjustment to Bereavement in Widowers and Perceived Social Support*, by Rosamond Lennox, included only two widowers who were noted to have children under eighteen [25]. The objective of this study, which focused mainly on older widowed men, was to note how men perceived society in helping them deal with their grief. The findings showed that there appears to be a correlation between their adjustment to their bereavement status and their perceived support from others.

The last study in this review is Betty Jane Lodge's *Role Adjustments to Single Parenthood: A Study of Divorced and Widowed Men and Women* [26]. This investigation was noteworthy because of the researcher's desire to better understand the American widower with school-age children. Lodge, in her research, addressed the issue of role and how widowed men respond to it as a part of being a single parent. The number of men was small and demographic information about the men was missing from this study. However, one of her major conclusions was that adjusting to single parent status is a process that one goes through by learning to cope with new demands of their parenting roles and by re-establishing their identity as a single person.

This literature review has established a starting point for studying men who become single parents by the virtue of a family crisis. Previous studies have provided important insights and views into single parenting and the unfamiliar roles, tasks, and functions that men must assume. The next section of this chapter presents a review and discussion of role theory and the interactionist perspective and an explanation of why they may be particularly useful in future research and clerical practice.

In American society, becoming a single parent through the death of a spouse is a statistically unusual, unanticipated life event [27]. Carolyn Balkwell, referring to becoming a single parent, states; ". . . role reversal may exacerbate any feelings of inadequacy or power-lessness which may be experienced by the surviving spouse" [28]. Today, the roles of the American father are more than ever being characterized by rapid change and uncertainty. Often, fathers entering into the new roles have few if any role models or reference groups [29]. It is interactions that people have with one another that helps establish how they will perceive their roles. These interactions often generate different expectations for the new roles, thus causing stress, conflict, and difficulty in adjusting to contrasting social positions that indi-viduals are placed in during their lives. This chapter also reviews the relevancy and application of role theory and the interactionist perspec-tive. Following the review of the interactionist perspective on social roles as they apply to widowers is a presentation of four propositions used to guide a specific research investigation that is described in detail later in the chapter.

Review of Role Theory and Interactionist Perspective

When men enter the role of single parenthood following the death of their wives it causes difficulty in many relationships with others. During this phase of the man's life he is being restructured at all levels, in both his personal and public life. It is at this phase of development that the implications of conflict, strain, and adjusting to his loss will have a direct effect on how the widower perceives himself and how others observe him. The implications and consequences for the widower and how he addresses the issue of being a single-parent are based largely on how he defines the new role through interactions with others.

Historically, men most often became custodial fathers to their children due to high maternal mortality. In large measure, the single dad role began centuries ago. Within this role, some men have experi-enced pressure to transfer responsibilities to a new wife or to give the children to relatives for their nurturing [6, 7].

Theoretical or practical aspects of widowhood for younger men have not been the focus of much research [4]. Hanson acknowledges that role theory can be useful in studying fathers in different social contexts [29]. She states that a person is able to understand and emulate the intri-cacies of behavior just by observing another significant person carry out that role. Orthner, Brown, and Ferguson state that because roles are not yet institutionalized in American culture for the single father, confusion and frustration are noted in the man's processing of roles [30]. Any man who attempts to perform roles of fatherhood is doing so without role clarity. Brim and Wheeler point out that a role is based on previously acquired desires by individuals to conform to the expectations and situations of others within the understood social setting [31]. Men in these settings use reference groups other than friends or family to maintain self-esteem.

Nye and Berardo have stressed that it might be time to look at a merging of interactional and situational frames of reference within the study of sociology [13]. This type of conceptual framework is referred to as "interstitial." It is the synthesizing of the two frameworks and the linkage of key concepts from both that would help establish an understanding of the process of transition, i.e., going from a nuclear family setting to a single-parent family by the nature of the crisis.

Interactionist Concepts Relevant to Single Parents as Widowers

Interaction helps to define the roles of humans based upon activities and settings. It is in these situations that the social roles are defined and played by others in the given setting. Within these situations and activities, it should be noted that social interactions are not governed just by cognition of social roles but also by intense human emotions [32].

Presented below are interactionist terms and concepts related to the situation of being a single parent widower with school-age children.

1. The widower holds a *position/status* that is common to others who share the same expectations associated with being widowed. Position refers to the collectively recognized category of persons for whom the basis for such differentiation is their common attribute, their common behavior, or the common reactions of others toward them [33]. Znaniecki argues that position is a way to classify social roles without inquiring into the person who is performing and those with whom he is interacting [34]. One limitation in applying this term to widowers is that it does not automatically recognize the broad range of permissible variation that exists among all those who occupy the same position. Also absent is a recognition of the gradual creative emergence in the course of history of new roles, with new standards and norms [34].

2. The role(s) of the widower is built to a great degree on the functions that are acquired or assumed to be acquired by the man. Roles are structured on *prescriptive behavior* which states how

someone should act, what is expected or not expected, and standards or norms for covert and overt behavior that are distinctive from other [33].

3. *Theatrical roles* involve interaction which revolves around and between the lead actor and the supporting actors. However, the lead actor is of no importance without other minor actors who support him by their circle of attention. Theatrical roles are products of drama. They are created by the author to visually and verbally recreate settings for players to reconstruct the roles that are culturally patterned by the author. The actors are to conform to the norms of what is understood as acceptable for the scene or meeting certain standards. The key actor must conform to his roles so that he adequately represents the drama the author has written. However, if the supporting cast does not follow the accepted norm or culturally recognized pattern, the key actor cannot be effective in his portrayal.

Theatrical roles and social roles are both based on culturally based individuals who will follow and learn what is expected of them so they may perform. Also the individual in the social roles has the difficulty if others do not learn and act according to the prescribed cultural expectations for behavior. The obvious difference between the two types of roles is in what is supposed to follow or occur. However, even when the actors follow the same cultural patterns their performances can vary from actor to actor. Why these various performances take place is open to speculation, but they cannot be ignored. In this discussion the central person is the widower with school-age children. The widower's social roles and relations will be constantly evolving and changing as he goes through the process of being a widower and disengaging himself from widowhood.

Four social role elements will be developed in this exploratory study: person, social circle, personal rights, and personal function. They are needed to better understand the evolution of the role of the widower.

Conceptual Components that Guide the Widower Role

The following concepts give guidance to understanding the role(s) of the widower and some of the associated changes that are required for adjustment.

1. *Loss of role:* The man loses the social identity of marriage and couple status when the label of "widower" is given to the man upon the death of his spouse.

2. *Change of role:* The man goes from the "known and understood roles" of marriage, father, husband, and joint parenting to "new,

different, and unknown roles" of a widower with school-age children.

3. *Isolation of role:* The man is separated and alienated from other individuals or groups in terms of interaction, communication, cooperation, and social and emotional involvement.

4. *Expectation of role:* Different sets of responses or behaviors are anticipated and desired in relation to a certain role(s).

5. *Adjustment of role:* Adjustment is the modification of one's understood behavior or attitude toward a role(s).

6. *Anxiety of role:* Extreme apprehensiveness, uneasiness, or fear are the result of not being able to clearly focus on or fulfill the demands of the role(s).

When considering these concepts that encompass the role of widower, it must be understood that role conflict is also likely to be experienced. Role conflict, ". . . is the incompatibility between two or more roles that an individual is expected to perform in a given situation. The performance of one role often interferes with or is antagonistic to another role. For example, the role of single parent can conflict with a new role of being uncoupled. The state of conflict may last only a short time and the conflicting demands may be met without much difficulty or it may be a persistent problem facing someone all his life." Stress also is commonly experienced when the widowers' roles interfere with the individual's usual pattern of behavior.

In addition to these important concepts, Znaniecki identified several principles of social roles that are particularly relevant to widowhood [34]. These principles help to provide a broader but more focused assessment of widowhood. These concepts and associated principles are presented below.

1. *Person:* An individual can perform a social role only if his social circle(s) judges him to be the kind of person who is fit for this kind of role. Such judgments are not made arbitrarily; they follow well-established cultural standards.

2. *Social circles:* A social circle is comprised of individuals who interrelate with the person (widower) and whose evaluation of him is valued.

3. *Personal rights:* Certain privileges are given to the individual by those in his social circle so that he may fulfill his responsibilities to his social role(s).

4. *Personal role behavior and function:* (a) Individual functions will relate directly to past experiences to given role(s) in which the person has functioned. (b) The person's failures or transgressions may interfere or have direct impact on other roles that are

performed. (c) A combination of points *a* and *b* may lead the individual to innovations that lead to the development of a new assortment of duties and how to carry them out [34, pp. 219-276].

Some of the other roles that single parent widowers might find in conflict during their adjustment need to be identified. These roles are directly related to family life.

1. *Socialization role* (social norms and mental well-being): Here the parents are expected to teach and instill social norms, desired behaviors, values, attitudes, skills, and roles that help shape the child and become integrated into his or her society [34, pp. 273-276].
2. *Child care role* (physical and psychic well-being): There is close interaction between the socialization role and the child care role. Both involve intimate association with the children along with teaching the children to be self-sufficient. The difference is that in the child care role the parent is instrumental in developing physically healthy children. The child care role is first. The socialization role follows when mental and physical maturity begins. As the child becomes older the child care role becomes secondary to the socialization role of the parent [35].
3. *Provider role* (economic well-being for goods and services): In this role the individual is responsible for obtaining or providing goods and services for the family members to function. This role has been traditionally assigned to the man-husband figure in the family; however, over the last number of years this role is becoming a joint role for the man and woman [35-37].
4. *Housekeeper role:* The role of housekeeper is built on the concepts of cleanliness and order in preparing or cooking food, and mending and caring for clothing and other household equipment. The housekeeper role also includes cleaning, laundry, marketing, and keeping financial records. However, the housekeeper role should not be confused with the housewife role. The two roles are often thought to be synonymous, because the housekeeper role takes place in the confines of the house where the housewife role such as child socialization, child care, or kinship take place [13, p. 36].
5. *Therapeutic role:* From the sociological and counseling perspectives there are four positive functions of the individual in the therapeutic role: 1) listening to problems, 2) sympathizing, 3) giving reassurance and affection, and 4) offering help to solve problems [3, p. 474].

Application of Znaniecki Principles of Social Roles to Adaptation to Widowhood

Four principles of social role according to Znaniecki are stated below. After each principle is a set of questions or statements that were then addressed in a research study.

Principle One: Person

A social role must be legitimized by the person who is the primary performer. The process that establishes the rank of widowerhood for men with school-age children contains seven variables. Each variable helps to bring into existence standards by which the widower may measure or be measured by his actions or responses. The following statements/questions follow from each principle.

- Information relating to a couple as husband and wife is often associated with the length of marriage.
- The length of widowhood gives the widower a time frame or reference point to measure change in his life since the death of his spouse.
- Caring for children who are eighteen years of age and under as a single parent makes the widower an atypical man in America.
- The age the man is widowed may be a determinant in how he will relate and adjust to his new duties and responsibilities.
- The total number of children in the family may cause stress and conflict for the man as he adapts to his new roles as a widower.
- The widower's education level may influence his ability to adapt to the role of widower with school-age children.
- The widower's gross income may be a factor which influences how the man adjusts to his new position and roles.

Principle Two: Social Circles

How different social circles aid the widower's needs can be measured by their means of usefulness and the guidance they give the widower as he adjusts to his roles. The social circles include the following groups: kin, kin by marriage, non-kin, and others. Kin includes mother, father, brothers, and sisters; kin by marriage includes the mother-in-law, the father-in-law, the brothers-in-law, and sisters-in-law. The non-kin grouping consist of personal friends, clergy, medical personnel, counselors, single parents, and other widowers. The other group includes television/radio programs, books, and support programs.

When an individual communicates to others symbolically his observations, feelings, or violations, he expects to be understood and to provoke some response. Indeed, mutual understanding through symbolic communication is an essential condition of social solidarity for sympathetic understanding. When something very painful or very pleasant occurs to an individual participant, he (or she) has the right to expect a manifestation of sympathy from his social circle—be it a large family or a circle of neighbors or acquaintances. Thus, after the circle learns of the death of an individual's father, mother, husband, wife, or other close kin, every participant is obliged to share in the common mourning [3, p. 103]. The following statements/questions related to this principle are addressed in this study.

- How the man adjusts to the death of his wife will help determine the amount of difficulty he will have with stress and conflict that accompanies the *loss*.
- The ability to adjust to the *change* of responsibilities of being a single parent will affect the amount of stress and conflict the widower will experience.
- The nature of the wife's death will affect how the widower adjusts to his loss. This ability to adjust will in turn influence to what extent he is able to accommodate the role of widower.
- Members of social circles have the ability to be helpful when *child care* (day care) is needed. How the widower perceives their helpfulness will aid the man when assistance is needed.
- During crisis situations, if child care is not in place the widower will need to acquire it. This consideration of hiring a relative or non-relative will likely be a *change* in normal task performance for the widower. Who the widower hires may be those who display the most understanding.
- The widower will associate with people in his social circles and seek their help in confronting different problems. The *isolation* the man feels about his widowhood will be confronted by talking to other people.
- The widower will be normally *isolated* by the nature of his crisis when he attempts to relate his loss to others. By talking to different individuals, the widower can rate how helpful and supportive they will be in understanding his loss.
- The lack of understanding by fellow workers of the feelings and emotions that are involved with the death of a wife may cause difficulty for the widower as he adapts to his *loss*.

- With the death of a man's wife, his responses to life and his perceptions of what is important are altered. The actions the widower takes may be viewed as his attempt to *change* his life due to his loss.
- The widower will seek out different sources of guidance to help him *adjust* to his new role as a widower. Some sources will be more useful than others for the man as he deals with his new and old roles. The sources which he regards as the most useful will be noted by positive responses from the widower.
- After the loss of a spouse the widower will experience a roller coaster ride of emotional highs and lows when it comes to dealing with his new single status. These mixed feelings may cause emotional conflicts which make *adjustment* difficult for the widower.
- Prior to becoming a widower with school-age children, the widower's social circle will include very few men who have experienced such a *loss*.
- Once a man with school-age children is widowed, he will seek out and find other men who have experienced a *loss* similar to his so that he may receive positive support and not be set apart by his new social position.
- Prior to leaving the rank of widower with school-age children, the individual must move toward the process of disengaging from the position of widowhood. One step for the widower to begin disengagement is dating. The dating process will cause *anxiety* for the widower when the time is right for him to look at the possibility of another relationship.
- The man may consider his social role of widower as an influence on the woman's decision of whether or not to go out with him. This social position of being widowed may cause *anxiety* for the man as he moves from the past to the present.
- The widower with school-age children must consider this additional responsibility when dating begins. This additional obligation of school-age children may be a difficulty which will cause *anxiety* in his ability or desire to leave the rank of widowhood.
- If a discussion of remarriage took place before the *loss* of his spouse, then the widower's attempts to date and possibly remarry will be less stressful for him.
- When the widower remarries or desires to remarry he is actively seeking a *change* that will disengage him from the social position of widowhood.

- The ability of the widower to adjust to both the physical and emotional *isolation* which is caused by the loss of his wife may be evidenced by how often the widower visits the cemetery.

Principle Three: Personal Rights-Economic

"Although some individuals are more, others less dependent, every individual throughout his life depends for his 'living,' i.e., the satisfaction of his wants, upon the aid of others who grant him certain economic rights. His rights are prior to his duties . . ." [34, p. 259]. The following statements relate to this principle.

- It is not unusual in times of crisis that people assist those in need with financial help. Those people who know the widower and/or his situation will feel compelled to help the man *adjust* by giving financial help. The amount of helpfulness they give will contribute to the widower's recovery.
- As a couple it is customary for the husband and wife to plan for their future by saving and investing money so they may adjust to the *change* in their lifestyle at retirement. One of these investments for their future may have been life insurance. Having this type of investment may or may not be a part of a couple's plan.
- If life insurance was a part of the couple's investments for their future, the amount of the policy may influence whether or not the surviving spouse will be able to maintain his old lifestyle as he *adjusts* to his new roles and social position.

Principle Four: Personal Role Behavior and Functions

Once the family unit has children, the parents must perform the tasks and functions of parenting that are culturally ascribed. When parenting goes from the "traditional two-parent arrangement" to single parenting due to the death of a parent, the remaining parent will take on tasks and roles which are alien to him. Nye states, "Traditionally, the mother has been closely associated with childrearing and child care more so than has the father. The traditional division of labor in the family has the *domestic roles* (house-keeping, child care, and child socialization role) as the major domain of the wife-mother, and the provider role as the primary activity and responsibility of the husband-father" [13, p. 36]. Along with the traditional roles the mother assumed, she usually is considered the primary care giver for therapeutic needs.   The following statements/questions are related to this principle.

- When a child is faced with the reality of death, specifically that of their mother, the child will have many questions and fears. A father's response to his children's queries which is less than honest may be caused by *anxiety* of the father.
- The ability to perform any given role is usually based in part on past performance, or partial performance, of the role. Being the sole parent will cause stress and conflict for the father as he goes about obtaining child care. This *change* in task experiences may or may not be stressful to the widower.
- When a man and woman marry, they customarily function in specific *domestic* roles that are considered traditional to each. But who decides what is traditional and what task is done by whom is up for debate. However, using hindsight, the widower can look back and see who performed certain tasks during his marriage.
- Previous experience with certain *domestic* tasks will dictate which task is now his easiest and which is the most difficult for the widower as a single parent to perform in the family.
- By performing different roles and tasks as a single parent the man will encounter different experiences where he will seek guidance. This guidance will be sought so that he may *adjust* to and fulfill these obligations. The usefulness of the guidance will vary because of the source that the widower uses.

METHODOLOGY

Given the target population of widowers with school-age children, it was necessary to establish the geographic limits for the research project. It was decided that because the population is very small, a national exploratory study would be most promising for locating the men in the target population. It was understood from the beginning that it would be difficult to locate the men to survey. The following criteria were used to determine if a widower could be included in the survey: 1) the widower had school-age children at the time of his wife's death, 2) the school-age children lived at home with their father after the death of their mother, and 3) the widower could still be widowed or remarried.

Sampling Design and Procedure

During the last week of August 1994, a preliminary attempt was made via FAX to acquire names and addresses of widowers who would participate in this study. The point of contact for this sampling technique was funeral homes. With permission from Eidsness Funeral Home in Brookings, South Dakota, a letter on Eidsness' letterhead was FAXed to twenty-five funeral homes in twenty-five different states. Funeral homes with a FAX machine on site, according to the 1993 National Funeral Directory, were randomly selected. A time frame of four weeks was allowed for a response from the funeral homes. At the end of this time frame no correspondence was received from any of the twenty-five funeral homes. This method illustrated the difficulty of developing a sampling process to find respondents for this type of research.

A second strategy was used to identify initial informants who would have information on widowers with school-age children. As a member of The Association of Death Education and Counseling (ADEC), this researcher acquired from ADEC headquarters a mailing list of all members. This list included more than 1500 names and addresses of members in the United States who work in a wide array of disciplines related to death and dying. The disciplines include professors, clergy, nurses, medical doctors, funeral directors, and hospice personnel.

A randomly selected number of ADEC members from the United States was drawn to create a snowball sampling procedure. These members were sent letters requesting their assistance with this research. A total of 200 letters were mailed to the ADEC members in September and October 1994.

Both mailings produced a limited number of names of potential subjects for this study. Therefore, a third strategy was implemented in December 1994. A notice was placed in the quarterly ADEC magazine *Forum*. This magazine is received by all currently active members. Thirty-one widowers were initially contacted through the 200 mailings and the notice placed in the *Forum*. These thirty-one men were sent survey packets to be filled out. An additional three widowers were found via *America On Line* using "Widower" as a search keyword. The remaining twelve men were brought to the researcher's attention by people who knew of the study and widowers who knew other widowers who wanted to participate in the study. In all, forty-six widowers with school-age children were found to participate in this national exploratory study. The respondents were living in twenty-one different states throughout the United States.

Research Instrument

Each survey packet contained the following materials: letter of introduction, instructions, survey, and a self-addressed stamped envelope for the widowers to return their survey. The surveys were sent back to the Department of Sociology at South Dakota State University so that participants would know that this research was a professional study.

Section one of the research instrument included thirty survey questions. Respondents were asked to respond to the questions by checking the response that "best fit them as an individual during the period of being widowed." Other questions asked the widowers to rate or rank their responses as they applied to them. Twenty of the thirty questions had space at the bottom of the question for the respondent to qualify his response in written form. The written narrative was considered to be significant. Asking for this type of response to questions was an attempt to allow men to relate their own experiences beyond that of a "yes" or "no" response.

Section two of the survey dealt with the collection of demographic information about the widower and his deceased wife. Information in this section covered the occupation of both the husband and wife, ethnicity of the husband, educational level of both husband and wife, religious affiliation of both, and the number of children and their ages. Additionally, information was requested concerning the deceased wife's cause of death, age at the time of death, and occupation. Widowers were also asked to sign a statement if they were interested in any future participation in a follow-up study on this same topic.

Independent Variables

This research focuses primarily on seven independent variables. How each of these variables were measured is described below. In some analyses the data were grouped into categories.

Length of marriage was measured in whole years. When a widower responded to the question of how long he was married, his answer was rounded down to the nearest year. For example if his answer was seven years five months, it was coded as seven years. (*Category I* = men who were married 10 years or less. *Category II* = men who were married more than 10 years.)

Length of widowhood was measured from the date of the wife's death until the date the survey was filled out or until the widower remarried. The length of being widowed was measured in whole months. (*Category I* = men who have been widowed 12 months or less. *Category II* = men who have been widowed more than 12 months.)

Number of children in the family includes all children of the widower. (*Category I* = widowers with 1 or 2 children. *Category II* = widowers with 3 or more children.

Care of children age eighteen and under was assessed by the current ages of his children. The length of widowhood was subtracted from the current age of the children to determine their age at the time of their mother's death. (*Category I* = widowers with children from 14 to 18 years of age. These children were considered to be latchkey children, capable of caring for themselves until their father was in the home. *Category II* = widowers with children less than 14 years of age. This age group was considered to need day care or supervision by an adult when their father was not present. *Category III* = widowers with children in both age groups. Widowers in this category would be confronted with both child care scenarios which would impact him differently than if he had children in just Category I or Category II.)

The widower's education level was determined by the widower's response on the survey regarding the highest educational level achieved. (*Category I* = men whose education level was less than a bachelor degree. *Category II* = men whose education level was a bachelor degree or higher.)

Widower's gross income was obtained directly from the survey by placing a check next to the income bracket that best fit them at the time they were widowed. (*Category I* = widowers whose income was $40,000 or less per year. *Category II* = widowers whose income was equal to or greater than $40,000 per year.) These categories were derived from figures published in 1994 stating that in 1992 for the "average earning of year-round, full-time workers: 1992" the median income was $37,180 [3, p. 474].

The age a man was widowed was obtained directly from the survey. (*Category I* = men who were 35 years old or less at the time of their spouse's death. *Category II* = men who were older than 35 when their spouse died.) Using the age of thirty-five as a break point for the two categories was based on statistics published in [3, p. 103]. This publication stated that the median age for an American male to be divorced in 1988 was 35.1 years of age. This information was used only as a reference from a heavily studied family crisis area where roles and marital status change.

Analysis Procedures

For analysis of this small sample population (46 men), the responses to the questions were collapsed, i.e., data reduction was used. This made it possible to infer findings for this small population where information and knowledge is lacking.

"Of all relationships affected by death, it is the death of a spouse that most changes the social identity of the bereaved. Husbands become widowers, and wives become widows. The existence of such a title reveals a fundamental change in one's social standing in the social order" [38, p. 483]. Although many questions were addressed in this study, only the most important and essential findings are presented here. The selected findings are those that reflect on the theory and its underlying assumptions about role changes and adjustments. Additional findings and more detail about specific analyses can be obtained directly from the authors.

Demographic Information

The demographic data collected on the survey represents information about the widower and his deceased wife. Except for one man who was African American, the remaining men surveyed were Caucasian. The men resided in both rural and urban settings in the United States. Most of the men were Catholic (N = 12), followed by Lutheran (N = 6), Methodist (N = 5), Presbyterian (N = 3), Other Protestants religions (N = 14), and Jewish (N = 3).

The occupations for the husband varied greatly, including college professor, chaplain, banker, self-employed, farmer, police detective, college student, salesman, and engineer. When asked if their deceased wife had been employed full-time outside the home setting, 85 percent of the men responded yes. Of the remaining 15 percent, four wives worked at least part-time outside the home with the other three wives being considered full-time housewives.

The age at which the wives died ranged from twenty-five years of age to forty-nine. The mean age for the wives death was thirty-eight years nine months. The educational level of the deceased wives ranged from high school graduate to law school graduate. Eleven (24%) of the women had a four-year degrees and nine (20%) of the women had completed a master's degree or higher. Eight (17%) of the women had received only their high school diploma or GED equivalent. The remaining eighteen (39%) of the women went on after high school to a vocational/technical school or took some college courses without completing their degree.

The most common cause of death was cancer, with 76 percent of the women falling into this category. The remaining 24 percent of the widowers lost their spouse by accidental death, suicide, or other natural causes.

At the time of their mother's death, the children's ages ranged from seven months to twenty-five years of age. The forty-six couples had a total of 114 children. Of these 114 children, 100 were eighteen years old or younger. When the mother died, the average age for these 100 children was nine years five months. Included in this group of children eighteen and under were two sets of twins and two step-children. The gender of the children was not requested on the survey.

The profile of the widowers surveyed was found to be the following at the time of the survey. Thirty-seven widowers were married longer than ten years while the remaining nine widowers were married for less than ten years. Thirty-two men were widowed more than twelve months while fourteen men had been widowed for less than twelve months. The number of children in the family for the widower showed that twenty-seven men had one or two children while the remaining nineteen men had three or more children. It was found that twenty-eight of the widowers had children who were thirteen or under for age, four men had children in the age group of fourteen to eighteen and the remaining fourteen men had children in both age groups. The eduction level of the widowers showed that thirty-five men had a B.S. degree or higher with the other eleven men having less than a B.S. degree. The widower's gross income level showed a split of twenty-three men earning greater than $40,000 a year and twenty-two men earning less than $40,000 per year. Lastly it was found that thirty-five men were widowed after the age of thirty-five with the remaining six men being widowed before they had reached thirty-five.

Highlights of Research Findings

The following were found to be the most significant findings for this national study of American widowers with school-age children.

Proposition I

Prior to the man actually being widowed, the study found:

1. Men widowed more than twelve months were more likely to recall having a discussion with their wife concerning his remarriage if she were to die first than those widowed less than twelve months.

2. Men who had one or two children were more likely to have a life insurance policy on their wife than men who had three or more children.
3. Men who had one or two children were more likely to have discussed with their wives the idea of remarrying if he were to be widowed than men who had three or more children.
4. The widower who had children thirteen and under was more likely to have a life insurance policy for his wife than widowers who had children age fourteen to eighteen or men who had children in both age groups.
5. It appears that regardless of the age group(s) of the children, a majority of men had discussed remarriage with their wives prior to their deaths.
6. The widower who had a bachelor's degree or higher was more likely to have discussed the idea of remarriage if she were to die first with his wife than widowers with less than a bachelor's degree.
7. All of the widowers (who had life insurance) agreed that having a life insurance policy on their wife helped to maintain their prior lifestyle.
8. Men widowed at an age of thirty-five or less were more likely to have discussed the possibility of remarriage if their spouse should die than men widowed at an age greater than thirty-five. This discussion is supported by the fact that the widower who was thirty-five or younger was more likely to remarry.

Proposition II

When the man became widowed and had school-age children to care for, the study found:

1. Widowers who were married more than ten years appear to have a stronger tendency to contact other widowers with school-age children than widowers married less than ten years.
2. Widowers appear to receive more support from kin than from any other groups, regardless of how long the man was married.
3. Widowers appear to receive little to no financial help from other groups, regardless of the widower's length of marriage.
4. When the number of children the widower had was considered, there appears to be no increase in financial assistance from those friends and relatives close to the widower.

5. Widowers who had children in the fourteen to eighteen age group date sooner than men with children thirteen and under and men who had children in both age groups.
6. Widowers who had children in the thirteen and under age group experienced more difficulty in meeting the right person to date than widowers with children in the fourteen to eighteen age group and widowers with children in both age groups.
7. Widowers with a bachelor's degree or higher were more likely to agree with the notion that women will date them just because they are a unique type of single man than a widower with less than a bachelor's degree.
8. Widowers who earn $40,000 or less per year appear to receive more useful guidance from kin when they begin to move on with their new lifestyle than widowers who earn $40,000 or more per year.
9. Men who had been widowed at the age of thirty-five or less found people to be more helpful when it came to someone to talk to than men widowed at an age greater than thirty-five.
10. Men who were widowed at an age greater than thirty-five stated that kin, kin by marriage, and non-kin were all considered not to be helpful with financial help while he was widowed, while men widowed at the age of thirty-five or less found kin and non-kin to be helpful.

Proposition III

With the reality of being a widowed man with school-age children, the study found:

1. Length of marriage appears to have played no importance in that most widowers had discussed remarriage with their wife before her death.
2. Men who were widowed for more than twelve months appear to have no previous knowledge of other widowed men with school-age children.
3. Length of widowhood appears not to change the perception among the widowers that being widowed makes them a unique type of single man.
4. Men who have less than a bachelor's degree were more likely to begin dating before the first anniversary of their wife's death, where as widowers with a bachelor's degree or higher were more likely to wait at least a year or use other criteria to start dating.

5. Kin and kin by marriage were more helpful to widowers who earn $40,000 or more per year when they needed to talk to someone than they were to widowers who earn $40,000 or less per year.
6. Men who had been widowed at an age greater than thirty-five were more likely to agree with the notion that women will go out with them because they are a unique single man than men widowed at the age of thirty-five or less.

Proposition IV

When men considered how others may look at them in their new role as a single man/parent because of being widowed, the study found that:

1. Widowers married ten years or more have more anxiety about the notion that women are inclined to date them because they are widowed.
2. Length of marriage makes no difference in the widowers apparent difficulty in finding the right person to date when his children are considered as a part of his life.
3. Men widowed for twelve months or less find kin to be very helpful when it comes to understanding their loss.
4. Widowers who had children in the thirteen and under age group perceive that women were more inclined to date them than did widowers with children age fourteen to eighteen and widowers who had children in both age groups.
5. Kin were more helpful for the widower whose education level is less than a bachelor's degree when needing someone to talk to than widowers who had a bachelor's degree or higher.
6. Kin were very helpful for widowers with less than a bachelor's degree when it comes to understanding their son's/brother's loss than men who were widowed and had a bachelor's degree or higher.
7. Widowers who earn $40,000 or less per year agreed with the notion that being widowed makes them a unique type of single man that women may be more inclined to date.

Proposition V

Regarding the impact of the man becoming a single man/parent due to the death of their wife, the study found that:

1. Widowers who were married more than ten years appear to adjust better to the death of their wife than widowers married less than ten years.

2. Men who were widowed for more than twelve months appeared to have a much higher desire to remarry than widowers widowed twelve months or less.
3. Widowers who had three or more children appeared to have more difficulty in adjusting to being a single parent than widowers with one or two children.
4. Regardless of the number of children, widowers perceive that being a widower makes women more inclined to date them, simply because they are a different type of single man.
5. Widowed men with child care concerns had more difficulty in adjusting to the death of their wife if they had children in the age group of thirteen and under.
6. Widowers who had a bachelor's degree or higher appeared to adjust with less difficulty to their wife's death than widowers with less than a bachelor's degree.
7. Widowers who had less than a bachelor's degree felt less guilt about the idea of being single because of their wife's death than did widowers with a bachelor's degree or higher.
8. Widowers who earn $40,000 or more per year appeared to experience more difficulty with their fellow employees when the subject of their deceased wife came up than did widowers who earn $40,000 or less per year.
9. Men who earn $40,000 or less per year found themselves feeling guilty more often when it came to being single again than widowers who earn $40,000 or more per year.
10. Those men widowed at the age of thirty-five or less found they had more difficulty in finding the right person to date than men widowed at an age greater than thirty-five.
11. Men who were widowed at an age greater than thirty-five felt less guilt for being single than men who were widowed at an age of thirty-five or less.

Proposition VI

With the label of widower being attached to the men, the study found that:

1. Men widowed more than twelve months have adjusted better to the fact of their wives death than men widowed twelve months or less.
2. Men widowed with children in the child care age group of thirteen and under had more difficulty in adjusting to the nature of their

wives death than the widowers with children in the other child care age groups.

3. The widower who earns $40,000 or more per year appeared to adjust to the death of his wife much sooner than the widower who earns $40,000 or less per year.

4. Obtaining child care appears to be more stressful for men who were widowed at the age of thirty-five or less than those men widowed after the age of thirty-five.

5. The nature of the wives death gave men widowed at the age of thirty-five or less more difficulty in adjusting to his loss than men who had been widowed at an age greater than thirty-five.

Proposition VII

In regard to becoming a widower with school-age children and having to run a household, this study found that:

1. Widowers who were married less than ten years appeared to have a higher stress factor when trying to locate child care and a higher difficulty in adjustment when dealing with the nature of their spouse's death than widowers who were married more than ten years.

2. Men widowed for twelve months or less found kin by marriage not helpful when it comes to child care.

3. Widowers agreed that when child care is considered for all the age groups the use of non-kin for child care was the most desired.

4. Widowers overall had a very difficult time adjusting to cooking and basic domestic responsibilities as a single parent.

Proposition VIII

Relative to the significance of the social position of being a widower along with being a single parent/man in American society, this study found that:

1. Regardless of the length of marriage, widowers appeared to select non-kin over kin for child care when returning to work after their wife's death.

2. The length of time that the man was widowed appeared to have no influence on the difficulty the men experienced in dealing with the responsibilities of being a single parent.

3. Men widowed with school-age children who had been widowed for more than twelve months found little difficulty in meeting the right person to date while men widowed twelve months or less had difficulty.

4. If a widower had three or more children, he was likely to know other widowers with school-age children.
5. Widowers who had children in school were more likely to know other widowers with children because of the school setting, whereas men whose children were too young to be in school knew few or no widowers.
6. Widowers who had a bachelor's degree or higher had more difficulty in adjusting to the responsibilities of being a single parent than widowers with less than a bachelor's degree.
7. Those widowers who earn less than $40,000 per year had a more difficult time when adjusting to single parent responsibilities than did men who earn $40,000 or more per year.
8. The widower who had been widowed at the age of thirty-five or less was more likely to make contact with other men who were widowed with school-age children than men whose age was greater than thirty-five when he was widowed.

Influences on the Widower

Social Circle

The influence of help and guidance by kin, kin by marriage, and non-kin is keenly observed by the widower. These individuals appear to have a greater influence on the widower than they likely realize. Their understanding or lack thereof appears to give direction to how the widower works toward his acceptance and understanding of his loss and his change of roles. Social circles as a whole are willing to help them and understand that the widower has to move on with his life. They also attempt to be positive in their active cooperation with the widower. However, what may be viewed as a positive influence by a member of a circle may not be received by the widower as such; thus, conflict and stress occur. An example in point is stated by one widower who said, "My father always irritated me when he said that he knew what I was going through and then related my loss to his divorce. No one knows your grief like you do." Another man wrote: "Most had little or no 'death' experience."

The influence of kin by marriage was less than a positive experience for many respondents. This was surprising in that when grandchildren are considered one would assume that in-laws would desire to maintain the social relationship with their son-in-law. If the parents of the widower's deceased wife desired to continue to be in the widowers social circle, their actions or lack of actions appear to be alienating many of them from both their grandchildren and their son-in-law. One respondent stated, "My in-laws tried to be uplifting but mostly cared about their loss. My friends cared for me."

Personal Rights—Economic

Those widowers who had a life insurance policy on their wife noted that having this financial life-jacket helped them maintain a form of stability in at least this social role. A widower who had a life insurance policy on his wife, stated: "A $100,000 life insurance policy on my wife made things much less stressful." Those widowers who had no life insurance policy on their wife or were in need of financial help after their wife's death would likely turn to their relatives or members of their social circles to find assistance. It is assumed by many people that in times of crises people give money to individuals to assist them. For the widowers surveyed, this appears not to have been the case.

Personal Role Behavior and Function

Widowers appear to view this area of social roles as their major stumbling block when adjusting and changing to their new lifestyle. When considering the issues of life after the death of his spouse the widower's primary concern is with the domestic roles at home. The necessity of the widower to adjust to roles that his wife had largely performed during their marriage, e.g., the cooking and house cleaning, caused him to adjust and prioritize his other roles; this brought stress to the men. The men acknowledged that tasks they had customarily performed now became difficult because of the additional tasks they had to perform. The men appear to function fairly well in all of the roles required of them as time passes. The task for which the widower is likely to go outside of his family structure for help is in the area of child care, where he will hire and rely on non-kin to assist him. Although the widower can find help in this task, the responsibilities, challenges, and difficulties that go with child care are prevalent as noted by the widowers. Relative to child care, one respondent stated, "Still a very difficult situation. One major reason for change in employment." Another man wrote: "I began using both my mother and mother-in-law. I had difficulty with my mother-in-law and had to stop using her. I work until 8:00 P.M. three nights a week. I have only found one profes- sional day care with hours I need." Another widower, said, "It was always a problem until they (the children) settled in. When a day care closed it was 'panic city.' Some arrangements weren't perfect." Widowers found help or guidance from other sources such as television or books not to be what they expected. A likely reason for this is that little is written for the widowed man that will assist him with this task and personal behavior.

Theoretical Implications

The implications of this research for role theory of widowers with school-age children are promising. The widower, based on his individual concepts and personal experiences, will mold his own social position. Znaniecki's social role theory makes the operationalization of the widower's social position possible. This possibility gives researchers a working formula for a sociological investigation of the widower from an interactionist framework. Using this approach makes a theoretical contribution to the knowledge base of what can be reasonably expected of an individual in the social position of being widowed with school-age children.

The contrasting difference between the theatrical role perspective and the social role perspective when dealing with widowers with school-age children is an important point to consider. By studying the widower in the social role, one is allowed to see the interaction between an individual and others who must learn from each other. This learning by both brings understanding and acceptance by all people who are involved with the change of a social position by a fellow member in their social circle. It is this interaction among those who are in supportive roles that makes social role theory more applicable to the widower as a social position.

Although theatrical roles and social roles are both based on culturally-based individuals who learn and perform as expected, differences occur when one attempts to enact roles in situations where substantial ambiguity relative to uncharted arenas for behavior is common place. Thus, while certain vague expectations and sterotypes about the role of widower may exist in the culture, the lack of precise statements of rights and obligations make appropriate behavior problematic relative to each new role.

Unlike the actor who modifies the written script through the interaction of his/her personality into the character, the widower must invent the character as he proceeds through a new and as yet uncompleted script. It is this lack of initial control by the men that gives the theory of social role by Znaniecki such significance. The impact of death, which results in the man becoming a widower with school-age children, is not often heard about nor rehearsed by the husband/father. The social roles and positions unfold and develop as the man adjusts to the influences, stresses, and conflicts that arise as the widower learns to function within his social circle, personal rights, and personal function.

Widowerhood is initially an individualistic role which expands to all facets of the man's life as he interacts with close friends, family, and his client at the office where he works. While other theories may have promise to explore a specific role of the widower, Znaniecki's "Social Role" theory is an excellent foundation on which to build a knowledge base of widowers with school-age children.

Limitations of Research

The greatest limitation of this research was locating widowers with school-age children in the United States. As previously stated, this population is rare. Locating men was accomplished by using ADEC members as the primary contact. Using members to locate widowers appears to have limits, as shown by the small number of men who responded to the survey. Other limitations are: 1) only one man of African heritage was included, 2) the men were highly educated, and 3) there was a notable void of respondents from the western and southeastern regions of the United States. However, when cost was considered as a factor in trying to locate the men, the means that were used proved to be quite successful.

Additionally it should be noted that forty-six respondents for a national survey may prove in future research to be too few to provide reliable data on widowers with school-age children in the United States. Finally, the survey questionnaire was built on present-day literature and knowledge from the areas of death and dying, single parenting, the traditional family, and Znaniecki's social role theory. It will more than likely have to be modified as more is learned.

In summary, the findings of this research are limited by the nature of this study, that being an exploratory study in an area for which little is written or known. This report represents a beginning so others may have an operational framework along with standard concepts in which to work when researching widowers with school-age children.

FUTURE RESEARCH

Future research may benefit from the topology which was used in this study, along with the addition of other independent and dependent variables. A quantitative examination of a larger widower population would attract researchers whose concerns and interests are the validity of measurements for this unresearched area. For the qualitative researcher, an in-depth narrative analysis of widowers would prove to be beneficial to link stress, conflict, and adjustment to the process of loss and how it affects the widower's role.

Future research should also consider the importance of what people know in general about death and dying and what impact it has on the survivors. This knowledge or lack of knowledge would be worthy of research with respect to how these people influence the widower with what they know of the process.

Finally, the term "widowed" more than any other term brings up the topic of death. It is the understanding of death and what impact it has, not just in sociological terms but also at multi-disciplinary levels, that is so lacking in American society. If America is to learn about death from a distance, let it not be from television, media hype, and movies, but from the efforts of parents, churches, schools, and universities where the reality of death and its impact can be taught to all.

REFERENCES

1. T. H. Holmes and R. H. Rahe, The Social Readjustment Rating Scale, *Psychosomatic Medicine, 11,* pp. 213-218, 1967.
2. Helena Z. Lopata, *Widowhood in an American City,* Schenkman, Cambridge, 1973.
3. U.S. Bureau of the Census, *Statistical Abstract of the United States, 1994,* U.S. Government Printing Office, Washington, D.C., 1994.
4. F. M. Berardo, Widowhood Status in the United States: Perspectives on a Neglected Aspect of the Family Life Cycle, *The Family Coordinator, 17,* pp. 191-203, 1968.
5. G. L. Greif, *Single Fathers,* Lexington Books, Lexington, Massachusetts, 1987.
6. S. M. Hanson and F. W. Bozette, Widowers as Fathers, in *Dimensions of Fatherhood,* J. Burgess (ed.), Sage Publications, Beverly Hills, California, pp. 416-434, 1985.
7. J. Burgess, *Dimensions of Fatherhood,* Sage Publications, Beverly Hills, California, 1985.
8. V. C. Fox and M. H. Quitt, *Loving, Parenting and Dying: The Family Cycle England and America, Past and Present,* Psychohistory Press, New York, 1980.
9. D. H. Morgan, *Social Theory and the Family,* Routledge & Kegan Paul, London, 1975.
10. B. Schlesinger, The Widowed as a One-Parent Family Unit, *Social Science, 46,* pp. 26-32, 1971.
11. F. Martinson, *Family in Society,* Dodd, Mead, & Co., New York, 1970.
12. R. O. Blood, Jr. and D. M. Wolf, *Husbands & Wives: The Dynamics of Married Living,* The Free Press of Glencoe, Illinois, 1960.
13. I. R. Nye and F. M. Berardo, *Emerging Conceptual Frameworks in Family Analysis,* Macmillan, New York, 1966.

14. R. A. Jones, *Emile Durkheim*, Sage, London, 1986.
15. A. M. Lee and E. B. Lee, *Marriage and the Family*, Barnes & Noble, New York, 1961.
16. A. L. Selig, Crisis Theory and Family Growth, *The Family Coordinator, 25*, pp. 291-296, 1976.
17. R. Hill, Social Stress on the Family: Genetic Features of Being Under Stress, *Social Casework, 39*, pp. 139-150, February-March 1958.
18. G. Theodorson and A. G. Theodorson, *A Modern Dictionary of Sociology*, Thomas Y. Crowell, Co., New York, 1969.
19. M. E. Lamb and A. Sagi, *Fatherhood and Family Policy*, Lawrence Erlbaum Associates, Hillsdale, New Jersey, 1983.
20. P. Bronstein and C. Cowards, Clinical Work with Divorced and Widowed Fathers: The Adjusting Family Model, in *Fatherhood Today: Men's Changing Role in the Family*, John Wiley & Sons, New York, 1988.
21. J. F. Arnold, Lone Fathers: Perspectives and Implications for Family Policy, *The Family Coordinator, 28*, pp. 521-528, 1979.
22. R. D. Gasser and C. M. Taylor, Role Adjustment of Single Parent Fathers with Dependent Children, *The Family Coordinator, 25*, pp. 397-401, 1976.
23. H. A. Mendes, Single Fathers, *The Family Coordinator, 25*, pp. 439-444, 1976.
24. J. W. Bedell, *Role Organization in the One-Parent Family: Mother Absent Due to Death*, thesis, California State College, Fullerton, 1971.
25. R. Lennox, *The Relationship between Adjustment to Bereavement in Widowers and Perceived Social Support*, masters thesis, School of Social Work: Atkinson College, York University, North York, Ontario, Canada, 1990.
26. B. J. Lodge, *Role Adjustments to Single Parenthood: A Study of Divorced and Widowed Men and Women*, doctoral dissertation, University of Washington, Seattle, 1976.
27. C. Lewis and M. O'Brien, *Reassessing Fatherhood: New Observations on Fathers and the Modern Family*, Sage, London, 1987.
28. C. Balkwell, Transition to Widowhood: A Review of the Literature, *Family Relations, 30*, pp. 117-125, 1981.
29. S. M. H. Hanson, Fatherhood, *American Behavioral Scientist, 29*, pp. 55-72, 1985.
30. D. K. Orthner, T. Brown, and D. Ferguson, Single-Parent Fatherhood: An Emerging Family Life Style, *The Family Coordinator, 25*, pp. 429-439, 1976.
31. O. G. Brim and S. Wheeler, *Socialization After Childhood: Two Essays*, John Wiley & Sons, New York, 1966.
32. J. H. Hewitt, *Self and Society: A Symbolic Interactionist Social Psychology*, Allyn and Bacon, Boston, 1984.
33. B. Biddle and E. J. Thomas, *Role Theory: Concepts and Research*, John Wiley & Sons, New York, 1966.

34. F. Znaniecki, *Social Relations and Social Roles,* Chandler, San Francisco, California, 1965.
35. I. R. Nye, *Role Structure and Analysis of the Family,* Sage, Beverly Hills, 1979.
36. G. Theordorson and A. G. Theordorson, *A Modern Dictionary of Sociology,* Thomas Y. Crowell, New York, 1969.
37. E. M. Duvall and B. C. Miller, *Marriage and Family Development,* Harper & Row, New York, 1965.
38. M. C. Kearl, *Endings: The Sociology of Death and Dying,* Oxford University Press, New York, 1989.

CHAPTER 11

Gender Differences Related to Sexuality in Widowhood: Is It a Problem for the Male Bereaved?

Kathryn Hustins

Most individuals lose a spouse through death at some time in their lives. In North America, approximately three million people are widowed annually. In Canada, 83 percent of those who are widowed are women and 17 percent are men [1]. Loss of a spouse through death often means loss of a loved one and a source of financial as well as emotional support. Changes also often occur in social interactions, especially if most friends and acquaintances are still married and their social activities are couple-oriented. Loneliness often becomes a major problem. Some evidence has shown that mortality and morbidity rates of surviving spouses tends to increase. Also, it is common for many men and women to experience a decline or absence of sexual feelings during the acute phases of their spouses's illness and in the period immediately following the death of their spouse [2].

This chapter presents some of the concerns and problems of sexuality raised during an investigation into psychological distress and social support in middle-aged Newfoundland widowed during the first year of bereavement [3]. Even though the primary focus of this chapter is on male sexuality during bereavement, it is important to make comparisons with the female experiences as well. These comparisons help to place the concerns into a broader context.

There is paucity of research into the issues of sexuality in bereavement and widowhood. It is, of course, an extremely personal and sensitive area. Also there are significant conceptual and methodological problems in measuring sexual behavior [4]. Is it frequency (e.g., the number of coital acts per week) or percentage (e.g., how many adults of a given age or given situation participate in sexual intercourse)? Or is it the level of intensity (e.g., the degree of physical arousal and excitement)? It has been suggested that perhaps a sound definition of human heterosexual behavior should also include less overt behaviors such as thoughts, fantasies, wishes, and affectionate touching [4]. As well, it has been suggested that we engage in sex for many reasons, such as the need to satisfy biological and reproductive drives, the need to obtain affection and intimacy, to exert power over another person, to escape boredom, to make up with a loved one after a fight, to gratify feelings of pride and self-esteem, or to confirm one's masculinity or femininity [5].

Until recently, very little has been known about sexuality and aging. It was widely assumed that there were no problems and there was nothing to know. Older adults were not supposed to have any interest in sex. When middle-aged and elderly patients complained of sexual difficulties or disinterest, health care professionals would respond with such comments as "Well, what can you expect at your age." This insensitive attitude was likely to feed on the patient's loss of sexual self-confidence, thereby creating a self-fulfilling prophecy so that sex in later adulthood became impossible because the individual believed that it was abnormal and unlikely [4].

During the last few decades, we have become increasingly aware that there is indeed sexual life during and after middle age. Some adults who have ambivalent feelings about sex may welcome advancing age as an excuse to abandon it. More often, however, the fear of losing the capacity to obtain sexual pleasure and intimacy is a very powerful one [4].

Research on male sexuality and aging indicates that male sexual activity declines with increasing age [6]. However, men are more likely to remain interested in sex through middle and old age if they enjoyed sex more often during young adulthood [7], if they are in good health [8], and if they believe that they can maintain effective sexual behavior as they grow older [9]. Research on female sexuality and aging indicates that while the sexual capacity of women declines relatively little with increasing age [10], their sexual activity decreases markedly and is significantly lower than that of men of similar ages [4]. Women who enjoy sex more during young adulthood and those who experience more coital organisms, are more likely to remain sexually active in later life [8]. Numerous studies have found that female sexual activity depends on the presence of a socially acceptable and sexually capable partner, such as a healthy spouse [8]. Physical health appears to have little influence on the sexual functioning of older women [7].

METHODOLOGY AND STUDY FINDINGS

In this descriptive and correlational study, thirty women and twenty-two men were interviewed two times within one year of losing their spouses. The first interview was conducted at three to six months and the second interview was at nine to twelve months following the death. Names were identified through obituary columns of local newspapers. Potential subjects were sent a letter inviting their participation in the study followed by a telephone call and visit to their homes. After obtaining informed consent the interview was conducted.

During the interviews the issue of sexuality arose as a major concern and problem for both widows and widowers. Questions were raised which addressed the following concerns and problems: 1) How does widowhood affect sexual response? 2) Does the actual state of widowhood cause a change? 3) Is the individual's emotional reaction responsible for a different sexual outlook? and 4) Does the health care professional sometimes set the stage for sexual troubles?

The women in this study (n = 30) responded with a grief reaction, depression, and decreased interest in all activities. Major problems included jealousy of old friends who were happily married, anger and resentment at their husband for dying and leaving, lack of money, and sexual adjustment based on attitudes, sexual drive, and opportunity. For some women, the death of their spouse was an escape or rescue from undesired sexual activity and abusive situations. Pfeiffer and Davis found 90 percent of women stopped having intercourse after their husbands became ill, disinterested, or died [8].

The widows talked about a number of sexual problems. Sexual outlets were difficult to find. Although society is slowly recognizing sexual activity outside of marriage, this activity, as well as marriage between older adults, is often viewed with disdain. They had difficulty finding sexual companionship since there are a relatively smaller number of older men available. Their inhibitions about assertively seeking out male friends also limited their opportunities.

The men in this study (n = 22) reported their problems somewhat differently. They experienced less social prohibition in seeking out female companionship. There also was more opportunity for them than for the widows. The major problem for most of these men was that they had no one with whom to share their sexual concerns or problems. A small number of those who masturbated to relieve their sexual tensions reported feelings of shame and guilt. Some men said that there was a conflict between wanting to marry and the financial limitations set forth by wills and certain pension plans. That is, some individuals would suffer considerable decrease in income with remarriage. For example, one widower who was living with a widow said that she would face a reduction in her $12,000 a year pension income if they married. He stated: "The thing that bothers me most about the sin versus marriage decision is that it forces us to put a price on virtue. For the $12,000 a year, we are willing to let it go and live in sin. If the sum involved $1,000-$2,000, we would marry tomorrow."

Sexuality is very sensitive to such threats as the illness or death of a spouse. One's sexual functions can tolerate being shut down for long periods of time without any irreversible damages to the human biological system [2]. Most men and women in this study experienced a decline or absence of sexual feelings during the acute phases of their spouse's illness and in the period immediately following the death of their spouse. The couples who lived through an extended illness prior to the death were affected by the illness itself, the treatment, and their personal reactions to the situation. Many of those in the study had been without sexual lives for a prolonged period before the death of their spouse. The following are some examples of the problems and concerns that were raised by the widowers during the interviews. Names have been changed to provide anonymity to the widowers.

> Albert's wife had been ill for about eighteen months before her death of brain cancer. She had been very tired and slept a great deal during this time. Albert had felt that it was not right to have sexual relations with his wife when she was so ill and the outcome was death. He said that he just shelved his sexual feelings because of his concern and love for his wife.

> Ben's wife had been institutionalized for three years before her death. She had a stroke at thirty-nine years of age and Ben had taken care of her at home for ten years before her admission to a nursing home. There were no opportunities for sexual relations or intimacy at the nursing home, nor was it "socially" acceptable to be thinking such thoughts at that time.

When sexual feelings began to emerge again, the men and women in this study reported that they had to deal with these feelings both psychologically as well as physically. Initially, the men and women found their initial reaction was one of surprise, reassurance, and frustration. There were also feelings of guilt combined with the pain of loss triggered by the returning sexual feelings and the memories that were associated with them.

> Chad's wife had been dead for six months when his sexual feelings returned. He was very confused and concerned as he

thought that it was "too soon" to be feeling this way. As well, he felt guilty that he had these strong feelings when he did not have his wife around anymore.

Don's wife had been dead for three months when his sexual feelings returned. "I tell myself that I don't have any sexual feelings, but I think sometimes at night when I wake up, that she is there beside me and I find I have an erection and don't know what to do.

Bereaved spouses deal with their sexual feelings in a limited number of ways. Many individuals in this study used suppression and distraction as defense mechanisms. Their energies were put into activities such as exercise, hobbies, and work. Others tried masturbation. The choice of a coping mechanism was highly dependent on the individual's personality and value system [2].

Evan tried to deal with sexual feelings by distraction. "I just try to forget and do something else. Most of it is at night when you go to bed and you are by yourself. There is nobody to turn to for comforting and love. Sometimes I get up and go read a newspaper or go for a walk. I feel guilty when I masturbate as it is against my religious beliefs."

The main reason that the men started to date and return to the coupled world was the need for companionship, someone just to talk with, to have dinner with, to fill the void of being without a partner. In talking with the widowed, I found that their advice to other widowed generally was: "Go out, mix with people, get involved, don't spend so much time alone. You have to get on with the rest of your life."

Twelve of the men (54%) and only two (7%) of the women in the study had developed some form of sexual relationship by the end of the first year of bereavement. These men and women had encountered few difficulties and reported satisfactory relationships. A number found casual dating difficult because they initially tried to recapture the same deep feelings with the same type of person as their spouse. As well, many expressed the fear of contracting AIDS. Some of the widowers found that other widows took the initiative in seeking casual dates by inviting them for a meal, bringing food to the house, and telephoning them frequently for reasons such as accompanying them to a social function. One man had remarried during the interval between Interview I and II, while one man was waiting until the end of one year of mourning before his remarriage. Almost all the men reported that they hoped to meet someone in order to resume a satisfying sexual relationship again.

Most of the women in the study, however, were not interested in becoming involved with anyone. The prospect of remarriage in the distant future was not identified as important or as a possibility.

CONCLUSIONS

How can we as health care professionals help the widowed to deal with sexual feelings after the death of a spouse? First, a careful sexual history is needed to distinguish between physical illness, sexual ignorance, genuine sexual disinterest, and short-term problems in sexual relationships after the death of a partner. Special effort should be made to assess the quality of the interpersonal relationship between the present sexual partners. Maintaining a good general health status is important. Be sure to check previous illnesses, surgeries, and medications because any of these factors may cause sexual dysfunction.

Second, it is necessary to dispel the myths and misconceptions regarding sexuality during the middle and later years as well as in widowhood. Information may be necessary about the physiological changes that take place during the aging process and the adaptations that the couple may need to make in length and type of foreplay. When no sexual partner is available, it may be helpful to educate a client about ways to masturbate effectively. It may be necessary to explore a wider range of sexual expression. Health care professionals also can serve as mediators if children object to a mother's or father's interest in remarriage after the death of a spouse.

Third, a useful framework which may assist those working with the widowed to promote a healthy sexual lifestyle is the PLISSIT MODEL developed by Annon [11]. This model advocates four steps in assisting older adults to develop and maintain a healthy sexual lifestyle: 1) Permission—permit the widowed to discuss issues related to sexuality in a comfortable informal way; 2) Limited Information—limit the information that you share to the concerns of the widowed adult, dispel any myths and stereotypes; 3) Specific Suggestions—give specific guidelines and/or techniques which prevent or alleviate a specific sexual problem (i.e., impotency); and 4) Intensive Therapy—referral to qualified sex therapist if the problem is beyond your expertise and then act as a client advocate [12].

In conclusion, the questions raised during this study have made us more aware of the difficulties which those who have been widowed have encountered. Those who are helped to overcome these difficulties can liberate themselves from negative stereotypes and self-defeating doubts to enjoy the pleasure of this most intimate aspect of adult relationships.

REFERENCES

1. Statistics Canada, *Canada Year Book,* 1994.
2. S. Shuchter, *Dimensions of Grief: Adjusting to the Death of a Spouse,* Jossey-Bass, San Francisco, pp. 253-262, 1986.
3. K. A. Hustins, Gender Differences and Bereavement, *The Canadian Nurse, 89*:3, p. 48, 1993.
4. R. Schulz and R. B. Ewen, *Adult Development and Aging: Myths and Emerging Realities,* Macmillan, New York, pp. 246-255, 1993.
5. G. Neubeck, The Myriad Motives for Sex, *Sexual Behaviour, 2,* pp. 50-56, 1972.
6. E. Pfeiffer, A. Verwoerdt, and G. C. Davis, Sexual Behaviour in Middle Life, *American Journal of Psychiatry, 128,* pp. 1262-1267, 1972.
7. R. E. Solnick and N. Corby, Human Sexuality and Aging, in *Aging: Scientific Perspectives and Social Issues,* D. S. Woodruff and J. E. Birrens (eds.), Brooks/Cole, Monterey, California, 1983.
8. E. Pfeiffer and G. C. Davis, Determinants of Sexual Behaviour in Middle and Old Age, *Journal of American Geriatric Society, 20*:4, pp. 151-158, 1972.
9. W. H. Masters and V. E. Johnson, *Human Sexual Response,* Little, Brown, Boston, 1970.
10. W. H. Masters and V. E. Johnson, *Human Sexual Response,* Little, Brown, Boston, 1966.
11. J. Annon, The PLISSIT Model: A Proposed Conceptual Scheme for the Treatment of Sexual Problems, *Journal of Sex Education Therapy, 2,* pp. 1-15, 1976.
12. E. Paul and J. O'Neill, A Sexual Health Model for Nursing Interventions, *Issues in Health Care of Women, 4,* pp. 115-125, 1983.

CHAPTER 12

Male Attitudes on Funeral Rites and Rituals

Paul Sakalauskas

When someone dies, survivors face situations of great stress. Among the first stressful decisions are those regarding rituals and disposition of the body. Mourning rituals become the public face of grief. Although these rituals can generate stress, they also provide opportunities for the expression of grief's emotions and allow individuals to channel their grief into accepted expressions of loss at a time when the death upsets previously predictable behaviors.

In Ontario, 45 percent of consumers have not made any decision about the type of funeral services they would select [1]. This means that many bereaved persons have no idea as to what they want and need to do or what the deceased may have wanted when it comes to making funeral arrangements. The decisions that are made most often depend on the survivor's perceptions of what is correct and proper and probability guesses as to what the deceased would prefer. This uncertainty adds considerable stress for the bereaved.

While there is a growing amount of research work done on differences between men and women in their grieving, very little is known about differences between men and women as they make arrangements for funerals. This chapter examines some aspects of these gender differences with emphasis on men and based upon perceptions of funeral directors and other professionals.

North American culture expects men to be in control, confident, more concerned about thinking than feeling, being rational and analytical, assertive, courageous, endure stress without giving up, express anger, bear pain, and to be a provider [2, pp. 12-13]. Many bereaved men are likely to make decisions that they hope will conform to what society expects of them. In some instances, they may neglect their own desires and needs. Therefore, it also is important to ask, "Do people feel the emotions they express or do people express the emotions they feel?" [3]. With a focus on gender differences, the question addressed in this chapter is, "Do men express their concerns and emotions in the same manner as women?"

It is important to understand what role the funeral rites and rituals play in helping the survivors deal with a death. J. William Worden [4] outlines four tasks that the funeral can do for the bereaved.

1. Funerals can help make real the fact of the loss. Seeing the body of the deceased person helps to bring home the reality of the death.
2. The funeral can give people the opportunity to express thoughts and feelings about the deceased. The things that they will miss and not miss about the individual.
3. The service can also be a reflection of the life of the person who is gone.
4. The funeral can draw a social support network close to the bereaved family shortly after the loss has occurred, and this kind of social support can be extremely helpful in the facilitation of grief.

The funeral service, if it is done well, can be an important adjunct in aiding and abetting the healthy resolution of grief [4]. The funeral director, being one of the first people the family might contact when a death occurs, is in a unique position of being a sounding board to families as well as an advisor when it comes time to arranging for a funeral. During the arrangement conference the funeral director will be asked to listen to what the family may have experienced prior to the death. They also will be in the position of advising a family on all their options and carrying out their requests.

Arranging for the funeral is probably one of the most difficult tasks many people must complete. Decisions will be made at the arrangement conference that could affect families for a long period of time.

A BRIEF SURVEY OF FUNERAL DIRECTORS

The Ontario Funeral Service Association asked fourteen of its members across the province of Ontario to complete a mailed questionnaire regarding their perceptions of the way individuals react when they must make funeral arrangements for someone who has died. We received eleven responses from funeral directors and one response from a bereavement counselor working at a funeral home. The respondents all worked at various funeral homes in the province of Ontario and were employed at funeral homes that collectively served over 3,600 families every year.

The questionnaire was brief and consisted of only eight questions. The respondents were asked to answer in regard to their observations of situations and actions that take place in the arrangement conference. The final question was a ranking of items that the funeral directors felt were important to the families they serve. The question asked respondents to compare the importance of these items to men and women. This is only a survey of impressions and observations. It was not intended to be a scientific study with generalizable conclusions. The responses to this survey, however, along with the personal experiences of the author, should be of interest and value to others who want to learn more about men and their views about funeral rituals.

The first question on the survey asked, "How do males and females differ when making funeral arrangements?" One respondent said, "If anything, I find most women are more willing to talk and men would like to get the business completed." Most of the respondents stated that they noted some very basic differences between men and women at the time of arrangements. The difference being, not what they choose for funerals but in the manner that they act. Men tend to be more interested in the facts and information about funerals. Women deal with more detail and are able to discuss more of the emotional aspects surrounding the death. Men are afraid to cry and express their emotions openly. Being strong for others is often reinforced as an honorable and admired quality.

Men will often ask the funeral director, "What is normally done for the funeral?" They appear lost and in need of guidance. Many men are afraid that they might do something that would offend family and friends. They want to do what is right.

Dr. Elizabeth Latimer, Palliative Care Coordinator for the Region of Hamilton-Wentworth, believes that men are more bewildered at the death of their spouse (personal communication). Women tend to share more. Dr. Latimer stated that if two men were dying and were in the same room, at some point their wives would share with each other their own experiences. It is very rare that two men would do the same if the roles were reversed.

Men are more task-oriented and look for a problem to solve. Generally speaking, men want to take care of the funeral arrangements quickly and leave. A man who loses a loved one often initiates action or engages in action immediately following the death. Endless case studies reflect a man's need to do something after the death, to take control of their loss [2, pp. 26-27].

Another question included in the survey was, "Is the main spokesperson usually male or female when several family members are present during the arrangement conference?" In a study conducted by John Bedell on reactions to mate loss he refers to several studies conducted in the past that note a sexual division of labor with the male being slightly superior [5]. It infers that because the male has final say, he has greater power. In another work about blue collar workers, Komarovshy found that the lower the educational level of the respondent, the greater the probability of a rigid sex role division of labor between mates [6].

The funeral directors responding to this question felt that the male usually takes care of the final decisions. One director responded; "Females usually do the talking during the arrangements, they seem to know what they want but will look to the male for approval." Although many of the responses noted that the male still has the final say, they felt that there is a greater tendency toward sharing the responsibility of decision making. Some noted that in many situations it is the individual with the most dominant personality that takes control and has the final say.

The third survey question asked, "Have you observed in your experiences a tendency for either a male or female to come in and make arrangements on their own without other family members?" Making funeral arrangements for someone that is very close can be very difficult. The majority of the families that come in to make arrangements come in with someone for support because they believe that they cannot do it alone. In Ontario, 76 percent of funerals are arranged "at need," that is to say that no arrangements were made in advance [7, p. 17]. Even when there is no preplanning or discussion about the type of services, there are times when individuals come in to make arrangements on their own. Usually this would be the male. They take upon themselves the responsibility of making all the decisions regarding services for the deceased. Many times when they are asked questions there is a need for them to consult with those who remained at home. Many of the males that come in alone usually do not talk to other family members or ask for their opinion beforehand. For example, a man who came in with his daughter to make funeral arrangements for his wife had an interesting previous experience. His daughter stated that she could not let her father come in alone. She related that several years previously her brother had died and her father came in alone to make the funeral arrangements. He had done this to protect his wife and he thought that it was his duty to take full responsibility. She said that her father had never gotten over that experience because it was so difficult.

Very seldom will a female make funeral arrangements on her own for an "at need" funeral. Although the funeral directors responded that men are most likely to make arrangements alone for an "at need" funeral, an interesting point was brought up. Over half the funeral directors indicated that women would usually come in by themselves to make "pre-need" funeral arrangements. In a consumer survey done in the United States, seven in ten said pre-arrangements should be made when someone is seriously ill or when you are making a will, 63 percent said following their sixtieth or seventieth birthday, 58 percent said when they are planning their retirement, and 55 percent said at retirement [8]. During these pre-need arrangements women said that they would like to make sure that everything was taken care of properly. In certain situations, their husbands did not want to be responsible and left it up to their wives.

The fourth question in the survey asked, "What differences, if any, are there in the arrangements selected for stillborn children if the father makes the arrangements alone or with the mother?" One respondent wrote, "The father certainly feels that the loss has to be acknowledged but rarely are there any arrangements beyond immediate burial or cremation." If there is one situation that exemplifies the difference between men and women in the type of rituals they choose, it is in the situation surrounding a stillbirth. The male's primary concern is to protect his wife. The general view is that they would like to spare the woman the ordeal of having any type of service. In Ontario, approximately 34 percent of the funeral homes do not charge for their services when they provide a stillborn service [7, p. 10]. Therefore, cost is not an issue for the parents when determining what they would like to have for the stillborn infant.

All the responses pointed to the male being business-like and protective. They stated that when the mother was involved in making arrangements with the father, the father would take a figurative step back. The mother would usually comment that she would like to have some sort of service. It did not matter if it was just a small family gathering in the funeral home or the cemetery. The male would usually be very supportive of his partner in any decisions she would make. The impression that most of the directors had is that women are more likely than men to have a clear idea of what kind of arrangements they want in these circumstances.

The fifth survey item was, "Are males more emotional than females during the arrangement conference?" In response to this question one person wrote, "It depends on whom they are making the arrangements for." There is a great deal of similarity between the arrangement conference and family meetings that are held on palliative care wards. Dr. Latimer noted that in these family meetings, where everyone is present, the male finds it difficult to discuss the situation at hand (personal communication). Men tend to hold back their feelings. To illustrate her point, Dr. Latimer gave the example of the young man who was diagnosed with terminal cancer. During one of these meetings she was talking to the family about the situation, the man's daughter broke down and cried. There was a pause, the man looked at his daughter then looked back at the doctor and asked, "So how long have you been a doctor?"

Most respondents felt that men try to be strong; it is difficult for them to break down in front of another person. They seem to be less emotional than women. They are all business and tend to be less verbal. According to Julie Brooks (personal communication), the Bereavement Councillor for Cresmount and Markey Dermody Funeral Homes, men tend to be more factual about the death and women tend to talk about their emotions. In the book, "The Widower," a young widower commented that he felt that men do feel the same types of emotions that women do but they don't want people to know [9]. It was noted by several funeral directors that older males are more emotional at the loss of a long time mate. Also, that younger men are starting to be more open with their own emotions.

Survey item number six asked, "How do males and females differ in their reaction to the death of a spouse?" A typical response to this question was provided by one funeral director who said, "Females will talk about the spouse and will cry in front of me. Males do not cry and do not talk a lot about the spouse." The following quote from an article written by a widow to other widows contained a critical piece of advice that illustrates another possible gender difference. "You will lean on those who come to see you through the initial period of shock. Somehow, all the bustle and confusion is a comfort—I'll always remember the squeeze of a hand, the neighbors kindness', the heartfelt 'I'm so sorry,' the physical closeness of the people I love" [10]. For many men this advice may be difficult to follow. Society does not encourage men to react to the death of a spouse in the manner above. The respondents stated that they felt men kept to themselves. Men will probably be matter of fact and may try to cover their feelings. They also felt that men were more devastated by the loss of a spouse.

Dr. Latimer stated that when a female patient is transferred home to die, the care is usually given by the children of the spouse (personal communication). Men are not as active in giving physical care to a dying person. Even after the death of their wives, husbands are usually very quiet. If adult children are present they are often the ones who ask most of the questions and do the talking. Men are often quiet during the arrangement conference as well.

Question number seven in the survey asked, "How do male and female parents differ in their reactions to the death of their child and how does this affect the choices and decisions surrounding the funeral?" Once again, the following quote emphasizes some common patterns or themes in their answers. "The male feels the need to take control, make decisions, worry about finances, yet is willing to accommodate his spouse. Whatever she would like is probably right and best for them. He tries to balance the responsibility of several issues and leave his needs last."

When a child dies suddenly, it is usually the father who is encouraged to go to the morgue to identify the body. If the mother states that she would like to go, she is usually discouraged. In hindsight, many parents wish they had gone together for the identification. Fathers who did not choose to view the body of their child felt that they failed their child because they lacked the courage to take on the "manly task" [11]. One funeral director related a story about a mother and father who came into the funeral home to view the body of their young son for the first time. The father did not want to go in the room. The funeral director said to the mother that she would leave her alone for a few minutes. The mother replied, "Please stay with me, I can't do this alone."

When both parents are involved in making funeral arrangements they are more likely to create a special meaning for the funeral service. They also try to involve others in planning and designing the funeral. They write letters to be placed in the casket and bring in belongings to be placed around the visitation room. Some mothers tend to take over the arrangements because of their need to continue to nurture the child after death.

Most of the responses to this question were similar to that of the stillborn situation. Fathers usually allowed the mothers to make most of the decisions. The mother may be more concerned about details like obtaining a lock of hair, selecting the right cards and verses. It appears that men offer support by encouraging their wives to lead in making most decisions and planning the funeral.

The final survey question asked the respondents to "rank" the following aspects of the funeral that you believe are important to males and females (1 = being most important; 5 = being least important). Table 1 shows the order of importance that funeral directors believe men and women view issues related to funerals.

Table 1. Order of Importance

Funeral Related Issues	Male Ranking	Female Ranking
Cost	1	6
Casket	2	3*
Funeral Service	3	3*
Appearance of Body	4	1
Support of Family and Friends	5	2
Visitation	6	4
Mode of Disposition	7	5

*Indicates a tie in the ranking.

The table clearly demonstrates that priorities are different for men and women. Apparently, men place a higher priority on the business aspects of the funeral service and physical actions. Women are most concerned about the appearance of the body and the social aspects of the funeral, particularly issues related to friends and family. The most important issue for men was the cost of the funeral, but it was the least important issue to women.

CONCLUSION

It should be remembered that the findings presented in this chapter do not represent the views or opinions of all funeral directors. Only funeral directors in one Canadian province were included. Their responses, however, did reveal that in various situations men act differently than women. It is interesting to note that when a spouse dies, men appear to be lost and bewildered. However, when men experience the death of a child or other family member they take on more of a role of protector and leader. Many men perceive it to be their duty to take charge.

As mentioned earlier in this chapter, mourning rituals are expected to be able to help bereaved individuals to resolve grief, to express and cope with their grief rather than making individuals act or perform in ways that make them uncomfortable or stressed. Men should not be forced into playing any particular or narrow roles related to funerals. Most often, men appear to prefer decisions that help them feel that they are doing what is correct, rather than what they simply "feel." This issue relates back to the questions asked earlier in this chapter.

Do people feel the emotions they express? Do people express the emotions they feel? Do men express their concerns and emotions in the same manner as women? Therese Rando writes that the male response to loss is different and should be respected. She states that women experience fewer conflicts between their traditional upbringing and the requirements of mourning. Many believe that men should react in ways similar to women. She advises, however, that men would be better served if they are allowed to express their grief consistent with their upbringing [12].

The funeral directors who responded to the survey noted that there are significant differences in the way men deal with various aspects of funeral arrangements. Julie Brooks, a bereavement counselor, stated that if we work on the premise that men tend to cover their feelings and not express them as openly, then men face a difficult task with the mourning process (personal communication). The best medicine we can give men is to help them to communicate their grief and not make them feel guilty about responses that we feel they should have.

REFERENCES

1. Canadian Consumer Research, *Today's Perceptions, Tomorrow's Opportunities,* Batesville, Toronto, Canada, 1992.
2. C. Staudacher, *Men and Grief,* New Harbinger, pp. 12-13, 1991.
3. D. R. Counts and D. A. Counts (eds.), *Coping with the Final Tragedy: Cultural Variation in Dying and Grieving,* Baywood, Amityville, New York, 1991.
4. J. W. Worden, *Grief Counseling and Grief Therapy,* Springer, New York, pp. 50-51, 1982.
5. J. Sirjamaki, Cultural Configurations in the American Family, *American Journal of Sociology, 53,* 1948.
6. M. Komarovshy, *Blue-Collar Marriage,* Vintage Books, New York, 1967.
7. The Ontario Board of Funeral Services, *Survey of Funeral Pricing Conducted in Ontario,* 415 Yonge Street, Suite 1609, Toronto, p. 17, December 1992.
8. Funeral and Memorial Information Council, *The Wirthlin Group Survey,* 2250 E. Devon Avenue, Suite 250, Des Plaines, Illinois, 1991.
9. J. B. Kohn and W. K. Kohn, *The Widower,* Beacon Press, Boston, p. 29, 1978.
10. T. S. Schoeneck, *Hope for the Bereaved, Understanding, Coping and Growing Through Grief,* Syracuse, New York, p. 122, 1991.

224 / MEN COPING WITH GRIEF

11. M. Kachoyeanous and F. E. Slader, Responses of Parents to Sudden Death, in *Spiritual Ethical and Pastoral Aspects of Death and Bereavement*, G. R. Cox and R. J. Fundis (eds.), Baywood, Amityville, New York, pp. 163-175, 1992.
12. T. A. Rando, *Treatment of Complicated Mourning*, Research Press, Champaign, Illinois, pp. 352-353, 1993.

PART III

Interventions and Helping Strategies

The final seven chapters in this book present information particularly valuable to those who want to help men deal more effectively with their grief. These authors and their specific topics represent a greater range in diversity than among the previous two sections. Some chapters are highly technical and geared for specific professional audiences while others present ideas and suggestions related to support groups and generic strategies to intervene. One chapter deals specifically with children, another with abused men, and still another on the topic of grieving reproductive loss. The final chapter, perhaps the most unique and creative of all, is the use of poetry to understand and treat grief.

The first chapter in this section, Chapter 13, "Assessment and Treatment of Grief States in Older Males" by Eric Rankin, provides a valuable introduction for all seven of these chapters because he places grief interventions within the broader context of loss and a developmental life course perspective. He does an excellent job of describing important guidelines for professional clinicians to follow when making assessments and diagnoses of pathological and non-pathological grief responses. The final parts of his chapter includes suggestions for general approaches to grief therapy with older men and makes use of interesting clinical vignettes to understand how they might be applied in specific cases. This chapter also is important to this book because Rankin's discussions illustrate the complexity of helping those with serious grief difficulties and the need for highly educated and well trained professionals to guide these interventions. Obviously, simply having good intentions is not sufficient to create effective helping strategies for bereaved persons.

Chapter 14, "The Bereaved Crisis Worker: A Sociological Practice Perspective on Critical Incident Death, Grief and Loss," by Robert

Bendiksen, Gregory Bodin, and Kathy Jambois extends the emphasis (of Chapter 13) on professionals and grief by examining the grief of front-line professional crisis workers. Crisis workers are those who usually respond first to critical incident deaths. They include EMTs, emergency nurses, medical examiners, trauma physicians, chaplains, funeral directors, national guard, police, firefighter dispatchers, and others. This chapter could have been included in Part I of this book because the authors provide a very useful conceptual framework, a sociological perspective, to understand the relevancy of male identity and role expectations in work as they impact bereavement and grief among crisis workers. Their chapter, however, is located in this inter-vention section of the book because the authors provide very useful discussions about education strategies, support services needed, and practical advice regarding on-site or situationally-specific behavior that will facilitate the grief process.

David Adams, author of Chapter 15, "The Grief of Male Children and Adolescents and Ways to Help Them Cope," has written an extremely valuable chapter that could have been included in the first section of the book as well. He provides a well-organized, thorough, and useful review of the relevant literature along with interesting clinical examples to help us understand how young boys and male adolescents learn to grieve. These discussions are valuable to describing and con-ceptualizing early grief experiences and recognizing how these may continue to impact each of us throughout our lives. Adams' chapter, however, is included in this part of the book because he presents extensive and useful suggestions about ways to help bereaved male children. He offers suggestions for family members, support groups and professional counselors. His sixteen practical suggestions for counsel-ing sessions is particularly valuable.

Chapter 16, "A Grief Unheard: A Woman's Reflection on a Men's Grief Group" by Peggy Anderson, is a most unique chapter. Anderson reports on her experiences of setting up an informal group for men to share their experiences regarding losses in their lives. She adds a nice personal touch to this section of the book as she describes the content and processes of group discussions and how the men shared and benefitted from their participation. She describes how these men were taught to internalize their feelings and were denied male companion-ship and empathy, yet they eventually became expressive, compas-sionate, and sensitive. Her chapter also conveys, through numerous quotes, the diversity of feelings among these men, their diverse life losses, and their vulnerability. She concludes with some practical advice for understanding men's grief and how we might consider making some changes to facilitate more satisfying grief experiences.

Kathleen Gray identifies another very unique loss situation for men and presents a thoughtful chapter discussing how husbands and wives are impacted by miscarriages, stillbirths, and perinatal deaths. In Chapter 17, "Grieving Reproductive Loss: The Bereaved Male," Gray argues that there is a gap between grief awareness in the literature versus grief awareness in the field, meaning that practitioners often lack the most in awareness. Her chapter helps fill this void by revealing another loss that men often experience but we know very little about. She identifies some ways in which men differ from women in their experiences of grief and coping and provides very valuable suggestions for how to help those in grief and professionals who work with them.

Chapter 18, "Grief of the Abused Male" by Alan Stewart, makes important contributions to this book by offering more of a religious or spiritual perspective to conceptualizing and treating grief and by broadening our views about many life experiences that create feelings of loss and grief. Specifically, Stewart examines men who were abused sexually, physically, or emotionally earlier in their lives and how it often results in a loss of identity and many other losses. These diverse reactions serve as another reminder of the multidimensional aspects of grief. He argues that being an abuse victim is another example of men being taught to keep quiet and not to express their emotions. Stewart concludes with some practical and generic suggestions for ways that we might help abused men deal with loss and grief.

The final chapter in this section and for the entire book is written by Michael Dilts. His chapter (19), "The Eloquence of Pain: Poetry of Bereaved Fathers Following a Perinatal Loss," is one of my favorite chapters because it is personal, informative, unique, and creative. Dilts examined poems written by fathers and mothers who experienced perinatal deaths to identify images and themes which help to describe the nature of their grief. The selected poems, including some of his own, are powerful, thoughtful, and insightful. The fact that Dilts reveals such compassionate and expressive poems written by men further indicates that while men may differ in some ways from women, they are quite capable of using strategies other than just the traditional masculine stereotypes. This chapter is included in this section of the book because Dilts also describes the value of using poetry as a form of therapy for facilitating the grief process. This chapter is a most fitting way to conclude the book.

CHAPTER 13

Assessment and Treatment of Grief States in Older Males

Eric D. Rankin

Reaction to a significant loss at any age can vary considerably from asymptomatic responses to major depressive disorders [1, 2]. Consequently, a comprehensive and thorough assessment is essential in evaluating individuals who have experienced a significant loss before considering potential diagnoses or clinical interventions. In later life, where significant losses are often ubiquitous, variability in the presentation of clinical syndromes further confounds the assessment, diagnosis, and treatment issues associated with grief reactions. Psychiatric disorders in later life are often characterized by symptoms that are non-specific to any one clinical syndrome or altered somewhat from their "classic" clinical presentation [3]. Changes in cognitive functioning, for example, are the hallmark symptoms associated with the dementias, but may also be a prominent feature in later life clinical depression (i.e., "pseudo-dementia"). Similarly, older adults with a clinical depression may not exhibit a dysphoric mood but rather increased complaints of somatic concerns or irritability [4, 5]. Therefore, any discussion of methods for assessing grief states among the elderly must first take into account the propensity for older adults to present with an altered presentation and identify non-specific findings. Furthermore, if this is the case for clinical syndromes like depression and dementia which can be characterized relatively easily by their symptoms, it becomes even more critical when considering clinical interventions with conditions like bereavement which inherently display greater variability.

The purpose of this chapter will therefore be threefold. Since loss is a pre-disposing condition (i.e., pathognomonic) in grief reactions and often pervasive in later life, the first objective of this chapter will be to examine the context and meaning of loss in older males. The second goal will be to provide some guidelines for conducting an evaluation of an older patient presenting with a significant loss, review current diagnostic criteria (e.g., the Diagnostic and Statistical Manual for Mental Disorders) associated with grief related syndromes, and present a clinical decision-tree (i.e., algorithm) for making a differential diagnosis of potential pathologic and non-pathologic responses to loss. The final objective will be to offer some suggestions regarding the general approach to grief therapy with older males as well as specific interventions and clinical vignettes.

LOSS AS AN ORGANIZING FORCE IN LATER LIFE DEVELOPMENT

Although there is some debate as to the exact age of "onset," most social and government agencies have used the arbitrary age of sixty-five to signify the beginning of later life. More recently, some authors have described the elderly in terms of the "young-old" (i.e., those age ≤ 75) and the "old-old" (i.e., those age ≥ 85). While this approach incorporates functional status into the concept of aging by introducing its relationship to chronic illnesses, it does not provide a conceptual framework for identifying the normative events and tasks associated with later life or their implications for bereavement during this phase of the life course. From a developmental perspective [6], each phase of life is punctuated by events of sufficient magnitude to disrupt current patterns of functioning resulting in the need to acquire and master new ones. The developmental events associated with the onset of later life include: 1) major and frequent interpersonal losses, especially of close sustaining relationships; 2) physical disability with functional decline; 3) loss of external manifestations of self (e.g., beauty, physical stature); 4) loss of social roles and resources; 5) loss of defensive outlets and options previously available to deal with intolerable affective states; 6) an increased reliance on others; 7) confrontations with the realities of mortality and death which were previously only fantasized; and 8) conflicts over the wish to live versus the wish for death [7, 8]. Other writers have simply described these events as various manifestations of loss, in particular narcissistic loss [9, 10].

The experience of loss, however, it is not unique to later life. Indeed many of the losses commonly associated with older adults (e.g., widowhood, retirement, physical disability) can and do occur in younger adults (e.g., divorce, layoffs, motor vehicle accidents). At least three critical areas differentiate later-life loss from other points in the life course. The first area refers to the context of loss, that is, the tendency for multiple losses to occur simultaneously across all three domains of functioning (e.g., physical, psychological, and social). Consequently, the process of experiencing and responding to a loss in later life is often confounded by prior and/or successive losses (e.g., intensifying or prolonging the grieving state). The second distinguishing factor is the increased likelihood for losses in later life to be chronic in nature rather than acute (i.e., leading to permanent disability/dysfunction rather than a temporary loss of function, status, etc.). For example, loss of ambulation in a younger adult following a traumatic incident like a motor vehicle accident is likely to resolve sufficiently so that the individual can return to (or close to) their pre-morbid level of functioning while a similar event in later life (e.g., a fall resulting in a broken hip) can often lead to permanent disability [11]. Moreover, in older adults there is often a "cascading" of losses precipitated by the initial event leading to increased disability and permanent loss of function. In the example of a hip fracture, previous clinical studies have reported increased incidence of nursing home placement and cognitive impairment following a broken hip in older patients [9]. The final area refers to the diminished reserve in bio-psychosocial resources available for older adults vis-à-vis other age groups to compensate for any particular loss. Death of a spouse at any age is extremely stressful; however, younger adults experiencing this loss often retain other personal and social support systems (e.g., families of origin and procreation, peer groups, employment, mobility, etc.) which can be very helpful in ameliorating the impact of the loss. Therefore, the depletion of an older adult's "bio-psychosocial reserve" due to age-associated and non-normative losses can interfere significantly with the individual's capacity to cope effectively with subsequent losses [6,12]. These characteristics have been presented schematically in Figure 1. The two boxes represent a mid-life adult and older adult (see Figure 1) while the arrows represent the number and chronicity of losses (pointing away from each box) and resources (pointing toward each box).

Having argued for a distinction between the experience of loss in mid versus later life, it remains important to emphasize that these differences are based on a developmental rather than chronological classification. For some elders losses in later life remain singular, isolated events. When significant losses (e.g., death of a spouse) are encountered by these older adults, there is evidence to suggest that the psychological impact may not be as intense compared to mid-life adults due to its "on-time" qualities [13]. As a result, the experience and impact of significant loss in later life can vary considerably more from other age groups ranging from milder reactions for those with adequate

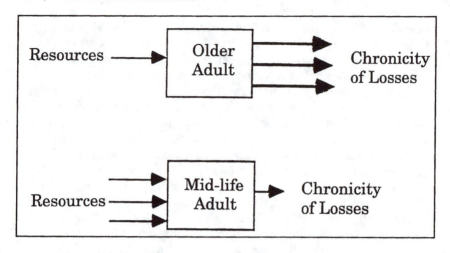

Figure 1. Comparison of biopsychosocial losses and resources
in older and mid-life adults.

resources encountering on-time losses to more extreme responses when
resources are diminished and/or losses are multiple. Therefore, from a
developmental and clinical perspective, it is not loss per se that distinguishes the experience of older individuals from those of younger ones,
but rather the manner in which these losses occur that makes their
experience intrinsically different from other points in the life course.

Multiple losses in later life are also thought to precipitate a new
series of developmental tasks and coping responses critical to successful aging. While the acquisition of new roles, relationships, and
abilities continue into mid-life, reaffirming and extending one's sense
of self [14], during the later phases of the life course older adults are
confronted with repeated losses of significant others, personal abilities,
and social roles that are critical to sustaining their core sense of self
[10]. Consequently, the primary developmental task confronting adults
in later life is the maintenance of self-identity and self-esteem in the
midst of multiple and significant losses [15]. Typically, coping with
multiple losses in later life has not been distinguished from coping with
major losses during other phases of the life course. Most authors
present a generic model identifying a series of tasks necessary for
the successful resolution of bereavement without regard to the
developmental context or meaning of the loss(es). For example, Levin
[16] described the process of successfully coping with loss in later life as
". . . the capacity to redistribute libido to new objects and new aims,"
while Havighurst [17] emphasized the need for older adults to adopt

new social roles as well as adapt old ones in response to their diminishing abilities. As previously noted, however, losses in later life usually require older adults, at some point, to relinquish long-standing attachments to core objects that have helped to define and sustain their sense of self. Moreover, the opportunity and ability to retain a sense of continuity of self by investing in alternative relationships becomes increasingly difficult in later life due to diminished capacities and limited resources. As a result, the psychological tasks and sources of conflict that must be successfully resolved are often unique to this stage of the life course. In sum, due to the increased variability in the type and manner of losses experienced and resources available in later life, the clinician can expect both greater range in the impact of significant losses and the tasks associated with adequately grieving these losses.

SOURCES OF CONFLICT IN RESOLVING LOSS IN LATER LIFE

Freud originally described mourning as a process in which memories and hopes of a lost loved one are brought up and "hypercathected" (i.e., the process by which libido becomes detached from each aspect of the lost loved one), ultimately resulting in the freeing of the ego to engage in new attachments [18]. From the psychodynamic perspective, successful mourning can be described as the resolution of two separate, but inter-related tasks. Initially, the reality of the loss precipitates a gradual and sometimes painful process of withdrawing libido from the lost object. Hence, the initial psychological task precipitated by a significant loss is one of detachment (i.e., de-cathexis). Once completed, the individual is free to initiate and sustain new relationships. Consequently, the final task associated with the resolution of a major loss is attachment to new objects (i.e., re-cathexis). Both Zarit [11] and Knight [19] have suggested that at least for some older adults, the multiplicity of losses in later life can protract the grieving process. In the clinical setting, it has been useful to consider this observation as a function of the resolution of conflict around issues of de-cathexis and re-cathexis. Sources of conflict that are likely to arise during the process of relinquishing core objects can be characterized by the following: 1) a diminished capacity for effectively coping with loss; and 2) a fear of psychological fragmentation or loss of personal control. Two potential areas of conflict related to the process of re-establishing core relationships include: 1) a tendency toward nihilistic thinking; and 2) the challenge of identifying meaningful replacements by discovering latent abilities. Given that these terms are clinical shorthand, a brief description of each is necessary.

1. Diminished Capacities

The term diminished capacities is used here to signify a diminution in an individual's capacity to cope effectively with stressors in later life due to a piling up of normative and non-normative losses. The cumulative effect of multiple losses across all three functional domains can significantly impinge upon an elder's ability to cope with successive stressors regardless of their personal meaning or level of disruption [12]. As Lazarus notes, "The skills, mastery, and powers, all painfully acquired which provided gratification as they functioned to effect adaptation wane in the last phase of life" [10, p. 110]. Furthermore, depletion of the individual's ego strengths and social support network can exacerbate sub-clinical neurotic tendencies into clinical states interfering further with their overall capacity to cope with the vicissitudes of later life [8, 20]. Under these conditions, an older person's capacity to tolerate the ambivalence and emotional distress associated with relinquishing core attachments may become partially or even completely compromised resulting in a pathological response to grief.

2. Fear of Loss of Control

The experience of a significant loss at any stage during the life course can challenge one's sense of mastery and control over personal events. It would appear that these perceptions also play an important role in the resolution of grief states. Hannson, Remondet, and Galusha have reported, for example, that perceptions of control are especially salient during the initial phases of grief [7]. During this period, acceptance of the reality of the loss as well as experiencing the associated emotional pain can be potentially overwhelming [21]. Avoidance of these tasks due to a fear of becoming overwhelmed emotionally or otherwise may interfere with the grieving process increasing the risk of pathologic response (e.g., physical illness, psychopathology) [1].

In later life, bereavement is often confounded by the occurrence of multiple losses within a relatively brief period of time. Sanders has noted that the experience of concurrent losses or stressors, per se, are potentially overwhelming and debilitating [22]. Therefore, the elderly's capacity to confront the reality and emotional pain of a particular loss is influenced, in part, by the number and meaning of previous losses. This may occur in at least two ways. First, the process of grieving previous losses may be incomplete depleting available resources for addressing new losses. Secondly, even if previous losses are being coped with adequately, the subjective experience of multiple losses in itself can heighten and exaggerate their personal sense of loss of control making it difficult to confront the painful and potentially overwhelming emotions associated with each new loss. As a result, efforts to engage older adults who have experienced multiple losses in the process of relinquishing attachments, even to those objects that would appear insignificant to others, is likely to be met with varying degrees of resistance as the individual attempts to retain some control over their subjective and emotional world.

3. Tendency toward Nihilistic Thinking

As previously noted, the process of grieving not only entails the painful process of withdrawing libido from the lost object, but also the re-cathexis of libido onto new objects or relationships [21]. When losses are multiple and involve core objects, the process of forming new attachments can also be a source of emotional pain, conflict, and ambivalence. This can be especially true for older adults whose emotional and intellectual investment in core relationships have evolved over a life time becoming increasingly enriching, but also delimiting. From this perspective, investment of self in relationships and activities is viewed by the bereaved as contributing directly to their current feelings of devastation, pain, and despair. While they may not question their initial motivation for establishing these attachments, in their current emotional state they may question the prudence of allowing themselves to once again risk the feelings associated with significant loss. Thus, following losses of long-standing core attachments, the geriatric patient may become resistant, either consciously or unconsciously, to engaging in the process of identifying and forming new attachments "since this will ultimately lead to new losses and pain." Shuchter and Zisook, for example, have referred to "fears of recurrent loss" as a source of resistance to forming new relationships after the death of a spouse [23]. If these nihilistic attitudes toward attachment become entrenched, they can interfere with the resolution of the grieving process resulting in an aloof and distant emotional posture toward available significant relationships.

4. Identifying Meaningful Replacements

Finding meaningful replacements following significant loss is a difficult and gradual process at any age [1, 21]. When losses are multiple and simultaneously involve various aspects of the individual's personal and social functioning, however, the opportunity to re-invest emotional energies from lost objects into other long-standing relationships or activities becomes correspondingly limited. As a result, many elders must explore new or marginal areas of self-expression for narcissistic maintenance and personal growth. Thus, while the process of de-cathecting from significant losses is difficult, when the loss is a singular isolated event the process of re-cathecting to new relationships is facilitated by activities and relationships independent of the loss which already hold meaning for the individual. For example, the elder coping with multiple losses including the death of a spouse, may not be able to invest in other personal and social activities (e.g., work or nurturer role, physical activity, peer relations) due to significant losses in these areas as well. As a result, the absence of ongoing meaningful activities and relationships during a significant loss can be an additional source of conflict and ambivalence in resolving significant losses.

Using loss as an organizing concept, the preceding section has attempted to establish a theoretical rationale for the importance of understanding contextual issues in later life bereavement. In particular, the influence of multiple and concurrent losses on the process of withdrawing libido from long-standing attachments (i.e., de-cathexis) as well as the re-investing in other relationships or attachments (i.e., re-cathexis) was examined. Four areas of potential ambivalence and conflict associated with these processes were presented. While each was described independently, they are often encountered concomitantly in clinical settings varying in their degree of intensity in relation to patient characteristics like developmental history and situational factors. The remaining sections of this chapter will explore the central role contextual issues associated with loss play in the assessment, diagnosis, and treatment of grief states in later life as well as highlight those issues most relevant to work with older males.

CLINICAL ASSESSMENT AND DIAGNOSIS OF GRIEF STATES IN THE ELDERLY

In general, the purpose of clinical assessment includes the following objectives: 1) to elicit information regarding the patient's presenting problems and clinical symptoms leading to the formulation of a diagnosis; 2) exploration of the patient's bio-psychosocial strengths and weaknesses to the extent necessary to guide the development and implementation of a treatment plan; and 3) understanding the individuality of each person seeking help. This would include an understanding of their ethnic identity, values, religious background, gender, family, and work histories. As Knight has noted, ". . . although therapy is generally problem-focused, one must not forget that it is a person that has the problem" [19, p. 92]. During the assessment process, clinical information usually consists of subjective and objective data.

Subjective data refers to patient, family members, and significant others perceptions of current/past psychosocial functioning, the circumstances surrounding the presenting problem (loss), and the patient's current mental status. Contextual factors identified in previous studies with the resolution of significant loss have included: the individual's emotional attachment toward the lost object; the occurrence of multiple losses leading to prolonged or incomplete grieving; the nature of the pre-loss relationship with high conflict being associated with complicated grief reactions; the circumstances surrounding the loss with the perception of an abrupt loss creating more psychological distress; and the quality of the bereaved person's social support network serving as a mediating variable [1, 11, 24]. Of particular interest to the present discussion are the impact of the patient's personal/familial history and gender.

Depending upon the therapist's theoretical orientation, efforts to collect a complete patient history from an older adult can result in either an overwhelming amount of information including early child developmental events or a minimal data set limited to a functional assessment of the targeted behavior. Regardless of one's clinical framework, however, some aspects of the patient's history remain salient in the assessment of later life grief states. Presence of a past psychiatric or psychological history is important in understanding the patient's areas of strength and limitations. While it is tempting to conclude when interviewing an older male, for example, who has recently lost his wife, suffers from multiple medical problems, and was in the process of being admitted to a long-term care facility, "that anyone would be depressed if they had all that happening to them." The reality is that most depressions in later life have had an early onset. That is to say, the individual suffered their first bout of depression prior to age sixty [25]. Thus, determining whether a patient similar to the one described above has had a previous history of depression has diagnostic as well as prognostic implications. Identifying the presence of a psychiatric history in older adults, however, is not always as straightforward as simply asking. As young adults, the availability of mental health services for this cohort was usually limited to state hospitals [19]. Consequently, asking an older patient if they were ever seen by a counselor or psychiatrist or prescribed an antidepressant is not adequate. A less cohort-biased approach is to ask if they have ever felt like this before and, if so, have they ever been unable to do their daily activities (either in the home or at work) because of the way they felt. In addition, since most older adults have already experienced some losses, it is useful to explore in some detail their response to previous normative (e.g., death of parents, retirement, etc.) as well as any potential non-normative losses (e.g., death of younger siblings, other "off-time" losses including major illnesses, etc.) as both have been shown to be predictors of current responses to loss [22].

Research into the relative influence of gender on the impact and resolution of later life losses has produced mixed results. Comparisons of elders coping with significant loss have been limited primarily to the experience of widowhood despite later life often being a time of multiple losses. While this may account for some of the apparent contradictory findings, it would not seem to be a sufficient explanation by itself. For example, increased psychiatric and physical morbidity in widowers has been reported in some studies [26, 27], while the opposite finding has also been reported [13, 22]. What appears to be a consistent finding across most studies is that men, in general, tend to report fewer psychiatric and physical symptoms than women and that they also rely more extensively on their marriage for social support. These differences in baseline functioning have led some writers to propose a distinction between general gender differences and grief specific reasons [23]. When gender comparisons have been limited to grief specific behaviors (e.g., yearning for deceased spouse), no differences were found [28]. Therefore, while bereavement appears to be equally distressful for both men and women, it would not be accurate to conclude that the effects of significant loss are necessarily the same across both sexes. Rather, males do appear to be at greater risk for psychiatric morbidity following significant loss, but this is due to the interactional effects of general gender-related differences with specific grief reactions. It is therefore extremely important to thoroughly assess the nature and extent of normative and non-normative later-life losses, especially in older males, since these individuals appear to have less extensive social support networks available to mediate the impact of the loss(es).

The final area of inquiry involving subjective information is an assessment of the patient's mental status following a significant loss(es). The fourth edition of the Diagnostic and Statistical Manual of Mental Disorders (DSMIV) [29] identifies six specific areas of functioning to examine when making a differential diagnosis between bereavement and psychiatric disorders (a detailed discussion of this information and a diagnostic algorithm or decision-tree will be presented in the next section). At this point of the discussion, it is useful to note that even though the DSMIV provides direction as to what areas of functioning to assess, considerable clinical judgment is still required. In particular, when considering positive findings from the mental status examination, the clinician must assess their relevance in terms of scope, persistence, and severity. Scope is used here to signify the range of the problem. For example, one area of clinical consideration is functional status. Questions concerning the scope of the problem would address how many activities and instrumental activities of daily living (ADL/IADL) are currently impaired (e.g., dressing, personal grooming, housekeeping, cooking, etc.). The persistence of these symptoms would examine issues of duration. In particular, the DSMIV suggests that a psychiatric diagnosis not be considered unless the symptoms have been present for at least two months following the loss. Issues associated with severity of symptom can be exemplified by the difference between a bereaved yearning to be with the deceased versus being actively suicidal. Clinical judgment also comes into play in terms of assigning relative value to the scope, persistence, and severity of a particular symptom. Active suicidal ideations do not have to exist for two months before considering a psychiatric diagnosis and treatment intervention.

Objective data refers to information collected using standardized assessment instruments. There are several advantages to incorporating the use of standardized instruments into an assessment protocol. First, identifying a set of instruments that will be administered routinely helps to ensure the consistency and comprehensiveness of the assessment protocol across patients. Second, many assessment instruments have cut-off points established which can facilitate clinical decision-making. And finally, standardized instruments often have normative data associated with their scales which enables the clinician to compare the clinical profile of an individual patient with a larger group of similar individuals. In our work in the Department of Behavioral Medicine and Psychiatry at West Virginia University, the assessment of grief-related problems in older adults includes the following standardized clinical instruments: the Geriatric Depression Scale [30] to assess the degree of affective disturbance in the patient; the Personal Mastery Scale [31] to assess the patient's perceptions of self-efficacy and self-worth; and either the Texas Revised Inventory of Grief [32] or the Inventory of Complicated Grief [33] to assess the potential type and degree of bereavement.

DIFFERENTIAL DIAGNOSIS OF GRIEF AND DEPRESSIVE STATES IN LATER LIFE

Generally speaking, considerable overlap exists between the symptoms in bereavement and clinical depression confounding the diagnostic process [2]. The co-existence of nomenclature based upon theoretical (e.g., pathologic vs. complicated vs. uncomplicated bereavement) and criterion-based (e.g., DSMIV) models also contributes to the confusion. Finally, the situation is exacerbated further with elderly patients due to the increased likelihood of an altered clinical presentation and/or non-specific findings. In older males, for example, the tendency to avoid affect-laden material or express emotions may lead the clinician to misinterpret the degree or severity of the patient's state of grief. While an attempt has been made to incorporate aspects of several models and perspectives into the diagnostic algorithm that follows (see Figure 2), it is not intended to be completely inclusive. Before discussing the content in Figure 2, it might be helpful to provide an overview of how it is organized. The algorithm is to be read from the top down. At each juncture point, a plus (+) and minus (−) sign appear on either side of the salient question to be explored. A plus signifies the presence of the clinical symptoms, status, etc. described below the query and a negative sign indicates their absence. The thicker lines ultimately lead to a diagnostic classification while the thinner lines below each diagnosis describe dynamic factors and treatment considerations.

Following a significant loss, the first clinical area to evaluate is the presence/absence of a mood disturbance. A mood disturbance has been operationalized in the algorithm to include nine of the ten symptoms identified in the DSMIV (suicidal behavior was excluded until later in the algorithm). Conceptually, the absence of a reaction to loss may occur when the individual refrains from expressing their response publicly, when there is a lack of true overt manifestations, or when there was little or no emotional investment in the lost object [1]. In the present algorithm, this condition has been classified as "asymptomatic bereavement." Regardless of the theoretical explanation, there is substantial empirical evidence that precipitating a grief reaction in individuals who do not manifest symptoms results in greater psychopathology and dysfunction [34]. Consequently, no treatment considerations are associated with this diagnostic classification.

Should a bereaved individual present with one or more clinical symptoms, however, the next question to examine is how adaptive is their response to a change in mood. Traditionally, at least four areas have been identified in the stress literature when clinically evaluating an individuals's response to a stressor (loss). These would include: 1) Does the coping response reduce or heighten the individual's level of anxiety? 2) Does the coping response enhance or impair their reality testing abilities (e.g., cognitive distortions, decreased self-esteem)? 3) Does the coping response lead to marked or prolonged functional impairment? and 4) Are the coping responses atypical or phase inappropriate (e.g., DSMIV cautions against considering an axis I diagnosis

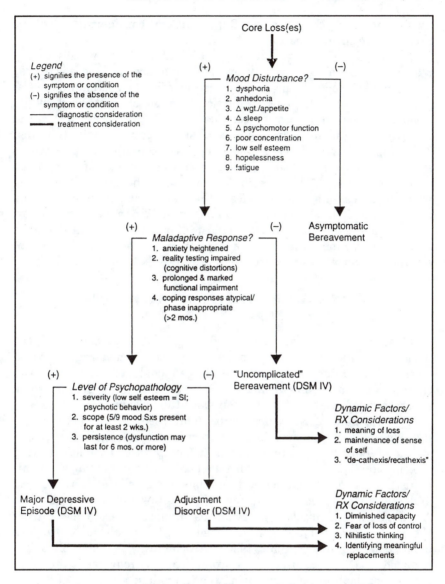

Figure 2. Differential diagnosis of depression and grief states.

if duration of symptoms are less than two months)? The absence of a maladaptive response would lead to a diagnostic classification of "uncomplicated" bereavement. This category is consistent with the DSMIV classification of bereavement. Such individuals may seek professional help even though the grief process appears uncomplicated by significant psychopathology [29] (treatment considerations will be presented in the next section).

If the clinical assessment suggests that the individual's coping responses are maladaptive, however, the final area to assess is degree of psychopathology. As previously described in the section on mental status, level of pathological function can be characterized by its severity, scope, and persistence. Based on DSMIV criteria, level of severity would include the presence of suicidal or psychotic thinking. The scope of the problem would be assessed by the number of symptoms present over the preceding two weeks (i.e., 5 or more mood related symptoms). And persistence of the pathological functioning would be assessed by the presence of these symptoms for more than six months. If an individual met or exceeded any of the criteria for severity, scope, or persistence, a clinical diagnosis of major depression should be considered, while a diagnosis of adjustment disorder could be considered if none of these criteria were present.

CLINICAL INTERVENTIONS WITH GRIEF STATES IN THE ELDERLY

Most treatment models developed for grief therapy begin with the basic assumption that bereavement is a process consisting of several distinct, but inter-related stages. Stage-models of grief and grief therapy are appealing to many clinicians since they provide some parameters of what to expect throughout the grieving process as well as specific clinical activities to be addressed during each stage. Worden, for example, describes the process of normal grieving as consisting of four tasks, beginning with the acceptance of the loss, feeling the emotional pain associated with the loss of a significant attachment, adjusting to changes in roles and relationships precipitated by the loss, and finally a reinvestment into new relationships and/or activities [21]. Although an individual may "revisit" each phase several times during the grieving process [35], it is assumed that the resolution of the loss ultimately requires specific tasks associated with each phase be resolved [21]. The treatment of uncomplicated bereavement therefore consists of facilitating/augmenting the individual's existing efforts at coping with the process of confronting and resolving the tasks associated with each phase of grieving. For older males coping with significant loss, this process may become complicated by age-associated aspects of loss and cohort-specific gender issues.

As previously described, it is not loss per se that distinguishes the experience of many older adults from other age groups, but the manner in which loss occurs. The increased tendency for multiple core losses to occur over brief periods of time interferes with the process of de-cathexing from significant relationships due to the concomitant piling up of losses and resulting feelings of loss of control as well as the process of re-cathexing to new relationships (e.g., nihilistic thinking, identification of meaningful replacements). Similarly, the tendency of many older males to eschew affect-laden issues or the expression of feelings as well as rely on a limited social network for support may limit further the ability of this group to relinquish significant attachments and form new ones. While these factors do not alter substantially the basic tasks involved in resolving grief states, they do require some modification in the clinical approach with uncomplicated bereavement and pathologic reactions to loss so that they are more consistent with the experiences of older adult males.

Treatment of Uncomplicated Bereavement in Older Males

Based on the discussion presented earlier, the term "uncomplicated" bereavement (refer to Figure 2) is used here to connote the absence of clinically significant levels of psychopathology following a core loss(es). While most of these individuals will not actively seek treatment from traditional psychiatric settings, they may come to the attention of mental health professionals via referral from primary healthcare providers or concerned family members (e.g., adult children). In these instances, concern over the intensity or expression of emotions by an older male family member is often a contributing factor in the decision to seek psychiatric or psychological consultation. While feeling emotional pain is a normal response following significant loss, for many older males the experience of such intense feelings is without precedent as is their family's experience of witnessing them in such an emotional state. This situation often accentuates concerns over a loss of control (e.g., increased liability in affect) and can exacerbate pre-existing perceptions of diminished personal control associated with concurrent age-associated losses. The following vignette illustrates the concerns of an older male and his family to his emotional response following the death of his wife.

Mr. A. was a seventy-one-year-old white male. He had worked as a building contractor taking a semi-retirement approximately five years ago. At that time, both of his sons took over the day-to-day operation of the family business. Following his "retirement," Mr. A. continued to assist with some construction jobs, volunteered at a local church-sponsored meal program, and went on extended trips with his wife of forty-seven years. Approximately two months ago, Mr. A.'s wife died after a two year illness. Following the wife's death, the patient maintained his high level of involvement in various work and social activities. More recently, however, his children have become increasingly concerned about their father's crying. He has weekly visits with them for Sunday dinner and reports crying at the "drop of a hat." Similarly, he reports becoming increasingly upset about returning to his empty home and will begin to cry during these times as well. The family reported that they had never witnessed their father cry before and were quite concerned, encouraging him to seek an evaluation. Mr. A. identified as his chief complaint "crying" and the worry that he "wouldn't be able to stop."

On evaluation, Mr. A. was pleasant and very engaging. His affect was broad and congruent with verbal content. When he spoke of his business activities, volunteer work, relationships with his children and grandchildren, and the care he had provided his wife, he expressed genuine pride and satisfaction. As soon as the topic of his wife's death was mentioned, however, there was an immediate change in his countenance and mood. Once the topic changed again, his mood returned to a more euthymic state (i.e., normal range). A review of personal and social functioning indicated no evidence of vegetative symptoms or change in functional status. Indeed, he appeared to seek out opportunities to be of assistance to others rather than withdraw from social contact. In essence, he was disturbed by the intensity of his emotional response to the death of his wife and the fear that these transient feeling states might overwhelm his day-to-day functioning at some point rather than a concern with an actual diminution in current psychological or social functioning. He reported no personal or family history of significant psychiatric problems.

The focus of the treatment attempted to address the normalcy of intense emotional responses following a significant loss within the context of aging. In this case, issues of loss appeared to be intensified by a general perception of loss of primary social role (provider) and personal control (labile affect). While the therapist provided a rationale for grieving and the steps involved for its resolution, these discussions took place only after securing the patient's permission to discuss the death of his wife. These included statements like the following: "I would like to talk about your wife a little more if that's all right with you. I know that this can be upsetting so if I ask you something you don't want to talk about, just say so. Also, if the discussion gets to be too much just say stop and we can talk about something else." It was hoped that by emphasizing the patient's control over the nature and content of the discussion of his wife's death, he would be more willing to risk working through the pain associated with his loss without fear of becoming overwhelmed or dependent upon others. While the therapist was encouraging of the patient to monitor his psychological status, the early sessions also required the therapist to be empathic and shift topics, if he felt the patient was becoming too distraught emotionally. Consequently, therapy sessions two through five began with the patient moving a box of tissues next to his chair. At some point during the session, the focus would shift to the death of his wife and he would break down and cry. Each of these early sessions would end with a query concerning whether the patient felt ready to leave the session or wished to stay a few minutes longer before going out as a further attempt to underscore his control of the situation and monitor his psychological status.

As he became more comfortable coping with the intensity of his emotions during the therapy sessions, the focus of the next several sessions turned to his emotional response outside of the sessions. An operant model of behavior was discussed describing the relationship between antecedents and consequences on behavior (crying). Once again, the goal of these discussions was to provide the patient with a paradigm for exerting more personal control over the manner in which he expressed strong emotional content. Strategies for predicting situations that were likely to precipitate these feelings as well as how to respond once he began to experience these emotions were discussed. During this phase of the therapy, the patient asked about bereavement groups. He was given the number of a local group and attended a couple of the sessions. While he felt the focus was on younger widows/widowers in general, he continued to have contact with some of the older members outside of the group's meetings. In addition, he called a close friend who had lost their spouse a year or so earlier to discuss and share their experiences. He reported to me that he felt he had been of help to several of these people by "just listening to them."

By the beginning of the third month of the therapy, the patient's affect would become constricted and mildly dysphoric when discussing his wife's death, but he no longer cried uncontrollably. Termination of the therapy ensued. During his last session, Mr. A. discussed his future interests and indicated to me that he would be available to talk with any of my future patients going through the loss of a spouse. Apparently, he had regained his pre-loss social identity, psychological equilibrium, and perception of personal control.

Treatment of Pathological Grief States in Older Males

The clinical concerns for older adults experiencing a pathologic reaction to loss extend beyond quality of life issues. The strong correlation between depression and suicidal behavior in older males underscores this concern. White males over the age of sixty-five presently have the highest suicide rate in the United States [36]. While various treatment interventions have been proposed for treating depressed geriatric patients, two of the models in particular provide a good match for working with issues related to the relinquishing of core objects and/or reinvestment in new attachments following multiple losses in later life. Cognitive-behavioral models have been demonstrated to be effective in treating older depressed elders by identifying and modifying distortions in thinking [28]. This approach can be very helpful in assessing and treating nihilistic thinking in older adults experiencing pathologic responses to core loss(es). Similarly, behavioral interventions can be useful in providing a graduated program for resuming meaningful activities or investing in new ones following significant losses. Brief therapies based on the principles of self-psychology may also be helpful in addressing multiple core losses in later life [10]. Functioning as a self-object, the therapist can meet the patient's need for an idealized caretaker following the loss of core objects as well as mirror the patient's remaining positive attributes. The patient's idealized relationship with the therapist can be extremely helpful to them in coping with fears of becoming overwhelmed by a loss of control. Similarly, the therapist's ability to empathically identify and reinforce the patient's remaining or latent abilities following core loss(es) can facilitate their efforts in finding meaningful replacements. The following two vignettes illustrate the use of these treatment models with an older male becoming increasingly nihilistic following the losses of physical and social functioning and one experiencing a piling up of stressors.

Mr. B. is a sixty-two-year-old white married male. He has been married four times to three different spouses. The patient has an extensive history of alcohol abuse, but has been abstinent for the past ten years. Approximately three years ago, he sustained a back injury at work and has been unable to return to his job as a foreman. The patient's back injury continues to be a source of physical pain and disability. He reports that he is unable to perform any household chores or leisure activities due to back pain. The patient's wife works full time and is presently the primary wage earner for the couple. Mr. B. identified his chief complaint as "I feel useless."

On evaluation, Mr. B. was casually dressed and well-kempt. He greeted the therapist with the comment "Are you ready for me?" The patient's affect was mildly constricted with some agitation related to verbal content (e.g., accident, loss of function). He described his mood as depressed and somewhat irritable. The patient's thinking was significant for poor self image/esteem, somatic complaints, increased agitation and frustration, feelings of guilt and self reproachment over current functional status, and passive suicidal ideation. He reported a significant personal and family history of alcohol abuse, but no prior psychiatric or psychological care.

The focus of the treatment attempted to address the patient's change in self perception, decrease in personal and social activities, provide strategies for coping with chronic pain, and monitor his suicidal ideation. As therapy progressed, however, the severity of the narcissistic injuries associated with his loss of function and role status became increasingly evident by his nihilistic ideation (e.g., "I don't know why my wife stays with me when I can't do anything?"). While both he and his father had had a problem with drinking, he had always been able to maintain a steady work history. Now that important distinction was gone.

Efforts to assist the patient grieve these losses as a first step toward ultimately identifying with new sources of narcissistic gratification were met with resistance. The patient argued vociferously the absence of any meaningful replacements in his life and the futility of searching for new ones. Without the hope of meaningful replacements, the patient was unable to relinquish his pre-injury self image. The therapist began to mirror empathical qualities in the patient that remained intact (e.g., intelligence, persistence in opinion, direct honesty). As the patient began to view these qualities as viable and accessible sources of narcissistic gratification, he began to mourn the loss of function and status associated with his injury. Although he continued to express sadness over these losses, his depression and passive suicidal ideation abated and Mr. B. enrolled in an electronics course at a local vocational-technical school and decided to pursue this interest as a hobby. The patient has maintained contact with me and as other significant disruptions or losses have occurred, he has continued to revert back to his previous style of coping. However, brief follow-up therapy has been very effective in providing him with alternative explanations for his situation and more reality-based strategies for coping.

The last clinical vignette illustrates the impact of a piling up of psychosocial stressors on an older male's capacity to grieve significant loss.

Mr. C. is a seventy-nine-year-old white married male. He has a college education and retired from a successful professional career. The patient has been married to his wife for fifty-eight years and the couple have four children. Approximately four months ago, the patient's wife suffered a cardio-vascular accident (CVA) resulting in a left-side hemiparesis and mild cognitive deficits. The patient decided to transfer his wife to a rehabilitation facility closer to their son. This required him to relocate as well and he moved in with his son and his family. The move offered his wife a better treatment facility, but effectively cut the patient off from his peer support group, familiarity of home and community, and access to primary activity since retirement (wood working). Since the move to his son's home, the patient reported a significant disturbance in appetite and sleep. He complains of increasing irritability and poor concentration. He describes his chief complaint as "depression."

On evaluation, Mr. C. presents nicely dressed but slightly unkempt. His affect was constricted and mood was described as dysphoric and anxious. The patient's speech was pressured. Thought processes were circumstantial with some tangential thinking also noted. Content was significant for feelings of being overwhelmed and apprehensive, ruminating over his wife's condition and obsessive-compulsive behavior. The patient reported no prior history of depression.

The focus of treatment attempted to address the overwhelming of the patient's coping repertoire and subsequent feelings of loss of control. The precipitous loss of functioning in the patient's wife and resulting efforts to cope with her care produced a significant dislocation in the patient's psychosocial support system. The patient attempted to cope with the resulting anxiety by becoming increasingly focused on unimportant details and exhibited excessive rule-governed behavior. He also refused to accept that there would be any permanent loss of function associated with his wife's CVA. The more distress he experienced, the more rigid and less effective he became.

In therapy, the patient immediately began to idealize the therapist and his opinion. While the patient had been very successful in both his personal life and career, he assumed a very dependent posture in the therapy. It soon became apparent that the patient felt in need of an ally. All of his wife's physicians and his family were telling him that he would have to accept his wife's disabilities as permanent. Although this was an accurate assessment of his wife's clinical status, the combination of losses following the move had overwhelmed Mr. C.'s capacity to grieve these unwelcomed changes in his wife and their relationship. Through the idealized relationship, the therapist was able to facilitate the grieving process by monitoring emphathically the patient's ability to tolerate each phase of the mourning process. Issues related to his wife's stroke were raised in a manner that were not totally overwhelming. In addition, significant portions of the sessions focused on the multiplicity of losses the patient had encountered, the need to slow the process of adjustment to one acceptable to him, and problem-solving techniques to assist in modulating affect and resolving crises. As the patient's wife progressed in her rehabilitation, he became more accepting of her condition and the couple ultimately returned to their own home.

CONCLUSIONS

In summary, the purpose of this chapter has been to present a discussion of the factors that distinguish loss in later life from other stages in the life course. The tendency for multiple losses to occur concurrently across all three functional domains was identified as the most salient characteristic in defining the experience of bereavement in later life. It was also noted, however, that the term "later life" was used to describe a developmental stage rather than a chronological category. Four areas of potential conflict associated with multiple losses were also identified. These included: a diminished capacity for effectively coping with loss; a fear of psychological fragmentation or loss of personal control; a tendency toward nihilistic thinking; and the challenge of identifying meaningful replacements by discovering latent abilities.

For older males, the resolution of these conflicts was predicted to be influenced by cohort-gender specific issues as well (e.g., the expression of affect, utilization of social support networks). It was argued that clinical assessment, diagnosis, and treatment could be enhanced by incorporating these concepts into existing diagnostic nomenclature (e.g., DSMIV) and treatment models (e.g., cognitive-behavioral therapy). Given the type and magnitude of loss experienced by some elders seeking counseling, mental health providers will also need to acknowledge the realistic limitations of their treatment interventions. The material in this chapter has been presented not to encourage hope where there is realistically none (i.e., regaining irreversible loss), but rather to offer clinicians a method for defining and treating later life losses in a manner that offers the older patient an opportunity to develop a greater understanding of what has been lost and what remains, coming to terms with the mourning process and experiencing a sense of closure, and instilling a sense of realistic hope that meaningful replacements exist and can be acquired once again.

REFERENCES

1. T. Rando, *Treatment of Complicated Mourning*, Research Press, Champaign, Illinois, 1993.
2. S. Zisook and S. Shuchter, Uncomplicated Bereavement, *Journal of Clinical Psychiatry, 54*, pp. 365-372, 1993.
3. C. Christison and D. Blazer, Clinical Assessment of Psychiatric Symptoms, in *Geriatric Neuropsychology*, M. Albert and M. Moss (eds.), The Guilford Press, New York, pp. 82-99, 1988.
4. E. Kim and B. Rovner, Depression in Dementia, *Psychiatric Annals, 24*, pp. 173-177, 1994.
5. G. Klerman, Problems in the Definition and Diagnosis of Depression in the Elderly, in *Depression and Aging: Causes, Care, and Consequences*, L. Breslau and M. Haug (eds.), Springer, New York, pp. 3-19, 1993.
6. M. Lieberman and H. Peskin, Adult Life Crises, in *Handbook of Mental Health and Aging* (2nd Edition), J. Birren, R. Sloane, and G. Cohen (eds.), Academic Press, San Diego, pp. 119-143, 1992.
7. R. Hannson, J. Remondet, and M. Galusha, Old Age and Widowhood: Issues of Personal Control and Independence, in *Handbook of Bereavement: Theory, Research and Intervention*, M. Stroebe, W. Stroebe, and R. Hannson (eds.), Cambridge Press, New York, 1993.
8. J. Sadavoy, Character Pathology in the Elderly, *Journal of Geriatric Psychiatry, 20*, pp. 165-178, 1987.
9. S. Cath and J. Sadavoy, Psychosocial Aspects, in *Comprehensive Review of Geriatric Psychiatry*, J. Sadavoy, L. Lazarus, and L. Jarvick (eds.), American Psychiatric Association Press, Washington, D.C., pp. 79-99, 1991.
10. L. Lazarus, Self Psychology: Its Application to Brief Psychotherapy with the Elderly, *Journal of Geriatric Psychiatry, 21*, pp. 109-125, 1988.
11. S. Zarit, *Aging and Mental Disorders: Psychological Approaches to Assessment and Treatment*, Free Press, New York, 1980.

12. S. Murrell, S. Meeks, and J. Walter, Protective Functions of Health and Self-Esteem against Depression in Older Adults Facing Illness or Bereavement, *Psychology and Aging, 6,* pp. 352-360, 1991.
13. S. Zisook, S. Schechter, P. Sledge, and M. Mulvihill, Aging and Bereavement, *Journal of Geriatric Psychiatry and Neurology, 6,* pp. 137-143, 1993.
14. E. Erikson, *Childhood and Society* (2nd Edition), W. W. Norton and Company, New York, 1963.
15. L. Lazarus, J. Sadavoy, and P. Langsley, Individual Psychotherapy, in *Comprehensive Review of Geriatric Psychiatry,* J. Sadavoy, L. Lazarus, and L. Jarvick (eds.), American Psychiatric Association, Washington, D.C., pp. 487-512, 1991.
16. S. Levin, *Equilibrium in Normal Psychology of the Aging Process,* International Universities Press, New York, 1963.
17. R. Havighurst, *Development Tasks and Education* (3rd Edition), McKay, New York, 1972.
18. S. Freud, Mourning and Melancholia, in *General Psychological Theory: Papers on Metapsychology,* Collier Books, New York, pp. 164-179, 1972.
19. B. Knight, *Psychotherapy with Older Adults,* Sage, Beverly Hills, California, 1986.
20. M. Rose, H. Soares, and C. Joseph, Frail Elderly Clients with Personality Disorders: A Challenge for Social Work, *Journal of Gerontological Social Work, 19,* pp. 153-165, 1993.
21. J. Worden, *Grief Counseling and Grief Therapy: A Handbook for the Mental Health Practitioner,* Springer, New York, 1982.
22. C. Sanders, Risk Factors in Bereavement Outcome, in *Handbook of Bereavement: Theory, Research, and Intervention,* M. Stroebe, W. Stroebe, and R. Hannson (eds.), Cambridge Press, New York, pp. 255-270, 1993.
23. S. Shuchter and S. Zisook, The Course of Normal Grief, in *Handbook of Bereavement: Theory, Research, and Intervention,* M. Stroebe, W. Stroebe, and R. Hannson (eds.), Cambridge Press, New York, pp. 23-43, 1993.
24. E. Rynearson, Psychotherapy of Pathologic Grief, *Psychiatric Clinics of North America, 10,* pp. 487-499, 1987.
25. J. Anthony and A. Aboraya, The Epidemiology of Selected Mental Disorders in Later Life, in *Handbook of Mental Health and Aging* (2nd Edition), J. Birren, R. Sloane, and G. Cohen (eds.), Academic Press, San Diego, California, pp. 28-74, 1992.
26. S. Jacobs, S. Kasl, A. Ostfeld, L. Beckman, and P. Charpentier, The Measurement of Grief: Age and Sex Variation, *British Journal of Medical Psychology, 39,* pp. 305-310, 1986.
27. K. Schaie and S. Willis, *Adult Development and Aging* (2nd Edition), Little, Brown and Company, Boston, Massachusetts, 1986.
28. D. Gallagher and L. Thompson, Cognitive Therapy for Depression in the Elderly: A Promising Model for Treatment and Research, in *Depression and Aging: Causes, Care and Consequences,* L. Breslau and M. Haug (eds.), Springer, New York, pp. 168-192, 1983.

29. American Psychiatric Association, *Diagnostic and Statistical Manual of Mental Disorders* (4th Edition), American Psychiatric Association, Washington, D.C., 1994.
30. J. Sheikh and J. Yesavage, Geriatric Depression Scale, in *Clinical Gerontology: A Guide to Assessment and Intervention*, T. Brink (ed.), Haworth Press, New York, pp. 165-173, 1986.
31. L. Pearlin and C. Schooler, The Structure of Coping, *Journal of Health and Social Behavior, 19*, pp. 2-21, 1978.
32. S. Zisook, The Texas Revised Inventory of Grief, in *Biopsychosocial Aspects of Bereavement*, S. Zisook (ed.), American Psychiatric Press, Washington, D.C., pp. 111-123, 1987.
33. H. Prigerson, P. Maciejewski, C. Reynolds, A. Bierhals, J. Newson, E. Frank, M. Miller, J. Doman, and A. Fasiczka, The Inventory of Complicated Grief: A Scale to Measure Certain Maladaptive Symptoms of Loss, *American Journal of Psychiatry, 152*, pp. 22-30, 1995.
34. C. Wortman and R. Silver, The Myths of Coping with Loss, *Journal of Consulting and Clinical Psychology, 57*, pp. 349-357, 1989.
35. D. Lund, M. Caserta, and M. Dimond, The Course of Spousal Bereavement in Later Life, in *Handbook of Bereavement: Theory, Research, and Intervention*, M. Stroebe, W. Stroebe, and R. Hansson (eds.), Cambridge Press, New York, pp. 240-255, 1993.
36. J. McIntosh, Older Adults: The Next Suicide Epidemic? *Suicide and Life Threatening Behavior, 23*, pp. 322-332, 1992.

CHAPTER 14

The Bereaved Crisis Worker: Sociological Practice Perspective on Critical Incident Death, Grief, and Loss

Robert Bendiksen, Gregory Bodin, and Kathy R. Jambois

HELPING THE BEREAVED MALE

This chapter presents a sociological practice perspective on front-line coping with critical incident deaths by crisis workers, such as police officers, firefighters, paramedics, ambulance drivers, and other crisis workers. Crisis work is not limited to these familiar roles, but includes first responders, EMTs, emergency nurses, medical examiners, trauma physicians, chaplains, funeral directors, national guard, police and firefighter dispatchers, and others. The primary focus here is on the emergency service roles of firefighters, police officers, and emergency medical workers.

Many crisis workers appear to respond to critical incident deaths predominantly in traditional male ways. Times are changing, with more and more women employed in crisis work. Many men are changing, too, but traditional models of coping are still with us, especially in front-line crisis work. More women are entering all emergency service occupations, but in greatest proportion among EMTs, paramedics, and related jobs. Fewer women are employed in police and firefighter positions, especially among volunteer departments and agencies.

Interestingly, EMT and paramedic work is closely related to nursing, which requires more education. When they work together, EMTs and paramedics not only report to charge nurses, they also have lower authority at crisis scenes where fire or police commanders take charge of the incident command system. The male model of work identity, as Sam Keen has described in his book *Fire in the Belly: On Being a Man*, continues to prevail in crisis intervention occupations [1].

CRISIS WORK IN SOCIOLOGICAL PERSPECTIVE

The social construction of reality is a perspective that allows us to identify and describe meaningful processes that people use to organize their world view and their work. Particularly important are the structural and psychosocial buffers, barricades, and banisters that are socially constructed by the type of work demands of crisis work. These can be maintained by crisis workers themselves, by managers and supervisors for whom they work, and even by well-meaning family and friends. Our sociological view builds on insights about male identity and role expectations in work and in bereavement. If there are any doubts about focusing on men in crisis work, we need only note how the media continue to remind us that male models of identity appear to rule the day in crisis work-role definitions and social expectations that constitute this particular social construction of reality.

The bereaved male is a fascinating and challenging topic because many men, in their emotional discourses with significant others, are becoming increasingly aware of male scripts, or what sociologists since Gerth and Mills have called their "vocabulary of motives" [2, p. 114]. Many men, today, are beginning to talk to one another, not just to trusted women in their lives, about positive and negative experiences of their roles and socio-emotional relationships as son, lover, husband, father, grandfather, friend, colleague, or fellow worker. Scores of books, articles, and conferences confirm this pattern and signal collective change in a multifaceted men's movement. More than a few men are learning, in their adult life, about how to start, build, and maintain relationships with other men and are having new experiences of socio-emotional equity in interactions with their significant others, both men and women.

Most men, it appears, find it harder than most women to talk of significant events in their life and of important memories from earlier life experiences either with close friends, colleagues, or even counselors. Women, in general, may seek out other types of support, where data show that more than half the clients of clinical counselors are women. When men informally get together, their discourse appears to be different from that of women in the same life situation or occupation. This has been a subject of psychosocial research from a feminist perspective for over a decade. Gender differences in perspectivity have been documented in terms of conversational discourse and moral concerns.

Deborah Tannen, in her 1990 book *You Just Don't Understand: Women and Men in Conversation*, claims that men tend to converse in "report talk" while women prefer to use "rapport talk" [3]. Carol Gilligan, in her early 1982 work *In a Different Voice: Psychological Theory and Women's Development*, characterizes the differences as an "ethic of justice" in male conversations, compared to an "ethic of caring" among women [4]. In contrast to many women, surprisingly few men, when asked, can identify a mentor or even a best friend with whom they share personal feelings and emotional expressions of joy, grief, or sorrow. Women might seek out a woman friend for their "rapport talk." Men appear to spar and enjoy one-up-man-ship more often than women who appear to prefer to attend more often to both the content and the form of the relationship itself.

We would do well to pay attention to the strengths of "report talk" and "ethics of justice," as we explore ways for men to develop their skills in "rapport talk" and their versions of "ethics of caring." With our tendency to stereotype in new ways, we must note that there are many exceptions to the patterns described by Tannen [3], Gilligan [4], and others. Yet, men, perhaps most, find private socio-emotional discourse difficult to initiate or to continue for more than a few minutes. Men who are articulate in a variety of topics related to work, leisure, or the news may quickly change the topic of a conversation if it gets too personal. If necessary, they prefer to seek out and talk to a woman who understands, even though these men may not attempt to have a similar conversation with men who are called "friends."

This pattern of male conversational interaction is particularly noteworthy, while focusing attention on Crisis Workers who tend to act as if a traditional male model of occupational identity is the only way to define role expectations. Changes are taking place, however, in not only role definitions, but also recruitment of more women as EMTs, paramedics, police officers, and firefighters. Crisis workers, both men and women, are being called upon to use their occupational expertise to respond to critical incidents that often involve injury, trauma, and death. Whether the critical incident is a crime scene, car accident, house fire, airline crash, or natural disaster, crisis workers are expected to bracket their personal reactions to horrors they face and do all that they can to save lives and treat the injured, often at the risk of life and limb [5].

Interestingly, traditional male models of occupational identity continue to dominate in the local culture of crisis work. Recent research challenges the efficacy of traditional male role expectations when socio-emotional needs are involved. Gender and occupational roles are being redefined in society, even as coping with critical incident death, grief, and bereavement also is changing. For example, the following case of emergency service workers who knew the victim of a sudden heart failure at home in a small Wisconsin community, as reported by Mark Hale and Diane Midland of the regional Critical Incident Stress Debriefing Program, illustrates these changing gender definitions.

In this instance, the first responder squad, the police officer and the charge nurse at the Trauma Emergency Center, personally knew the forty-six-year-old male victim of heart failure and his family. The squad included a female and a male, which is typical of the increasing gender equity found among ambulance personnel. The female first responder, it turned out, was the best friend of the victim's wife, and her male colleague was well-acquainted with the family. The police officer responded quickly because he was at home next door, and the charge nurse at the regional hospital also knew the family very well. The impacted crisis workers at the scene and in the hospital did all they could, but failed to keep the victim alive. This case is reported in a twenty-minute video produced by Gundersen Lutheran Medical Center in La Crosse, Wisconsin, where the CISD program is located.

First responders, as all emergency personnel, are trained to cope with medical crises like this by following prescribed procedures, a protocol practiced and used many times. What makes this intervention different are the relationships that each of the emergency people had with the victim, his wife, and his children and the psychosocial strain of grief that each one experienced during the critical event and after-wards. Each of these emergency workers became a bereaved crisis worker, an experience they only expected to observe in what one described as the "truly bereaved" family.

In this brief documentary, the women crisis workers described their close friendship to the victim's wife and how they had to bracket their emotions in order to attempt life support. One of them said that she couldn't look his wife in the eye during CPR because she was afraid that she would start to cry. The male first responder, while expressing his close feelings for the victim's wife and children by a hug, was somewhat preoccupied with whether or not he had done his job cor-rectly. In his "justice ethic," he said that he was "questioning myself over and over and over again for a week. I wasn't prepared for some-thing this hard. It had a deep effect on me and I look at things quite differently because of its' emotional effect on me."

Although caution must be exercised about generalizing from single cases, it is important to note how differently the male first responder and police officer described their grief compared to the female first responder and charge nurse. Perhaps we need to look more carefully at how men and women respond to loss during their bereavement experiences [6]. Sometimes, front-line crisis workers experience grief and bereavement because they know the victims, as with the case in rural Wisconsin. Other times, they are bereaved because they can identify with the victim's family, as in the case of children who die. And sometimes, crisis workers are bereaved because fellow firefighters, police officers, or others died in a response event, such as in the 1949 Mann Gultch Montana fire described in the best selling book *Young Men and Fire* by Norman Maclean [7], in the 1986 FBI shoot-out in Miami, or in numerous other examples across the United States.

In crisis situations, it is not always easy to isolate the psychosocial strain of grief and bereavement from the external stress of demanding crisis work itself. To emphasize the social-psychological aspects of this issue, it might be more appropriate to use the term "strain," rather than the more commonly used "stress," to focus our attention in the interaction setting where crisis workers actually live. Bereavement is the status and role of people who are in a position of loss. Bereaved people often experience intense strain in their personal identity and social interaction with significant others as they respond to the impact of external stress from critical incident deaths. With this focus on psychosocial strain caused by critical incident death, several questions come to mind:

1. What do we know of the bereaved crisis worker?
2. How do traditional male models of occupational identity shape responses to critical incident deaths?
3. What is done on-site and later to cope with occupational grief and loss?
4. How might improved organizational strategies reduce occupational and psychosocial strain of critical incident deaths on crisis workers?
5. In what ways might decision-makers creatively respond to demographic changes of gender ratio (i.e., more women among front-line crisis workers) when developing CISD programs?
6. How might changes in the local occupational culture impact the psychosocial strain of critical incident deaths among bereaved male crisis workers, as well as their bereaved female colleagues?

These, and perhaps many other questions, should be addressed as we look at crisis workers as the potential victims of occupational and psychosocial strain in coping with critical incident death and loss. As one crisis worker has so aptly said, "There is no dignity left in death, not when you are working on a rescue call." This is in contrast to those who are more fortunate to be able to die in a hospice setting. As one hospice patient in Greg Owen's 1980 study of hospice in Minnesota so aptly said, "Do you have to die to get that kind of care?" [8]. To this hospice patient's question one might answer "no, not just die, but die under the right circumstances," because many people are sudden critical incident victims who are cared for by well-trained and well-meaning crisis workers.

CRISIS WORKERS TO THE RESCUE

What firefighter, emergency medical technician, paramedic, police officer, or other front-line crisis worker hasn't heard the following, or something very similar? "I close my eyes and see the charred bodies of three children and their mother upstairs under the bed!" This particular tragic recollection, a vivid memory picture, comes from a seasoned firefighter chaplain who was paged, during an on-call evening, to a metropolitan townhouse fire because firefighters and police officers at the scene were unable to deal with a bereaved husband's emotional expressions of grief and loss. Upon arrival, the firefighter chaplain, who is also a volunteer EMT in his home community, soon learned some important facts about the situation: that the bereaved victim's husband was not the father of the dead children, and that he had been arrested and taken to jail because of acting strangely and of having an empty gas can in his car at the fire scene. The first dilemma faced by this counselor was whether the situation was one of critical incident bereavement or of jail ministry.

This firefighter couldn't forget the image of children, who were the same age as his, lying dead under that charred bed. Critical incident injuries and death, as this case shows, often involve complicated social interactions in the human drama of responding to victims, survivors and even those called upon to help. Most highly skilled crisis responders do not, and ought not, remain unmoved and unaffected by the intense and persistent occupational and psychosocial strain of responding to severe injuries and loss of life on a regular basis. It should not be surprising that the most difficult deaths to personally cope with, according to crisis workers, are deaths of children, deaths of other victims who share similar life circumstances with the crisis workers, and deaths of fellow workers in the line-of-duty. According to specialists, it is the death of fellow crisis workers in the line-of-duty that has the most intense reactions, most often [9, 10].

Consider another case, that of crisis workers who must respond to the acute grief of a father of two of three children killed in a day-care apartment fire. Seven children were being cared for by a young adolescent girl whose mother, the day care provider, had left her in charge during a trip to the grocery store. It was a quick, intense fire started by children playing with matches in a back room. Both the adolescent girl and her mother were suffering from guilt and shame. The bereaved father expressed his shock, rage, and emptiness by pounding a nearby wall. Rather than subdue him, as police officers started to do, the firefighter chaplain moved closer to the grieving father and responded to the waves of grief that emanated from him by placing supportive hands on the pounding fists, and then held him in an embrace as exhaustion led to sobs of emotion. Soon after, this bereaved man, accompanied by the chaplain, was able to go and announce the tragic deaths of the children to his wife who was still at her place of work.

Not all police or fire departments have clinically trained chaplains on-call, as was the case in this metropolitan area. One of the most significant roles that fire and police chaplains contribute is in making a death notification to families. Many times they accompany another official, such as a sheriff's deputy, to make these very difficult calls on bereaved family members.

Firefighters, emergency medical technicians, paramedics, first responders, police officers, and other disaster workers like to plan and prepare for disasters, crashes, traumas, and fires, assuming someone else is the victim. But, what happens when the rescuers are the victims, and they become the physical or emotional casualties of their own rescue work? Who, then, will rescue the rescuers? Who will put out the inner-fire that can burn-up and burn-out the EMT, the firefighter, the police officer, or other emergency personnel? How, under these circumstances, will crisis workers be able to competently respond to burnt, bruised, broken, bloodied, and dead bodies, as well as to the grief and bereavement of victims' relatives or friends? And, what of rescuers being killed in the line-of-duty and the resultant grief and loss of colleagues and friends.

Crisis responders are not immune to consequences of their work. Rescue workers are human beings who are not supermen and wonderwomen, though sometimes even they like to believe they are. In Robinson and Mitchell's study of responses to the debriefing process, a participant stated that, "Other tough guys' have coping problems, too" [9, p. 377]. It is not uncommon for the media to portray frontline crisis workers as machines or robots who are unaffected by the tragedies they face on-the-job. Contrary to this public perception, firefighters, EMTs, paramedics, police officers, and other crisis responders are subject to emotional pain and suffering in their work, which may impact other relationships both at home and at work. Traumas, tragedies, and dilemmas often emotionally touch them, or at least ought to, if they are responding in healthy ways. These are professionals who know the full range of normal human emotions, including fear, anger, joy, sorrow, depression, anxiety, and grief, which they experience in rescue work [11].

Intrapersonal and interpersonal acknowledgment of human vulnerability is often the first step a rescue worker can take in dealing with occupational and psychosocial strain of grief and loss. Admitting their own vulnerability to loss may be difficult for many crisis workers because of their work-related responsibilities, as well as their clearly defined job descriptions, protocols, and role-expectations that are rooted in traditional male models of identity [10].

Sociologist Robert Fulton reminds us that "Death asks us for our Identity!" [12]. The personal affront of death to psychosocial identity and spiritual meaning in the lives of critical incident victims and their families is no less true for front-line crisis workers who deal with critical incident injury, death, and loss more often than most of us ever have or ever will. A major challenge to crisis workers and their supervisors is to organize ways to identify and respond to occupational and psychosocial strain of critical incident deaths at work. The first responder emergency workers in the rural Wisconsin rescue effort were personally surprised at finding themselves with symptoms of grief, including not wanting to eat, not sleeping, having an upset stomach, and diarrhea. One way to approach the challenge of dealing with critical incident death and bereavement is to review the occupational hazards in critical incident loss that are often found among people in this line of work.

A critical incident is any event which has emotional power sufficient enough to overwhelm a person's usually effective abilities to cope. According to Jeffrey T. Mitchell, critical incidents are situations faced by emergency service personnel that may result in reactions which have the potential to interfere with a crisis worker's ability to function in the present situation or in other circumstances [13]. This could be due to a major disaster, but it might also be due to one-on-one crisis interventions. All that is necessary is that the incident results in psycho-social reactions in the emergency workers. Examples of critical incidents, according to Mitchell, include:

1. Serious injury or death of an emergency team member in the line of duty.
2. Serious injury or death of a civilian from emergency service operations. This would include a shooting by a police officer or a civilian injury or death caused by the collision of emergency units responding to a fire or EMS call.

3. Almost any case which is charged with profound emotion such as the sudden death of an infant under particularly tragic circumstances.
4. Any loss of life which attracts extremely unusual attention from media.
5. Any loss of life which follows extraordinary and prolonged expenditures of physical and emotional energy in the rescue.
6. Any incident which can be considered a serious physical or psychological threat or a sudden loss to the rescuers.
7. Almost any incident in which the circumstances are so unusual or the sights and sounds so distressing as to produce a high level of immediate or delayed emotional reaction that surpass the normal coping mechanisms of emergency personnel [13, p. 29].

A case in point is the Hackensack, New Jersey, 1989 fire at a car dealership that resulted in the death of three firefighters. Three men had entered the upper floor of the garage and were trapped. Their radio transmissions for assistance were not heard or understood and they died a violent death in the fire. Witnesses at the scene saw rarely-expressed grief and mourning among surviving firefighters. It had been decades since the Hackensack Fire Department had lost a firefighter in a fire. One survivor thought there might have been a sense of invulnerability before these deaths, while another sensed some survivor guilt among fellow firefighters who could have made a serious attempt at rescue, if they had received the distress message. The funeral and support group discussions that followed gave full expression to the grief and mourning of family members and colleagues alike.

Socio-emotional trauma is a blow to one's identity that breaks through personal defenses suddenly and with such force that one cannot respond effectively. Socio-emotional trauma occurs when an event or situation suddenly tears through protective psychosocial insulation and the person feels vulnerable in personal relations with others. Every crisis responder has seen what physical trauma can do to a body. Too many, however, are not aware that socio-emotional trauma can be just as destructive to the spiritual, psychological, and sociological dimensions of a rescue worker's life.

The intensity of the impact of critical incident death depends on several critical factors that affect how a loss is experienced. According to Hodgkinson and Stewart, these include:

1. The degree of personal loss (i.e., personal investment in or identification with victim or place, when the crisis hits close to home);

2. Duration of the loss (i.e., a rescue or resuscitation effort that is long and hard, so it hurts; or the permanency of failed rescue efforts, where one can handle almost anything, if there is a happy ending);

3. Degree of personal threat (i.e., danger or hazard to oneself or fellow workers at the scene); and

4. Degree of terror or horror (i.e., the sights, sounds and smells of death and destruction in the situation) [14, p. 69].

The Kansas City Hyatt Regency Hotel disaster in 1984 is another case in point. A Kansas City firefighter was assigned to recover bodies on the second day after three walkways collapsed killing scores of party goers. The temperature that summer day was 94 degrees. The firefighters had been briefed on what to expect as rubble was pulled away, even with photographs, in an attempt to inoculate against the horror of the sights, sounds, and smell of death and destruction. It didn't work. As the crane that was extended through the lobby lifted a major section of walkway, they found seventeen bodies rather than the predicted six or seven. The firefighters actually slipped and slid across the Hyatt lobby floor which was red from body fluids. But, it was the smell in the 94 degree heat that assaulted the rescuers. One firefighter, who is now involved in critical incident debriefing work, said that she took repeated daily showers and changed clothes frequently for six weeks in an attempt to get rid of this olfactory memory of death. In critical incident debriefings, crisis workers will often remark on the impact of the sights, sounds, and smells when asked about the worst part of the event for them.

Socio-emotional trauma can either be vented or remain pent-up. If psychosocial ventilation of emotional trauma is done adequately, there can be a healthy release of inner feelings. Through talking, tears, hugs, and physical exercise within twenty-four hours, a lot of pressure can be released in constructive ways. But if a person tries to hold in an emotional trauma, to suck it up, some kind of dysfunction or destruction will occur [6, 15]. There appears to be an emotional law of gravity that demands that there be no such thing as an unexpressed emotion, as it will come out someway. In this situation, there is the choice to let it out in healthy ways or become unhealthy to some degree. Pent-up emotions can lead to several outcomes, to psychosocial change, such as growing isolation and cynicism, to psychosomatic illness or to strained relationships with significant others. Emotional trauma is serious business; its victims literally need advanced life and love support.

GRIEF AND BEREAVEMENT SERVICES AMONG CRISIS WORKERS

Sociological data on bereaved crisis workers are difficult to find in the many articles written for police officers, firefighters, emergency medical workers, or other crisis intervention roles. An exception to this dearth in data is a 1993 survey conducted by Mark Hale and Diane Midland who conduct Critical Incident Strain Debriefings in the seventy-five mile service area of Gundersen Lutheran Medical Center in Wisconsin [16]. Hale and Midland are currently analyzing data from 1,118 questionnaires received from EMTs/first responders (38.0%), firefighters (36.5%), police officers (15.5%), and hospital emergency nurses (10.0%).

More than seven out of ten of the respondents were male crisis workers, giving a distinctly male orientation in the overall results. Greater gender balance, however, was approximated among the emergency medical workers where 40 percent were female and 60 percent were male. Fully 95 percent of the firefighters and the police officers were male, whereas 95 percent of the hospital emergency nurses were female. In general, two-thirds of the 1,118 respondents were trained volunteers. This sample of crisis workers in mostly rural Wisconsin included a large sub-group of volunteer firefighters (85.5%) and volunteer emergency medical workers (76.0%). Seventy-five percent were between the ages of twenty-five and fifty. Even though the response rate included only 40 percent of the departments and agencies in their service area, 80 percent of the respondents from this essentially rural area reported that they had personally experienced bereavement as a crisis worker in a critical incident death of a victim whom they had known before the event.

The most interesting results from this study relate to the questions that allow comparisons in grief symptomatology. The researchers asked the crisis workers to indicate which of a list of twenty-eight psychosocial symptoms generally associated with grief and loss they had experienced after assisting someone not known to them and who was critical or in a life-threatening situation. A second list of symptoms, then, was presented with the request to the respondent to think of one critical/life-threatening incident involving an individual who was known to them and check any of the twenty-eight listed symptoms that they experienced as a result of that death. More than four-out-of-ten of the respondents experiencing both of these situations reported that they continued to visualize the event days and weeks afterward. A cluster of symptoms that many have associated with responses of grief were reported somewhat less frequently by a significant minority of respondents. These included: uncertain about what to say, increased heart rate, knot in stomach, feelings of inadequacy, problems sleeping, and unusually quiet behavior.

Not surprisingly, the critical incident deaths of a known victim produced more frequent grief symptoms than the deaths of victims unknown to the crisis workers. For example, the reports of visualizing the event increased from 41.5 percent to 47.6 percent, a six point increase. An even greater increase in reported grief symptoms was found in the list of six common responses to loss, mentioned previously, where responses increased an additional 8 to 15 percent when the victim was personally known. For instance, reports of being unsure of what to say increased from 25.8 percent to 39.8 percent when the victim was known. A knot in the stomach increased from 24.4 percent to 38.9 percent, while problems sleeping increased from 21.6 percent to 29.3 percent.

However, the most significant change in symptomatology was with the self-reported symptom of grief, which was left undefined. Only 12 percent of the respondents reported that they had experienced what they understood as grief in the cases of critical incident deaths of unknown victims. When the victim was personally known, however, nearly three times the number of respondents (33.9%) said that they recognized grief in their own personal adjustment to these deaths. As the first responder in the video mentioned earlier said, this experience of grief was misplaced, as it was the family that was truly bereaved.

Bereaved crisis workers are in unique critical incident situations, especially when they know the victim and even when they had never met the victim before the event. According to Hale and Midland, knowing the victim can provide comfort to families who feel that friends, who might have been familiar with medical or social history, were there to do what could be done to help [16]. At the same time, knowing the victim increases the risk of being impacted. The more intimate the relationship with the victim the greater the potential for psychosocial strain in grief and mourning. During the resuscitation attempt, given a reasonable chance of success, the rescue worker who is grieving will find it increasingly difficult to keep emotions bracketed during vigorous CPR efforts. Recall, again, the first responder who made extra effort to not look into her friend's eyes during CPR compressions on her best friend's husband. Recall, also, the increased sense of responsibility from the male first responder who, for days, visualized the event as he searched his mind for what he felt might have been mistakes in recovery efforts that failed.

What, then, can be done to respond to bereaved Crisis Workers, both male and female, who experience organizational and psychosocial strain in critical incident deaths? There are, according to critical incident experts [13], five types of intervention that are effective in helping firefighters, police officers, EMTs, paramedics, and other emergency workers cope with loss: pre-incident education strategies; on-scene support services; brief critical incident event-defusion discussions; large event demobilization briefings; and a psychosocial process of structured critical incident stress debriefing groups (i.e., CISD).

Pre-Incident Education Strategies

Pre-incident education involves three primary audiences: education of line personnel on critical incident strain recognition and reduction; education of command personnel on critical incident strategies for field control of psychosocial-strain responses; and education of a firefighter's family and/or close friends on coping with critical incident deaths and on ways to enhance, enrich, and support the crisis worker's relationships. Ongoing support requires that crisis workers do their part in maintaining their relationships. Male mentors in socio-emotional equity can be extremely helpful to younger male crisis workers who are beginning to deal with issues of death, grief, and bereavement.

On-Scene Support Services

In order to provide direct support to obviously distressed personnel, the professional support person most highly recommended is the fire or police chaplain for all departments that can be called to the scene. The president of the Midwest Region of Fire Chaplains Association, Gregory Bodin, recommends that the support person function as an observer and advisor, watching for the development of acute stress and strain reactions. The support person, in most cases a fire or police chaplain, along with trained peer counselors working at the scene, briefly check on the well-being of personnel, offering encouragement and psychosocial support. They look for the "thousand mile stare" or those who wander off alone, as well as reactions like confusion or acting out (e.g., hitting a tree or kicking an airpack or any behavior that seems unusual). A typical response of many males in this setting is a blank stare or even anger, which is due to complex gender role issues and lack of experience in emotion-talk.

The professional support person should spend time with those who are resting, using a lot of tact and avoiding probing or interviewing techniques. Helpers helping helpers should be careful of their own need to be needed and of the temptation to other inappropriate or untimely counseling. The effective fire and police chaplain is open and available, then or at a later time, if individuals choose to ventilate or share their reactions. The key to successful on-scene facilitation is keeping one's eyes open and having a good listening ear, as this ought to be a supportive ministry of presence. Support persons also need to be professional resources to command officers, where they can suggest to the command staff which individuals or groups need a break or rotation off duties.

In major disasters, twelve-hours-on and twelve-hours-off is the national rescue standard, with at least one-half hour rest breaks after two hours of intense work [17]. This should be real rest away from the scene or at least facing away from the scene so they are not focused on it during the rest period, even turning their radio off. It is important to keep them in a place where they are readily accessible, as they may be quickly needed. It is often difficult to get rescue types away from the scene once they have started working a disaster. Research studies have shown that if rescuers stay more than twelve hours, there is a higher risk for injuries and mistakes [17]. In cases of very rough and prolonged disaster work, rescue workers should have shorter exposures to the setting and should be rotated in stages. The down-side of this is that more rescue workers are exposed to these extreme situations and more will experience the personal strain.

Experienced support staff recommend that the professional support person direct staff to follow the cardinal rule: "If you don't have to see it, don't look." It is not essential to needlessly expose oneself, staff, or bystanders to critical incident trauma or death. This recommendation is not easy to follow because curiosity is very human. At fire and disaster death scenes, there is often a veritable parade passing by the burnt and charred remains. The medical examiner and arson investigators, in particular, aren't helped by having an audience as they do their work, as it might disrupt a crime scene. It is best for everyone on the fire and disaster scene to focus on doing their own job, their mainframe task, and function as a team player to get the job done as quickly and safely as possible.

Critical Incident Defusion Discussions

A brief critical incident defusing discussion is best done one to two hours after an event, preferably eight hours, and at most twelve hours [18]. It often happens spontaneously back at the fire or police station or in the ambulance quarters. People who have just returned from a critical incident intervention soon start talking about the incident, they check out with their peers what they saw and did, and sometimes even how they felt. Reviewing and rethinking is very appropriate. The primary need for many at this time is to tell them they did a good job, as people look for affirmation and reassurance soon after a traumatic event from peers and supervisors. A defusing discussion is not a time for criticizing personnel or critiquing the incident. No responsibility for malfunctions should be assigned to any team members at this time [14].

Defusing is simply a time to offer understanding, to check on each other's well-being, and provide support and friendship to those who seem hardest hit by the incident. Before the defusing, people need time to meet personal needs (e.g., refreshment and relaxation). At an appropriate moment, the core group of crisis workers gather together and begin a defusing discussion that lasts one-half hour to one hour at the most, as these people still need to carry out their work responsibilities [18]. During the defusing process, one should be cautious not to tear down individual psychosocial defenses. This group discussion is not group therapy or psychotherapy [18]. Everyone should beware of the facilitator who wants to do counseling here, as the goal is to stop bleeders, not to remove calluses. There is a natural tendency for this type of group to fall into blaming at this point. The facilitator must gently and firmly stop this natural tendency by some to assign fault and to shame others. It is essential to remind the group that this type of psychosocial autopsy should be saved for another context.

If there is a lot of group guilt and shame, then it must be dealt with in the group setting. The leader should try an approach known as "refragmentation," which is emotionally taking a hammer and smashing the collective image of failure, especially if the fact-finding phase has brought out the group's negative judgment. When group members have begun to see all the pieces of the event during the fact-finding phase, they may collectively share a feeling of guilt and shame. The discussion leader should take advantage of the group being together to break up this emotional image that generates the guilt and shame. In the end, each person in the crisis event should leave with the knowledge that they had their own piece of the event. Everyone in this type of situation should be reminded that, at the time they were in the action, they could not see the whole picture to base their decisions and actions on and therefore need not be shamed or feel unnecessary guilt.

Large Event Demobilization

De-escalation or decompression support is reserved for very large events, such as a full-scale disaster, where there is a long scene-time and demobilization is done immediately after the event. Personnel are brought directly from the scene and will not be returning to the scene for further work. The demobilization center is a large room, half for food and talking and half for small-group facilitation. Small group discussions are structured, with each engine or truck company or working team seated around one circle. This type of deceleration should never be more than one-half hour, with ten minutes for talking and teaching and twenty minutes for rest and food as a transition to help reentry [18].

A Traumatic Events Information Sheet is handed out and the group leader goes over it quickly in the first ten minutes to give people information [18]. Someone has described this as a little gift to help move them from the awful to the routine. The team leader may say: "We know you are tired and you have just experienced a tragic event. Here are some things you may or may not experience and some things you can do for yourself." In effect, large event demobilization is a brief guided learning experience of re-socialization that aims at normalizing a very abnormal experience for a large group of crisis workers. When brief support programs are limited, the opportunity of a longer structured critical incident strain debriefing (i.e., CISD) is an additional option for crisis organizations.

Critical Incident Strain Debriefings

A critical incident strain debriefing is a routinely scheduled group meeting of emergency personnel that aims to defuse the potential for post traumatic stress problems. Structured discussions in CISDs emphasize that emergency personnel are experiencing normal responses to abnormal events. Emergency workers are reassured that they are not crazy or unique for having reactions and symptoms. These debriefings are based on the processes of socio-emotional ventilation and educational prevention. The goal of a debriefing is to mitigate the impact of a horrible event in the recent experience of rescue workers and to accelerate the normal recovery of normal people with normal reactions to abnormal events [18].

The major tasks and functions in the socialization of bereaved crisis workers in CISDs include: 1) education about critical incident strain reactions; 2) socio-emotional ventilating of feelings and perceptions; 3) reassuring participants that responses are normal; 4) forewarning of what they may experience; 5) reducing fallacy of uniqueness about experience; 6) reducing fallacy of abnormality in reacting to event; 7) building positive contact with peers; 8) increasing knowledge of professional support available; 9) achieving inter-agency cooperation; 10) preparation for future critical incidents; 11) screening for socioemotional vulnerabilities; and 12) referring problems to appropriate professionals [19, 20].

The CISD model is based on the pioneering work of Jeffrey T. Mitchell on critical incident stress debriefings which has been adapted and adopted in many CISD programs [20]. Critical incident death and loss is a major event in many crisis workers lives. Many bereaved crisis workers have been helped by critical incident strain debriefings that provide a guided normative structure for telling stories, comparing experiences, sharing emotions, and supporting peers in making personal sense to what might be impossible to ever fully understand. Male firefighters, police officers, EMTs, and other crisis workers may need this type of protocol to give themselves permission to learn how to do the socio-emotional work of mourning.

The Hackensack, New Jersey fire, where three firefighters were killed, demonstrates the effective use of a debriefing team. A line of duty death, such as the Hackensack fire, is the only scenario where there would be an actual formal debriefing on the day of the event. A brief defusing discussion is simply not adequate for this kind of pain and loss, so there should be another formal debriefing three to five days later, allowing for a few days to pass after the funeral. The teaching portion of CISDs focuses on education about the long-range grief process and bereavement. This is a process of re-socialization where there is a positive bridge between teaching and re-entry. Bereaved crisis workers are often helped by having a brief memorial service, which is a meaningful way to say "good-bye" after being debriefed.

CONCLUSION: CRISIS WORKERS AND CRITICAL INCIDENT DEATHS

Firefighters, police officers, and emergency medical workers are shaped in their response to critical incident deaths by what sociologist Norman Denton calls "positionality" (i.e., the social location and expectations that affect their identity and responses). Front-line crisis workers must use their expertise, combined with socio-emotional bracketing, to get their front-line crisis job done. Too little attention has been given by social scientists, emergency service leaders, and crisis workers themselves to grief and bereavement caused by deaths of children, deaths of victims in similar life circumstances, and deaths of fellow workers in the line-of-duty. Crisis work has traditionally been men's work, although that is changing, as we have noted. Crisis intervention is high risk, technical, physically demanding, and essential for the safety and well-being of individuals, families, and community. It fits the warrior image. Men in crisis work are aware of gender expectations, but many are unable to talk about their own socio-emotional needs even with friends. Fortunately, new male models of identity are emerging that are challenging both radical feminist charges of male complicity in violence and anomic male responses to socio-emotional equity.

In most departments and agencies, it is business as usual when it comes to organized responses to the socio-emotional impact of critical-incident deaths on crisis workers. New opportunities for intervention are available as some chiefs, supervisors, and other administrators have developed protocols for support. These include: 1) pre-incident education of newly-hired personnel and at entry to a crisis scene; 2) on-scene support services by Firefighter and Police Chaplains and Trained Peer Counselors; 3) brief critical incident defusion discussions shortly after an event; 4) large event demobilization briefings to alert personnel about critical incident strain; and 5) structured CISD support groups led by experts and trained peers. In addition, regional networks could be developed to educate and be on-call to conduct critical incident strain debriefings. Training workshops on death, grief, and bereavement could be an integral part of scheduled inservice programs. Staff positions might be funded for clinically educated chaplains in police and fire departments and in emergency medical programs. Social workers in trauma emergency services could develop workshops and organize CISDs for their service area. Clinical sociologists might consult and lead creative problem solving groups of crisis work leaders and decision-makers in policy development.

Many full-time police and fire departments have hiring guidelines that mean more women will be hired to work alongside men in front-line crisis work. Volunteer departments seem to be much slower in changing gender ratios. On the other hand, gender equity is much more common among EMTs and paramedics. This type of social change demands that attention be given to adapting to the expectations and needs of both new and old personnel. Women who are first to enter departments or agencies often must be even better at their work than the old timers. Decision makers would do well to pay extra attention to the need for men in their units to develop socio-emotional equity in dealing with peers. New interest in coping more effectively with occupational and psychosocial strain in critical-incident death and loss is a promising first step in responding to changing gender ratios.

This chapter has assumed throughout that the organizational culture of departments, agencies, and units does more to influence how crisis workers cope with critical-incident death and loss than any other factor. It appears that there is a residual group of crisis workers who may be at risk for potential damage in post traumatic stress disorder

[19]. The overwhelming majority of crisis workers are helped by more adequate support from informed and caring peers and professionals, and for many this means bereavement support in structured critical incident strain debriefings. Grief and bereavement take their normal course with or without professional help for most, so many crisis workers are not in need of professional grief counseling when they experience critical incident death and loss. They, like the rest of us who are coming to terms with who we are as men and women, are in need of psychosocial support and socio-emotional equity as we experience human joy, sorrow, grief, and loss. "It's about time!" that we as men do our part in helping the "Bereaved Crisis Worker!"

REFERENCES

1. S. Keen, *Fire in the Belly: On Being a Man,* Bantom, New York, 1991.
2. H. Gerth and C. W. Mills, *Character and Social Structure: The Psychology of Social Institutions,* Harcourt Brace, New York, 1953.
3. D. Tannen, *You Just Don't Understand: Women and Men in Conversation,* William Morrow, New York, 1990.
4. C. Gilligan, *In a Different Voice: Psychological Theory and Women's Development,* Harvard University Press, Cambridge, Massachusetts, 1982.
5. J. M. Manson, Aiming for "Detached Concern"—How EMT's and Paramedics Cope, *Journal of Emergency Medical Services,* 6:1, pp. 6-23, 1981.
6. L. Lister, Men and Grief: A Review of Research, *Smith College Studies in Social Work, 61*:3, pp. 220-235, 1991.
7. N. Maclean, *Young Men and Fire,* The University of Chicago Press, Chicago, 1992.
8. G. Owen, *A Study of Hospice in the Twin Cities,* University of Minnesota Sociology Department, Minneapolis, 1990.
9. R. C. Robinson and J. T. Mitchell, Evolution of Psychological Debriefings, *Journal of Traumatic Stress, 6*:3, pp. 367-382, 1993.
10. S. Cannon, T. W. Durham, E. J. Allison, Jr., and J. E. Williamson, Emergency Workers' Cognitive Appraisal and Coping with Traumatic Events, *Journal of Traumatic Stress, 1*:3, pp. 353-370, 1988.
11. B. Raphael, *The Anatomy of Bereavement,* Basic Books, New York, 1983.
12. R. Fulton and R. Bendiksen (ed.), *Death and Identity* (Third Edition), Robert J. Brady Company, Bowie, Maryland, 1994.
13. J. T. Mitchell, R. A. Cowley, and H. L. Resnik, *Emergency Response to Crisis,* Brady Communications, Bowie, Maryland, 1987.
14. P. E. Hodgkinson and M. Stewart, *Coping with Catastrophe: A Handbook of Disaster Management,* Routledge, New York, 1991.
15. G. Caplan, Loss, Stress, and Mental Health, *Community Mental Health Journal, 26*:1, pp. 27-48, 1990.
16. M. Hale and D. Midland, *Gundersen Lutheran Medical Center Study of Crisis Workers,* unpublished, 1993.

17. G. Bodin, personal interview, 1993.
18. J. T. Michell and G. S. Everly, *Critical Incident Stress Debriefing: The Basic Course Workbook,* International Critical Incident Stress Foundation, Ellicott City, Maryland, 1995.
19. G. S. Everly, Jr. and J. M. Lating (eds.), *Psychotraumatology: Key Papers and Core Concepts in Post-Traumatic Stress,* Plenum Press, New York, Chapter 16, 1995.
20. J. T. Mitchell, When Disaster Strikes: The Critical Incident Stress Debriefing Process, *Journal of Emergency Medical Services, 13*:1, pp. 43-46, 1983.

CHAPTER 15

The Grief of Male Children and Adolescents and Ways to Help Them Cope

David Adams

One Friday after school, my friend Tommy, an athletic, venturesome, mischievous ten-year-old was missing from our usual softball game. His absence was acknowledged by our neighborhood group, but the idea of going to his home to remind him of our game was quickly dismissed with "he knows where we are," "he always comes," and "maybe he will just be late." When I arrived home, my mother informed me that a radio announcement stated that Tommy had been injured by a truck and taken to a hospital. A few hours later it was confirmed that he had died under the wheels of the truck while hitching a ride on a metal casting beneath it. The next day, in a very "matter of fact way" my mother suggested that I call our teacher and ask if I should go to the funeral to represent the class. The teacher thanked me warmly but politely declined my offer saying the funeral would be held on Monday and that she alone would attend. At the school assembly the principal said everyone felt sad and the school flag was lowered to half mast. I remember picturing in my mind how horrible his death must have been but no one ever talked about it. Tommy was quickly forgotten.

I was nine years old when my aunt died. When I went to the funeral home on a Sunday morning with my father and grandfather, the funeral director, sensing that I was bored, showed me some pieces of human skull bone. Then I looked at my poor old aunt. I was not permitted to be present at the funeral service, and it seemed to be taken for granted that it was not necessary for me to be there. I was to remain at home. School attendance was forbidden and viewed as disrespectful.

When my grandfather died I was fourteen. He had lived with us all of my life, and his death at age eighty-eight, after a short period of intense suffering, generated feelings of both sadness and relief. Before the funeral, I was given money to buy a black tie and I gained minor disapproval from my father because it had a red motif. I was allowed to be an usher, and as we waited for people to come my father said to me: "David, keep a stiff upper lip. You must be a man." I watched my father's tearful eyes and I did as I was told.

I was eighteen when I was assigned to a chronic ward in a psychiatric hospital and my first patient died the day I started. I was helping him down the hall when he suddenly became cyanotic and fell dead at my feet. A kindly male attendant sat with me and told me I was not to blame and that the man was going to die anyway. He said that he once had a similar experience and death was to be expected as part of the job. The discussion ended. Despite his reassurance, I was devastated, I slept very little that night and found it difficult to return to the same environment the following day. I remember wondering how often patients died this way and whether I could deal with such deaths again.

Collectively, these experiences were cast in the mould of *C'est la guerre*—this is war—life must go on.

Fifteen years later my father died suddenly and I found myself locked into the model engrained within me. Don't cry in public, be strong for your mother and sister, pay attention to details, feel angry instead of sad, don't talk about your father, and get the legal and practical issues in place so that life can continue.

Despite the knowledge and experience I had acquired over the years as a clinical social worker involved in the care of the dying and bereaved, and despite my commitment to open communication and expression of feelings, I matched Carol Staudacher's picture of how men grieve: keep silent, mourn alone, cry in secret, cover up visits to the grave, be strong and protective, and spare others your pain [1].

The lessons we learn as children are powerful and pervasive, especially when we learn them from a parent or other influential adult of the same gender. In many cultures, fathers and grandfathers continue to serve as role models who are expected to educate male children concerning the beliefs of the culture and indoctrinate them into accepted traditions and practices. Grieving and the process of bereavement are no exception. However, because Western society has changed markedly in the past several decades, it has been suggested that gender may now be a less intense and prevalent influence on the behavior of children and adolescents [2]. Perhaps, enlightened modern-day parents of both genders who are the nurturers, role models, protectors, and controllers of children can help them discuss their grief openly and express their feelings in a supportive environment [3]. Perhaps, fathers as part of this process are more involved with their children and more sensitive to their grief. It can be suggested that death is certainly more visible in television and videos and more frequently referred to in modern music [4]. However, I wonder how far we have progressed. Do we really know enough to help grieving male children? Are boys truly different from girls in their reaction to loss and how they mourn? Are male children mirror images of their fathers? If there are differences, how and when are these manifested?

This chapter will promote an understanding of the grief and mourning behavior of male children by making reference to the literature, integrating personal clinical experiences, and elucidating how grieving male children and adolescents think and feel. The final part of the chapter provides some practical guidelines for professional counselors, therapists, and bereavement facilitators. These are directed toward helping youngsters to learn to reconcile their losses. They must experience their grief, actively mourn, and learn to live with the loss. However, before examining grief experiences it is imperative to explore in brief what is known about male children.

MALE CHILDREN AND THEIR DEVELOPMENT

There is a consensus that despite all of the changes in Western society there continues to be specific gender differences that are reflected physically, cognitively, socially, psychologically, and behaviorally. The literature also reflects that gender differences are most often induced and maintained through acculturation and socialization [5]. For some, there may be room for doubt fueled by beliefs that gender differences are associated with heredity and genetics. Indeed, many adults, including some professional counselors and therapists, harbor these beliefs when they see similarities in appearance, mannerisms, gait, emotional disposition, and a host of other traits that remind them of grandparents and other relatives who may have died before the birth of a child who behaves in a certain manner. In the literature such observations and speculations receive limited support. However, some questions emerge concerning the influence of hormonally driven behavior differences, particularly during adolescence [6].

In support of factors linked to acculturation and socialization, Kohlberg suggests that in the first year of life children develop their gender identity. This is reinforced as they develop gender stability or "constancy" during the subsequent four years [7]. Stillion notes that:

> Like a rolling snowball, growing larger and more solid as it moves along, children use these core understandings about gender activity as salient factors in organizing their worlds. Thus by the time children reach school age they have entered sex-typed worlds and are knowledgeable about, and comfortable with, gender role stereotypes [5, p. 33].

Kaufman suggests that "masculinity is unconsciously rooted, is reinforced as the child develops and then positively explodes at adolescence" [6, p. 36]. Clearly boys are indoctrinated through exposure to cultural and social rules for male conduct that shape and reinforce their identity and influence their thoughts, feelings, and behavior for the rest of their lives.

The Societal Expectations of Male Children

Despite efforts to change socialization patterns of male children in Western society and to provide greater equality between the sexes, boys have continued to receive advantages and opportunities based on their gender. They continue to be excused for a range of behaviors that in many instances are deemed to be inappropriate for girls. The majority of boys readily become part of their gender roles. Society promotes, reinforces, and rewards the underlying freedom for male children to be less disciplined, less compliant, more secretive, and more venturesome than their female counterparts [5, 8]. Boys are generally expected to be:

- physically strong and capable of holding their own or overpowering opponents;
- emotionally strong, unbending, and able to handle major emotional set backs;
- brave and bold, willing to take risks and stand up for their rights,
- protective of others, especially females or friends who are deemed to be weak or defenseless;
- responsible and trustworthy, to follow through, to do their duty and succeed in practical matters;
- effective problem solvers who can excel academically in maths, sciences, or technical pursuits;
- resourceful and capable of using their imagination and creativity;
- assertive, action-oriented, able to promote themselves and succeed;

- tough and durable, able to manage themselves under duress and endure;
- humorous and entertaining, willing to laugh, have fun, and be one of the boys;
- intolerant of others, especially males deemed to be weak and incapable of coping like a male should cope;
- competitive, to want to win;
- aggressive, to lash out and vanquish when reason and assertiveness are no longer effective; and
- sponges, who absorb all types of information, hold it, hide their thoughts and feelings from the outside world and release them only when they deem it to be appropriate [5-9].

David and Brannon suggest that American male children are taught to live by these rules of thumb:

1. "No sissy stuff"—you must learn to take your "licks" and your chances;
2. "Be a big wheel"—success should be yours, act the part;
3. "Be a sturdy oak"—you must learn to prevail in the face of adversity; and
4. "Give 'em hell"—be more powerful than others, use muscle power and bravado, use violence if necessary [10].

It is no surprise that males may find themselves entrapped in dilemmas such as former U.S. President George Bush's conflict between wanting a peaceful benevolent society at home and advocating "kicking butt" abroad [11, p. 22]. Most disturbing is the fact that in contrast to what might be anticipated in contemporary Western society, male traits, including those that are least desirable, have remained intact and have been consistently portrayed across the past two decades [12]. They have also been found to be firmly in place in twenty-five different cultures around the world [13].

IDENTIFICATION PROCESSES AND SOCIALIZATION OF MALE CHILDREN AND ADOLESCENTS

The fact that boys are expected to be non-communicative, inexpressive, unable to give, competitive, dominant, and potentially aggressive raises questions concerning the identification and socialization processes of male children.

The Identification Process

Theories of attachment and identity have been influential in shaping our understanding of child and adolescent development, with the former being linked to childhood and the latter to adolescence [14-16]. Research by Benson and his associates with late adolescents of both genders adds new understanding concerning how the two theories interface, particularly how attachment influences the identification process [16]. In their study:

- identity achievement—the successful exploration of alternatives and making a commitment to a gender—was found to be strongly associated with attachment to mother. Mothers were viewed by both genders as being more trustworthy and a greater source of security than fathers. Male adolescents tended to have lower identity achievement than females and to have weaker attachment to mothers than their female counterparts;
- attachment to mother appeared to be helpful in resolving identity crises of both sexes and making a commitment to a gender;
- attachment to both mother and father offered a measure of protection against an inability to explore gender issues or make a commitment to a gender;
- strong attachment to father was linked to premature gender commitment and inhibition of the exploration of gender related issues by both sexes; and
- attachment to father also influenced life satisfaction for both genders. Both sexes reflected broad variations in life satisfaction and the researchers speculated that late adolescents may carry out peer comparisons pertaining to "the perception by adolescents of discrepancies between their idealized and actual attachment to fathers" [16, p. 201].

On the surface, these findings may be viewed as a direct contrast to Kohlberg's constructs of "gender identity" and "gender constancy" [7]. However, gender identity may also be viewed as a progression along a continuum. It is a process that has its underpinnings early in life, is closely linked to attachment, is modified continually throughout childhood, and reaches maturity in late adolescence and early adulthood. Of particular relevance is the fact that boys appear to have weaker identification processes and reach "identity achievement" more slowly than girls [7]. As a result, it can be speculated that boys may also be more vulnerable to male stereotypes that are perpetuated by loving mothers and fathers in keeping with societal expectations. Both parents may lock male children into the cognition and rules of conduct previously articulated in this chapter, with fathers functioning as the role models who inhibit healthy exploration and require a premature commitment to the male gender [16].

The Socialization Process

In order to relate to others and the community, male children are guided by the nuclear and extended family and an array of other systems such as day care and nursery school, elementary and secondary school, clubs and other organizations, and their peers. From school-age on, and in pre-adolescence and adolescence in particular, the influence of peers and other adults who have values and beliefs that are seen to be in contrast to those of parents may become more dominant. These values and beliefs may give license to male behavior that is destructive or socially unacceptable [6, 17-19]. In some instances, these less desirable influences simply build on behavior that has been encouraged since early childhood. Often fathers are the major advocates for male behavior, wanting their sons to live up to what they think boys should be—almost as if boys are their emissaries, representing the family in the community. What fathers often fail to acknowledge are the consequences of such behavior. A "give 'em hell" approach can readily reinforce hostility, aggression, and ruthlessness as a way of life [5, 6]. Obviously, there is a need for fathers to be available and involved, to provide a check and balance, and to do so even amidst the turbulence of adolescence. Socialization that encourages self-sufficiency, responsibility, independence, initiative, and other positive behavior is very much in order in the development of male children and adolescents, especially when balanced with stereotypical feminine behavior traits concerned with caring, intimacy, and a willingness to communicate feelings as well as thoughts [5, 20]. Achieving this balance is a difficult and taxing process for both parents and male children.

As Koocher noted, boys are expected to achieve success based more on "external achievement than personal fulfilment" [21, p. 404]. This external focus means that they must struggle with themselves in the process of learning to be intimate, forming nurturing relationships, and denying dependency [21, 22]. Strong family ties complete with open communication, emotional support, moral and spiritual beliefs, and the ability of parents to act together in implementing and continually modifying suitable boundaries frequently helps male children to develop and manage themselves in a socially acceptable manner. However, in some dysfunctional families such ties may be limited or non-existent so that children are increasingly vulnerable to negative influences within and beyond the family. In single parent families, the check and balance provided by male and female influences may also be weak or lacking. Continuing socialization by a consistent father figure may become a major challenge given difficulties associated with post divorce weekend fathers or fathers who exit from their children's lives completely [23]. Recently, problems have also been identified in intact, "normal" families in which the father's behavior is fraught with discomfort in the "new father role" of child care provider which in turn impinges on the socialization of male children in particular [24, p. 56].

Toys, games, music, and the media are all potential sources of gender stereotyping that indiscriminately support traditional male characteristics and behavior in childhood and adolescence. For example, early in life boys are frequently socialized with toys that encourage aggression, violence, and destruction and participate in games such as lacrosse, hockey, and football that value competition and aggression [5]. Wass and Miller estimated that adolescents in grades seven through twelve spent 10,500 hours listening to rock music, and in a sample of 894 students from grades nine through twelve found that males were more apt to listen regularly to rock music containing suicidal, homicidal, or satanic lyrics [25]. When consistent parenting or the presence of a positive father figure is lacking, films, videos, and television programs may be particularly influential in developing and maintaining male behavior traits that are undesirable or socially unacceptable. Media stereotyping frequently highlights the value of aggression and violence through portrayals that are dramatic and compelling. Wass states that such portrayals "become scripts, scenarios, and maps for behavior" early in childhood [4, p. 97]. For instance, a recent report suggests that in United States "the average child has watched 8000 televised murders and 100,000 acts of violence before finishing elementary school" [26, p. 44]. This same report also notes that "children under the age of eighteen years are 244 percent more likely to be killed by guns than they were in 1986" [26, p. 44]. It stresses how children grow up afraid. Alarmingly, television is rapidly becoming a worldwide force that even in developing countries is demonstrating, reinforcing, and perpetuating the acceptance of aggressive male behavior and violence as a way of life [27].

The reality of this destructive phenomena for male children and adolescents is highlighted by Stillion, who suggested that:

> It is clear from statistics in accidents, homicide, and suicide that males live in more violent worlds than females do and that a significant amount of the sex differential in longevity is caused by

the difference in death by violence among male children and adolescents [5, p. 39].

Her findings are supported by the fact that in the United States:

- "aggression and violence form the core of suicidal and homicidal behavior and are also contributing factors in death by accident" [5, p. 37];
- boys are twice as likely as girls to die from accidents between ages one and fourteen and three times as likely between ages fifteen and twenty-four;
- homicide is the cause of death for twice as many boys as girls during childhood and adolescence;
- white males between ages fifteen and twenty-four are four times as likely to be murdered than white girls;
- Afro-American males in the same age range are seven times more apt to be murdered than their female counterparts and seven times more likely to be murdered than white males; and
- the suicide rate is three times higher for males than females ages one to fourteen and six times higher in the age range of fifteen to twenty-four [5, 17].

THE BEHAVIOR PROBLEMS OF MALE CHILDREN AND ADOLESCENTS

As we begin to examine the consequences of male traits and behavior for grieving male children and adolescents and to understand how they grieve, it is worth noting that concerns about how boys think, feel, and act are legitimate. For example, in studies of preschool children it has been shown that boys are more aggressive, react aggressively when attacked, and approve of aggression more than girls [5].

Pierce and Edwards found that when children were allowed to express themselves freely toward resolving conflicts without pressure from their environments, boys used more violent means of resolution whereas girls used more reasoning and analysis [28]. The problems of male children were delineated previously in the work of Offord and his associates in the Ontario (Canada) Health Study in which more than 3000 children were studied between 1983 and 1987 in order to determine the incidence of psychiatric disorders in the general public [29]. These data show that boys ages four to eleven years, as opposed to their female counterparts, were one and one-half times as likely to have a conduct disorder (6.5% vs. 1.8%); three times as apt to be hyperactive (10.1% vs. 3.3%); almost equally prone to emotional problems (10.2% vs. 10.7%); and one and one-half times more likely to be experiencing more than one problem (19.5% vs. 13.5%) [30].

For adolescents in this study, boys were two and one-half times as likely to have a conduct disorder (10.4% vs. 4.1%); more than twice as likely to be hyperactive (7.3% vs. 3.4%); but only one-third as apt to suffer from emotional problems (4.9% vs. 13.6%); and less than one-half as likely to experience somatic distress (4.5% vs. 10.7%). Almost as many boys as girls had difficulty with more than one problem, with boys remaining consistent with earlier ages and girls increasing slightly beyond boys (18.8% vs. 21.8%). In this age range it is suggested that boys may tend to externalize and act out their feelings, whereas girls may internalize them, thus partially accounting for the differences between genders [30]. The amount and degree of male violence and the frequency of male behavior problems has increased since these earlier studies. Stillion, citing aggression as the most destructive male trait, suggests that:

> We have conclusively shown that we have been conducting a huge social experiment across the last several decades. We have conclusively shown that exposing children to violence accelerates their personal behaviors in a more violent world. Thus it should not be surprising to note that one in six youths between the ages of ten and seventeen has seen or knows someone who has been shot [5, p. 36].

PERCEPTIONS OF CHILDREN
CONCERNING WAR

In an interesting study that links perceptions, cognition, and feelings of male children, Cox and his associates studied the impact of the Gulf War on American primary school children [31]. In their research, 492 children in grades three to five were asked to complete a simple questionnaire, use descriptive words and provide drawings expressing their thoughts about the war, provide a brief explanation of their drawings, and document their name, gender, and grade. It was revealed that boys were more apt "to name weapons, give violent terms as answers, and not react negatively to the war" [31, p. 113]. In addition, boys tended to draw pictures of weapons more frequently than girls and draw people less frequently. When they did draw people, boys tended to draw soldiers with expressionless faces. Girls were much more likely "to identify with the people associated with the war, as well as respond with more hope and a more positive attitude" [31, p. 113]. The expressions on the faces drawn by the girls reflected concern and sadness.

In this study, the use of violent terms or drawings of weapons of war increased with age in both sexes but remained most predominant in male children. The researchers noted that the tolerance of the war and artistic and written representation of violent acts and weapons raises concerns about how children are being socialized toward the acceptance of aggression and violence.

THE FEELINGS OF MALE CHILDREN

Thus far this chapter has focused heavily on male identity, socialization, and problems associated with male behavior traits. An integral part of the difficulties encountered by male children and adolescents is the expectation that they will: deny that they are fearful, not react outwardly to pain, hide their sadness, and express anger and hostility as a release for pent up frustration when they encounter disappointment or loss [6]. When males are expected to keep their feelings inside, they may feel anxious and fearful due to their inability to cope, guilty if they fail to measure up to traditional expectations, or prone to self-hatred. When they encounter losses and must grieve, the unmanageable emotional and unattainable behavioral expectations that confront them place male children and teens in opposition to what may help them most.

Unfortunately, research concerning children's understanding of death and how they cope with dying and bereavement has seldom focused on systematic study of reactions by gender [5]. Consequently, in order to explore what happens to bereaved male children, it is useful to briefly examine how children of both genders perceive death at various stages as a benchmark for our understanding. A brief review of how children are disadvantaged as grievers and recognition of some specific problems leads us to a review of useful information from the literature concerning bereaved children and adolescents that becomes more specific to male children as we progress.

CHILDREN'S UNDERSTANDING OF DEATH

Since the early research reported by both Anthony and Nagy, the literature has consistently stressed the value of using stages of cognitive development as a framework for understanding children's perceptions of death [32]. However, more recent studies suggest that caution is needed in this approach as children may be able to comprehend sub-concepts of death such as universality (everyone dies), irreversibility (death is final), non-functionality (all body activities cease), and causality (why people die) at an earlier age than previously anticipated and for some sub-concepts with less clarity [33]. Nevertheless, the cautious use of the cognitive developmental approach helps to comprehend what children think and feel about death at different ages.

Infancy Through Adolescence

Prior to the age of six, most children view death as reversible, associating it with sleep or short term absences. The dead are believed to have all of their bodily sensations and functions intact. Lonetto suggested that as part of this process, young children see life and death as interdependent and circular [34]. One cannot be present without the other. Young children are prone to linking death with their greatest fear, the fear of being separated from their parents, especially their mother. Other fears may also be present as young children frequently associate death with being good or bad, or with darkness or evil. This tendency to think concretely and to blend fact with fantasy may result in children giving a diverse range of explanations concerning death. Causes of death may include accidents, bad behavior, evil or violent acts, monsters, kidnapping, or the consequences of hospitalization or physician behavior [34].

From ages six through eight, many children recognize that everyone dies including themselves, see death as final, understand that all body functions cease, and expand on their knowledge of causes of death to incorporate a range of rationale including accidents, illness, killings, and old age. Children also tend to be concerned with being maimed or mutilated and frequently attribute death to external and frightening forces [34].

From nine to twelve years, almost every child will recognize the universality of death, the finality of the process, and the complete range of reasons for death. However, recently it has been noted the irreversibility of death is called into question by new life saving technologies that add uncertainty to the belief that death is forever [35]. Children in this age range also become more interested in life beyond death and concerned about burial rituals, pain and suffering, and body disintegration after death. Lonetto pointed out the importance of the child's fear of suffocation during this period [34]. He is also one of the few researchers to discuss gender, noting that in artwork and discussions boys in this age range tend to concentrate on the terrifying, horrible aspects of death whereas girls see death as scary and heart breaking [34]. This age range is also marked by achievement of abstract thought and reasoning, and, as Lonetto suggested, blackness, doom, and death-related symbolism reflect the presence of abstract thought in children's art. He supported the belief that boys tend to be more externally oriented, externalize their feelings concerning the death, and ward off internalizing distress in contrast to girls who may take the tragic loss of a loved one to heart.

During adolescence, death is often seen as disruptive, devastating, and anxiety provoking for both genders. It frequently triggers a fight or flight response. Teens may lash out in anger if death comes too close, or retreat, using denial, physical escape, or a wall of silence as they seek solitude to mull over what has transpired. During this response, girls are usually more prone than boys to episodes of tearfulness, sadness, and depression in keeping with their tendency to be more in tune with their feelings, more demonstrative, and willing to talk [34, 36].

In the early and middle phases of adolescence, it is recognized that dependency on parents decreases, compliance declines, emotions fluctuate, and independence is a stimulus for experimentation. During this turbulent testing-out period, risk-taking behavior with resulting injury and death, day-dreaming and anxiety provoking thoughts concerning death, and confusion regarding the status of being dead may all be present [35, 37]. The former is particularly relevant as males frequently may be induced by peers or driven by personal anger to "push the envelope" and be vulnerable to tragic, untimely deaths [5, 37].

BEREAVED CHILDREN AND ADOLESCENTS

The Tasks of Bereaved Children and Adolescents

When children are bereaved, the late Sandra Fox suggested that they have four tasks:

1. to understand;
2. to grieve;
3. to commemorate the death by participating in rituals; and
4. to go on with life knowing that it is all right to maintain a linkage with the deceased person in their minds and actions [38].

Although these tasks appear to be simple and straightforward, they are just the opposite. As Rando suggested, children are "disadvantaged grievers" [39, p. 200].

Children and Adolescents as Disadvantaged Grievers

There is no question that bereaved children and adolescents are compromised by their perceptions and may be:

- apt to emulate the coping behavior of bereaved parents;
- dependent on adults, often delaying their own grief in order to protect and support their parent(s);
- lacking the coping mechanisms necessary to reconcile their grief in a single phase of childhood;
- prone to mixing fantasy with reality, particularly early in their lives before their ability to think in abstract terms matures and parallels the cognitive processes of adults;
- liable to think in literal and concrete terms so that they may assume that they have in some way contributed to a death;
- devoid of the necessary life experiences and time orientation, particularly in the pre-school period, to recognize that loss is permanent;
- lacking in emotional maturity that is required to deal with ambivalence. They must often shed tears, ask questions, and run off and play—mourning in brief episodes of sadness;
- overlooked as mourners by relatives and friends who tend to be preoccupied with the grief of adults, particularly their mothers;
- excluded from rituals that commemorate and memorialize the death; and/or
- compelled to grieve repeatedly through mourning during ensuing phases of their development and to varying degrees throughout their lives. Their grief may be intense and manifested at times when adults fail to recognize or understand its connection with a loss in the past [39-41].

Problems of Bereaved Children and Adolescents

Although children and adolescents are disadvantaged as grievers, it must be recognized that grief and mourning are normal phenomena. Those who benefit from family stability, parental consistency, open honest communication, compassionate role modeling, inclusion in death-related rituals, and freedom to grieve longitudinally over time, can mourn effectively and learn to live with what has transpired.

However, as part of the process of mourning difficulties may be encountered *en route*. These may include:

- emotional lability and a tendency toward mood swings;
- death-related anxieties and phobias concerning themselves and their families;
- isolation and alienation from family and peers;
- confusion about the death and their relationship to the deceased;
- nightmares or startling dreams of the deceased;
- daydreaming or seeing life-like visions of the deceased;
- somatic distress manifested through symptoms such as "tummy aches," anorexia, headaches, and/or enuresis;
- preoccupation and inability to concentrate so that school performance declines;
- being accident prone;
- regression to earlier stages of behavior; and/or
- loss of self-confidence [41-43].

Reactions of Bereaved Siblings

Findings from several studies validate the intensity of difficulties faced by bereaved siblings across childhood and adolescence. For instance, Martinson and Davies found that in studying bereaved siblings ages two to fourteen, seven years after the death of their brother or sister, many felt guilty, lonely, encountered problems with school performance, and thought that they had been responsible in some way for the death. Approximately 30 percent of the siblings had residual psychosocial problems that restricted their ability to function. Interestingly, gender was not deemed to be a significant variable in their findings. This raises questions concerning whether or not bereaved boys and girls do grieve differently and whether or not time is a levelling factor that erases differences that are present immediately following the death [44].

In another study of bereaved siblings, Rosen examined the reactions of college students whose sibling had died while the student was in adolescence [45]. Her research revealed that three-quarters of her subjects felt isolated and had not spoken with anyone concerning their thoughts and feelings about the death. Instead, one-third had provided comfort for their parents, one-quarter coped with the withdrawal of their fathers, and one-third endured life with mothers who experienced prolonged depression. More than one-half of the students felt guilty about:

- their inability to resolve past disagreements with the deceased sibling;
- having wished that the sibling would die;
- being a survivor; and/or
- feeling jealous of their parents' grief for their dead child.

Death phobias, cognitive disturbances, and distorted concepts of death, illness, doctors, and hospitals were present in varying degrees within the sample. Although information concerning gender differences in the study were limited, Rosen noted that many surviving siblings harbored anger and males were more likely to express it aggressively [45].

The intensity of reactions in these studies are similar to the findings of Cain, Fast, and Erickson from the 1960s [46]. Krell and Rabkin later expanded on their work [47]. They suggested that bereaved siblings may be:

- *haunted* by silence and lack of discussion about the dead brother or sister. For example, Ben, age eighteen, stated; "My father shut down all communication about Kenny (his brother who had died 5 years before) as if he never existed. Kenny stayed bottled up in my mind";
- *bound* by the overprotective behavior of parents. James, a twenty-three-year old, told me that he was seventeen when his nineteen-year-old brother Barry was killed on his motorcycle. He said; "Suddenly I lost all of my freedom as my parents clamped down on me. My father became rigid and controlling and my mother became my watchdog, wanting to know everything about my plans—where I went, what I did, and who my friends were. She made me go places with the two of them (both parents) like a twelve-year-old. It was like being put in prison without any recognition of who I was or what I felt. I was a good kid . . . I was really hurt"; and/or
- *resurrected* as the embodiment of their dead brother of sister and expected to perform as well as or better than the deceased sibling. For instance, at the age of fourteen, Brent, a quiet boy with interests in music and literature, was vulnerable to his father's desire to see him play hockey. Three years previously his brother, Terry, had died from leukemia following a brief illness. Brent's father continually reminded him how much Terry was missed, how Brent was failing to carry on a family tradition, and how he was missing a great opportunity by being a "wimp" and a "bookworm." His father's disappointment became an obsession. Brent was "missing the boat." He had athletic skill in his genes, like his father, Uncle

John, and both grandfathers. They were all good hockey players, but none were as good as Terry had been. Terry would have been a "pro." "He was almost there when God took him and robbed him of his life." Brent said: "My father made my life miserable that summer. He made so many demands on me to be like Terry that I finally gave in. I signed up for hockey. I was awkward on skates. Instead of my father being understanding and helping me, he was critical and most of the time made me feel like a failure. I was miserable ... everything I did was either wrong or praised out of proportion. I started to hate hockey, my father, Terry, and myself. Even my mother made me feel that I should have been like Terry. No one would let me be myself. I hurt inside, I looked for ways to escape . . . I became bitter . . . a person I was never meant to be."

Reactions of Children and Adolescents to Parental Death

The majority of studies of bereaved children and adolescents focus on the death of a parent, as approximately 5 percent of North American children and teens encounter parental death. Studies from the 1970s and 1980s suggested that from one-third to one-half of these children encounter serious difficulties including:

- severe emotional and behavioral disturbances characterized by emotional lability, rage, poor impulse control, and a tendency toward hyperactivity or withdrawal [48];
- poorly developed self-esteem and self-image [49, 50];
- increased need for psychiatric consultation [51];
- increased suicidal ideation and behavior [52];
- higher incidence of alcohol and substance abuse [53]; and/or
- reduced productivity and competitiveness at school [54].

The majority of these studies either do not make reference to gender or suggest that gender is of limited or no consequence in their findings.

Reactions of Children and Adolescents to Parental Loss Including Death with Reference to Gender

In a study by Raphael and her associates, 2158 Australian adolescents were divided almost equally by gender. Approximately one-quarter had encountered some type of parental loss. These included death, uncertainty if the parent was alive, loss of contact, and separation with some contact. Ten measures of personality, self-image, emotional, and family problems were used in the study [55]. In their findings, the researchers pointed out that:

- adolescents from disruptive families had "more emotional problems, lower self-esteem, higher rates of mental health consultation, and poor perception of their school performance than those from intact families" [55 p. 698]; and
- there was little difference between adolescents' responses to the various types of parental losses or between those "who did or did not have an alternative parental figure" [55, p. 698]. This suggests that "the details of the loss event and subsequent family structure do not predict adolescent adjustment" [55, p. 699].

The researchers also noted that when genders are compared males appeared to have fared better. They suggested that:

Females reported more general health problems, had higher neuroticism scores, had a poorer body image, and were more impulsive. They were also more likely to have a negative perception of their school performance, to have reported psychological problems in their family, to have consulted a professional themselves, and to say that they have not been sexually active [55, p. 695].

Separation and Divorce

The work of Raphael and her colleagues raises concerns about the severity of boys' reactions to parental loss and death. How do boys react to separation and divorce? The literature reveals that:

- boys experienced greater difficulty adapting than girls especially at the grade five level (age ten) [56, 57];
- six years following divorce boys were less socially competent than girls and demonstrated more antisocial behavior [57];
- boys under age ten who were aggressive during separation or divorce had the greatest difficulty in adolescence [23, 58, 59];
- when conflict between estranged parents was rampant, regression and aggression increased in children of both sexes. Older children and adolescents were more restless, tense, and anxious. Boys, in particular, were more prone to "zombie" behavior in order to insulate themselves from the conflict [60, 61]. This behavior has also been attributed to children living in poverty who are exposed to repeated acts of violence;
- boys tended to be more dependent on peers than their female counterparts [57]; and/or

- the importance of gender differences declined through time, and after five years one-third of adolescents of both genders were moderately to severely depressed [23, 58, 59].

Overall, regardless of the level of intelligence or socioeconomic status, boys displayed less appropriate behavior, less work effort at school, less happiness, and more behavioral problems.

Post Traumatic Stress

A study by Harris Hendriks and her associates examined post-traumatic stress disorder (PTSD) and other mourning behavior of bereaved children and adolescents after their fathers killed their mothers [62]. PTSD symptoms included seeing distressing images and being susceptible to "flashbacks" triggered by memories or reminders in their environment. Numbness, detachment, withdrawal, hyper-vigilance, insomnia, and cognitive impairment were also common. The researchers suggested that "unlike most psychiatric conditions in childhood, girls of all ages seem more vulnerable to PTSD than boys, but boys may show more behavioral disturbances after exposure to trauma" [62, p. 17].

The researchers noted that even when murder is not involved, violence between parents may result in increased vulnerability for boys of violent fathers. Their vulnerability includes:

- over-emphasis on attachment to mother, a process that may impinge on their identity formation;
- acting aggressively due to biological and social factors;
- the risk of rejection by mothers, as such behavior emulates the actions of the violent father; and
- the fact that boys mask their distress with their behavior.

When their fathers are murderers, boys may be expected to be rough and more aggressive than their peers. Their behavior may become increasingly dangerous as their actions may mirror the murderous event [62].

MALE CHILDREN AND ADOLESCENTS AT RISK

In light of the disadvantages and problems children and adolescents face as grievers, bereaved male children are exposed to psychological and emotional risk due to factors that emanate from the following seven contextual variables:

1. The nature of the loss—the more sudden or violent the death, the greater the impact. In accidental death, suicide, or homicide, boys are especially prone to alienation and isolation as they retreat into themselves. Since boys are expected to be responsible and protective of others, they may be blamed to some extent for a death and made a scapegoat. The blame within families may be overtly expressed or hidden in parent-child interactions that are subtly punitive. When this occurs, feelings of shame and guilt may pervade. Boys may be further alienated by family pressure to keep the details of a death secret. Alienation is most apt to occur in situations where income is low and family cohesion is lacking. The lack of control in such situations may intensify the parents' need to absolve themselves of guilt. In instances involving sudden departure of a parent from the home and a resulting separation and/or divorce, lack of forewarning may also have devastating effects. However, careful probing may reveal that visible parental conflict had been present for months or years and children denied that separation was possible. This phenomena has been articulated verbally or in drawings by children of nursery school age.

2. The nature of the relationship—extremes in love or hatred of the "lost" or dead person may increase the intensity of the child's or adolescent's reactions. When male children are faced with the departure of a father figure, the impact may be particularly devastating when the influence of same sex role modelling is at peak levels, especially in mid-latency and early adolescence. Similar intensity may also be found in the deaths of same sex siblings as siblings tend to link their fate to each other [63].

3. Family functioning before and after the disruptive event. Family dysfunction may result in a deprivation of psychological and emotional support, role clarity, boundaries, and decision-making mechanisms necessary to guide children and teens in their mourning. Pre-adolescent and adolescent males are especially vulnerable to the influence of peers and to releasing their feelings through anti-social, aggressive, and destructive behavior. The latter may be fueled by anger and the need for retribution resulting in a repetition of traumatic events [37, 60, 62, 63]. When parents are in conflict, the risk of accentuating and prolonging maladaptive mourning behavior rises markedly. Parents may model impulsiveness and aggression, engage children in collusion against each other, or use them as a conduit for communication. Male children and teens are especially vulnerable when they enter into the conflict in order to either protect their mothers or to emulate aggression by their fathers in order to remain in favor or avoid retribution.

4. Lack of parental guidance, in addition to scapegoating and antisocial behavior, may lead to complicated grieving characterized by distortions of reality and self-concept, object relations difficulties, self-destructive behavior, and overidentification with the deceased person [60, 62]. Due to the tendency for boys to have difficulty processing emotionally laden information, they may be especially susceptible to reality distortion. Joseph, now age twenty-four, was nine years old when his father died. Reflecting on his father's death, he said; "For years I blamed myself for my father's death, I hated him so much. I wished he would die. I believed God heard me and killed him with a heart attack. I was afraid to tell anyone what I believed I had done."

5. Difficulty with object relations. Tim, age ten, three years after his father's suicide by hanging, said; "My father died. He killed himself . . . he used to yell at me and not my sister . . . he must have hated me, otherwise he wouldn't have passed away. Sometimes I think he is watching me and I am afraid . . ."

6. Distorted self-concept. Jeffrey, age nineteen, recounted; "When my brother Kevin drowned, I was eleven and he was nine. I hated myself. I thought I was ugly . . . it was as if my guilt was etched in my face and polluted my mind. At one point, I had nightmares . . . I was killing him every time."

7. Self-destructive behavior. This may be fueled by severe depression leading to sleep disturbances, low frustration tolerance, feelings of helplessness and hopelessness, poor impulse control, and aggression. Mark, age twenty, said; "When I was seventeen my girlfriend, Carol, was killed when she fell from her horse and broke her neck. I was so upset. I thought my life was over. Three weeks after she died, I took my father's car and drove it as fast as I could. I lost control and rolled it over. I guess I really didn't care if I lived or died. I was lucky I only broke my leg."

The cases which follow offer two scenarios that are typical examples of how bereaved male children and adolescents respond to a death. In the first example, Billy is the surviving sibling following the accidental death of his brother. In the second example, Larry grapples with the death of his father from illness.

Billy, Age Seven

When they were bicycle riding, John, age nine, guided his brother Billy down a busy street that was off limits. John rode ahead and was hit by a car and killed instantly. According to his parents, "Billy seemed to take the situation in stride." He was tearful and went to the funeral home and the funeral service, but said little to his parents about the death.

Three months later, Billy lashed out at other children, started to swear, wanted to sleep in his brother's bed, and refused to go to school. He also began abusing the family's cat by pulling her tail and tormenting her ruthlessly.

When Billy came to see me with his mother, Sally, she was still extremely distressed about John's death. She was barely able to cope with family responsibilities, cried continually, expressed feelings of guilt for allowing the boys to ride to the grocery store, was angry that John had not taken the back roads as promised, and frustrated that her husband, Gary, would not talk about the accident. He had returned to work and was aloof and irritable.

Sally had tried to talk to Billy with limited success. She argued with her husband about Billy's bicycle riding and his aggressive behavior. She insisted that he be restricted to the street where they lived and be reprimanded immediately. Her husband then began to yell at Billy for hurting the cat and getting into trouble at school. Finally, after several weeks of conflict, the couple agreed to seek assistance for Billy with father's reluctant agreement that sessions with the family would likely ensue at my discretion.

At first, Billy was extremely restless and evasive, wanting his mother close to him. In the third session, after drawing a picture of the family, he told his mother she could leave. In subsequent sessions, he drew more pictures and talked about:

- the accident, usually briefly and then he switched the subject, returning to it later on;
- his anger that his brother was dead and that God had taken him away;
- his uncertainty about where his brother was and if he would return;
- his feelings of responsibility for the death;
- his recognition that if he talked about his brother, his father would avoid the subject or become angry and his mother would cry;
- his recurring dreams about his brother and how they frightened him;
- his anger at his brother for dying;
- his "hurting inside" when he became angry;
- feeling guilty for tormenting the cat; and
- being upset when he went to school—being alone, going past the street where his brother died, and being in the school and playground all made him want to run home.

Larry, Age Sixteen

Larry was thirteen when his father, David, developed lung cancer and died a year later. During this time, his father, who had been the baseball coach, scout leader, and companion for his children, gradually deteriorated and was bedridden. His father had been the mentor for Larry and his ten-year-old brother, Tim. He had taught them canoeing and baseball skills and helped them to rebuild bicycles. When he became ill, the family was forced to rely on his wife Jenny's job and move to low-income housing, a change that seemed at first to have little effect on Larry. According to his mother, Larry's only problem during his father's decline was that he became increasingly more irritable and restless.

After his father's death, Larry readily took on more family responsibility. He was helpful and protective of Tim and his sister, Penny, age six. He was a model son and his uncle spoke about Larry with pride at family gatherings, saying that Larry was a "real man." "He just took over without skipping a beat." In the months that followed, Larry comforted his mother, babysat, and did more than was asked of him.

Shortly after Larry's sixteenth birthday, he changed radically. He became irritable and preoccupied. He was involved in several thefts, skipped school, was caught speeding excessively, and joined a gang at school that carried weapons.

Because of the time lapse of three years since his father's death and Larry's move from elementary to secondary school, the event had been forgotten in the school system. Larry was quickly labeled by the high school principal as a problem teenager, "a juvenile delinquent" who constantly misbehaved and was threatened with suspension. However, to everyone's surprise, Larry managed to maintain average grades. It was also noted that at times his behavior became less erratic and he was more cooperative. This was particularly true in the class of one male teacher and when his uncle Bob, his father's younger brother, stayed with the family for a few days every couple of months.

Concern about Larry peaked one day when his mother dated a male friend. Larry became extremely hostile and acted as if his role was being threatened. He muttered that "if that guy comes back, I'll kill him."

His mother was very distressed when I met them at our first session. It was clear that Larry was upset and resented the fact that his mother had brought him to see a counselor. Working with him was not going to be easy. After his mother left the room, we discussed my interest in helping him and the ground rules for our sessions. To my surprise, he returned in the weeks that followed. It became clear that Larry was having a difficult time dealing with:

- growing up so fast. He was frightened of the future and fearful of his responsibilities at home and school;

- his need to manage his feelings. He recognized that his friends did not really understand what he was experiencing;

- his anger with his father for dying and leaving him with "all this responsibility";

- baseball. He dropped out at age fifteen, calling it "a stupid game." A few sessions later, he admitted that his feelings were linked to missing his father. Memories of their times together were haunting him;

- the gang and the stealing. Belonging, feeling needed, doing the same thing as everyone else, getting even for "losing my father" and obtaining material goods as satisfaction, were all part of Larry's grieving. Larry admitted that the knives that gang members carried frightened him. They were "a power thing." He stated that weapons were "O.K. for show," then added that he could never stab anyone;

- memories of his father and feelings of fear and anger. In combination they triggered his desire to speed. Excitement, wanting to run, a need to destroy, and feeling powerful were all confusing but compelling forces;

- sightings. Several times he thought he saw his father and twice his Dad appeared in Larry's dreams. Once he told Larry to stay in school and once he just appeared, waking Larry with a start; and

- problems at school. These were connected to an inability to concentrate and being "fed up with his mother's nagging about his need for an education." However, guilt seemed to keep him functioning in school as he told me that his father would have wanted him to be successful and "make something" of himself.

After telling his story, examining his feelings, and learning to be honest about what he had done and why, Larry blurted out that he knew his father was watching him. He also said that the beginning of baseball season, Father's Day, Christmas, and every time his mother was ill, even with influenza, still upset him.

Larry reported one day that he had begun to talk in private with his father. This experience and dialogue with me had helped him recognize that he needed to return to playing sports and "clean up his act." He also admitted that he was still angry with God for taking away his father and felt guilty about his behavior toward his mother. He said that he still could not believe that she would try to replace his father. He still wanted to protect her. He added that he would continue his counseling sessions.

WHAT HELPS BEREAVED MALE CHILDREN

The Influence of Family

In addition to the need for family stability, consistent parenting, love and affection, open communication, and moral and spiritual guidance, grieving male children and adolescents like their female counterparts, benefit from preparation for pre- and post-death experiences. These may include visiting a dying relative in the hospital, facing death at home, visiting the funeral home, attending a funeral, or witnessing a burial. They also manage best when they are given choices regarding the nature of their involvement in such experiences, are helped to maintain or return to regular activities within a short time, and receive the type of emotional support from parents that enables them to grieve.

Given the tendency of male children to be less communicative than girls, to react with more anger, and to be more difficult to de-brief following upsetting experiences, the need for preparation is especially important.

Bereavement Support Groups

One of the most effective ways to help children from school age to pre-adolescence to express their feelings and work through their grief in a safe, supportive environment is to enroll them in bereavement support groups [64, 65]. Within these groups, children recognize that they are not alone, learn why they feel the way they do, receive peer support and adult guidance, and are exposed to a range of planned activities that help them express their thoughts and feelings in order to mourn their losses. As a prerequisite, it is helpful for group facilitators to meet bereaved children in their homes. This helps to prepare children for the group, provides them with a familiar person when they arrive at the group, and helps to reduce their anxiety. For boys in particular, this process may help to minimize their resistance to participating and dealing with painful, hidden thoughts and feelings.

Although the process for involvement of adolescents in bereavement support groups relies more on individual initiative and peer encouragement, as Johnson pointed out [65], the informal intake interview serves a similar purpose to the home visit. Johnson also suggested that having both male and female participants in the same group facilitates discussion and release of feelings. Girls act as catalysts and role models in the group, making it more natural for boys to risk becoming part of the group process. In children's groups, the same process takes place. Girls provide emotional support to boys, encouraging them to express their feelings, and, in some instances, help them to face their problems more rationally.

The Role of Professional Counselors

To individually counsel bereaved children and adolescents, we need to evaluate exactly what is needed and insure that alternative measures such as support groups are considered. Sometimes groups are more effective than individual or family counseling as children may find greater support, encouragement, and safety in the presence of peers who are in similar situations. In some instances, alternatives may be limited, non-existent, or inappropriate due to the nature of the child or teen's grief reaction and parental perceptions of the value of other approaches.

Clinicians are frequently challenged by two major questions when counseling bereaved male children and adolescents:

1. If they are quiet and pull away into themselves, is it best to leave them alone and respect their need to mull over what has transpired? If so, for how long?
2. If they are angry and acting out physically or lashing out verbally, should this behavior be overlooked at the risk of reinforcing and perpetuating the release of hostility?

The need for boys to pull away to sort out their thoughts and feelings is normal, as some measure of withdrawal accompanies regular patterns of mourning. However, depending on the nature of the loss and the child's psychological adaptation and behavior prior to and following it, extended withdrawal or total refusal to share their thoughts or feelings with anyone may be a warning sign of difficulty yet to come. For example, such behavior may signify a high level of anxiety, intense sadness or depression, anger, overwhelming feelings of guilt, or a combination of emotions that are too difficult to express overtly.

When confronted with this scenario, counselors need to pay attention to what parents, particularly the mother, perceive and how they interpret such perceptions at the time of intake. Mothers often know their children best, are more perceptive than fathers, and serve as a barometer in respect to the seriousness of concern about their children.

Face-to-face assessment is in order when parents are worried and withdrawal or silence is protracted or seriously disrupts the regular functioning of their children.

If bereaved male children and adolescents use physical or verbal aggression to express their anger, it is imperative to evaluate the circumstances related to aggressive acts, their severity, how often destructive or hurtful behavior has been manifested, and when such acts took place. It is also necessary to determine if such behavior was present prior to bereavement and whether or not it is linked to other factors such as family dysfunction, peer influence, poverty, or other sociocultural factors.

Anger is a normal, often necessary part of the grieving process. It may be confusing, readily increased by frustrating circumstances, and difficult to manage. Irritability, occasional outbursts, and minor aggression are common and are often viewed by adults as acceptable behavior for grieving male children and adolescents. Difficulties arise most frequently when anger is driven outward. Impulsiveness and uncontrolled acts of violence may result in damage to property, personal injury, or even homicide. On the other hand, when anger is retained and directed inward, it may accrue and fuel anxiety and guilt reactions that may lead to suicidal acts, substance abuse, or other means to escape from the anguish.

The extremes of external and internal direction of anger place bereaved male children and teens at risk. Unlocking the anger and unleashing it constructively may avoid severe consequences as vestiges of grief reactions last to varying degrees for a lifetime. Bereaved youngsters need to know to the greatest degree possible why they may be reacting in a specific manner, what they may expect to think and feel, and what they need to do in order to mourn in ways that do not place them in jeopardy.

HOW WE HELP

The remainder of this chapter offers suggestions for helping bereaved male children and adolescents. These should only be construed as applicable to boys encountering mild to moderate difficulties during the mourning process. Bereavement counselors and therapists must be clear about what they are prepared to provide, willing to individualize approaches to bereaved male children and adolescents based on their expertise, and able to recognize their own limitations. When encountering distorted grief reactions characterized by self-punishment, self-destructive tendencies, severe mood or conduct disorders, or extremes of guilt, agitation, hostility, withdrawal, or cognitive impairment, an interdisciplinary approach that includes psychiatric consultation may be in order.

Professionals who provide individual or family counseling to bereaved male children and adolescents and their families are at a disadvantage. Too often these children are frustrated by parental concern and coercion to seek professional assistance. Resistance to participating in counseling and withdrawal may be combined, resulting in refusal to take any risks in communication. When this happens, a call directly to the child or adolescent requesting a meeting often results in a willingness to attend an initial session.

Establishing Rapport

From the outset, boys need to feel secure in the presence of the counselors and to perceive them as interested, approachable, caring, trustworthy, and flexible adults. In most instances involving children and pre-adolescents, counselors should encourage the parent(s) to accompany their child to the first session or two, and, depending on the clinical approach, allow them to provide the safety and comfort that enables the child to participate in age-appropriate methods of communication. It may also be important for children to bring a comforting toy or stuffed animal to the sessions as it adds to a child's comfort and may become a valuable part of the communication process. Adolescents may prefer to include a sibling or close friend instead of a parent. In most instances, such inclusions can be helpful in facilitating communication.

In the first session, the ground rules should be established for what will ensue. These should include recognition that continued involvement of additional persons may be limited in keeping with what needs to be accomplished and the comfort level of all concerned, particularly the child and the counselor. Next, it is important to learn as much as possible about the child or teen, their likes, dislikes, interests, and life at home, school, and in the community. Special attention should be given to their perceptions and interpretation of what has happened to them and what they find hurtful and difficult. Listening carefully, being non-judgemental, making eye contact to show that the counselor is not afraid of discussing what has transpired and will not be pushed away, and empathizing based on having been in similar grief-related circumstances are all necessary in establishing rapport. Boys are especially responsive to adults who are gentle, firm, persistent, and unwilling to accept at face value the "I'm all right, Jack" stance common to bereaved males.

Practical Suggestions for Counseling Sessions

Once rapport is established, clinicians need to:

1. Identify and work on de-mythologizing the taboos. Boys need to understand that they are not weak or inadequate if they seek assistance or openly express their sadness.
2. Provide them with permission to grieve and show their feelings in the shelter of our sessions together. For older children and adolescents this may require that no one else be present.
3. Help them to recognize that their confidentiality will be respected and that the counselors are not emissaries or clones of their parents. However, it may be appropriate to ask for their permission to communicate with or seek the assistance of their parents.
4. Tell them that their privacy will be respected when they need time to contemplate what they wish to share or to temporarily delay discussion of a painful subject.
5. Assist them in the process of linking thoughts and feelings in order to reduce their tension and pain.
6. Encourage them to use the phrases, *I feel, I wish, I need, I miss* as key communicators.
7. Facilitate the release of thoughts and feelings through age-appropriate expressive modalities. Male children may act out intense feelings through play, drawings, or music.
8. Encourage them to construct and recount in their own words positive and negative stories about their lives with the deceased. They should include how they felt then and how they feel now. Memories are an essential part of healing and facilitate the gradual process of separation.
9. Help them to reality test by having them ask family members questions about what transpired surrounding the death. Counterbalance any tendencies to assume inordinate responsibility for contributing to the death or the emotional distress of others.
10. Encourage them to discuss their need to protect grieving parents, siblings, or other family members. Protecting is often an assumed mandate of male children and adolescents.
11. Give them permission to discuss how they are affected by family secrets pertaining to the death. Families may be especially demanding of male children when death involves a suicide or homicide.
12. Be patient when thought processes are distorted. Facilitate discussion of their beliefs and determine how and when to help

them reframe their thoughts so that distortions are gradually eliminated. It is not usual for a death to be construed as a breakdown in trust or punishment for destructive wishes or wrongdoing.

13. Help them to clarify and work through their confusion in areas such as object constancy and object relations. Earlier in this chapter, Larry struggled with object constancy and his need to regain his sense of self and his place in a world that was instantly changed by his father's sudden death. His autonomy and sense of omnipotence were removed. He grappled with an intense need to assume his father's roles and responsibilities, and to be independent and self-sufficient. He also contended with uncertainty about his relationship with his father. Despite an intense need to lash out and rebel, he wanted to succeed in life in order to please him.

14. Encourage them to discuss their dreams and visions. The intrusion of hallucinatory visions, dreams, and feelings of presence are part of grieving and are usually anxiety provoking, haunting, difficult to acknowledge, and even more difficult to share. Grief compounds and complicates the tendency of male children and teens to retreat within themselves in order to sort out their thoughts and feelings and determine how to confront their difficulties. Grief is the ultimate retreat into oneself. Acknowledging that it is not unusual to encounter such experiences may release a flood of memories and concerns accompanied by great relief. The acknowledgment also provides an opportunity to assure bereaved children and teens that searching for and wanting to maintain contact with the deceased is a normal part of mourning.

15. Help them to regain self-confidence and control of their lives. Provide positive feedback about their ability to manage their mourning constructively and encourage their continuance in activities that help them to feel self-sufficient and competent.

16. Urge them to manage their anger constructively. Competitive sports have helped many boys with destructive tendencies to redirect and release their anger.

The clinical dialogue with bereaved boys should advise them that they will encounter mood swings, may be ambushed by intense feelings when they least expect it, and may need to revisit the same issues several times. When counselors open up extremely painful issues, or identify or precipitate bizarre, harmful, or impulsive behavior, they must be prepared to deal with the consequences. As part of the interaction, counselors must also accept that they may be prone to love or hate reactions. The former may be closely related to role modeling, the need for affection and other components of transference, whereas the latter may be linked to a resistance to pain manifested through hostility. At every step clinicians must allow time for fun and humor in keeping with the need for respite from grief.

Male children and adolescents must learn to manage their mourning in the external world. Parents, family members, and in some instances, peers are their main sources of support. If family members are receiving ongoing assistance themselves to deal with their grief, each will become knowledgeable about the process. When this is not feasible, selective involvement in the counseling sessions by family or peers may be helpful in clarifying information and providing ongoing emotional support and guidance. Regardless of the family situation, it is helpful to have at least one positive male father figure who is deliberately or inadvertently part of the continuing role modeling process at home or in the community and is tuned into meeting the needs of the bereaved child or adolescent.

The establishment of a strong support system facilitates the bereaved male child or adolescent's adaptation and transition back to the community. Through time this system will continue to be important as the bereaved child or adolescent will need to deal with feelings that were unresolved during counseling, revisit and reinterpret their grief at future developmental stages, and cope with the flood of feelings that may be precipitated by even the smallest loss.

CONCLUSION

There is ample evidence that bereaved male children and adolescents frequently differ from their female counterparts and are vulnerable because of the way they have been socialized and acculturated. Professional counselors often have the skills necessary to help them manage difficulties during mourning and gradually reconcile their grief. However, as this chapter illustrates, information concerning gender differences in child and adolescent bereavement, and male reactions in particular, is difficult to find. Findings are scattered throughout the literature usually appearing as minor observations emanating from a study of many variables. In most instances, description of the methodology is sparse or lacking and conclusions are so brief that they are of limited value. Scientific evidence as well as clinical experience is required in order to enhance the quality and effectiveness of our intervention. In addition, every effort must be made to break down the barrier of male silence so that today's generation of fathers

and sons can express their thoughts and feelings openly and constructively, and change the way that male children and adolescents grieve.

REFERENCES

1. C. Staudacher, *The Grief of Males,* paper presented at the Bereaved
   Families of Ontario Conference, Carleton University, Ottawa, Canada,
   June 1991.
2. B. Thorne, Girls and Boys Together. . . . But Mostly Apart, in *Men's Lives,*
   M.S. Kimmel and M.A. Messner (eds.), Macmillan, New York, 1989.
3. D. W. Adams, The Suffering of Children and Adolescents with Life-
   Threatening Illness: Factors Involved and Ways Professionals Can Help,
   in *Beyond the Innocence of Childhood Volume 2: Helping Children and
   Adolescents Cope with Life-Threatening Illness and Dying,* D. W. Adams
   and E. J. Deveau (eds.), Baywood, Amityville, New York, 1995.
4. H. Wass, Appetite for Destruction: Children and Violent Death in Popular
   Culture, in *Beyond the Innocence of Childhood Volume 1: Factors Influencing Children and Adolescents' Perceptions and Attitudes Toward Death,*
   D. W. Adams and E .J. Deveau (eds.), Baywood, Amityville, New York,
   1995.
5. J. M. Stillion, Gender Differences in Children's Understanding of Death, in
   *Beyond the Innocence of Childhood Volume 1: Factors Influencing Children
   and Adolescents' Perceptions and Attitudes Toward Death,* D. W. Adams
   and E. J. Deveau (eds.), Baywood, Amityville, New York, 1995.
6. M. Kaufman, The Construction of Masculinity and the Triad of
   Men's Violence, in *Men's Lives,* M. S. Kimmel and M. A. Messner (eds.),
   Macmillan, New York, 1989.
7. L. A. Kohlberg, A Cognitive-Developmental Analysis of Children's Sex-
   Role Concepts and Attitudes, in *The Development of Sex Differences,* E. E.
   Maccoby (ed.), Stanford University Press, Stanford, California, 1966.
8. E. M. Hetherington and R. D. Parke, *Child Psychology: A Contemporary
   Viewpoint,* McGraw-Hill, New York, 1993.
9. M. Messner, Boyhood, Organized Sports and the Construction of
   Masculinities, in *Men's Lives,* M. S. Kimmel and M. A. Messner (eds.),
   Macmillan, New York, 1989.
10. D. S. David and R. Brannon, *The Forty-Nine Percent Majority: The Male
    Sex Role,* Addison-Wesley, Reading, Massachusetts, 1976.
11. R. K. Lore and L. A. Schultz, Control of Human Aggression, *American
    Psychologist,* pp. 16-24, January 1993.
12. D. J. Bergen and J. E. Williams, Sex Stereotypes in the United States
    Revisited 1972-1988, *Sex Roles, 24,* pp. 413-423, 1991.
13. J. E. Williams and D. L. Best, *Measuring Sex Stereotypes: A Multinational
    Study,* Sage, Newbury Park, California, 1990.
14. J. E. Marcia, Identity in Adolescence, in *Handbook of Adolescent Psychol-
    ogy,* J. Adelson (ed.), Wiley, New York, 1980.

15. S. M. Quintana and D. Lapsley, Adolescent Attachment and Ego Identity: A Structural Equations Approach to the Continuity of Adaptation, *Journal of Adolescent Research, 2*, pp. 393-409, 1987.
16. M. J. Benson, P. B. Harris, and C. S. Rogers, Identity Consequences of Attachment to Mothers and Fathers Among Late Adolescents, *Journal of Research on Adolescence, 2*, pp. 187-204, 1992.
17. J. Taylor Gibbs, Young Black Males in America: Endangered, Embittered, and Embattled, in *Men's Lives*, M. S. Kimmel and M. A. Messner (eds.), Macmillan, New York, 1989.
18. T. Attig, Death Themes in Adolescent Music: The Classic Years, in *Adolescence and Death*, C. A. Corr and J. N. McNeil (eds.), Springer, New York, 1986.
19. M. S. Kimmel, Rethinking "Masculinity": New Directions in Research, in *Changing Men: New Directions in Research on Men and Masculinity*, Sage, Newbury Park, California, 1987.
20. L. Steinberg, Single Parents, Stepparents, and the Susceptibility of Adolescents to Antisocial Peer Pressure, *Child Development, 58*, pp. 269-275, 1987.
21. G. Koocher, Talking with Children About Death, *American Journal of Orthopsychiatry, 44*, pp. 404-411, 1974.
22. J. M. Stillion, *Death and the Sexes,* Hemisphere, Washington, D.C., 1985.
23. W. F. Hodges, *Interventions for Children of Divorce: Custody, Access and Psychotherapy*, Wiley Interscience, New York, 1991.
24. R. F. Levant, The New Father Roles, in *Gender Issues Across the Life Cycle*, B. Rubin Wainrib (ed.), Springer, New York, 1992.
25. H. Wass and M. D. Miller, Factors Affecting Adolescents' Behavior and Attiudes Toward Destructive Rock Lyrics, *Death Studies, 13*, pp. 287-303, 1989.
26. J. Adler, Kids Growing Up Scared, *Newsweek*, pp. 43-49, January 10, 1994.
27. S. B. Henen, *Multiple Losses and PTSD Among Children Affected by Violence in South Africa,* paper presented at The International Work Group on Death, Dying, and Bereavement Conference, Oxford, England, June 1995.
28. K. Pierce and E. Edwards, Children's Construction of Fantasy Stories: Gender Differences in Conflict Resolution Stratagies, *Sex Roles, 18*:7/8, pp. 393-399, 1988.
29. D. R. Offord, M. H. Boyle, J. E. Fleming, H. Munroe-Blum, and N. J. Rae-Grant, Ontario Child Health Study: Summary of Selected Results, *Canadian Journal of Psychiatry, 34*, pp. 483-491, 1989.
30. D. R. Offord, M. H. Boyle, P. Szatmari, et al., Ontario Child Health Study II: Six-Month Prevalence of Disorder and Rates of Utilization, *Archives of General Psychiatry, 44*, pp. 832-836, 1987.
31. G. R. Cox, B. J. Vanden Berk, R. J. Fundis, and P. J. McGinnis, American Children and Desert Storm: Impressions of the Gulf Conflict, in *Beyond the Innocence of Childhood Volume 1: Factors Influencing Children and*

Adolescents' Perceptions and Attitudes Toward Death, D. W. Adams and E. J. Deveau (eds.), Baywood, Amityville, New York, 1995.

32. C. A. Corr, Children and Death: Where Have We Been? Where are We Now?, in *Beyond the Innocence of Childhood Volume 1: Factors Influencing Children and Adolescents' Perceptions and Attitudes Toward Death*, D. W. Adams and E. J. Deveau (eds.), Baywood, Amityville, New York, 1995.

33. A. Lazar and J. Torney-Purta, The Development of the Subconcepts of Death in Young Children: A Short-Term Longitudinal Study, *Child Development, 62*, pp. 1321-1333, 1991.

34. R. Lonetto, *Children's Conceptions of Death*, Springer, New York, 1980.

35. M. W. Speece and S. B. Brent, The "Adult" Concept of Irreversibility, in *Young People and Death*, J. D. Morgan (ed.), The Charles Press, Philadelphia, 1991.

36. D. W. Adams and E. J. Deveau, When a Brother or Sister is Dying of Cancer: The Vulnerability of the Adolescent Sibling, *Death Studies, 11*, pp. 279-285, 1987.

37. A. K. Gordon, The Tattered Cloak of Immortality, in *Adolescence and Death*, C. A. Corr and J. N. McNeil (eds.), Springer, New York, 1986.

38. S. Fox, Helping Child Deal with Death Teaches Valuable Skills, *The Psychiatric Times*, pp. 10-11, August 1988.

39. T. A. Rando, *Grieving: How to Go on Living When Someone You Love Dies*, D. C. Heath and Company, Lexington, Massachusetts, 1988.

40. D. W. Adams and E. J. Deveau, *Coping with Chidlhood Cancer: Where Do We Go from Here?* (New Rev. Edition), Kinbridge, Hamilton, Canada, 1993.

41. T. A. Rando, Anticipatory Grief and the Child Mourner, in *Beyond the Innocence of Childhood Volume 3: Helping Children and Adolescents Cope with Death and Bereavement*, D. W. Adams and E. J. Deveau (eds.), Baywood, Amityville, New York, 1995.

42. D. W. Adams, *Childhood Malignacy: The Psychosocial Care of the Child and His Family*, C. C. Thomas Publishers, Springfield, Illinois, 1979.

43. R. R. Ellis, Young Children: Disenfranchised Grievers, in *Disenfranchised Grief: Recognizing Hidden Sorrow*, K. J. Doka (ed.), D. C. Heath and Company, Lexington, Massachusetts, 1989.

44. B. Davies, Long-Term Follow-Up of Bereaved Siblings, in *The Dying and the Bereaved Teenager*, J. D. Morgan (ed.), The Charles Press, Philadelphia, 1990.

45. H. Rosen, *Unspoken Grief: Coping with Sibling Loss*, D. C. Heath and Company, Lexington, Massachusetts, 1986.

46. A. C. Cain, I. Fast, and M. E. Erickson, Children's Disturbed Reactions to the Death of a Sibling, *American Journal of Orthopsychiatry, 34*, pp. 741-752, 1964.

47. R. Krell and L. Rabkin, The Effect of Sibling Death on the Surviving Child: A Family Perspective, *Family Process, 18*, pp. 471-477, 1979.

48. M. Kaffman and E. Elizur, Bereavement Responses of Kibbutz and Non-Kibbutz Children Following the Death of the Father, *Journal of Child Psychology, Psychiatry and Allied Disciplines, 24*, pp. 435-442, 1983.

49. D. M. Rosenthal, C. J. Peng, and J. M. McMillan, Relationship of Adolescent Self-Concept to Perception of Parents in Single and Two-Parent Families, *International Journal of Behavioral Development, 3*, pp. 441-453, 1980.
50. D. R. Dietrich, Psychological Health of Young Adults Who Experienced Early Parental Death: MMPI Trends, *Journal of Clinical Psychology, 40*, pp. 901-908, 1984.
51. R. Seligman, G. Gleser, J. Raun, and L. Harris, The Effects of Early Parental Loss in Adolescence, *Archives of General Psychiatry, 31*, pp. 475-479, 1974.
52. K. S. Adam, A. Bouckams, and D. Streiner, Parental Loss and Family Stability in Attempted Suicide, *Archives of General Psychiatry, 39*, pp. 1081-1085, 1982.
53. M. A. Burnside, P. E. Baer, P. E. McMaughlin, and A. D. Pickering, Alcohol Use by Adolescents in Disrupted Families, *Alcoholism: Clinical and Experimental Research, 10*, pp. 274-278, 1986.
54. A. M. Ambert and J. F. Saucier, Adolescents' Perceptions of Their Parents and Parents' Marital Status, *Journal of Social Psychology, 12*, pp. 101-110, 1983.
55. B. Raphael, J. Cubis, M. Dunne, et al., The Impact of Parental Loss on Adolescents' Psychosocial Characteristics, *Adolescence, 25*, pp. 689-700, 1990.
56. E. M. Hetherington, M. Cox, and R. Cox, Long-Term Effects of Divorce and Remarriage on the Adjustment of Children, *Journal of the American Academy of Child Psychiatry, 24*, pp. 518-530, 1985.
57. J. Guidubaldi and J. E. Perry, Divorce and Mental Health Sequelae for Children: A Two-Year Follow-Up of a Nationwide Sample, *Journal of the American Academy of Child Psychiatry, 24*, pp. 531-537, 1985.
58. J. S. Wallerstein, Children of Divorce: Report of a Ten-Year Follow-Up of Early Latency-Age Children, *American Journal of Orthopsychiatry, 57*, pp. 199-211, 1987.
59. J. S. Wallerstein and S. Blakeslee, *Second Chance: Men, Women and Children a Decade After Divorce*, Tichmor and Fields, New York, 1989.
60. R. E. Emery, Family Violence, *American Psychologist, 44*, pp. 321-340, 1989.
61. J. R. Johnston, L. E. G. Campbell, and S. S. Mayers, Latency Children in Post-Separation and Divorce Disputes, *Journal of the American Academy of Child Psychiatry, 24*, pp. 563-574, 1985.
62. J. Harris Hendriks, D. Black, and T. Kaplan, *When Father Kills Mother: Guiding Children Through Trauma and Grief*, Routledge, London, 1993.
63. S. P. Bank and M. D. Kahn, *The Sibling Bond*, Basic Books, New York, 1982.
64. E. Ormond and H. Charbonneau, Grief Responses and Group Treatment Interventions for Five-to-Eight-Year-Old Children, in *Beyond the Innocence of Childhood Volume 3: Helping Children and Adolescents Cope with*

Death and Bereavement, D. W. Adams and E. J. Deveau (eds.), Baywood, Amityville, New York, 1995.

65. C. Johnson, Adolescent Grief Support Groups, in *Beyond the Innocence of Childhood Volume 3: Helping Children and Adolescents Cope with Death and Bereavement*, D. W. Adams and E. J. Deveau (eds.), Baywood, Amityville, New York, 1995.

CHAPTER 16

A Grief Unheard: A Woman's Reflection on a Men's Grief Group

Peggy M. L. Anderson

GENDER AND GRIEF

After the death of my husband, I spent six years learning about bereavement personally, read, researched and studied thanatology, and interviewed widowed women professionally in order to write a book about women coping and growing after the death of a husband. Having my own experiences of loss and grief confirmed by the experiences of other women over those years was healing for me and the catalyst for my beginning a bereavement counseling and consulting practice in London, Ontario. Initially, much of the individual and group work I did was with widowed men and women. In this context, I had the opportunity to see parallels and differences between men's and women's grieving styles.

The subject of gender and grief surfaced for me again in 1992 when I did a publicity tour in the western provinces of Canada to promote my book, *Wife After Death* [1]. Most of the interviewers who talked to me were men. These men had read my book. Repeatedly they asked me, "Why no men's stories in here? Where is the book like this for men?" I had made a conscious choice to write about women only, because I had experienced loss as a woman. I wasn't a man. I couldn't write about men's experiences of loss! In time I stopped being defensive about the questions men out west and elsewhere were asking and began to hear what they were really saying. They were not criticizing my work. They simply wanted someone to look at their losses, grief, and pain as seriously as I had looked at women's losses in *Wife After Death* [1]. Like women's anger which did not find a serious voice until the feminist movement, men's pain had never been clearly articulated or separately studied. I had not seen many men's stories of losing a son, mother, wife, or father on bookstore shelves. Now men were saying to me, "We want our grief to be heard."

Back home after my publicity trip I asked my male friends about the subject of men and loss. These men said that they had seldom been given the opportunity to deal with personal losses and grief in their lives. They were open to the possibility of exploring the subject further. So was I. With this in mind, I began to read everything I could about men and the men's movement, paying particular attention to insights and theories about men's pain and grief. In reading the opinions of recognized authorities like Sam Keen [2], Robert Bly [3], and others, I sensed an awareness of the enormity of men's pain, but the topic was largely left there, unexplored. To further investigate I decided to do some searching myself. I would ask particular men about particular losses. I wanted to learn about men's grief from the inside, from their own experiences. With this goal in mind I invited several men whom I knew personally to form a men's circle where grief would be the focus. And I wanted to be present with them to witness the process.

THE PROJECT: CHALLENGES

When I began this work I wondered if I were expecting too much! First, I would be asking men to meet and confront their pain in the presence of several other men whom they did not know well or at all. Would they do this? In addition, I wanted to be there with them in order to observe the group from the inside. Would they function as a men's group with a woman, therefore an "outsider," in their midst? Also, I knew that my role would be ambivalent at first. Because I needed to facilitate the group in the beginning to get the process up and running, I would begin as its facilitator but would have to pull away from this role as the group progressed so that it would become truly a "men's" group. Mid-group I would have to leave the role of facilitator, a comfortable one for me because of my many years of working as a grief group leader, to become a silent observer. Would my role change be too jarring? Finally, I realized that as a woman whose prime loss experience was the death of a spouse, my gut knowledge about the bereavement process was inevitably gender specific. Worse yet, I knew I carried certain prejudices about bereavement and coping styles:

- "Women know how to grieve," I thought.
- "Men aren't as good at grieving as women."
- "Men find partners more easily after the death of a spouse."

- "Men are economically less hard hit than women after the death of a spouse."
- "Men avoid grief."
- "Men never share their grief with other men."
- "Men don't do their own personal grief work after loss."

Looking at my preconceived notions honestly was an eye opener! I could never get into men's loss experiences if I continued to hold such misconceptions. To do this work with integrity, I would have to abandon all gender bias about loss and bereavement; I would also have to (try to) become androgynous!

I faced other challenges as I contemplated doing this work. In an all men's circle I would be attempting to establish empathy and intimacy with several men at one time. As the only female present I would need to keep my center despite the gender imbalance in the group. I would not want to "mother" the men who told me their pain nor would I want to carry their pain with me. Protective mechanisms would be important if I were to survive this experience intact. I wanted to learn about men's loss without losing myself in the process.

Having a clear set of goals at the outset of the project helped me to minimize the difficulties of the undertaking. There were certain questions I wanted to answer. These questions became my personal anchor. I wanted to know:

1. What is men's grief?
2. How do men grieve?
3. Is our currently accepted grief model sufficient for men?
4. How do men help each other through grief?
5. What kind of grief group model will work for men themselves?

Now that my goals were clear, I was ready to start.

THE PROJECT: "SIX REALLY SAD GUYS AND TOM"

My first step was to write letters to ten men outlining the project and asking if they would be willing to participate with me to learn more about men and loss. Eight men answered my invitation positively and we set our first meeting date. After the second meeting, one participant decided to opt out of the project because of time commitments and a feeling that he was repeating grief work already done. The remaining seven men who participated in the group ranged in age from thirty-nine to seventy-one years. Four men were married, one was living with a life partner, another was separated, and one was divorced. None of the men had formal grief education although four had exposure to the grieving of others in their workplace settings. The men had careers as a social worker, a pastoral counselor-in-training who worked as a diner cook, a self-employed landscape artist, an insurance underwriter, a psychotherapist/MD, a marriage and family therapist, and a retired physical education teacher. All of the men had pre-project experience in group process work either through men's groups or personal growth and/or retreat work. Five group participants belonged to men's groups during the time period of this research.

Our group met monthly for eighteen months. All of our meetings were audiotaped with the permission of the participants. A total of forty-two hours of meeting time was transcribed. All participants agreed to allow me to use their stories in part or in whole. They also chose to use their actual names in any reporting of the men's group project. Because there were two Toms in the group, I have called one Tom A. and the second Tom E. in the manuscript to differentiate between them. All quotations which I use in this chapter are taken verbatim from transcriptions made during the men's group sessions. Each man in the following pages speaks his own story in his own words.

My intent was to explore all kinds of loss, including but not limited to loss through death, during our group time. When the group began, none of the participants had lost a child or spouse to death. Several had lost grandparents, one his sibling, and one his father prior to the group's beginning. None of these losses had been in the immediate past. During the time we met, several group members suffered major losses, including the unexpected death of Bob's father, Ken's diagnosis of cancer and his subsequent treatment, Tom A.'s sudden marriage breakup, and Ralph's decision to change his life pattern by admitting his alcoholism and attending Alcoholics Anonymous. The men generally seemed interested in the project and were anxious to get started.

Mild tension arose at first because this group had no clear agenda. This tension abated after the first few meetings. In addition, Tom E. stated concerns which did not seem to be shared by the other participants. He said that he felt he did not fit in, did not understand grief, had no grief of his own, did not choose to think about the negatives in his life because he had so many positives, and might not return after the first meeting. His stated preference was to be active as a group, to DO something with the group like singing or painting rather than just talking. The group exerted no pressure on Tom to stay or leave. Tom chose to stay. Through the course of our meetings he often shared deeply. We discovered in time that when Tom E. was sixteen his older brother died in Palestine. Tom had also been a fighter pilot in the Royal Air Force during the Second World War when he was about nineteen.

He survived this War when many of his war buddies did not. Much later he had a close brush with death when immediately before our group began he experienced serious complications following knee surgery. Tom eventually realized that he had had numerous losses which he'd neglected when he admitted, "I'm discovering I don't know what grieving is about."

Tom E.'s presence was very important to the group. He was its senior member, always totally honest about himself and others. He became a valued and regular participant in the group, like a mentor to the others. In fact, because of Tom's philosophy, the group jokingly called itself "six really sad guys and Tom!"

THE PROJECT: GETTING STARTED

Each night for the first few meetings we began the group by discussing why we were meeting and how we were going to achieve our aims. I took on the facilitating tasks, convening the group and making it an emotionally safe place. Building a sense of community which valued the confidentiality of the information shared in the group was essential. Without an atmosphere of trust, little useful sharing could occur. I used several techniques to get started. For example, in week one I led a quiet meditation/visualization exercise in which I had the men relax to music, then return on the screen of their minds to the scene of the first loss experience they could recall. After this exercise each man wrote in silence describing the memory that surfaced during the visualization and how his family of origin handled (or avoided) this loss. These were often very early recollections which took the participants into interesting places and set a firm foundation for sharing past losses. The following example reflects the detailed nature of one visualization.

> (Stuart: age 60) I was between three and four when my mother's only brother, Russell, died of tuberculosis in Detroit. And I can still remember the scene in full Technicolor: the pattern on the kitchen floor at home and the color of the green stool that my mother was sitting on in front of the sink while she peeled potatoes. The whole thing was so vivid because this was my first exposure to grief! She was absolutely grief stricken, totally! And I guess I had a feeling of helplessness because I couldn't do anything. All I could do was weep with her, I guess. And for me, you see, I'd never seen Uncle Russell. I'd only heard about him. Sounds of my mother grieving. Sadness because of her pain.

The group became less structured over time. Often we shared informally letting the conversation move where it would. Once the group process was well established my role became less leader-facilitator and more participant-observer. So I did little more than make the coffee and plug in the tape recorder. I was able to focus my attention primarily on how the men dealt with their loss among themselves. Just be there and listen. I spoke infrequently, and when I did speak it was as one of the group, not as analyst or expert. Essentially my silence was crucial so that the men were free to support each other in their own way, without female modeling.

The men responded with heartfelt compassion and surprising skill to the losses which surfaced spontaneously from meeting to meeting. I also learned from transcribing and studying the taped material after each meeting that an evening's conversation which seemed to ramble aimlessly in session had direction and focus after all. The digressions were part of the process of laying the groundwork for telling the untellable, their stories of loss. Now, after several group meetings, the men were confronting their pain and celebrating their joy. I was moved by their insights and sensitivity to one another and felt privileged to be in their midst. Yes, these were special men. But, given the opportunity, perhaps all men can be so.

THE PROJECT: LOSSES DISCUSSED

Over the course of the eighteen months the men shared more loss experiences than I had anticipated. They spoke of:

- loss of persons (i.e., father, mother, spouse, sibling, aunt, uncle, grandparents);
- separation from place;
- separation from freedom and autonomy;
- separation from family members;
- loss of a dream, a vision, the future;
- loss of body reliability (i.e., aging);
- being unseen and unheard within the family of origin;
- terror of not being;
- terror of living in unbearable pain;
- terror of losing the old self;
- missing important life markers (i.e., birth of child, initiation into manhood);
- anticipatory losses (i.e., joining AA, imminent death, wife's leaving the marriage);
- loss of a love;

- shame for the past (i.e., the heritage of others: alcohol, illness, grief, unwanted or illegitimate pregnancy, abuse);
- loss of the unknown (i.e., uncle's death, not knowing the father/ uncle/grandfather at all, or better, or more fully).

While I had expected that all men felt some loss and pain, I had no idea that they had experienced so much of it. One man would tell his story and another would follow and another and another. It seems that being invited to share loss, grief, and pain was the catalyst for these men to recount many aspects of their life histories that had not previously been told or shared, except perhaps with a spouse or partner. To share these facts and the feelings unleashed by them with other men was unrehearsed and unusual. Most men, as Paul tells here, were accustomed to dealing with losses alone.

> (Paul: age 48) This early memory for me was when I was five or six years old so this is going way back. I had a friend who lived next door and in the morning I was running out and around to the steps and knocking on his door and there was no answer. There is this positive anticipation of playing with my friend and there's no answer and there's no answer . . . thinking maybe he's not there and then going home and being told by my mother that they've moved away. I was shocked; it was quite devastating at the time because he had moved far away to Calgary. He was gone. I remember feeling a disbelief and then a feeling of helplessness, loneliness in a sense, because really he was my only friend. And then there was anger and betrayal. No one was concerned. My mother hadn't twigged to the severity of the loss for me. I did not have anyone who shared in that loss. That was a very low period in my life and I can remember turning to the bush and the woods. Often I was by myself. There was solace in that.

Ralph remembered many boyhood losses, too.

> (Ralph: age 46) When I was seven or eight I came home from school in late February. What sticks in my mind is that cold weather, just gray. It wasn't snowing: just cold and dark, around four o'clock. My procedure was always to change my clothes and help with the chores. We had horses. This day the animal disposal truck was there and the last of our heavy horses went down, very unceremoniously; it was shot in the head and taken away from the farm. My father was crying. It was the last horse. Just then I recognized that it would never be the same again. The aloneness was there and my way of coping with it was just to do my chores, work hard, try not to think much, become very quiet. Be a man: put your shoulder into it.

Later my uncle killed himself and when I was doing the chores in the barn that night I remember screaming at my Dad, why was I like this; why couldn't I be like a cow? A cow was not feeling as bad as I was. Of course, he didn't have the answer! I certainly didn't.

Like Paul's mother, Ralph's father was unable to help him understand his feelings with the result that both boys internalized their pain. Men carry an incredible load of pain. And most carry it alone, often unspoken, to the grave. Ralph, Paul, and the other men in our group were breaking the silence of generations by sharing their pain in a circle of men. They were finally getting back what had been denied them by their forefathers: male companionship and empathy. To speak, to be heard, and to have one's experiences validated, is crucial to healing the deep wounds of the soul. For men to have these experiences validated by another man is soul satisfying.

LOSSES DISCUSSED AND PALPABLE GRIEF

Many other stories vividly expressed the pain that these men had carried with them for many years. The pain of having to deny tears in order to be a man is one Tom E. told.

(Tom E.: age 71) You're talking about me 20 years ago. Tears for me were just weakness, absolute weakness. A man crying? Oh God! That was me not very long ago, about fifteen years ago. I finally did break down and cry one day.

(Ralph) I have to ask the question: "What made you cry fifteen years ago?"

(Tom) I was sitting at the kitchen table, this is when (I wanted to cry but I could always swallow it, stiff upper lip) my wife and I had separated but I was back at the house and we decided we would have supper together. I was going to say grace. I wasn't feeling too happy about the situation so I started to say "For what we are about to receive" and this lump came up and this time I couldn't swallow it. It got stuck; the tears came. And what happened was, my three kids came around me, instead of leaving me, they came around me, and by that sort of action I realized what I thought was weakness was not weakness. They did not leave me, they came around me! They were with me. That was the first time. It isn't as if I probably hadn't wanted to cry. I felt it coming on but I wouldn't let it happen because I am a man. Crying is a weakness. If I start crying, the whole place, the whole place will collapse.

Ken shared what living with cancer and chemotherapy treatment did to him.

(Ken: age 48) I've gone through cancer treatment all summer and very certainly there are some losses associated with that. In terms of loss the one was the loss of my hair and my beard. I'm not talking as much about the loss of it, as what it symbolized. After my first treatment my hair was coming out in chunks and so when I saw that happening I went to the barber and got it buzzed, actually and it stayed that way and just didn't grow, just this ugly gray, peach fuzzy looking hair.

It was a loss of identity; to other people too. People did not know me. I'd tell them who I was. That was a new experience. With three old friends at a Christmas party this year when I sauntered up to them, I could see they didn't have a clue who I was so I introduced myself. It really was a loss of identity.

The one loss was the identity. The other would be, I guess, what I would call the loss of immortality. I carried the notion around that bad stuff happened to other people. I'm young and my body is in good shape; look at me: hardly a stomach on me and I'm almost 50: that sort of stuff. I had a kind of arrogance about my body and then to suddenly realize that I've got this potentially deadly disease. I didn't know I had it; it's obviously been there for a while and what caused it. That was probably the most devastating loss, just realizing that, hey, I have a mortal disease. Something that could take my life. I'd never felt that mortal before. Suddenly you're looking at the potential of something that could take life. That was probably the biggest loss.

Tom A. told about the fear for his own survival when his wife decided suddenly to leave the marriage.

(Tom A.: age 39) Well, I'm afraid I'm checking in with a disaster on my hands. I'm going to have to though. Lynda announced to me that she no longer wants to be a couple with me. Last week was devastation for me; this week I feel rage. She told my daughter without my being present. I was ready to f—— kill her! I'm not thinking very clearly. I'm glad I'm getting the bitch out of my life. It's hard to hear myself say those words. I'm full of doubts. I'm doubting her, I'm afraid I won't survive.

Ralph told about carrying a shame from a past generation.

(Ralph) I carry a huge shame inherited from my mother. My mother's father, my grandfather, drank in the thirties. My first memory of that was when I was six or seven, he died of a heart attack. My father had to talk my mother into going to the funeral. She hated her father and was ashamed of him. Nothing was said to me specifically but it's what I could hear and feel and I have been living with that ever since.

Ralph went on to describe the fear of his grief.

(Ralph) I'm scared shitless of this grief: my loss of life as I know it, my loss of control. It's like all these years I've been searching for another option and it seems like I've finally found it. I have to trust the process or go back to the old (drinking) way and I will be alone. And I will lose my soul.

Dick spoke of his loss of confidence as a child when his mother stopped protecting him in the world.

(Dick: age 56) I am about four. A friend of my mother's is in for afternoon tea. She's brought her son, slightly older and larger than I. We were sent out to the back yard. This kid is attacking me and is now holding me pinned down on the grass. The women come out. I call to my mother. She says I have to learn to fend for myself when the other mother wants to do something about her son's viciousness. I am dismayed. I lost the faith I had in my mother that she would protect me. It was also the first in a series of experiences as a child when the rules were quoted after the fact. I had no knowledge that I was to fend for myself. After that incident I was given no help to do that. On the contrary, I was often criticized for trying to do that. Apparently, I was to fend for myself without getting angry. Damned if I do and damned if I don't. I soon lost confidence that I could make realistic judgments how to act or react. As I reflect on this its like a loss of innocence. I was there and I was safe and I was protected. This event came along and when I expected protection I was just yanked away.

Bob shared poignant feelings concerning his relationship with his father and his father's very recent death and funeral.

(Bob: age 48) Even though he was in a coma when I got there I was able to be with him on a compassionate level. That is about as close as I can remember being to him. Even though I couldn't speak with him I had so much feeling for him. It was very peaceful.

I was struck by the esteem in which he was held. It's given me a new insight on who he was. I saw other sides of him as well, the person. It's like it broadened the picture of who the man was. It's almost like a gift in those remembrances, a witnessing, a testimony: I did not know that about him. Somehow all of his life was separate. I'm starting to sense how rich his inner life was; pretty rich. (Long silence and tears) It's strange the distance between us seems less now that he's gone. I don't know.

As I say, I spent a long time being angry with him because of that distance and that distance became my distance, and I knew that and I couldn't break that down. Part of me was hurting but I came to accept that. In a strange way I feel closer to him now than I ever have. Right now I feel a great sense of release.

THE PROJECT: WHAT MEN NEED IN A GROUP

In order for men to share their deepest hurts and losses they must have a few basic needs met in the group setting. First, they need to be invited to be present and to share their losses. Second, some explanation of why grief work is important may be helpful to men considering whether to join a men's group like the one described in this chapter. For instance, my plan to use the group for conducting research and writing a book gave the group viability, and lent credibility to their participating in it. Their work will have an end product which will be useful to society. Third, men should have an understanding at a cognitive level of the importance of men meeting together to discuss their pain and shame. Fourth, men need to have a safe place in which to meet and talk. The group setting must be comfortable, not austere (as in a hospital or funeral home location), and private. Fifth, men need to be reminded of their losses in many ways at the beginning of the group. Keeping a loss inventory is not a high priority in most men's daily lives! I used several exercises in the group. These methodologies are described in detail in my Grief Support Manual [4]. Sixth, men need to be reminded that grief has a physical component and that in the process of discussing past losses they may feel pain or tension in their bodies. Finally, I believe that men need to trust the power of the group process. This trust can be instilled in a number of ways, by assuring confidentiality for one, but most simply, trust grows when one person in the group believes strongly in the value of the process and shares that belief with others.

FEEDBACK: COMMENTS FROM THE MEN THEMSELVES

I asked the men to describe what they were learning about men and loss through our group meetings. Their comments are presented below:

- men say that women can't take seeing them in tears;
- men feel deeply; men feel loss deeply;

- men feel deep shame over the past darkness of their forefathers;
- men personalize these past shames and carry the grief from it;
- men feel the lack of male mentors and would have benefited from having them in their lives;
- men feel lack of connection with male relatives;
- men want the father connection;
- men feel ambivalence around the father/mother connection because of their strong need for differentiation and autonomy;
- men may see the authoritarian father parallel to, but ironically caught in, the authoritarian institution, corporation himself;
- men realize that they themselves are in the same bind now;
- men who as boys see one or the other parent's tears and deep grief for the first time, carry a deep and lasting impression of this intrapsychically;
- how men's earliest grief experience is handled by support people and caregivers in their past, influences present responses to loss and life;
- men think women have unreal expectations of them;
- for men the relationship of intimacy and grief is connected;
- men allow silence around sharing deep grief;
- men do allow and accept other men's tears, terror, grief;
- men help one another by being together, doing or saying nothing;
- men ask hard questions of one another;
- men can deny feelings;
- men can ignore their bodily reaction to loss (i.e., ignore somatic symptoms);
- men can and do say "I love you" to one another when it is felt; and
- men who experience loss without denial become more passionate and compassionate individuals.

FEEDBACK FROM PEGGY

- I did not expect to be so moved by men's recounting their earliest loss experiences;
- my response is subjective not academic;
- women's loss seems to be more connected with the loss of person or perhaps self through another person;
- men's losses are many but chief among them are loss of innocence, ideals, missed opportunities, boy-to-man transitions;

- men don't talk about grief, loss, pain, shame: this does not mean they don't have it or feel it;
- men don't talk about the above because sharing has not been modeled to them historically;
- because men don't as a rule talk about their grief, there is a sense that they are carrying something; women are more apt to put it out;
- men in this group found the process of communicating is in itself enlightening;
- men in this group report that having grief witnessed is healing and helpful;
- a lot of grief was discussed in this group;
- each person deals with each different loss in a unique way;
- the grief model we hear most about and teach in grief courses tends to be the feminine model;
- there may be other models of healthy grieving;
- there is intimacy in this men's group which includes the silences— long ones; the sharing of stories; telling parallel stories; the courage to ask hard confrontative questions (ones which in a women's group setting I would be hesitant to ask);
- the courage to answer them (straight up); the trust in the group and group process which allows this;
- the humor and giddiness (which I loved);
- I was very moved by the men's interaction and supportive way with one another in the group;
- when I sit with a group of men discussing intimate issues I experience something different from when I do the same thing with an all-women's group;
- men can get into more "head" stuff;
- men have ways to avoid the other (i.e., "How about those Jays?") whenever the subject gets a little too personal or emotional;
- when I hear men's grief I feel it in my body;
- men often ignore their very physical reactions to emotional pain;
- men's tears are powerful; they have the power to move me;
- couples grieving the same loss can be very out of sync;
- although many of the men in this group are in healing professions, they aren't much aware of the grief process or their own loss issues and grieving styles.

I felt privileged to be allowed a seat in the men's circle.

SOME CONCLUSIONS:
ANSWERING THE QUESTIONS

When I set goals for myself at the beginning of this project, I hoped to find answers to five questions. Summarized, here is what I have discovered through initiating and observing a men's group which has grief as its major focus.

1. What is Men's Grief?

Men feel loss over many things in their lives. They also feel many losses carried forward through generations. In this regard they are not so different from women. However, compounding men's loss is the fact that men are more likely to be socially conditioned to repress feelings associated with loss, and not to tell their stories in order to avoid the feelings associated with them. By repressing the feelings associated with loss men do two things. First, they do not allow grief, like a festering sliver, to work itself out. So the poison seeps inside. Second, they deny to themselves a part of their history. By avoiding the whole and repressing a part of their immediate and distant past, they prevent themselves from "knowing themselves" fully. Not to know fully who you are makes it almost impossible to share oneself fully. Feedback earlier from the men showed they felt there must be a connection between intimacy and grief. This is it. By remaining silent about their own loss and pain and shame and fear and terror, men can never be fully seen, never be fully validated for themselves, therefore, never fully loved. Perhaps this is the shadow of maleness; that men have been forced into denying their vulnerability. Little wonder that our world is suffering from an abundance of male violence. Perhaps men's biggest loss in ignoring their grief is the loss of a very important part of themselves.

2. How do Men Grieve?

Others have studied men's grief and found that men's grieving style comes largely from socializing and conditioning [5]. My work suggests that this grieving style will change when men become conscious of their patterns and take a different path. When men begin to share losses with one another as the men did in our circle, they take a first step onto a new path.

Men grieve in many ways. Men cry. Men rage. Men hurt inside. Men deny their pain and speak very little about it. Until now they have done this alone because that is what has been modeled to them. That is what was safe for their fathers. However, as men discover that old patterns exact a high price, many, like the pioneers in my group, may want to try another way. Their choice may be to speak and be heard. It is a unique and healing experience for a man to have his stories heard and validated by other men. Men may choose to take a new path for the sake of their own sons or for the sake of the women in their lives. Because I love men, it is my hope that they will do it chiefly for themselves!

3. Is our Currently Accepted Grief Model Sufficient for Men?

No, it is not. Neither is it sufficient for women. Grief is unique. It is not uniquely feminine and uniquely masculine, it is individually unique to each man and woman. It is a process which is dynamic and never ending. We need a model which encourages an acceptance of differences and allows each man and each woman to choose his or her unique path to healing and wholeness. Men and women also need to realize that loss and grief is normal, natural, and a healthy part of being alive. Men, with their pain and grief like women with their anger, will need courage and determination to speak out, to dare to be heard!

4. How Do Men Help Each Other Through Grief?

Participating in and observing my men's circle has led me to conclude that men help one another through grief simply by being present for one another. More specifically, in our circle, I found that men helped each other by talking together about their loss, grief, pain, shame, fear, and terror. They also listened to one another as each man spoke his story. They witnessed for one another what had happened and what had been felt. They did not abandon one another as the group process unfolded. They told parallel stories to reinforce and validate each other's sense of loss. They often asked difficult questions of each other for clarification or confirmation. They offered difficult answers when asked difficult questions by their peers. This means they were fully honest and particularly vulnerable with each other in the context of the group.

They often used humor to diffuse an emotionally charged moment. Humor, by the way, should be encouraged in groups such as this. Humor can restore safety to a group when terror or anger threatens to overload it and blow it apart. Men are adept at sharing wild stories to do just this. Men also helped one another through grief by staying through difficult times and issues. Tom A. told the group immediately after his wife announced she would leave him, "I'm afraid I won't survive." The group listened to Tom in silence. Then slowly one man began to elicit more information from Tom; another challenged him when he did not make sense. Like seasoned counselors, they seemed to know just how far to go with Tom. Despite Tom's desperate state, he found help in the group. When I asked Tom just how the group had helped him, he simply replied, "They let me speak and they did not leave."

Men expect to be abandoned when they show their deepest feelings. Finding that other men can hear them and not flinch gives them power to go through their feelings and to come out the other side. Tom survives. Other men will too.

5. What Kind of Grief Work Model Will Work for Men Themselves

Out of the project I have compiled a manual called *Six Really Sad Guys and Tom* [4], which is the model for the grief work group for men piloted in London and explained in part in this chapter. The *Manual* includes detailed outlines for meetings, a guide for the facilitator, resource material, and a bibliography. Questions and comments concerning either this chapter or the *Manual* mentioned above can be mailed to the author in care of Sophia Publications, 83 Victoria Street, London, Ontario, N6A 2B1.

CONCLUSION: A GRIEF UNHEARD

There are many ways for men to grieve. Men do carry much grief and have carried it silently for centuries, believing that this was the only way. They have been silent sufferers because no other way has been modeled to them; no other way seemed safe. Men can and do help other men through grief, given the opportunity. A men's group with grief as its focus is a helpful tool for men who wish to break the silence for themselves and for the ones they love.

In concluding, there is a noteworthy caution. Group work like ours must not be undertaken lightly. Those wanting to initiate such a group should have considerable group processing skills, preferably including some past experience as a group participant, should have done their own grief work, and should be firm believers in the healing power of sharing among men in a group setting. Compassion and integrity are always important attributes for facilitators of grief groups, especially so when men are to be encouraged to become vulnerable by sharing their pain and grief, their fears and terror.

Traditionally, men and women have not heard men's grief because we have not wanted to hear it. In order to hear from men themselves about their deepest fears and losses, we must first ask. In order to hear from men, we must make it safe for them to tell. And finally, in order to hear, we must not be afraid *to listen*.

REFERENCES

1. P. M. L. Anderson, *Wife After Death: Women Coping and Growing After the Death of a Partner,* Sophia Publications, London, Ontario, 1991.
2. S. Keen, *Fire in the Belly: On Being a Man,* Bantam Books, New York, 1991.
3. R. Bly, *Iron John: A Book About Men,* Random House, New York, 1990.
4. P. M. L. Anderson, *Six Really Sad Guys and Tom: A Manual for a Men's Grief Group,* Sophia Publications, London, Ontario, 2000.
5. C. Staudacher, *Men and Grief: A Guide for Men Surviving the Death of a Loved One; A Resource for Caregivers and Mental Health Proefssionals,* New Harbinger, Oakland, 1991.

CHAPTER 17

Grieving Reproductive Loss: The Bereaved Male

Kathleen Gray

The study of grief as a basic universal human emotion had been, until recently, a neglected area of research [1]. It is interesting to note that until 1972 "grief," as a distinct heading, was not listed in the subject index of *Psychological Abstracts*. In 1973, "grief" appeared for the first time as a separate subject category. Those early entries on grief in 1973 were restricted to fairly common experiences of grief, experiences which were familiar to most people—bereavement, widows and widowers, cultural differences, bereavement, etc. The first listing of grieving due to perinatal loss appeared in 1974 [2].

Since that time, however, the range of grief experiences, that is those involving loss, has expanded considerably. There seemed to be a growing awareness of additional areas in which a person could or would be allowed to grieve. The recognized range of grief experiences has been expanded to encompass not only perinatal death, including stillbirth, but also other early reproductive losses due to miscarriage and abortion. In general, spontaneous and induced abortion have been overlooked as grief issues [3, 4]. Regarding miscarriage or spontaneous abortion, Stack observed, "Grieving following spontaneous abortion is common, but generally not recognized by family, friends and professional caregivers" [5].

Thus, with the expanded range of grief experiences, by 1985 the number of grief entries had grown from seven in 1973 to ninety-eight, filling one and a half pages in *Psychological Abstracts*.

GRIEF AWARENESS EXPANDED

The current thinking of what constitutes normal grieving and the grieving of reproductive losses, especially in popular writings, seems to allow for a much greater latitude and variety of manifestations of grief. It appears that some of what was considered at an earlier time to be complicated grieving would now be included in the continuous range of normal grieving. At the 1993 Conference on Death and Bereavement at King's College in London, Ontario, Dennis Klass stated that "complicated grieving is in the process of being redefined." Judging by the number of books and articles, both professional and popular, that are written today on the topic of grief, it would seem that we are somewhat more aware of and sensitive to grief issues related to reproductive loss. However, our society still does not allow grievers sufficient time to process their grief or even to recognize many reproductive losses as grief issues. What appears to be common sense is not necessarily common practice.

Although there has been progress in this area of grief awareness—the annual conference sponsored by the Centre for Education about Death and Bereavement at King's College in London, Ontario, is but one example—there still exists today a gap between grief awareness in the literature versus grief awareness in the field.

While there are many compassionate, caring health professionals who are aware of grief reactions in reproductive loss, we know from the examples that our clients present to us at the Centre for Reproductive Loss[1] that we still have a long way to go to bring this awareness to the practitioners. This lack of awareness is illustrated in the following example.

One of our clients who had miscarried told her obstetrician how much she was helped by grief work at the Centre for Reproductive Loss. Because she thought that he would like to know this in order to help other women by passing on the information, she gave him one of our brochures. After looking at it, he promptly handed it back to her

---

[1] The Centre for Reproductive Loss, a non-profit, non-denominational, registered charitable organization was founded in Montreal in 1992 by three health care professionals. "It was established in order to respond compassionately to the emotional, spiritual, or psychological distress of individuals and families affected by such reproductive losses as miscarriage, stillbirth, abortion, adoption and infertility." We believe that these reproductive losses are not only women's issues. In fact, the word "woman" does not appear on our brochure. From the beginning we have recognzied that these are men's issues as well. Even children are affected, not to mention other family members, including grandparents. Our address is: Centre for Reproductive Loss, P.O. Box 282, Station Côte St. Luc, Montreal, Quebec, Canada H4V 2Y4; telephone (514) 486-6708.

saying, "You're making a big deal out of this. Most women don't react like you. Why don't you go home and get pregnant again so you won't be so emotionally involved." There is a lack of awareness of grief for women and reproductive loss, but it is far greater regarding bereaved men and reproductive loss.

EMOTIONAL IMPACT OF REPRODUCTIVE LOSS

The experience of reproductive loss, such as miscarriage, stillbirth, and perinatal death, has been compared to being hit by an emotional Mack truck. At a time when grieving parents are most vulnerable, they need to hear the healing and compassionate words of acknowledgment of their emotional pain due to these tragic losses. Unfortunately, many grieving parents report encounters with some health professionals that are not only insensitive but border on cruelty. In addition, there are some family members and friends who mean well, who have no intention to harm but often create the harm they do not intend. Consequently, the parents' grief is compounded and intensified by insensitive comments, clichés, or by lack of any recognition and even abrupt dismissal. These grieving parents not only experience profound sadness but anger as well. Health care professionals, in particular bereavement counselors, need to be aware of these emotions and help parents to recognize and appropriately express this sadness and anger which are essential in order to facilitate the grieving process.

DIFFERENCES IN GRIEVING

Traditionally, research and clinical interventions have focused upon how the mothers dealt with these losses while the fathers' grief was often not even acknowledged. Both men and women need to realize the importance of grieving these losses. While men also grieve, for the most part they do so in different ways. Being aware of some of these differences can bring about an understanding of the bereaved male and of the ways to help him to grieve reproductive losses.

Men's response to loss as a father in general differs from a woman's response as a mother. Studies in the literature support this. The first of these, "Parents' Grief Following Pregnancy Loss: A Comparison of Mothers and Fathers," examined gender differences in bereavement following such reproductive losses as miscarriage, ectopic pregnancy, stillbirth and neonatal death [6]. Using the Perinatal Grief Scale, fifty-six couples were interviewed at two months, one, and two years post-loss [7]. Their findings indicate that, while both men and women grieved these losses, women's grief was significantly higher on this scale. They also found that fathers tended to deny their grief and internalize their feelings of loss rather than openly express them.

Another study, "Parental Grief Reactions and Marital Intimacy Following Infant Death," examined the grief reactions of bereaved mothers and fathers following the death of their infant [8]. These findings, consistent with others in the literature, revealed that "mothers and fathers experience the death of an infant differently. Their expressions of grief are different as is the intensity of many of their reactions and the manner in which they deal with their loss. The major issue raised by these findings is that there is a need for different models to explain the grief experience for mothers and for fathers" [8, p. 252]. Of the several clinical implications raised in this study, one stands out in importance for bereavement counseling, which is that "clinicians need to be attuned to the differences and similarities of the grief reactions experienced by bereaved mothers and fathers. Thus an important aspect of grief counseling should include helping each parent to understand and respect his or her own grief reactions as well as those experienced by the spouse" [8, p. 252].

In her book *Men & Grief*, Carol Staudacher has observed that the differences in the way fathers grieve can be attributed largely to cultural expectations [9]. Men are "not expected to express loneliness, sadness or depression" nor are they "expected to exhibit helplessness or to cry openly" [9, p. 20]. These "cultural expectations for men directly correspond to solitary or secret grief" [9, p. 20]. Thus, men grieve alone and in secret. Another factor which may account for these differences is that "men are usually more adept at masking their emotions and—as a natural outcome—may underreport emotional issues and reactions. In addition, the dissimilarities in grief reactions after an infant's death may arise from differing degrees of intensity in the mothers' and fathers' bond with the infant" [9, p. 122].

Staudacher has also included several responses which have been identified with grieving fathers.

- Fathers tend to be private in their grief and reluctant to talk.
- Fathers "keep busy" after the death.
- Fathers are inclined to exhibit more anger and aggression than their wives and to mask their other prominent feelings.
- Fathers are not inclined to ask for compassion, support, or affection.
- Fathers do not as frequently seek professional help.
- Fathers return to "normal functioning" more quickly than mothers.

When surviving an infant's death:

- Fathers will usually experience less guilt than mothers.
- Fathers' grief reactions are more likely to be of lesser intensity and shorter duration [9, p. 122].

MARRIAGE RELATIONSHIP AFFECTED

The death of a child, even from miscarriage, can affect the marriage relationship. It is a well-known fact that the divorce rate is extremely high in marriages in which a child has died. For some, however, the marriage will become stronger. The following story of a reproductive loss from a man's perspective reflects the impact on a person's life and marriage. John wrote about his experience in *The Grief Recovery Handbook* [10]. Part of his story follows.

> The divorce happened because we had no idea how to deal with the grief caused by all the changes in our lives. We were newly married, new parents, and new grievers at the same time. The death of our son was the straw that broke the camel's back.
>
> . . . I had no skill or practice at being able to talk about what I was feeling. I felt isolated and alone, yet truly believed that I was supposed to be strong and keep it all inside. Since that was all I knew, that is what I did. With that type of pressure building up, arguments became common. Hurt feelings were then added to the fire, and more arguments followed. . . .
>
> When communication breaks down in a marriage, no matter the cause, it is only a matter of time before divorce occurs. When the divorce takes place, we have yet another grieving experience to deal with, so the cycle continues. . . .
>
> Friends didn't want to talk about the death. They made the topic of my son's death off-limits. Years later, I asked them why. They said, "Talking about the death would rekindle old pain."
>
> They didn't want to see me hurt any more. They thought they were loving me.
>
> None of these well-meaning people knew that by trying to make it easier for me, they were making my grief more intense. They thought that they were loving me, but in fact they almost loved me to death.
>
> I kept all that pain inside until I was ready to explode. It was very much like being a time bomb.
>
> Somehow, I knew that talking about my feelings would be good for me, even though it frightened me. But everyone around kept acting like it wasn't appropriate to talk about my painful feelings.

With enough messages of this nature, I soon began to question my
own sanity. I decided something was wrong with me. I couldn't see
any end to the pain. I began to entertain the idea of ending it all
[10, pp. 72, 82-83].

While some marriages may end in divorce after the death of a child,
there are couples who can grow from that experience and whose marriages are strengthened by it.

The tragedy of losing a baby can also be an emotional challenge for
future pregnancies [11]. Parents report feeling vulnerable, "a loss of
innocence," and even frightened that the pregnancy will end in miscarriage again. The sense of joy and optimism is often diminished and
parents have a difficult time bonding with the child in utero and, in
some cases, even after the child is born.

One father tells his story of how he dealt with his own anxiety of
pregnancy after two miscarriages.

> I believe my wife and I felt equal measures of hope and fear,
> but we dealt with them in profoundly different ways. Anne, for
> whom the last four years have seemed like one long first trimester
> punctuated by D&Cs, told everyone the news immediately. No
> matter what happened, she wanted people to acknowledge the
> pregnancy. I, on the other hand, like the baseball fan who doesn't
> want to call attention to a no-hitter for fear he'll jinx it, would have
> preferred not to mention it at all—for the whole nine months, if
> possible.
>
> She called what was inside her "the baby," I referred to "the
> pregnancy," "the fetus," or merely "it."
>
> When I forced myself to touch her tummy, it was not the tender,
> prolonged caress of the first pregnancy, but a timid, tentative
> touch, the way a child pats the head of a strange and possibly
> dangerous dog. Slowly but surely, I realized this nineties' new man
> had become the emotional equivalent of the cigarette-puffing father
> of the fifties, who paces the waiting room while his wife sweats out
> the details in the delivery room.
>
> My wife was understandably hurt and accused me of ignoring
> the pregnancy. I wasn't ignoring it; I could think of little else. But
> like husbands in some other cultures I've read about, I believed
> that to show concern was to court disaster.
>
> Although we are now well into the Indian summer of the second
> trimester, we know from friends who have had stillbirths that we
> are far from home free.
>
> Even with these small misgivings, I feel closer to Anne now;
> although I still leave more unspoken than she would wish, our
> parallel lives are converging. As our son grows, I find myself think-
> ing of the two girls we lost, and I know that if—will I ever be able to

say when?—he is born, they will in some way rest more easily in my memory. And I vow to make up for all the kisses I was never able to give them [12].

LOSS NOT ACKNOWLEDGED

There are other reasons that grieving fathers do not reveal their own grief and that is due to the lack of acknowledgment of their grief and pain by family, friends, and, sadly, even by some health care professionals themselves. At one of our reproductive loss support groups, there were five couples present. These men told us that they were ignored and dismissed by health care professionals, they were not encouraged to seek help, and those who did try to seek help were not welcomed into women-only groups. These men wanted to be recognized for their fatherhood but were not. Because such reproductive losses are not easily shared, the bereaved father may experience loneliness in his loss and may suppress his feelings of grief and anger. When grief is not acknowledged, when it is denied, dismissed, minimized, or disenfranchised, and when those feelings are buried, there can be serious and detrimental consequences which could result.

Some grieving fathers may try to avoid the pain of loss through drugs, alcohol, food, keeping busy, or other forms of acting out, including aggressive and sometimes violent behavior. At our Centre, we often encounter situations of this nature. The following is just one such example and reflects the experience of several women.

A woman who had experienced a stillbirth came alone to our support group because her husband thought that it was stupid to talk about the death of a child. He did not think the support group was necessary even though his wife was being helped by it. His wife knew that he felt jealous that other men were there. She also said, "He blamed me at first. He cried only twice. To him, it's over. He keeps everything inside. He doesn't want to face it. He's very aggressive towards me—more so since this happened."

Worden recognized the consequence of buried grief, as he stated in *Grief Counseling & Grief Therapy* : "[G]rief often surfaces as the underlying cause of various physical and mental aberrations. People seek physical and mental health care without necessarily recognizing that there may be a grief issue underlying their particular physical or mental condition" [13, p. 1]. Worden cites the psychiatrist John Bowlby who also believed that underneath many psychological conditions there may be an unresolved grief reaction: "Clinical experience and a reading of the evidence leave little doubt . . . that much psychiatric illness is an expression of pathological mourning . . ." [13, p. 1].

REPRODUCTIVE LOSS INTERVENTIONS

The implications for health care interventions following reproductive loss are significant, therefore, especially as they pertain to
medical and family history. With each of the clients at the Centre for
Reproductive Loss, we always take a reproductive history as well as a
history of grief and loss experiences, including the coping responses of
the individuals to those experiences.

When the bereaved father can face the pain and walk through the
grief, he can recover and even grow from that grief experience.
Although most of the counseling we do at our Centre is with women on
a one-to-one basis, it is still possible to help the grieving father by
working with the woman and by working through the woman.

Grief education as an intervention is extremely important to
recovery. We have found it helpful to teach the woman about the
grieving process and its manifestations, as well as the differences in
the responses of men to grief. Her understanding of her own grief as a
normal response to loss, in addition to the assurance that she is not
"going crazy," a feeling she often reports, can lessen the tension in their
relationship. When she can understand and respect her husband's
grief, then she can let go of the expectation that her husband must
grieve exactly as she does and allow him the space he needs to grieve in
his own way. She can understand that his different mode of grieving is
not to be construed as a lack of caring. It is difficult enough for grievers
to have sufficient energy to help and support one another, because they
usually don't know what to do to help themselves, much less their
spouse.

Bibliotherapy is another helpful intervention. Articles and books
on grief and reproductive losses are made available to clients at
our Centre. One that we use quite often is Christine Moulder's book
Miscarriage [14]. Usually the woman will read it first and pass it on to
her husband. One client's husband disliked reading so she read to him.
Another man read the same book himself, and came to understand the
grief he and his wife were experiencing after the miscarriage of their
son at twelve weeks. He told his wife that he sometimes talks to the
baby. When she asked him what he said to the baby, he replied, "That's
between me and the baby." In addition, he was the one who suggested
planting a tree in the garden in memory of their son. They both agreed
that facing the pain of this loss not only saved their marriage but
strengthened it.

Men seem to take comfort in knowledge of the facts, of statistics,
and information in general. It's helpful to know that other couples who
experience reproductive loss have similar feelings and that they are not

alone. One man's reaction to his wife's miscarriage is told in Allen and Marks' book *Miscarriage: Women Sharing from the Heart* [15].

> I just did not believe it. I felt confusion, shock, and disbelief because I had never considered miscarriage as a possibility. I was under the mistaken impression that it was a very, very rare occurence.
> Then I learned that, statistically, it was not uncommon. And we spoke with others who had miscarried. I realized I was not such a rare, rare, one-in-a-thousand. That was a comfort [15, p. 98].

Before the process of letting go can occur, connecting with the child in this relationship needs to be done. Naming, seeing, and holding the child helps to establish the relationship with the child. Many hospitals in Canada and the United States encourage this as part of their perinatal bereavement protocol. It is also helpful to have a photograph of the child to make real this event. Having a memorial service for the child or some kind of ritual, even an informal one of the parents' choosing or designing, can bring a great deal of comfort also.

The significance of contact with the miscarried child is movingly described in Reed's story.

> At the hospital they asked, "Would you like to see the baby?" At first that seemed ridiculous. But then I saw the baby. He was 16 weeks; and he was dead. I started to cry. I played with him. This was a person.
> Under 20 weeks of pregnancy in California a baby is called a "lab specimen." But Jillian was treating the baby just like he was a baby, a human being. He was a human being, and we did treat him as one. We named him. Jillian wanted to have him buried. The priest came. He said a nice prayer. We buried the dead. I am so grateful she thought of that. I felt a lot of relief!
> This miscarriage is the worst thing I have ever experienced. I feel confusion about why I was being lied to that the baby was just a lab specimen, that it wasn't a baby. The worst was the ignorance: The state considers a baby a lab specimen. I wish they had told us of the option to have and bury our baby. They take away from you any right and responsibility. You *can* have your baby's body! It's your baby no matter what its age. Go to a hospital and see one of the babies from a miscarriage! Look at the baby and face it. I can't describe the feeling I had about our whole country. I was ashamed of our system, that we would handle miscarried babies that way.
> If I hadn't seen him, I'd say I didn't experience the death of a child. I definitely think I'm a father. If someone asks me if I'm a father, I'll say, "I have two children and one died" [15, pp. 101-102].

This father was asking for acknowledgment. He was asking for acknowledgment and recognition of his fatherhood. He was asking for acknowledgment of the reality of the loss. The first of Worden's four tasks of mourning is to accept the reality of the loss [13, p. 10]. While Worden describes this as the task of the griever, it should apply to the health care professional as well. Many parents object to the terms "fetal tissue" or "products of conception" or "contents of the womb" when physicians, nurses, or others use them to refer to their miscarried child. When a woman calls the Centre to say she miscarried, our response is to offer condolences about the loss of her baby. Her reply is, "You're the first to call it a baby."

Long after the physical wounds have healed, acknowledgment is what will be remembered. It will be remembered as being hurtful if it is lacking. It will be remembered as healing when it is present. The healing process can begin when acknowledgment is given with attentiveness and sensitivity. A recent study which examined the recommended interventions at the time of pregnancy loss—miscarriage, ectopic pregnancy, stillbirth, or newborn death—found that the attentiveness and sensitivity of health care personnel was more significantly related to greater satisfaction with overall care than were the total number of interventions alone [16].

Acknowledgment is perhaps the single most effective healing intervention that grieving fathers and mothers need in order to begin the healing process when grieving reproductive losses. Acknowledging another's grief and pain is such a powerful healing force. It not only recognizes the loss as a grief issue, but also it gives the person permission to grieve. Contemporary psychologists tell us how important it is to give people permission to grieve. Another contemporary had already given that permission a long time ago, when He said, "Blessed are those who mourn for they shall be comforted."

At the Centre for Reproductive Loss, we see many people who are hurting and grieving because of reproductive losses. When we help them face the pain and walk with them through that grief, we can help bring about grief recovery and healing. The phrase that appears on our brochure, "In the grieving is the healing," reflects what Isaiah the prophet said in the Old Testament, "to bind up the broken hearted." And that probably best summarizes what we do in the area of reproductive loss—"to bind up the broken hearted."

These losses are heart breaking. Although our work is difficult, we ourselves are the ones who are blessed when we can bring comfort to those who mourn.

ACKNOWLEDGMENTS

I am indebted to my partners Anne Kiss and Nancy Paré, who joined me in founding the Centre for Reproductive Loss with their "shared wisdom," and who gave of their time, talent, and energy to this labor of love.

REFERENCES

1. C. H. Shackleton, The Psychology of Grief: A Review, *Advances in Behaviour Research and Therapy, 6,* pp. 153-205, 1984.
2. P. M. Seitz and L. H. Warrick, Perinatal Death: The Grieving Mother, *American Journal of Nursing, 74,* pp. 2028-2033, 1974.
3. S. S. Joy, Abortion: An Issue to Grieve? *Journal of Counseling and Development, 63,* pp. 375-376, 1985.
4. I. Kesselman, Grief & Loss: Issues for Abortion, *Omega, 21*:3, pp. 241-247, 1990.
5. J. M. Stack, The Psychodynamics of Spontaneous Abortion, *American Journal of Orthopsychiatry, 54,* pp. 162-167, 1984.
6. K. M. Stinson, J. N. Lasker, and J. Lohmann, Parents' Grief Following Pregnancy Loss: A Comparison of Mothers and Fathers, *Family Relations, 41*:2, pp. 218-223, 1992.
7. L. Toedter, J. Lasker, and J. Alhadeff, The Perinatal Grief Scale: Development and Initial Validation, *American Journal of Orthopsychiatry, 58*:3, pp. 435-449, 1988.
8. A. Lang and L. Gottlieb, Parental Grief Reactions and Marital Intimacy Following Infant Death, *Death Studies, 17,* pp. 233-255, 1993.
9. C. Staudacher, *Men & Grief,* New Harbinger, Oakland, California, 1991.
10. J. James and F. Cherry, *The Grief Recovery Handbook,* Harper & Row, New York, 1988.
11. L. Hager, Pregnancy After Miscarriage, *Parenting,* pp. 97-103, February 1995.
12. G. H. Colt, The Silent Partner, *Parenting,* pp. 100-103, February 1995.
13. J. Worden, *Grief Counseling & Grief Therapy,* Springer, New York, 1991.
14. C. Moulder, *Miscarriage,* Pandora Press, London, England, 1990.
15. M. Allen and S. Marks, *Miscarriage, Women Sharing from the Heart,* John Wiley & Sons, Inc., New York, 1993.
16. J. N. Lasker and L. J. Toedter, Satisfaction with Hospital Care and Interventions After Pregnancy Loss, *Death Studies, 18*:1, pp. 41-64, 1994.

CHAPTER 18

Grief of the Abused Male

Rev. Alan Stewart

We live in a world that often refuses to view men as victims. The following two hypothetical cases (actually the composite experiences of several men) can serve as illustrations of several important issues related to grief of the abused male. These early abusive experiences produce effects that may last through the remainder of their lives. Abuse creates multiple lifelong losses.

The first man, in his thirties, suffering from depression, finds himself in court. His wife has alleged that he has assaulted her. He loves his son, lost his job, pretends that he is in control, but conversation with him shows confusion. He is not in touch with the reality of life and what is actually happening to him. He even yells at the judge in the court room. His second attempt at marriage was also a failure. His wife and her family seem to be the focus of the rage he holds for all who have wronged him in the past. He has never received counseling. He sees himself as a "victim of circumstances" but does not see how he contributes to his problems. He has no intimate friendships. To survive, he lives in a fantasy world. It is all that he knows.

The second man, in his late forties has gone the gamut of all the 12 Step programs. Convinced that they all point to his multiple-cross addictions, he is bright and articulate about his problems. Married with children, he has done well in the profession of his choice. Still, he struggles in much pain about how to relate to his spouse, and is unable to see the high level of his intellectual ability. In spite of all his self-help work, he seems to continue to get himself into situations where he is betrayed by co-workers. He is extremely open about himself and has no difficulty in being open and vulnerable to those he meets. He is loving, kind, and receptive as a person and presents a confident appearance to those he engages at work. Most of his relationships seem intimate, but he doesn't understand why he "acts out" his sexuality in unacceptable ways. When he gets stressed out, he goes to the phone for sex.

What do these two men share? Is there a common thread in their experience? What are the communalities and metaphorical similarities? They have both been abused earlier in their lives and continue to live out of that victim situation even though the original situation has long since passed. In fact, the men have taken over their abusers role with both themselves and others as victims. The abuse has been transformed from the childhood realities to more insidious adult manifestations. Neither man recognized that he had been abused. The first man was beaten for years by his father and humiliated by other family members. It took a meeting with a relative to remind him of the years of beating that he had forgotten. He used to make mistakes in his school exams on purpose so that he would fulfill the prediction of his father that he would never amount to anything. He kept his marks artificially low to coincide with the taunts of his family. He would not take his acne medication so that he would be as ugly as possible. He felt he was to blame for the "discipline" he received. No one had ever pointed out the abuse of his father and how his mother betrayed him by letting it go on and not taking him to safety. He had no idea how all of his childhood experience affected his adult life. The second man was sexually abused by members of his own family by perpetrators of both sexes. He never realized that he was not to blame. Like most men who have been abused, he just saw it "as the way it was" and was unable to identify and articulate the consequences in this struggle. Like many men, he just thought that he started sex "at an early age."

Both men grew up not comprehending the word "trust," living out their lives like a ship crossing the Atlantic, full steam, without a "rudder," unable to navigate the mine fields or avoid the collisions of the journey. No one comprehended the confusion and identity issues that these men suffered. There were two reasons for this. First, their experience had never been understood as "abuse" so that they could then move into responsible behavior understanding how that experience was harmful to their lives. They needed to know that the skills they had learned to survive the abuse in childhood were not helpful in mature adult relationships. Second, the experience of being male and being abused confounds the cultural paradigm that says men are in control, strong, aloof, unfeeling, and cannot be hurt. Men are taught that they cannot be victims.

One day while I was working with these men, I came to a sudden realization. From the men I had worked with in jails and from men I had talked with who lived on the street and simply wanted "a jug" to get them through the night, began to emerge a clear pattern. This may have been through the influence of my alcoholic father or from the men themselves who told me about their abuse. The puzzle began to unfold. Men do feel, and these men turn to alcohol and other substances to numb their feelings. As one man put it, cocaine was the only release he had from the pain of his life. Even if it was for only a few moments, it was worth it.

The "masks" of the abused man may vary from life in the park to the business suit in the financial tower. They may live in the suburbs or in jail. They may be handsome or seem to ooze pain from every pore. They may be of any age, but the ability to hide the pain decreases with age. The costs of not being able to be intimate with people in their lives begins to take its toll on their relationships. What makes the problem of the abused man "invisible" to most people is that the manifestations of their abuse vary from one individual to the next. While a knife wound to the arm will make the arm bleed, abused men "bleed" in many different ways.

The abuse is somatized by seeming to become part of their bodies and how they live out their lives. Because the abuse is part of them, they are unable to see their behavior as a survival response to problems that no longer exist. Like a cancer, the abuse infiltrates the adult male in various components of his life: his spousal or partner relationships, anger, violence leading to incarceration, sexual acting out, depression, problems with authority figures at work or in the family, fear of the father role, and all the problems related to non-existent self-esteem.

What many men have in common is their lack of an emotional vocabulary to explain their life experiences. Hard work and substance abuse may be the way they numb their pain, but never having known trust, they are confused in relating on an intimate level with the men and women in their lives. With a desperate need to have some control and maintain their masculine identity, they must try to hide their abuse at all costs. They live in constant fear, but cannot reveal this fear. They are scared. To reveal their abuse is to lose themselves. This is the primary grief of the abused male—the loss of self-identity.

Previously abused men often have problems with anger. This may stem from either the impossibility of expressing it at all or the opposite, being an inappropriate expression of anger that is either self-destructive or damaging to others, or both. When one man's stepfather was diagnosed with cancer, he smashed his fist through the bathroom wall. The family thought he was upset at the news of his stepfather's illness. When it became revealed that the man had sexually abused him, it became clear that the rage was over the loss of the opportunity for revenge and confrontation that had been brewing for twenty-five years and was never able to surface. Now it was impossible. How can you beat up an old man with cancer?

While it might be interesting to ask what questions would reveal the abuse, it is more important to list the factors that facilitate the disclosure. Some of the most common contributors to disclosure are listed below.

- The listener must be seen to be safe by the victim (i.e., seen as understanding of abuse and non-judgmental of the victim).
- The listener must be attentive, realizing that this opportunity may not happen again for decades if it ever happens again in the person's lifetime.
- The listener must understand the courage it takes to disclose.
- Disclosure often occurs during or after a life crisis (i.e., marriage breakdown, arrest or incarceration, illness, family death, anxiety attack, addiction traumas).
- Disclosure occurs in a safe place (i.e., often a public place, coffee shop, by phone, an intimate moment with a partner, or a place where the victim determines he is safe).

GROUPS FOR ABUSED MEN

In order to learn more about abused men and to discover effective ways to assist them, I placed a small ad in the local paper to identify other men to join two that I was already assisting. It brought about thirty calls. Many could only talk with the anonymity of the phone and could not meet me for an interview. Some could come to the interview, but could not attend a meeting. Others could only attend a few meetings. Abuse teaches a man that taking care of himself is the last priority on his list. His self-esteem is so battered that he lives his life through the feelings and the expectations of others. The only safety control mechanism is to live through the expectations and perceptions of others. Long ago the abused man learned that his perception and feelings were not valid. Some men find it easier to open up to a woman first, a spouse, counselor, or a friend. The safety of their manhood is less threatened by a woman. This same threat points to the need for the expression of the abuse to another man, and the healing component of that revelation that a woman cannot provide because of her gender. It is vital for women to know that they might be a "bridge" in the healing journey of the man who has disclosed his greatest fear. The anonymity of a phone call helps others.

Understanding and treating the grief of abused men must be based on a multidisciplinary model because of the severity of the grief and the damage inflicted on his gender identity. Whether men have been abused sexually, physically, or emotionally by men or women, the losses they have experienced seem to be similar. The following list of losses shows the multidimensional effects of abuse:

- loss of trust
- intimacy (can't get close to people)
- boundaries
- childhood
- spontaneity
- privacy
- self-respect
- confidence and serenity
- hope
- family
- happiness
- feelings (resist and deny their existence)
- the ability to deal with anger
- the primary loss of the abused man is of manhood, of identity, of self

It is vital to understand the important role of gender in facilitating the healing process for abused men. While women often serve as a crucial bridge in breaking the silence and identifying the underlying existence of the abuse and may facilitate the healing process, men must be involved because each man has to see himself as a man. A woman can help a man to understand how he is seen by women, but only men can help him to see himself as other men see him, which in turn can heal how he sees himself. He has to see that other men have experienced his loss and still survived. He needs to see, hear, and experience the male mode of emotional expression modeled for him, so that he has permission to grieve his own losses and move beyond the grief. He is able to grieve without losing himself in the grief, as this was his fear.

Abuse teaches a man that he cannot grieve, that it is not his right to express the pain and the loss of his abuse. This is taught by our societal denial of the male as victim and teaches him to pretend that his abuse did not happen. He feels that pretence must be maintained at all costs. This is why the silence is usually only broken at a time of life crisis. Whether a man has been abused by males or females, the one constant is that his own manhood is at stake. Therefore, an integral part of the healing must come from other men. He can only be comfortable as a man in knowing that he is accepted, loved, and blessed by other men. It has been this way since the beginning of time. One of the men in my group went into a bar and witnessed another man being very obnoxious and angry. Assuming that this stranger must be abused he told the man his own story. The angry obnoxious man broke into tears. His revelation allowed the angry man to grieve.

Treatment of abused men also involves both group and individual work. It requires a collaborative process where counselors, psychiatrists, clergy, and partners recognize the depth and need for care that involves a multidimensional approach. Men need to experience care from an intensive strategy that helps them recover what was lost. Those who help abused men need to be caring persons who support that process. The therapist, the facilitator, the other men in the group, the partner, they all complement each other in this process. They all fill a need. They must recognize that the abuse compromises the man's normal personal, psycho-social, and spiritual development. Issues may be delayed, deferred, or stuck. A thirty-five-year-old man may still be waiting for the chance to sit on his father's lap and cry like a three year old, because he never had that healing experience in his own life. Each man's story has to be deconstructed and reconstructed, so that he may gain insight into his own experience. This process allows him to step outside of the experience so that he can then articulate it, and use it to get the power back that he lost when he was abused. Abuse is essentially the loss of power, and recovery involves getting back the power.

SPIRITUALITY AND TREATMENT

The recovery process is much more than just going through stages. It is a journey, and the journey of a lifetime begins with a single step. It is like a path being made through the woods, the path is made by walking on it. The repetition of the steps create the pathway. The "path" is a spiritual path. When I use the term "spiritual" I do not mean religious in the conventional controlling sense of the word. I mean spiritual in the sense that all people are spiritual. Many men talk about God and prayer, so the key ingredient in my understanding of "spiritual" is "belief." A belief in God is what helps these men to hold on at times when no one else is there. The healing comes from being "like-God" for each other; that is to say, "To believe in each other." God being infinite, can be a tree or Neil Diamond recordings. God is that spark of belief.

OTHER GROUP FEATURES

With profound gratitude to the AA program and how it brought great healing and health to my own family, I have attempted, in my own treatment groups, a recomposing of the AA "path." I am giving a somewhat different interpretation of the steps on the path to recovery from abuse. The traditional 12 Step Groups fulfill a different need than groups for men who have been abused, but they complement each other. (Table 1 shows the 12 steps for my groups for abused men.) While these steps are not read at every meeting, they point to spiritual strength, awareness, responsibility, hope, and healing for men who did not know that this was available for them. The movement from victim, to independence, to interdependence needs support at every level.

Therapy, group, and individual support all help to change the context of the man's life and help him to create a new paradigm for living his experience, so that he can learn to do something different with his pain from what he has done in the past. In the transition from victim to victor, the changes may be positive for men but may prove difficult for some of their relationships where they might have been more compliant in the past. Support is needed for the confusion that results from this paradox. He is getting better but some people sense the change and feel threatened by it.

The helpers must always be concerned that conversations do not degenerate into blaming, as this is counterproductive in teaching adult responsibility and response to past and present experience. When a man starts blaming, there is a power shift. His power returns to his abuser. It could be that the Liberation Theology of the sixties has created a cultural ethic of blame with its rally cry to "hang the perpetrator." When we do that, we become the perpetrator and the cycle continues to the next generation. We need to develop an intergenerational understanding of what is occurring. We need to recognize that our sexism, stereotyping, mistaken assumptions, and blaming, supports and perpetuates the abuse of both men and women in our culture. We must learn how to stop the pain from being passed on.

Abuse teaches a man that trust and safety do not exist; therefore, the more safe times, safe places, and caring people, the better. The more his normal need and desire for self-expression and the more his own giftedness and the achieving of power in his life are realized, the better for him to know who he really is. In short, the more this takes place, the more "normal" he can feel. This is a process where these men reclaim their own power so that they can be who they are.

Table 1. Twelve Steps on the Path . . .
For Men Who Have Been Abused

1. We admitted that we had been made powerless by others at some point in our lives.

2. We came to believe that a Power greater than ourselves could lead us out of a life living as a victim, to one of wholeness where we were able to make free choices.

3. We made a decision to turn our will and our lives over to the care of God, as we understood God to be; replacing the survival tactics learned from the abuse, to healthy ways of relating.

4. We made a searching and fearless investigation of how we relate to others as a victim and how we might better relate as men.

5. We admitted to God, to ourselves, and to another human being the exact nature of how we had been harmed.

6. We were ready to have God and others who believe in us to help us learn healthy ways of living.

7. We accepted our Sonship as a man of God, and believed in ourselves and the reality of getting better.

8. We made a list of all the persons who had harmed us, to understand and become aware of how the abusers had taught us wrongly.

9. We undertook to confront these individuals in ways that were empowering to us, and kept us in a position of safety.

10. We continued to explore our lives in safe places, with safe people, at safe times, so that we would not injure ourselves or others.

11. We sought through prayer and meditation to improve our conscious contact with God, as we understood our Higher Power to be, praying only for knowledge of God's will for us, and the power to carry that out, being the best men we are able to be.

12. Having had a spiritual awakening as to the reality of healing in our lives, we tried to carry this message of hope to others, and help them build their own safety with the men and women in their lives.

Groups for abused men can help to create a place of safety, of non-competition, a place where intimacy and confidence may be developed, where reconciliation may be learned. While most cultural places for men tend toward competition, the group can be a place where men can talk about how to father their own children, where an understanding of personal commitment may be fostered, where brotherhood may be experienced, and where the men can leave feeling empowered. The group setting needs to be a place of non-judgment, as well as loving confrontation. One man recently told me that he was quitting the group, but then realized that the confrontation over boundary-setting was done for his benefit. He returned when he realized that it was part of the healing process. It must be a place where men can come and go.

Men can learn much from the Women's Movement about speaking out about their abuse. Of the 250 abused men who have disclosed abuse to me, only one of them has ever pressed charges in the courts against their abuser. A few have been trying, but it is only recently that this has happened. Because of the social shame and isolation that abused men experience they do not report the abuse. It is common to believe that abused men become abusers and should be feared. My experience is more that they are wounded and in need of healing. Their behavior is more self-abusive than it is toward others. They often take over their own abuse from their perpetrator and act it out in various forms of self-abuse such as activities that lead to incarceration, substance abuse, and painful guilt-laden self-hatred that causes more pain both to themselves and those they love.

Abuse is not acknowledged because our attitudes suppress it. When we change our attitudes it can be released and healing will take place. Our culture needs to reclaim the positive attitude of male nurturing, teach generative models about what a man is, and give men the right to have safety and freedom of intimate expression as part of their life journey, from boyhood onward. This is a positive and masculine concept. Men have feelings and needs. This is what made them vulnerable to abuse in the first place. A predator makes use of a child's natural need to be touched, affirmed, and experience closeness. The adult fear of male intimacy needs to be exposed for what it is, a fear. The development of this healing paradigm for abused men has given a gift that will benefit both men and women. The warmth and nurture of a generative male has been, and is, a positive and masculine beneficial aspect of a healthy culture. It is not something to be feared, but rather to be embraced both by men and by women.

ACKNOWLEDGMENT

A special word of thanks to the many men who had the courage to trust me with their stories and their pain, in the hopes that the telling will relieve others of their grief.

CHAPTER 19

The Eloquence of Pain: Poetry of Bereaved Fathers Following a Perinatal Loss

Michael Dilts

The grief that accompanies the death of an unborn or newly born child is often quite different in character and intensity from the grief associated with other forms of bereavement. The startling juxtaposition of birth and death seems a freakish and arbitrary event which defies all of our well-worn rationalizations. Miscarriages leave virtually nothing in the way of memories or tangible mementos. If they are lucky, the bereaved parents of a stillborn or newborn infant will end up with a lock of hair, a certificate of death, and maybe a photo or two—all that remains of their dreams, their hopes, the fleeting bliss of expectant parenthood. As they try to pick up the shattered pieces of their future and return to what is left of their lives, a couple whose pregnancy has ended in sorrow find that for many of their friends, family members, and business associates, not to mention government agencies, their loss doesn't really "count." Because their child was not born alive or lived only a few days, she or he is not regarded as a real person. Therefore, they cannot be feeling true grief and are not entitled to the same compassion and support offered to other mourners. For references on perinatal bereavement see [1-4].

Bereaved parents find many ways to cope with the sometimes overwhelming emotions which are kindled by their loss. A surprising number of them turn to poetry as an emotional outlet. In this age of blockbuster movies, music videos, and interactive multimedia, poetry is fast becoming a vestigial art form. It is certainly not at the forefront of our consciousness as a culture. There is something about the deliberate use of words and rhythm, however, which echoes the native vocabulary of the heart. It is almost as if these suffering parents, many of whom never thought much about poetry before and may have deliberately avoided English Lit. as students, are driven by instinct to take up rhyme and meter as a means of unloading the burden of their loss.

THE CORPUS

This study was based on a corpus of seventy-five poems written by members of Helping After Neonatal Death (H.A.N.D.). Founded in 1981, H.A.N.D. is a peer support group for bereaved parents and families with chapters in five Northern California counties. So many poems are submitted for publication in the H.A.N.D. newsletter, *Helping Hands*, that one out of every three issues is now entirely devoted to poetry. Poetry also plays a very important role in the annual Service of Remembrance sponsored by H.A.N.D. to acknowledge the brief lives of our children. Although grandparents, siblings, and family friends contribute some of the poems which appear in the newsletter or are read at the service, the majority of the authors are mothers or fathers of the deceased child.

Only poems in the latter category, poems written by a parent, were included in this study. Twenty-two of these, or roughly 29 percent, were written by fathers. A total of forty-nine authors are represented in the corpus, of which ten, or about 20 percent, were men. This percentage is consistent with the participation rate of fathers in our support group meetings. Men typically constitute 10 to 20 percent of the parents in attendance on any given evening. The fathers who attend support group meetings are not necessarily the ones who write the poems, of course, although there may be some overlap. For many if not most of the male authors, poetry serves as the primary form of therapy. In this regard it is interesting that one-third of the fathers contributed multiple poems compared with only one-fourth of the mothers.

A careful reading of the poems in the H.A.N.D. corpus reveals significant differences in the way that fathers and mothers put their poems together, in the vocabulary that they use, and the images and themes they employ. There are also a few areas where little or no difference can be identified. Most studies of perinatal grief have focused on bereaved mothers. The poems in this study provide a unique opportunity to listen to the voices of fathers rising up alongside those of mothers, adding another level of depth and richness to the choir.

HOW DO MEN WRITE?
POETIC STRUCTURE AND DICTION

One of the first observations that can be made about the H.A.N.D. parents' poetry is that fathers were much more likely than mothers to make use of standard poetic devices such as rhyming verse and the kind of antiquated vocabulary and syntax typically associated with "serious" poems (see Table 1). The fathers used rhyming verse fully half of the time, as opposed to the mothers who relied on rhyme in a little more than one quarter of their poems. At the same time, "poetic" language showed up in almost a third of the father's and in a quarter of the mother's poems. Almost a fifth of the fathers' poems were couched in the form of a prayer, compared with only one poem written by a mother. A number of the men adopted childlike vocabulary and syntax, as if speaking to or for a child. This is something the mothers never did.

The following excerpt from a father's poem illustrates the use of poetic language and rhyme. The poet is speaking of a tree planted in memory of his child.

> Through its strong branches you shall never get to climb
> Nor feel its soft cool summer's shade
> Your soul runs deep like life's great root unseen by us—
> Forever timeless beauty nature made.
> (Robin Davis, *The Blue Spruce of Vasona*)

In one poem, the father attempted to describe his young son's reaction to the death of his daughter by writing from the child's point of view.

> Where did baby sister go?
> Mommy is very very sad
> Daddy plays with me more now
> Grandma and Grandpa came over
> And we had a party
> I ate meatballs and rigatoni
> And I got a brand new car
> (Felix Berenberg, *Where Did Baby Sister Go?*)

We have seen that rhyme and archaic diction each appeared in one quarter of the mothers' poems. What other poetic devices did the women poets employ? In well over half of the mother's poems, repetition of words, phrases, or even entire lines was a primary poetic device. A fourth of the mothers' poems were written in a very informal, almost conversational style practically indistinguishable from everyday prose. Among the men, three made a significant use of repetition, but none at

Table 1. Frequency of Using Poetic Devices in Men's and
Women's Poems

Poetic Device	Men (%)	Women (%)
Rhyming Verse	50	26
"Poetic" Language	32	25
Prayer-Like Forms	18	2
Childlike Language	9	0
Repetition	14	59
Conversational Style	0	25

all came close to the conversational style used by so many of the
women. In the following verses from a mother's poem, conversational
prose and repetition are used simultaneously:

> I called the hospital where I had you, Ivette.
> They put me on hold.
> I called again wanting to know more about you.
> They put me on hold.
> After being on hold for a few minutes,
> Someone hung up the telephone.
> I'm no longer on hold.
> I called back so mad wanting to scream my head off.
> They put me on hold.
>
> (Angelica Labrado, *I Called to Hold You, Ivette*)

WHO SPEAKS? WHO LISTENS?

Another feature worthy of examination is the context of the discourse implied by the parents' poems. How does the poet identify him
or herself? To whom is the poem addressed? As can be seen in Table 2,
the differences between fathers and mothers are somewhat less
pronounced here than in the case of structure and diction, but some
interesting patterns do seem to emerge. The majority of both fathers'
and mothers' poems were written exclusively in the first person singular ("I, me, my"), indicating the intent of the poets to communicate an
intensely personal experience. Men, however, were somewhat more
likely than women to extend their expression of grief to other family
members by using the first person plural ("we, us, our"). A more or less
comparable minority of fathers and mothers used the first person
singular in combination with a reference to another person ("my wife
and I," "John and I"), and a similar minority avoided the first person
and used "you, they, she, he," etc. In a handful of cases, the poet

Table 2. Identity of the Speaker and Audience Addressed in the Poems

	Men (%)	Women (%)
Speaker		
"I" Exclusively	59	70
"I" and Someone Else	9	8
"I" as Someone Else	5	6
"We"	23	15
"He," "She," "You"	5	2
Audience		
Child	55	53
Generic	41	49
God	10	6
Parent	0	4

assumed the identity of another person altogether, speaking from the point of view of one of the baby's siblings, as in the example cited above, and even from the baby's point of view.

In these lines from a father's poem, the first person plural is used along with a specific reference to "my dear wife."

> Elizabeth Ann, our child, has breathed her last,
>   this long moment will not stay in the past.
> For me, her proud Daddy, and my dear wife,
>   this precious child has changed our life.
>   (Jim Zoland, *A Child I Can No Longer Hold*)

The question of the audience, implied or explicitly named by the poets, is one of the few areas in which there were no significant divergences between the fathers and the mothers. In both cases just over half of the poems were addressed to the baby herself or himself. I believe this quite striking phenomenon reflects the parents' need to validate the existence and personhood of the tiny child they barely knew. It is almost as if the audience actually reading or hearing the poem is being asked to stand witness to the fact that the poets are faithful parents who have not abandoned the memory of their children. Most of the remaining poems address a generic, unspecified audience, although a few are addressed directly to God, and in one poem the parent addresses herself from the baby's point of view. Note that there is actually some overlap among these cases since several authors address the baby, God, and/or an unspecified audience at various points in the same poem.

WHAT ARE MEN SAYING?–IMAGERY

Turning now from the form to the content of the poems, a number of the images used by parents to describe the pain of their loss recur in poem after poem. These are outlined in Table 3. Here again the similarities and differences between the choices made by the male and female poets provide revealing evidence of the influence of gender on the interpretation of the same tragic experience. Images drawn from nature were quite common, occurring in nearly half of the fathers' poems and in a significant number of mothers' poems. Some parents used nature as a symbol of brutality, senseless destruction, and inexplicable tragedy, while others saw regeneration and hope. Many of the most powerful poems in the corpus relied heavily on nature imagery.

The following two examples of nature imagery were produced by the same father, but are separated by six years.

> On the beach a sun-scoured bone
> Dissolves from chip to powder
> Like a hundred-year whisper
> Shattered shells cup no more songs
> ...
> No footprint remains before or behind
> Sand and salt have no memory
> We have entrusted her name to the blind, illiterate wind
> She who was taken and given at the same moment
> (Michael Dilts, *A Walk on the Beach*)

> You are lighter than air
> The sky is your playground
> Your laugh in the wind shakes the trees
> You play tag with the clouds
> You slide down a rainbow
> The sunshine sticks fast to your honey bright hair
>
> Wherever I go
> You know where to find me
> You enter my soul with each breath
> When we meet in the moonlight
> Let me wrap you in beauty
> And whisper my lullaby words soft and low
> (Michael Dilts, *Song for Malka*)

Also typical of the men's poems were more-or-less stereotypical symbols of childhood: toys, stuffed animals, baby clothes. Bereaved fathers spoke of not being able to play ball with their children, of

Table 3. Frequency of Types of Imagery in Men's and Women's Poems

Image	Men (%)	Women (%)
Nature	46	15
Symbols of Childhood	30	9
Roles and Relationships	36	36
Anger	18	15
Gift or Legacy	14	11
Religious	27	45
Body Metaphors	5	21

Note: Since a single poem often contained multiple images, column totals exceed 100 percent.

sandboxes lying idle, of heavenly games of tag in the clouds. The mothers who used imagery of this sort seemed to have younger children in mind—infants with bows in their hair, babies crawling on the "never clean" carpet. Note the images chosen by a father in the next excerpt to symbolize the broken promises of childhood:

> He never kissed a little girl.
> He never flew a kite.
> He merely came and took one look,
> Then faded into night.
>
> (John Mote, *Please Don't Ask If I'm OK*)

Compare these with the more immediate image of the empty nursery used by a mother in the lines which follow:

> Mommy cries out for you.
> Her arms ache to hold you.
> Her breasts ache to nurse you,
> But the rocking chair stays empty
> in the cold and dreary room.
>
> (Karen Hansen, *Love Holds My Heart*)

Images having to do with the role of parenthood and the relationship between parent and child show up in fathers' poems just as frequently as they do in those of mothers, a fact which is somewhat surprising considering that our culture tends to assign the responsibility for defining and maintaining family relationships to women. Men and women were equally likely to give examples of the ways in which the child was still part of the family or to speak of the birthday parties they would have held, the lullabies they would have sung. Here is how a father speaks of his unfulfilled parental role:

> What a great joy it would be to hold you all even once again
> And say "good night" when another day is done
> We wonder are you kids today still happy?
> Are your souls somewhere OK?
> Can you see the inside falling
> Tears which never fade away?
>
> (Robin Davis, *Marking the Time*)

Occurring in fathers' and mothers' poetry with more-or-less equal frequency were images associated with anger. In most cases the anger was muted and indirect, often focusing on surrogate targets such as inconsiderate people in line at the supermarket or switchboard operators at the hospital who put people on hold. The one significant exception was, interestingly, provided by a bereaved mother's poem. Her anger was directed at pregnant women and their unborn babies and was not at all muted. In fact, it was not so much anger as it was unbridled rage, which found expression in graphic fantasies of violence. The poem was so extreme in its tone and content that I did not include it among the seventy-five poems used in this study. In the following excerpt, which is typical of the corpus, a mother complains about encountering still-pregnant women in public following her loss. Note her focus on the bodies from the neck down—she is angry at the shapes she sees, not at the people behind them.

> They confront me everywhere
> Round and bloated bodies assert themselves
> With the force of a spoiled child
> gloating over some victory
>
> (Elanah Kutik, *Body Images*)

Both fathers and mothers often described the child's brief life as a gift and spoke of a precious if intangible legacy remaining after the child's death. The following example was written by a father.

> Allison—you were so young
> You gave us so much and your life had just begun.
>
> You were with us ten days which wasn't enough
> but you gave us a lifetime of strength,
> just showing how you fought.
>
> (David Maxwell, *Allison Clare's Poem*)

Women were more likely than men to insert descriptions of heaven, to compare their children with angels, to imagine them living among the angels, or to use other overtly religious images. Not surprisingly, mothers also relied more heavily than men on body metaphors, comparing their empty wombs to their empty hearts, describing bodies which, like their owners, seem to be in denial over the unexpected termination of the pregnancy. Here is an excerpt from a mother's poem.

> I am empty now, where he once lived
> I was turned inside out, my uterus scrubbed of all life
> That holy light that dwelled within me
> Extinguished in one long exaggerated . . . push!
>
> (Lyn Smith, *Birth*)

WHAT ARE MEN SAYING?–THEMES

The parents covered a broad range of subject matter in their poems, and some of the most common topics are listed in Table 4. As was the case with the images employed in the poems to express these ideas, there seem to be some gender differences in the distribution of the themes, which reflect the differing concerns of bereaved fathers and mothers.

Proportionally more fathers' poems than mothers' poems dealt with the issue of the baby's post-mortem location and well-being. Fathers seemed to need more assurance than mothers that their baby is in a safe place and is being cared for. Two uniquely male themes which were present in a small number of fathers' but in none of the mothers'

Table 4. Frequency of Specific Themes in Men's and Women's Poems

Theme	Men (%)	Women (%)
Where is Baby?	18	9
Baby Spared Life's Trials	9	0
Does Baby Know Me?	9	0
Why?	14	11
Injustice	18	17
Emotional Paradox	18	15
Anatomy of Pain	27	30
Will Memory Survive?	18	40
Description of Baby	9	28

Note: Since a single poem often addressed multiple themes, column totals exceed 100 percent.

poems were: 1) that the baby was in some way fortunate to have been spared the normal vicissitudes of life; and 2) a concern with whether or not the baby is aware of the parent's existence and/or of the parent's love for the baby. The former theme is very much in evidence in the following lines.

> Life's cruel injustice can't touch you now.
> And know that we'll miss your smile.
> Be tranquil my son and take your time.
> There's nothing left to prove.
> Your battle is over, your race is run,
> And God will care for you.
>
> (John Mote, Restful)

A number of the topics in the list occur with more or less equal frequency in both the fathers' and the mothers' poetry. Both parents asked that most basic and least answerable of questions: Why? Why did it happen? Why a baby? Why me? Here is how one mother phrased the question.

> Oh Brianna, I miss you so,
> Why did you say goodbye before hello?
> Daddy and I we love you so,
> Why did you have to go?
>
> (Gina M. Glenn, Brianna—Why?)

The related issue of the injustice of death for such a young child was also shared by male and female parents. Many parents of both sexes also spoke of experiencing a strange set of conflicting emotions after their child's death. Even in the midst of their profound sorrow, they felt an overriding sense of awe and wonder at the birth process itself and/or they felt gratitude for the baby's presence in the world, however brief. Here is how a father describes this sense of ambivalence.

> That flicker of love and joy runs off like
> raindrops down the shut closed window pane.
> Turning back cannot rediscover that rare, fleeting,
> magical mix of life, passion and love.
> I can only hope time may bring another,
> but never this lost chance, this love, this child.
>
> (John Mote, A Lost Chance)

Surprisingly, fathers were almost as likely as mothers to use their poems to make a record of the grief process, often describing their suffering in considerable, almost clinical detail (in Table 4, this theme is referred to as the "anatomy of pain"). In the following example a father speaks of the surreal world of sorrow into which the mourner is suddenly thrust.

> I do not know the difference anymore
> Between pain and not-pain
> The darkness in my eyes
> Outlasts the morning
> And deepening afternoon brings no change of light
> (Michael Dilts, *Notes for a Therapy Session*)

One theme which is found to some degree in a significant number of mothers' poems but considerably fewer fathers' poems is a concern with how long the parents' memories of the baby will last. Overt expressions of this concern are often accompanied by a very detailed description of the baby's appearance and clothing. Some poems even mention the baby's distinctive smell. The poem itself seems to be intended as additional insurance against the fading of memory. A mother writes:

> Where have you gone
> My tiny one?
>
> I search for you
> As you drift away
> From me in a river of red.
>
> Desperately I long to
> find you,
> Knowing I will never see
> or hold you.
>
> But no one can deny
> Your presence I feel
> In a gentle breeze
> Or in the flowering tree
> Planted in your Memory.
>
> (Sue Salutric, *Adam*)

BREAKING THE SILENCE:
ANALYSIS AND INTERPRETATION

Authors who have conducted in-depth studies of the male grief response (see especially [5]) have commented upon men's tendency to remain silent about their inner experiences, their preference for solitary mourning, and their need for action, which can take the form of physical exertion, pursuit of litigation, or immersion in their work. Even among the fathers whose poems we have been examining, men who "broke the silence" and put their pain into words, the influence of male cultural conditioning seems to be at work. We have seen that the male poets are more likely to take on the linguistic strictures of rhyme and meter and to avoid everyday vocabulary and syntax in favor of self-consciously poetic diction. Why don't they just say what they mean? Aren't these literary trappings just another way for men to mask their deepest and truest selves? There is of course some justification for this point of view. The traditional poetic structures do provide a ready-made mold into which the amorphous and unfamiliar emotions of grief can be safely poured, and that very sense of safety could have helped to free our poets' tongues.

It may be, however, that there is more to men's reluctance to put their grief into words than meets the eye. When all is said and done, is the language we use in everyday conversations truly an adequate medium for capturing the full anguish, the deep hidden anger, the profound despair which accompanies the death of a child? It may be that for most men it is more honest to remain silent than to attempt expression of such feelings in the same words which are used for idle lunch room chatter. For those who attempt the task, only the transcendent tools of metaphor and verse have any chance of doing it justice. No less a poetic talent than Tennyson seems to have shared this sentiment:

> I sometimes hold it half a sin
> to put in words the grief I feel;
> For words, like Nature, half reveal
> and half conceal the Soul within.
> (Alfred Lord Tennyson, *In Memoriam*)

The fact that fathers were more willing than mothers to extend ownership of the experiences documented by their poems to other family members can be interpreted as another artifact of cultural conditioning. Part of the role of the male as head of the family is that of the spokesman, the representative of the family unit to the outside world. Projecting his own feelings onto his female partner or his children also permits a father to talk about his despair and confusion in a way which is not threatening to his image as the strong and fearless protector. Even in their poetry, fathers seem to be satisfying the social expectations of the male role. Here, again, there is another way to view these facts. Were the fathers who acted as family spokesmen simply following the typical male pattern of denying their own emotions, or does the empathy they demonstrated for the suffering of others show that they were more successful than the female poets at breaking through the self-absorption of the grief response? Could it be that their traditional role as defenders of the family unit actually heighten fathers' sensitivity to the pain of their spouses and children so that their own grief truly includes and is intensified by the grief of those around them?

The differences between the imagery and themes of fathers' and mothers' poetry may have less to do with cultural conditioning than with basic physiology. There is just no getting around the fact that a mother's physical experience of pregnancy is not at all comparable with that of a father. To say that the mother is more intimately involved with the process is, of course, a gross understatement. For her the child is no longer an idyllic fantasy of the future but an everyday reality. Thus, it is not at all surprising that mothers tend to internalize their response to a pregnancy that ends in tragedy while men externalize their response to the same event. The father sees himself as part of a cosmic tragedy, swept away by a natural catastrophe over which he had little or no control. The mother, however, feels betrayed by her own body and is unable to avoid a sense of personal failure. These differences were clearly reflected by the predilection of the male poets for nature imagery while the women's preference was for body metaphors. At the same time, the tendency of fathers to wonder what happened to the baby they never knew while the mothers struggled to remember each tiny detail speaks poignantly of the parents' contrasting sense of the child's reality. Even when they addressed the same topic, the fathers and mothers approached it from very different angles. For example, the men tended to see the injustice of their child's death in the context of the blind cruelty of life in general. The women's sense of injustice, however, was much more specific. They wanted to know what couples with living children had done to deserve their good fortune.

POETRY AS THERAPY

The authors represented in the H.A.N.D. corpus wrote poems for a variety of reasons, some of which overlapped for a given parent or a given poem. For many, the poem was a way to say goodbye to the baby and provided an opportunity to thank the baby for her or his brief visit or to ask forgiveness for real or imagined failings on the parent's part. Some parents used the poem as another forum for telling their story yet another time in yet another way, while others seemed intent on documenting their experience of the grief process as if making a journal entry in verse. The minority of poems which were not actually addressed to the baby often asked for understanding and compassion from the public at large or contained reassurances intended for the parent him or herself. These reassurances sometimes included an acknowledgment that the parent's grief was gradually abating, that healing was taking place.

Evidence of healing can also be seen in sets of poems written over time by the same author, a slow and steady movement from bitterness to despair to resignation and, finally, a faltering step toward resolution. For such poets it is obvious that creation of verse had an important therapeutic value in and of itself. Parents who write poetry may not think of it as therapy at the time, of course. Occasionally poems were written for special events—a memorial service, an anniversary date. For the most part, however, the impulse to write was spontaneous and for some parents it came as rather a surprise. None of the authors, either male or female, was a professional writer, and only one or two had ever published poetry before.

While poetry writing is not a formal part of H.A.N.D.'s current peer support program, parents do bring in poems to read from time to time. Poetry readings are a traditional component of our annual Service of Remembrance, although we have found that most parents are unwilling to attempt a live reading of their own work for fear that they will break down and be unable to continue. We also invite parents to contribute poems and other writings to our newsletter, and, as was mentioned in the introduction, we now devote one out of three issues exclusively to poetry. It seems that the best way we can encourage bereaved men and women to engage in this kind of writing therapy is to provide examples of what others have written. A side benefit of this approach is the secondary healing that takes place for those who read the poems and discover, without even attending a single support meeting, that they are not alone in their pain.

CONCLUSION

While this study has placed emphasis on the differences between women's and men's grief, it is important to acknowledge the many overlaps and similarities. The need to speak to the beloved just one more time, the anger at death's injustice, the frustration at the indifference of the world at large, the secondary grief for a relationship which exists no more, the eternal question "why"—all of these are common to both genders and thus constitute the universal language of bereavement, the essence of pain. Parents who turn to poetry find neither a cure for their anger nor any answers to their questions, though some may insist, not always convincingly, on their willingness to submit to "God's plan." What parents' poems do seem to provide is a measure of release, a measure of comfort, and a first step on the long journey of healing.

ACKNOWLEDGMENTS

I would like to thank the parent-poets whose poems have been excerpted for this chapter, as well as all of the fathers and mothers who have contributed poetry to *Helping Hands* and to the Service of Remembrance over the years. The following items have individual copyrights and are used with the permission of the authors: *A Walk on the Beach,* copyright 1985 by Michael R. Dilts; *Song for Malka,* copyright 1991 by Michael R. Dilts; *Body Images,* copyright 1985 by Elanah Kutik; *Notes for a Therapy Session,* copyright 1985 by Michael R. Dilts; *Adam,* copyright 1988 by Sue Salutric. All other poems except for Tennyson's *In Memoriam* are copyright 1989-1994 by H.A.N.D. of Santa Clara County and are used with the permission of H.A.N.D.

REFERENCES

1. L. G. Peppers and R. J. Knapp, *Motherhood and Mourning: Perinatal Death,* Praeger, New York, 1980.
2. S. Borg and J. Laske, *When Pregnancy Falls,* Beacon, Boston, Massachusetts, 1981.
3. J. Defrain, et al., *The Invisible Death,* D. C. Heath, Lexington, Massachusetts, 1986.
4. H.A.N.D. of Santa Clara County, *Health Provider's Manual for Helping after Neonatal Death,* H.A.N.D. of Santa Clara County, Los Gatos, California, 1987.
5. C. Staudacher, *Men and Grief,* Harbinger, Oakland, California, pp. 11-41, 1991.

Contributors

DAVID W. ADAMS, MSW, CSW, CGT, CDE, is a professor in the Department of Psychiatry and Behavioral Neurosciences, McMaster University, Faculty of Health Sciences and Executive Director, Hurst Place: The Employee Assistance Program. He has an extensive background as a clinician and educator and is especially noted for his work with ill and bereaved children, adolescents, and their families. David is a certified grief therapist and certified death educator. He is co-editor of *Beyond the Innocence of Childhood,* a three volume series related to understanding of death, life-threatening illness, palliative care, and bereavement in childhood and adolescence. He is also co-author of *Coping with Childhood Cancer: Where Do We Go From Here?* and is internationally known as a workshop facilitator and lecturer. David is past chair of the International Work Group on Death, Dying, and Bereavement (IWG) and a member of the CHIPPS Psychological/Spiritual/Bereavement Group of the National Hospice Organization.

SUSAN ALLEN received her doctorate in counseling from the University of North Texas, and is currently on the psychology faculty at Baylor University in Waco, Texas. She teaches courses in developmental psychology and counseling theory and method.

PEGGY ANDERSON is an author, teacher, and bereavement consultant in London, Canada. Her publications include *Wife After Death* (1991; 1993), *Alone and Growing* (1997), *Communicating with the Dying and the Bereaved* (1997), and *Grief Support Groups* (1997). She has also written for various publications including a chapter in Baywood's *Readings in Thanatology, Working with Widows in Groups.* She is currently an instructor in the University of Western Ontario's Palliative Care and Thanatology Program. As a bereavement counselor in private practice, Peggy specializes in working with the widowed. She especially enjoys group work and facilitates/participates in several grief-related groups each year.

ROBERT A. BENDIKSEN is a professor of sociology at the University of Wisconsin–La Crosse and research associate at the University of Minnesota's Center for Death Education and Research. He has co-edited (with Robert Fulton) *Death and Identity* (Charles Press, 1976 and 1993) and co-edited (with E. Clark, J. Fritz, P. Rieker, and A. Kutscher) *Clinical Sociological Perspectives on Illness & Loss: The Linkage of Theory and Research* (Charles Press, 1990). Dr. Bendiksen is certified in clinical sociology, and he has published articles and conducted numerous workshops on "Death, Grief, and Bereavement" and "Creative Problem Solving" for health personnel, teachers, and administrators in the United States and Norway. He is currently the chair of the International Work Group on Death, Dying and Bereavement.

ANGELINE BUSHY, RN, CS, PH.D., is currently the Bert Fish Endowed Chair in Community Health Nursing at the University of Central Florida. She received a BSN degree from the University of Mary in Bismarck, North Dakota, an MN Degree from Montana State University, and a Ph.D. from the University of Texas. Her primary areas of expertise are in rural health nursing and community health.

JACK BUSHY, MS, MSW is clinical coordinator at the Bismarck Veterans Center. His area of expertise is treating clients with war trauma and specifically past traumatic stress disorder. He attended Eastern Montana University where he earned a Master's Degree in counseling and also received an MSW from the University of Kansas.

MICHAEL CASERTA, PH.D., is an associate professor at the University of Utah Gerontology Center in Salt Lake City. He has co-authored numerous journal articles and book chapters in the areas of spousal bereavement, family caregiving, and health promotion and self-care. His most current work focuses on ways to improve the self-care practices of older widows and widowers "Pathfinders". He is an active member of the Association for Death Education and Counseling (ADEC), the American Society on Aging (ASA), the American Association for Health Education, and the Gerontological Society of America where he has co-convened an interest group on Death, Dying, Bereavement, and Widowhood.

MICHAEL R. DILTS holds degrees in linguistics from the University of California at Berkeley and from Harvard University, where he was an NSF Graduate Fellow. During his career in the computer industry, Michael worked for such companies as Texas Instruments, Wang Laboratories, and Apple Computer. After the stillbirth of his first child he became involved with Helping After Neonatal Death, a parent support organization in the San Francisco Bay Area. In addition to editing the organization's newsletter, he authored *Unsung Lullabies: A*

Parent's Guide to Healing After Childbearing Loss, publication of which was partially funded by a grant from the March of Dimes.

KENNETH J. DOKA, Ph.D., is a professor of Gerontology at the College of New Rochelle. Dr. Doka's books include *Disenfranchised Grief: Living with Life Threatening Illness; Living With Grief: After Sudden Loss; Death and Spirituality; Living with Grief: When Illness is Prolonged; Living with Grief: Who We Are, How We Grieve; AIDS, Fear & Society; Aging and Developmental Disabilities; and Children Mourning, Mourning Children.* Dr. Doka is the associate editor of the journal *Omega* and editor of *Journeys,* a newsletter for the bereaved. Dr. Doka has served as a consultant to medical, nursing, hospice organizations, as well as businesses, educational, and social service agencies. As senior consultant to the Hospice Foundation of America, he assists in planning, and participates in their annual teleconference. In 1998, The Association for Death Education and Counseling (ADEC) presented him the Outstanding Educator Award. He is a past president of ADEC, Chair of the International Work Group on Death, Dying & Bereavement and is an ordained Lutheran clergyman.

KATHLEEN GRAY, RN, BS, M.Sc., M.Ed., a nurse and bereavement counselor, is president of the Centre for Reproductive Loss which she founded with two other colleagues in Montreal in 1992. In addition to her nursing background of clinical experience and teaching, her expertise lies in counseling individuals who have suffered such reproductive losses as miscarriage, stillbirth, abortion, infertility, etc. She has also designed a seminar on grieving reproductive losses; several seminars have already been given in the Montreal area to health professionals and volunteers of the Centre. She is currently writing a book on *The Healing Process: Grieving Reproductive Loss* for Baywood Publishing.

JOHN E. HART, M.Ed., CAS, LCSW, is a certified trainer, licensed social worker, an certified bereavement facilitator. He is the former program director of the Mobile AIDS Resource Team (MART), a training component of the Massachusetts Department of Public Health's AIDS and Substance Abuse Bureaus. He is currently working as a consultant and as a guest lecturer in the HIV Specialty of the graduate level nurse practitioner's training program at the Massachusetts General Hospital's Institute for Health Professions. His work on homophobia, grief, and loss has been presented at many local, national, and international conferences.

BERT HAYSLIP, Jr., is a Regents Professor of Psychology at the University of North Texas, where he teaches graduate and undergraduate courses in adult development and aging, life span development, death and dying, and gerontological counseling. He is a fellow of the Gerontological Society of America and of the American Psychological Association. He has had grants from the National Endowment for the Humanities, the National Institute on Aging, and the Hilgenfeld Foundation. He is co-author of *Hospice Care* (1992) and *Adult Development and Aging* (in press, Krieger Publishers). His interests range from grief and bereavement to the assessment of death anxiety to intellectual functioning and later life.

KATHY JAMBOIS-RANKIN is a certified oncology nurse, currently practicing in Radiation Oncology at DeKalb Medical Center in Decatur, Georgia. She is also a member of the Charles B. Eberhart Cancer Support Team, and the Quality of Life Committee at DeKalb Medical Center. She holds a Masters Degree in Community Human Services from the University of Wisconsin–Green Bay, and a Bachelor's degree in Nursing from Winona State University, Winona, Minnesota. Her revised Master's thesis titled "Critical Incident Stress Debriefing: An Examination of Public Services Personnel and Their Responses to Critical Incident Stress" is to be published in 1999.

SAM KEEN, PH.D., was over-educated at Harvard and Princeton and was a professor of philosophy and religion at various legitimate institutions before becoming a free-lance thinker, lecturer, seminar leader, and consultant. He is the author of a dozen books, was a contributing editor to *Psychology Today,* a co-producer of the award winning *Faces of the Enemy,* and the subject of a Bill Moyers PBS Special, *Your Mythic Journey with Sam Keen.* He has marked disrespect for accepted boundaries, tired answers, uncritical ideologies, and the sacred jargon of various professions. When not writing or traveling around the world lecturing and doing seminars on a wide range of topics on which he is not necessarily an expert but a skilled explorer, he fiddles with horses and growing things on his farm in the hills above Sonoma.

KENT KOPPLEMAN graduated from the University of Nebraska and taught high school English and social studies in Nebraska, Iowa, and Connecticut before earning his Ph.D. from Iowa State University. He accepted a position at the University of Wisconsin–La Crosse where he still teaches about issues related to diversity and multicultural education. In 1988 he was selected "Teacher Educator of the Year" by Wisconsin's Department of Public Instruction. In 1989 his son Jason was killed in an accident on the way home from work which resulted in a book entitled *The Fall of a Sparrow: Of Death and Dreams and Healing.*

DALE A. LUND, PH.D., is a professor of gerontology and sociology and director of the University of Utah Gerontology Center. Dr. Lund is internationally known for his research, publications, and presentations on coping with difficult transitions in later life, particularly family caregiving and spousal bereavement. He edited and authored *Older Bereaved Spouses* which was one of the first research-based books to address grief in later life. Dr. Lund is the founder of the Bereavement Interest Group within the Gerontological Society of America and is a member of the International Work Group on Death, Dying and Bereavement and a past recipient of the Outstanding Researcher Award presented by ADEC. He is a past-president of the Utah Gerontological Society and current president of the Utah Alzheimer's Association.

TERRY L. MARTIN, PH.D., is an assistant professor of psychology at Hood College in Frederick, Maryland. He is a licensed clinical professional counselor and certified grief therapist specializing in issues surrounding dying and bereavement and serves as a consultant to hospices and hospitals. He is a certified death educator and has taught various death-related courses for over twenty years, including an advanced grief counseling certification course for the Association of Death Education and Counseling (ADEC). Dr. Martin has several publications about different patterns of grief including chapters (with Ken Doka) in several books and journals.

DR. MENDELSOHN is a professor of sociology at South Dakota State University. At the graduate level, he teaches sociological theory and the sociology of deviant behavior. For undergraduates, he offers courses in the sociology of death and dying, domestic violence, and popular culture. In addition to examining the role behaviors and conflicts confronting widowers with children, his current research interests focus on graduate student academic advising, the role adjustments among transgendered persons, and domestic abuse within Native American communities.

DOUGLAS E. O'NEILL received his Ph.D. in Sociology from South Dakota State University, Brookings, in 1996. His dissertation *American Widowers with School-Age Children: An Exploratory Study of Role Change and Role Conflict,* earned Dr. O'Neill the William E. & Harriet B. Gould Memorial Scholarship Award for the most outstanding dissertation in the Sociology Department. His interest in the topic of widowers with school-age children is the result of his personal experience of being widowed when his wife, Demetra died of breast cancer, leaving behind a husband with six children, age fourteen months to twelve years of age.

ERIC D. RANKIN, PH.D., is an associate professor and director of clinical gerontology in the Department of Behavioral Medicine and Psychiatry at West Virginia University. His clinical and research interests have focused on mental health problems in later life including dementia, mood, anxiety, and substance disorders. Dr. Rankin has received funding for research from The National Institute on Aging, private foundations, and pharmaceutical companies. He is a fellow in the Gerontological Society of America.

LAURA McCOY ROBERTS received her doctorate from the University of North Texas in counseling psychology. She is currently on the staff at the Counseling and Testing Center at Southern Methodist University in Dallas, Texas.

PAUL SAKALAUSKAS has been a licensed funeral director in Ontario for twenty-four years. He is involved in many community organizations related to bereavement, including Past Chair of the Bereavement Working Group for Hamilton Wentworth, Past Chair for the Regional Palliative Care Advisory Group for Hamilton Wentworth, member of the Ontario Funeral Service Association and sat on the board of the association for eight years. He is presently a board member of the Hamilton Wentworth Regional Cancer Center Foundation.

REV. ALAN STEWART has been the minister of Westview Presbyterian Church in Toronto since 1990. During this time, Rev. Stewart became keenly aware that there was a huge problem that men were experiencing, neither noticed nor named; men sleeping on the streets and languishing in our jails had been *abused*. Growing up, they had been beaten, raped, molested, humiliated, and were in great pain. These men were victims. For six years Rev. Stewart has facilitated a group for men who have been abused and has spoken on this topic at Queen's University in Kingston, Kings College in London, Ontario as well as community groups, on local radio, and has lead retreats and events on men's issues.

NEIL THOMPSON teaches in the School of Health and Community Studies at North East Wales Institute, United Kingdom, and is a Principal Consultant with Ashley Maynard Associates. He has over seventy publications to his name, including the books, *People Skills* and *Promoting Equality* (both published by Macmillan). He has been a speaker at conferences and seminars in Britain, Greece, Canada, the United States, and Australia. He is a member of the International Work Group on Death, Dying and Bereavement.

Index